500 Activities for the Primary Classroom

Contents

Macmillan Education
4 Crinan Street
London N1 9XW
A division of Macmillan Publishers Limited
Companies and representatives throughout the world

ISBN 978-1-4050-9907-3

Original design by Anthny Godber
Illustrated by Kathy Baxendale
Cover design by Andrew Oliver
Cover photography reproduced with the kind permission of
Alamy/Stock Connection Distribution.

The publisher would like to thank Susan Norman and Melanie
Williams for reading the draft manuscript and for their
invaluable suggestions and ideas.

The author and publishers would like to thank the following
for permission to use copyright material:
Extracts - 'Food Groups' and 'The Water Cycle' from The
Magic Pencil website by Carol Read and Timothy Ackroyd
copyright (c) The British Council, reprinted by permission of
the publisher. Going to the Zoo – Words by Tom Paxton
copyright © Harmony Music Limited/Cherry Lane Music Inc,
reprinted by permission of Bucks Music Group, UK. All rights
reserved. Adapted rhyme 'I Wiggle My Fingers' from Bright
Ideas Language Resource, by Leonora Davies and Frankie
Leibe, copyright © Leonora Davies and Frankie Leibe 1987,
reprinted by permission of the authors. Poem 'Now we are six'
by A.A.Milne, copyright © The Trustees of the Pooh
Properties, published by Egmont UK, London, reprinted by
permission of The Trustees. Extract from 'Managing Children
Positively' by Carol Read, copyright © Keyways Publishing
Limited 2005, first published in English Teaching Professional
magazine May 2005 www.etprofessional.com, reprinted by
permission of the publisher. Adapted extracts from Hello
Robby Rabbit 1 Teacher's Book by Carol Read & Ana Soberón,
copyright © Macmillan Publishers Limited 2002, reprinted by
permission of the publisher. Adapted extracts from Superworld
1 Teacher's Book by Carol Read and Ana Soberón, copyright
© Macmillan Publishers Limited 2000, reprinted by permission
of the publisher. Song 'Two Little Butterflies' from Superworld
1 Pupil's Book by Carol Read and Ana Soberón, copyright
© Macmillan Publishers Limited 2000, reprinted by permission
of the publisher. Adapted song 'Put your litter in the bin!' from
Superworld 2 Pupil's Book by Carol Read and Ana Soberón,
copyright © Macmillan Publishers Limited 2000, reprinted by
permission of the publisher. Extract 'The Kraken' from
Superworld 3 Teacher's Book by Carol Read and Ana Soberón,
copyright © Macmillan Publishers Limited 2000, reprinted by
permission of the publisher. Extract 'The Pizza Train' from
Superworld 3 Pupil's Book by Carol Read and Ana Soberón,
copyright © Macmillan Publishers Limited 2000, reprinted by
permission of the publisher. Extract from Superworld 4
Teacher's Book by Carol Read and Ana Soberón, copyright
© Macmillan Publishers Limited 2000, reprinted by permission
of the publisher. Extracts from Little Bugs 1 Teacher's Book by
Carol Read and Ana Soberón, copyright © Macmillan
Publishers Limited 2004, reprinted by permission of the
publisher. Photocopiable Worksheets from Bugs 1 and Bugs 5
Spanish edition, by series authors Carol Read, Ana Soberón,
Elisenda Papiol and Maria Toth, copyright © Macmillan
Publishers Limited 2004 and 2005 respectively, reprinted by
permission of the publisher. Extract 'Play the can you…?
Game' from English Club 1 Student's Book by Carol Read and
Sagrario Salaberri, first published by Heinemann 1992,
copyright © Macmillan Publishers Limited, reprinted by
permission of the publisher. Extract from English Club 2
Teacher's Book by Carol Read and Sagrario Salaberri, first
published by Heinemann 1993, copyright © Macmillan
Publishers Limited, reprinted by permission of the publisher.
Adapted extract from Macmillan Children's Reader 'Penguins'
The Race to the South Pole, original text by Luther Reimer,
copyright © Macmillan Publishers Limited 2005, reprinted by
permission of the publisher. Poem 'I'm a Grown Man Now'
by Roger McGough, copyright © Roger McGough 1983,
reprinted by permission of Peter Fraser and Dunlop,
(www.pfd.co.uk) on behalf of Roger McGough. Adapted poem
from Action Rhymes & Games from Bright Ideas for Early
Years series, copyright © Max De Boo 1992, reprinted by
permission of Mrs Max De Boo. Extract from The Incentive
Value of Theory in Teacher Education by H. G. Widdowson,
copyright © Oxford University Press 1984, first published in
ELT Journal 1984, Volume 38 used by permission of Oxfords
University Press. Extract from 'Monkey Puzzle' by Julia
Donaldson and Axel Scheffler, copyright © 2000 Pan
Macmillan Children's Books, reprinted by permission of the
publisher. Extract from 'Dear Zoo' by Rod Campbell,
copyright © 2001 Pan Macmillan Children's Books, reprinted
by permission of the publisher. Material from 'The Gruffalo'
by Julia Donaldson and Axel Scheffler, copyright © 1999 Pan
Macmillan Children's Books, reprinted by permission of the
publisher. Extract from 'Tandem Plus (Teacher Resource
Material)' by Carol Read and Alan Matthews, copyright
© Pearson Education 1997, reprinted by permission of the
publisher. Poems 'A Thousand Hairy Savages' and 'A Baby
Sardine' by Spike Milligan, copyright © Spike Milligan
Productions Limited, reprinted by permission of Spike
Milligan Productions Limited. Material reproduced from
The Usborne First Cookbook' by permission of Usborne
Publishing, 83-85 Saffron Hill, London EC1N 8RT, UK www.
usborne.com, copyright © Usborne Publishing Limited 1987,
1997, reprinted by permission of the publisher.

Although we have tried to trace and contact copyright holders
before publication, in some cases this has not been possible. If
contacted we will be pleased to rectify any errors or omissions
at the earliest opportunity.

Printed and bound in Thailand

2016 2015 2014
16 15 14 13

About the author

I am an educational consultant, teacher trainer and writer based in Madrid. I am also an assessor of courses leading to the Cambridge ESOL young learner teacher qualifications, the CELTYL and YL Extension to CELTA. As a teacher, I have worked with young learners in several different countries, including Venezuela, Portugal and Spain. Teacher education has long been one of my main interests and I have many years' experience working with teachers, teacher trainers and educational managers in a wide range of contexts in both the private and state sectors. I have also frequently run teacher education courses for organizations such as the British Council and the Council of Europe, as well as Ministries of Education and other teaching institutions, in many different countries in Europe, Latin America and Asia. Over the years, I have co-authored several course books (including a multi-media project, *Bugs*, which won a British Council Innovation Award) as well as written supplementary materials and numerous articles about teaching children.

Thanks

This book reflects over twenty years of working with children and owes much to the many people who have shaped my thinking and classroom practice both directly and indirectly. I would specially like to acknowledge and thank the following people who, through their books, conference sessions and/ or seminars, have had a tangible influence at particularly formative times: Lynne Cameron, Bruce Campbell, Robert Fisher, Howard Gardner, Edie Garvie, Carolyn Graham, the late Susan Halliwell, and Penny Ur.

In turning classroom experience into a book, I would like to thank the Series Editor, Adrian Underhill, and everyone at Macmillan who have given me so much help: in particular, Kate Melliss for her commitment to the project; Anna Cowper for her sensitivity in helping to shape the material initially and for her support throughout; Jill Florent for her wise guidance and understanding at every stage of writing and for her dedicated help on the Index; and Alyson Maskell for her superbly insightful and meticulous editing. I would also like to thank Karen White for managing the editorial process, Balvir Koura for managing the design, Hazel Barrett for managing the permissions and Cindy Kauss for very kindly stepping in beyond the call of duty to help with these.

Huge thanks are also due to the following colleagues for generously contributing their expertise and insight in comments on draft versions of the introductions to different sections: Kay Bentley, Gail Ellis, Dr Janet Enever, Chris Etchells, Jayne Moon, Shelagh Rixon and Scott Thornbury, although any remaining shortcomings are of course my own. I should also like to thank the two anonymous readers of the draft for their useful feedback and constructive advice.

Last but not least, very special thanks to my family – to my husband, Alan Matthews, who acted as an initial reader of the introductions to each section and who, together with our (now grown up) children, Jamie and Hannah, gave me constant encouragement and support, and without whom the book might never have got beyond being an idea.

Dedication

For every teacher who tries to bring out the best in every child.

About the series

Macmillan Books for Teachers

Welcome to Macmillan Books for Teachers. The titles are written by acknowledged and innovative leaders in each field to help you develop your teaching repertoire, practical skill and theoretical knowledge.

Suited to newer and experienced teachers, the series combines the best of classic teaching methodology with recent cutting-edge developments. Insights from academic research are combined with hands-on experience to create books which focus on real-world teaching solutions.

We hope you will find the ideas in them a source of inspiration in your own teaching and enjoyment in your professional learning.

Adrian Underhill

Titles in the series

An A–Z of ELT
Scott Thornbury

Beyond the Sentence
Scott Thornbury

Children Learning English
Jayne Moon

Discover English
Rod Bolitho & Brian Tomlinson

Learning Teaching
Jim Scrivener

Sound Foundations
Adrian Underhill

Teaching Practice
Roger Gower, Diane Phillips & Steve Walters

Teaching Reading Skills
Christine Nuttall

Uncovering Grammar
Scott Thornbury

700 Classroom Activities
David Seymour & Maria Popova

Blended Learning
Barney Barrett & Pete Sharma

General introduction

No printed word nor spoken plea
Can teach young minds what they should be.
Not all the books on all the shelves
But what the teachers are themselves.

RUDYARD KIPLING

There are two phrases which are quite commonly used
by teachers, as if they were in some way conclusive.
One of them is 'It works'. The reaction to this ought
always to be 'Why?' The fact that something works
is no more interesting than the fact that something
does not work. What we need to do in both cases is
to enquire about the conditions for success or failure,
and to make them as explicit as possible so that they
can be tested by other teachers in different teaching
situations. The phrase 'It works' should mark the
beginning of enquiry, not its conclusion.

HENRY WIDDOWSON [1]

1 About the book

Aims of the book

This book is a compendium of activities for
primary language teachers of children aged 4–12.
The main aims are:

- to provide a wide-ranging resource of practical
  ideas which are easy to use and which can be
  adapted flexibly and creatively in different
  contexts and situations
- to provide support for primary language
  teachers in their own professional development
  through encouraging them to use the activities
  as a springboard for personal investigation
  and enquiry into what 'works' for them in their
  own classes.

Who the book is for

The book is suitable for:

- primary language teachers working in the
  state or private sectors
- candidates following teacher education courses
  such as the Cambridge ESOL CELTYL, the YL
  Extension to CELTA and the Trinity Certificate
  in TESOL
- language teachers who have been trained to
  teach adults and who are being asked to teach
  children for the first time.

The approach of the book

The main approach of the book is to provide
immediate, workable ideas and solutions to the
perennial question of *What on earth am I going
to do with my class tomorrow?* Parallel to this, the
approach emphasizes developing an awareness
of the complex factors involved in working
effectively with classes of children and laying a
solid foundation in primary language teaching
skills.

The activities are designed to take into account
the learning and development of the whole child,
rather than simply to provide a series of 'recipes'
for narrowly focused language practice. This is
reflected in the aims and procedures, as well as in
the comments and suggestions that follow each
activity, and in the scope of the Index, which also
includes reference to learning skills and attitudes,
as well as language, topics and lexical sets. The
activities are designed to be used creatively and to
generate a range of further personalized teaching
ideas. They are also designed to act as a guide
and support in developing your own criteria
for selecting and using activities appropriately
in class.

Description of the materials

General introduction

This is divided into two parts. The first part,
About the book, includes an outline of the aims
and approach, as well as a brief description of
the materials and how to use the book. The
second part, *Working with children*, contains
sections on creating optimal conditions for
children's learning, managing children positively
and general guidelines for setting up and using
activities in class.

Sections of the book

The book is divided into ten sections which reflect
key areas in primary language teaching. These
are: *Listening and speaking, Reading and writing,
Vocabulary and grammar, Storytelling and drama,
Games, Rhymes, chants and songs, Art and craft,
Content-based learning, ICT and multi-media,* and
Learning to learn. Each section introduction gives
an overview of methodological issues related to
the topic and invites you to reflect, analyze and

evaluate the teaching and learning that results from doing the activities.

Activities within each section

The activities are organized to reflect the topic and title of the section to which they belong. However, there is also some overlap between the sections in the sense that, for example, listening skills (Section 1) are also developed through activities in other sections such as *Storytelling and drama* (Section 4) and *Rhymes, chants and songs* (Section 6); reading and writing skills are also developed through activities in other sections such as *Content-based learning* (Section 8) and *ICT and multimedia* (Section 9). Similarly, activities which involve drama are also included in *Games* (Section 5) and *Rhymes, chants and songs* (Section 6) and activities which contribute to the development of children's *Vocabulary and grammar* (Section 3) also appear in several other sections of the book.

Overall, throughout the sections, there is a balance in activities suitable for children of different ages and levels. This balance varies depending on the section. For example, the sections on *Reading and writing* and *ICT and multimedia* contain fewer activities for very young children, whereas the sections on *Rhymes, chants and songs* and *Storytelling and drama* contain more. For each activity, information is given under the following headings: *level, age, organization, aims, language focus, materials, procedure, comments and suggestions*. Time is not included as part of this information since this is very variable and depends on the level and age of the children, the size of the class, as well as other factors relevant to individual activities, such as the number of vocabulary items in a game or the length of a story or text.

Level The level of activities is specified in relation to the Council of Europe's Common European Framework (CEF) bands and these are sub-divided into A1.1, A1.2, A2.1, A2.2, B1.1, B1.2. However, since the CEF has been developed with older learners in mind and the learning contexts and domains for children are somewhat different, and likely to be more limited in scope, this specification is approximate. The levels given for activities in each section are those that children are currently working towards, and not levels which they have actually attained. For example,

an activity which is specified as level A1.1 may be done by children who are almost complete beginners and just beginning to work towards level A1.1, rather than having already reached it.

In terms of recognized public YL exams which children may be working towards, the specified levels correspond in the following way: level A1.1 – equivalent to Cambridge ESOL Starters or Trinity ESOL Grade 1; level A1.2 – to Cambridge ESOL Movers or Trinity ESOL Grade 2; level A2.1 – to Trinity ESOL Grade 3; and level A2.2 – to Cambridge ESOL Flyers and Trinity ESOL Grade 4. Level B1.1 is equivalent to Trinity ESOL Grade 5 and level B1.2 to Cambridge ESOL Preliminary English Test and Trinity ESOL Grade 6.

Age Each activity includes the age range for which it is likely to be appropriate. It needs to be stressed, however, that this is likely to vary in different contexts and cultures, depending on a range of factors such as the age children start school and the approach to literacy in their first language (L1). For many activities, the age range specified is quite broad, eg 6–12. This indicates that the same technique or procedure may be suitable for different ages depending on either the materials used, or the way it is realized, or both.

Organization This explains how each activity is organized, eg whole class, pairs. Alternative forms of organization are also given, where appropriate, in the comments and suggestions which follow each activity.

Aims The aims specified for each activity include language aims as well as broader educational aims such as cognitive, content, social and attitudinal aims. Through considering learning aims in a holistic way, activities go beyond the narrow confines of isolated language practice and take into account children's overall education and development in a more rounded way.

Language focus This shows the main language that children will use during an activity. Where alternative language may be used, this is also stated and additional explanations provided in the comments and suggestions as necessary.

Materials These are designed to be easily available and/or easy to prepare. Photocopying is not usually necessary. Examples of materials to use or adapt are frequently provided, including sample texts, simple illustrations, diagrams, grids or mind maps to copy.

In some cases, optional materials such as, for example, puppets, real objects or other props are also suggested.

Procedure The procedure for activities is set out in steps which are easy to follow and/or adapt in ways which are suitable for your class. In some cases, the procedure described is for a generic activity, illustrated by an example, which you can then either use or apply in other ways.

Comments and suggestions These include such things as a commentary on the nature of the activity, guidelines and tips for doing it successfully in class, ideas for variations and follow-ups, suggestions of when it may be appropriate to use the activity and ideas for adapting it for older or younger children and/or different levels.

The Index

The Index is arranged into four alphabetically organized sections: *Language, Topics and lexical sets, Learning skills and attitudes, Activity titles*. The Index is designed to help you identify and select appropriate activities. The inclusion of learning skills and attitudes as part of the Index underlines the relevance of these in children's overall education and learning. References to these link in with the aims which are specified for activities.

Further reading

Suggested further reading is included on page 320.

How to use the book

The book can be used in a number of ways. If you want a general overview of a range of methodological issues on different topics related to teaching children, then you might like to read the general introduction first, followed by the introductions to each section, and familiarize yourself with the kind of issues and activities that each one contains. As a compendium, the book can be used flexibly to supplement a wide range of course books and syllabus-types (eg structural, functional, story, content- or topic-based) and dipped into whenever you want ideas for activities.

You can find what you need easily, either by looking in a specific section or under an appropriate heading in the Index. For example, if you have decided to use a specific story book with the children and are looking for ideas of how to exploit it, then it will be best to go directly to the section on *Storytelling and drama* and identify the activities that you think will be most suitable. If, on the other hand, you are doing a specific topic with the children, eg rainforests, or a unit of work which focuses on a particular lexical set, eg parts of the body, or an aspect of grammar, eg comparative adjectives, then you can find potentially suitable activities to use by looking these up in the Index. Alternatively, you can also use the Index to access activities which develop particular cognitive skills, eg classifying, or which are designed to promote social skills, eg collaborating, or activities which develop children's confidence and self-esteem.

Before using an activity in class, you might like to read the general guidelines for setting up and using activities (see *General guidelines* on pages 14–15). After using one or more activities from a particular section, you might like to reflect, analyze and evaluate the children's response to the activity, and your own, by answering the questions in *Reflection time* which are included at the end of the introduction to each section. These questions are also suitable to use as the basis of workshop discussions with colleagues. If you get into the habit of regular reflection as an integral part of the way you approach teaching–learning processes with children, you will find that over time you will build up conscious awareness of your own personal theories of teaching and learning. In this way you will develop a set of principled beliefs about what 'works' best in your classroom which is rooted in your own professional practice.

2 Working with children

Creating optimal conditions for children's learning

There is no definitive research evidence or universal agreement about the best age to start learning a foreign language and, as has been said[2], it is optimal conditions rather than an optimal age which counts. All children are unique in what they bring to the classroom and in their ability to process information and learn through different facets of their Multiple Intelligences[3]. They are also unique in their personal preferences and emerging learning styles. Whether you are working with four-year-olds or twelve-year-olds or any age in between, you may like to consider the ingredients of the

'C-Wheel'[4] (see figure 1) as a tool for helping you to create optimal conditions in order to maximize children's learning and enable everyone in your classes to blossom and thrive, both as engaged, responsible learners and as people.

Figure 1 **The C-Wheel**

The C-Wheel takes as its starting point the centrality of the child and the child's learning. It is made up of eight principal segments showing a range of factors which contribute to creating optimal conditions for children's language learning. All the ingredients of the C-Wheel start with the letter 'C', hence the name. There are also subordinate 'C' ingredients included in the description of some segments. The C-Wheel segments clockwise round the wheel are as follows:

1 Context

Children make sense of the world and of language through the context they find themselves in. Children pay far more attention to the whole situation than to language, and the younger they are, the truer this is[5]. It is only as children get older that they are able to deal with disembedded language, and this is often one of the problems with the transition from primary to secondary school. The context in which children carry out activities in the primary classroom needs to:

- be natural, real or understandable
- be relevant and make sense to the child

- allow for the discovery and construction of meaning
- allow for learning to be active and experiential
- encourage the use of language as a vehicle to do things which have a real purpose
- support children's understanding, for example, in the way visuals in a story book or body language, mime and gesture can do.

2 Connections

Optimal conditions for learning may be created when you actively look to build in connections within and between lessons in a number of ways. These include connections:

- to other areas of learning, eg science, maths (that is, when you build in real *content*, another 'C' ingredient)
- to the child's real life experience at home and at school
- to the way the child's life, language and *culture* (also a 'C' ingredient) compares and relates to English-speaking peoples and cultures
- to what has gone before and what will follow in the teaching–learning sequence
- between what the child already knows, about the language and about the world, and what is to be learnt
- between *what* is learnt and *how* it is learnt (that is, when there is also an integrated focus on helping children learn how to learn (see Section 10).

3 Coherence

Coherence is a factor in creating optimal conditions for learning in both the short and longer term. One way of making learning coherent is through creating meaningful contexts and making connections to other areas of children's learning and experience in ways described above. In terms of the internal coherence of what is being learnt, it is important that learning should never seem bitty or fragmented to children. At the same time, it needs to be broken down into appropriately sequenced steps, so that children don't feel overwhelmed. Over the course of the primary years it is important to ensure that there are plenty of opportunities for children to acquire and learn language in meaningful, comprehensible and supported ways. You also need to ensure that learning does not become fossilized at the level of language chunks or isolated lexis, but rather that patterns and regularities in the language system gradually emerge once the child is conceptually ready to perceive them (see also introduction to Section 3).

Coherence is also achieved when activities provide reasons for doing things that children can understand and perceive as relevant, and when the relationship of the outcomes to their own learning is made explicit and explained (see also introduction to Section 10).

4 Challenge

It is important to get the level and balance of linguistic and cognitive challenge right for children (and *cognition* is another C-ingredient here). If activities are too easy, children will simply become bored, de-motivated and possibly disruptive. If activities are too difficult, children are likely to become anxious, and also de-motivated and possibly disruptive.

The concept of the **zone of proximal development (ZPD)**[6] (see figure 2) is helpful in pitching activities and learning sequences at an appropriate level of challenge for children. In an everyday classroom context, the ZPD can be paraphrased simply as the gap between a child being able to carry out an activity without any help or support and an activity which is simply out of reach for the child at the moment and cannot be attempted without guidance from someone who is more knowledgeable or skilled.

Level of potential development as determined through problem-solving under adult guidance
ZPD
Actual developmental level as determined by independent problem-solving

*Figure 2 **The ZPD (based on Vygotsky, 1978: 76)***

There is no point teaching below the bottom of the ZPD because the child can already function in a competent and independent way here and no new learning will take place. Equally there is no point teaching above the top of the ZPD because

the difference between this and the child's current level of competence is too great. In this way, the ZPD provides a valuable conceptual framework for situating the level of challenge in activities that may be appropriate for children at any one time – activities which stretch and extend learning, but at the same time are also achievable and allow for success.

'Flow'[7] is another relevant factor in relation to challenge and creating optimal conditions for children's language learning .'Flow' is to do with feeling emotionally positive and motivated towards a learning activity and your own performance. It's the feeling you have when you're 'on a roll' with an activity you may have to do, such as writing a report or an essay, or even preparing a lesson! 'Flow' is a kind of feeling towards an activity and your own performance that says something along the lines of 'yes-it's-a-challenge-but-I'm-into-it-and-I'm-determined-to-do-it-and-I'll-feel-great-when-I-do-it'. Preconditions for creating 'flow' have been described as 'a perfect balance between available skills and challenges'[8]. When children experience 'flow', they feel a sense of positive energy, pleasure and self-motivation towards their own learning. This drives and inspires them from within, rather than as a result of any external reward, and can be a powerful motor for sustaining persistence and effort in learning over the longer term.

When the level of challenge is right and children experience 'flow', this leads to a sense of achievement and success. As the saying goes, 'success breeds success', and this in turn helps to build up *confidence* (another C-ingredient) and self-esteem and also often to positively influence behaviour and heighten levels of performance too.

5 Curiosity

Closely related to the concepts of challenge and 'flow', it is also important to arouse and maintain children's curiosity, to generate a desire to learn and find out about things, and to make the act of learning interesting, relevant and enjoyable in its own right. In order to maximize learning we need to sustain children's interest and curiosity in appropriate age-related ways. This curiosity can extend to all kinds of topics, as well as to other people, cultures and language itself. The way you realize different classroom techniques, activities and procedures should provide opportunities for children to be curious, investigative and experimental. It should also create a climate in which asking questions and finding out for yourself is encouraged rather than suppressed.

6 Care

Another essential factor in creating optimal conditions for learning is the affective climate created in children's learning environment. As has been said, 'Children don't care how much we know until they know how much we care.'[9] All children need to feel treated and cared about as individuals rather than as a group to be controlled. In large classes this may sometimes be difficult, but can be got round by developing strategies for finding time for personalized moments in which you can convey that you know and care about each child. (see also *Relationships* p.11 and *Respect* p.13).

Care for children also manifests itself in the extent and nature of the support you give children while they are learning. Scaffolding[10] is the metaphorical term often used to describe the special kind of help given by the teacher at any one time to make it possible for the child to progress from imitating, repeating or copying, to being able to perform more competently and independently, in other words to cross the ZPD referred to earlier. In language classes, support or scaffolding for children's understanding and developing language use may be provided by, for example,

- using visuals and real objects
- using mime and gesture
- modelling processes to carry out activities
- recasting and expanding children's language in a natural way
- providing opportunities for rehearsal and experimentation
- asking questions appropriately
- responding to children's meaning
- providing encouraging feedback
- appropriate and constructive praise.

Using positive language is another important factor in creating an environment of care. You may like to reflect on the number of negative or critical comments, as opposed to positive or supportive comments, that you give children during lessons. In the findings of a small-scale study[11], it was found that on average children receive 460 negative or critical comments and 75 positive or supportive comments every day. Through thinking about ways in which we can comment positively and supportively about what children are doing appropriately or getting right, rather than focusing and commenting on what they are not doing appropriately or getting wrong, it is possible to create a shift in the emphasis of care we give children. This can potentially have a hugely beneficial impact both on their attitudes and their learning.

7 Community

Community is the superordinate for three other important C-ingredients: *communication*, *collaboration* and *cooperation*. In order to create optimal conditions for learning, we need to work towards creating a sense of community in the classroom where:

- activities are shared experiences and events
- children are encouraged to cooperate and collaborate, and to help and respect each other
- diversity is positively valued and there is recognition that all children will contribute and participate in uniquely different ways
- there is natural and real interaction and communication in a social environment
- children are given opportunities to respond in personal, divergent ways and to choose what they want to say or do.

8 Creativity

The mention of personalized, divergent responses leads naturally to the last, but not least, segment of the wheel – creativity. All children come to class with creative potential, and developing creative thinking skills as an integral part of language lessons:

- allows 'hidden talents' to emerge
- increases personal investment and ownership – thus helping learning to become more memorable
- develops fluency and flexibility in thinking
- allows for humour and fun.

Opportunities for creativity are often lost as children get older. In order to create optimal conditions for learning, we need to include activities which develop creativity, fantasy and imagination that are so much part of the world of primary-aged children and which can lead to positive new learning. Even when children only have very limited linguistic competence in

English it is feasible to include activities which develop creativity, fantasy and imagination (see references to developing creative thinking skills in the Index for some examples) and the outcomes are frequently both inspired and inspiring.

Around the C-Wheel

Teaching and learning never take place in a vacuum. Around the edge of the C-Wheel, therefore, are factors which provide the parameters and filters for shaping the ways in which optimal conditions for learning may be realized appropriately in different cultures and contexts.

As a reflective activity, you may like to think about how the C-Wheel applies to your own teaching and children's learning where you currently work. As you use the activities in the book, you may also like to extend, adapt or reinvent the C-Wheel to show the factors that, from your own experience of classroom practice, seem to provide optimal conditions for children learning in your context.

Managing children positively

The main aim of managing children positively is to create and maintain a happy working environment in which the norms and rules of classroom behaviour are respected and children are engaged in purposeful activity and feel secure and motivated to learn. Maintaining a balance between children's enjoyment and acceptable behaviour is often one of the greatest challenges primary language teachers face.

As children move up through the primary years, it can be helpful to see classroom management as a continuum. At one end of the continuum, with very young children, classroom management is essentially implicit, with the main focus on socializing children who are new to a school environment. This includes establishing learning routines and the formation of good habits, such as learning to pay attention and learning to share. By contrast, at the other end of the continuum, once children are in upper primary and familiar with school life, classroom management can be much more explicit, with well-established expectations of behaviour, and reference to rules and norms which children understand and are largely willing to accept.

With any age group, however, it is important to be aware that managing children positively is a complex, interactive process in which a dynamic web of relationships and interrelated patterns of behaviour are built up over time. As part of managing classes of children positively, it is important to take initiatives to establish clear working parameters as soon as you meet a new class for the first time. In order to do this, you may find it useful to consider the seven 'R's [12] : Relationships, Rules, Routines, Rights, Responsibilities, Respect and Rewards.

Relationships

The relationships that you establish with the class as a whole, and with the individuals that make up each class, lie at the heart of establishing a healthy and happy working environment and managing children positively. In a small-scale survey conducted with children between the ages of six and eleven in Spain [13], children most frequently identified qualities of good teaching that reflected their relationship with the teacher. These included someone who is fair, patient, caring, affectionate, kind, funny, listens to you, helps you, makes you work, treats you as a 'person', tells you off if necessary, but doesn't get angry or shout. These qualities, identified by children themselves, provide a useful basis for thinking about the kind of relationships you intend to establish with your classes. Although every teacher has their own unique personality and 'teaching persona' and will go about establishing relationships in different ways, the following general points help in getting off to a positive start.

- Learn the children's names as soon as you can and always use them.

- Avoid having favourites (or at least make sure that this doesn't show).

- Listen to what children have to say. (If a child wants to tell you something at an inappropriate moment, postpone till later but don't then forget, as this will give the message that you're not really interested.)

- Build up children's confidence and self-esteem and encourage them to believe they can succeed.

- Be patient if you need to explain or give instructions more than once.

- Create time for personalized moments in which you convey that you know and care about each child as an individual. This may be, for example, at the start or end of lessons, before or after formal teaching begins or while children are working individually.

- Model behaviour that you would also like the children to adopt. For example, be polite and courteous, use 'please' and 'thank you' when you ask them to do things, smile and greet them whether in or out of the classroom.
- Use praise appropriately to provide constructive feedback and encourage participation and effort.
- Use inclusive language, eg *Let's ... / Today we're going to ...*
- Use humour and show a sense of fun.
- Be fair and firm about enforcing rules and insisting on children's adherence to classroom norms.
- Keep calm at all times; try not to raise your voice or shout.
- If you tell a child off, make it clear it's their behaviour that you don't like, not them.
- Be consistent. If you say that you or the class will do something, make sure it happens.
- Mark and return work promptly. Be constructive in your comments and respond to children's intended meanings, rather than just language accuracy or spelling.

As you develop your relationship with different classes and children, it is a good idea to get into the habit of monitoring yourself and how things are going. Through reflection and analysis of your own behaviour (the only person in the class whose behaviour you can actually change), you will be able to identify aspects of this that make your relationships work better and produce a more positive response in the children.

Rules

Rules may either be imposed by the institution or established as part of your working parameters. It is usually best to have as few rules as possible and to make sure that the rules themselves, eg *We must put up our hands if we want to speak*, as well as the reasons for the rules, eg *If we all talk at once no-one listens to what we have to say*, are clear to everybody.

It is important that any rules you establish are perceived as fair by the children and that you can actually enforce them. For example, a rule which states *We must always speak English in class* may, at some moments, be perceived as unfair by the

children if, for example, they have something they desperately need to say. It may also at times be neither desirable nor possible for you to enforce. In this case, a communication rule formulated differently, eg *We must ask if we need to speak Spanish (May I speak Spanish, please?)* may be more effective. This version of the rule will not only establish English as the main language of communication in the classroom but will also encourage the children to think twice before giving you a signal that they need to resort to their mother tongue.

The most effective rules are ones which are expressed using inclusive language (*our* rules for *our* classroom) and for which the children feel ownership. It also helps when rules can be expressed positively rather than negatively in order to highlight desired behaviour. For example, in a rule such as *We mustn't shout in our classroom*, the immediate association is to think of shouting, whereas if it is expressed positively, eg *We must talk quietly in our classroom*, the same rule is more likely to work to better effect.

The best way to establish rules as part of your working parameters is to involve the children in decisions about which ones will apply. Depending on the age and level of the children, the procedure you use to do this can vary (see 10.14 for an example).

Routines

Routines are established patterns of behaviour in which everyone knows what is expected of them and what they should do. The introduction of classroom routines is instrumental in setting up working parameters which function effectively with all ages. With very young children they play a particularly important role. In order to introduce and establish routines successfully, you need to have a clear plan of the areas these will cover and the form they will take. For example, you may like to think of routines for such things as:

- greeting the children
- taking the register
- starting lessons
- getting into pairs or groups
- moving from one part of the classroom to another
- doing particular activities, eg ones involving movement or stories

- getting the children's attention
- starting and stopping activities
- giving out and collecting in materials
- looking at and/or correcting children's work
- collecting in and returning homework
- going to the toilet
- tidying up
- ending lessons.

Familiar routines help to make children feel secure and confident in the classroom. They promote cooperation as, for example, when we all help tidy up together. They also foster a sense of community and belonging, in the sense that we all know and share the way we work and do things together in the classroom. Routines can also play an important role in providing opportunities for natural language acquisition. For example, in a routine at the start of lessons where you ask and talk about the weather, over time children will naturally acquire the language to do this without being formally taught. As children become increasingly familiar with routines and what is expected of them at different stages of learning, they act with greater autonomy. This helps you to manage your classes positively. It also helps save your energy and voice (highly important if you are teaching full-time) as, in some areas at least, once routines are established, children will only need a prompt to know what to do.

Rights and responsibilities

Rights and responsibilities are often two sides of the same coin. Here are some examples from the children's perspective. If you have the *right* to join in the lesson, then you also have the *responsibility* to remember to bring your books. If you have the *right* to speak in the classroom and have others listen to you, then you also have the *responsibility* to listen to others when they do the same. If you have the *right* to use the classroom scissors, crayons and glue, then you also have the *responsibility* to share them with others when they need to use them as well. If you have the *right* to have a turn in games, then you also have the *responsibility* to respect the turns of others when they play. If you have the *right* to see the pictures when the teacher tells a story, then you also have the *responsibility* not to block the view of others. If you have the *right* not to be mocked or laughed at,

then you also have the *responsibility* not to mock or laugh at others, and so on.

Although it is unlikely to be appropriate to talk about rights and responsibilities explicitly with children, it is important to model through your own behaviour the way you value these. For example, with responsibilities, if a child constantly forgets their book, it may be necessary for the teacher to issue frequent reminders and reprimands. However, what typically happens is that on the one day the child remembers to bring their book, the teacher may well not comment at all. If you wish to positively reinforce the child's sense of responsibility in this area, then you need to show explicitly that you value this. A quiet word of praise, eg *Well done for remembering your book today, Juan!* is much more likely to reinforce the behaviour you want than saying nothing, which may leave the child wondering why he bothered to bring his book anyway or whether you even noticed or cared.

Similarly with children's rights, it is important to show through your behaviour that you value these and are willing to protect them. If, for example, a child mocks or laughs at another child in the class, you need to make it clear that this behaviour is completely unacceptable. In this case, it may also be worth explicitly discussing the reasons for this, possibly in a private moment after the class, and inviting the child to consider the situation from the other child's point of view by asking how they would feel if the same happened to them. In encouraging children to reflect on their behaviour and see things from others' point of view, they are more likely to act towards others in a responsible way.

Respect

Respect is the glue which holds together all the other 'R's. Respect cannot be taught explicitly but it can be modelled in all your behaviour, such as using the children's names, being polite, respecting personal space, valuing diversity, recognizing that children contribute and participate in different ways and understanding that they have feelings and 'off days' just like you. The most important thing about fostering an atmosphere of mutual respect as part of managing children positively is to remember that respect works two ways. If the children feel that you respect and treat them like individuals rather than a class to control, they will also respect and respond to you as individuals, rather than with a collective group mentality which is always much harder to manage positively.

Rewards

It is usually best not to use any system of extrinsic rewards to raise motivation levels and/or ensure good behaviour, at least at the outset. This gives a positive message that you expect everything to go well. However, there may be times with some classes when introducing a reward system can be an effective way to reinforce appropriate behaviour and/or to add an additional, motivational, feel-good factor to things that are already going well.

Reward systems can be devised in all kinds of different enjoyable ways, eg using stars, stickers, points, smiley faces, raffle tickets or marbles in a jar. If used effectively, they can help promote collaboration, appropriate behaviour and individual as well as class effort. However, if used without care, they may also have the opposite effect and create a divisive atmosphere of 'winners' and 'losers', in which some children become obsessed by collecting stars or points, or whatever it is, while others adopt a strategy of opting out, which has a correspondingly negative effect on their motivation, effort and behaviour in class.

The kinds of reward systems which generally work most effectively are ones where individuals are rewarded and the reward contributes cumulatively to a prize which is won by the whole class. For example, in the case of collecting marbles in a jar, individual children, pairs or groups may be awarded marbles during lessons for, for example, working well, making an effort to speak English, helping others, completing their work carefully. As soon as the jar is filled with marbles, the whole class gets a prize. This may be something as simple as watching a favourite video, having a quiz, playing a favourite game, or whatever else you and the children choose. The jar for the marbles should not be too big, so that the prize or pay-off is attainable over a reasonably short period of time, eg a week or, maximum, two. If it takes a whole term (a long time in the life of a child!) to fill up the jar and earn the prize or pay-off, then they are likely to lose interest and enthusiasm. When giving a reward, this is best done instantly as an ongoing part of your teaching, so that the association

between the reward and the reason for it is always fresh in the children's mind, eg *Great work, Daniel and Antonio. I only heard English in the game! Two marbles in the jar for you!*

The effect of individuals collecting rewards for the benefit of the whole class creates an atmosphere in which there is positive peer pressure to make an effort, work well and produce appropriate behaviour. A collaborative reward system like this can also be made fun by your challenging the class, eg *Can you fill the jar by Friday? I don't think so! Show me I'm wrong!*

If you do decide to use a reward system such as the one above, it is a good idea to regularly vary the system you use for accumulating rewards, eg marbles, raffle tickets, stars, as, if you always use the same, it is likely after a while to lose its associations of pleasant expectation, surprise and fun. It is also essential always to use reward systems in the positive way in which they are intended, ie as rewards, rather than negatively or punitively, for example, by taking, or threatening to take marbles back out of the jar once they have been awarded.

When planned for and implemented together, the seven 'R's provide an integrated framework for managing children positively and creating a happy working environment in which teaching and learning take place in an effective and harmonious way. As a reflective activity, you may like to note or think of practical ways in which you can implement the seven 'R's in your own classes.

General guidelines for setting up and using activities

Once you have selected the activity or activities you are going to use in class, the following is a general checklist of things you may need to do:

- **Prepare the language** you will use to set up activities before going into class.
- **Use a familiar signal** to get the children's attention (this may be a gesture, a tambourine, a clap of the hands, a bell, a rhyme, standing in a special place or putting on a special hat).
- **Wait** until everyone is quiet and attentive before starting to explain what to do. Try and use neutral body language and facial expression as you do this. Don't give up – at least one child will notice that you are waiting to start and do your management for you.

- **Announce the general nature and purpose of the activity**, eg *We're going to … play a game / do a group survey / act out a role play in order to …*

- **Establish or create a context** and use this as an opportunity to, for example, pre-teach vocabulary, elicit what children know, encourage them to predict or guess answers, etc.

- **Divide the class** into pairs, groups or teams, if this is relevant for the activity. Use gesture, names and/or numbers to reinforce children's understanding of intended groupings and to show the physical organization if necessary, eg if children need to turn round their chairs.

- **Give clear instructions** appropriate to the language level of the children. Keep instructions short and chunked into stages. Use simple language patterns and accompany your instructions by gesture, mime or visuals to clarify meaning.

- **Demonstrate** how the activity works in practice. In the case of a pairwork game, for example, this may mean inviting one or two children to the front of the class either to play part of the game with you or each other while the rest see how it works, or playing the game with the whole class once or twice before they play in pairs.

- **Check** that the children understand what to do before they start the activity. If relevant, it is also worth double-checking that they know their partner, group, team or role. If you speak the children's L1 but don't want to use it yourself in class, you may like to ask a child to tell you the instructions briefly in their own language. This enables you to check the children have understood and has the added bonus of giving those children who may need it the opportunity to hear the instructions repeated in their own language.

- If appropriate, **model** aloud procedures or thinking processes that children will need to go through themselves in order to be able to carry out an activity or task successfully.

- As soon as you are sure everyone clearly understands what to do, **give a signal to start** the activity.

During and after the activity

- Allow the children to carry out the activity independently and responsibly and make it clear that you expect them to do this.

- Monitor discreetly and be ready to encourage, give help or stop any trouble developing if necessary, but don't make the children feel you are watching them too closely.

- Train the children to look up in order to let you know when they have finished doing a task or activity and always be ready with something else for them to do while others finish.

- Use a signal for stopping the activity before moving on. Always stop while children are still engaged and enjoying the activity and before interest has waned.

- Vary the way you give feedback, check answers or invite individual children to report back or tell/show the rest of the class what they have done. Keep up a pace to this in order to avoid the children becoming distracted or losing interest. Actively look for positive things to comment on about the way individual children or the whole class has worked in order to convey how much you value this.

- Conduct a learning review (see introduction to Section 10) as a follow-up to the activity if appropriate.

Conclusion

Every teacher, every class and every child is different. This is what makes primary language teaching a unique and dynamic ongoing learning experience, not only for the children but for you. This book suggests ideas for creating optimal learning conditions for children, ways to manage children positively and over 500 activities to use in class – at the end of the day, however, in mediating and making it all 'work' successfully, your best resource is most definitely YOU!

References

1 This quotation is from Widdowson H. 'The incentive value of theory in teacher education', ELTJ Vol 38, 1984.

2 Rixon, S. 1999 *Young Learners of English: Some Research Perspectives.* Harlow: Longman

3 Gardner, H. 1983 *Frames of Mind: The Theory of Multiple Intelligences.* London: Fontana

Gardner, H. 1999 *Intelligence Reframed: Multiple Intelligences for the 21st Century.* New York: New York Basic Books

Howard Gardner's theory of Multiple Intelligences currently identifies eight different intelligences. These are: verbal-linguistic, musical, logical-deductive, visual spatial, kinaesthetic, interpersonal, intrapersonal and naturalist.

4 I originally developed the C-Wheel to use on teacher education courses with primary language teachers. See also Read, C. 'Towards Whole Learning' in *Creating a Positive and Practical Learning Environment,* Eds. Gika & Superfine, IATEFL 1998

5 Donaldson, M. 1978 *Children's Minds.* London: Collins/Fontana

6 Vygotsky, L. 1978 *Mind in Society.* Cambridge Mass: Harvard University Press

7 'Flow' is a concept originally developed by Csikszentmihalyi and other American psychologists working at first on the peak performances of athletes. See Csikszentmihalyi, M. 1990 *Flow: the Psychology of Optimal Experience.* New York: Harper and Row

8 van Lier, L. 1996 *Interaction in the Language Curriculum: Awareness, Autonomy & Authenticity.* Harlow: Longman

9 Andrés, V. de 1999 'Self-esteem in the Classroom or the Metaporphosis of Butterflies.' In Arnold, J. (ed.) *Affect in Language Learning.* Cambridge: Cambridge University Press

10 Wood, D., Bruner, J. & Ross, G. 1976 'The role of tutoring in problem-solving.' In *Journal of Child Psychology and Psychiatry* 17/2: pp 89–100

11 reported by Jack Canfield in DePorter, B. & Hernacki, M. 1995 *Quantum Learning.* London: Piatkus Books

12 Read, C. 'Managing Children Positively.' In ETP Issue 38, May 2005

13 Read, C. 'What makes a teacher special for you?': unpublished survey of 120 primary school children that I carried out in Spanish in January 2000 at Arturo Soria School, Madrid, with the help of Ana Soberón.

Section 1 **Listening and speaking**

When children start learning English at primary school, there is usually an emphasis on developing listening and speaking skills. Through listening to English, children are led naturally into speaking. From using single words and formulaic language, children gradually develop the ability to produce language and to interact with others in a more extended way.

Learning to listen

When learning to listen in English, children are actively engaged in constructing meaning and making sense of what they hear. To do this, they use not just language but their knowledge of the world and clues provided by the context, for example:

- their expectations about the intentions of the speaker
- predictions about what they will listen to
- the speaker's use of voice, mime and gesture
- the reason and purpose for which they are listening
- other features in the immediate environment which support their understanding, eg flash cards, story or course book illustrations, posters, real objects, puppets, sound effects on a CD, or the visual setting of a DVD.

Essentially, young children need plenty of opportunities to listen to language embedded in engaging and meaningful contexts. Through listening, children become familiar with the sounds, rhythm and intonation of English. Listening also allows children to recognize, understand and respond to language non-verbally before they produce it themselves.

Classroom talk as, for example, when you give instructions, organize and manage different classroom activities and give the children feedback, encouragement and praise is a major source of listening material for children. As far as possible, it is advisable to use English for this kind of classroom language. Through repetition and routines, you will build up an expanding repertoire of language that children understand and respond to as part of everyday communication in class.

In addition, you can use: Storytelling and drama (Section 4), Games (Section 5), Rhymes, chants and songs (Section 6), Art and craft (Section 7), and Content from other areas of the curriculum (Section 8), to develop children's listening skills. Ideas for these are included in each section. The listening activities in this section include ideas which do not fall directly into those categories and also ideas which can be adapted and applied to listening texts from other sources, such as the course book.

Developing listening skills

In L2, as in L1, children develop listening skills before speaking skills. It is enriching to expose them to language that is ahead of their productive competence, as long as their understanding is guided and supported, for example through mime, illustrations and/or the activity they are asked to do. From the outset, it is important to use a variety of different spoken text types: instructions, rhymes, stories, songs, dialogues, conversations, descriptions. It is also important to build up confidence and show children that they can be successful listeners without necessarily understanding every word. The use of longer texts, such as stories, can also help develop children's extensive listening skills, where listening is motivated by pleasure rather than information (see Section 4, Storytelling and drama).

When you do a listening activity, it is often useful to plan for the following three stages: *before*, *while* and *after* listening.

Stage 1
Before listening, you need to create a clear context which interests and motivates the children and you need to establish a reason and purpose for listening. It may be appropriate to introduce new language or vocabulary which occurs in the listening text at this stage too. Children can also be encouraged to predict and make active guesses about the listening, based on pictures or other clues.

Stage 2
While listening, children do one or more activities to develop listening sub-skills such as listening for global understanding or gist,

listening for specific information or detail, listening for mood or attitude, and to show their understanding either verbally or non-verbally or through a written response, such as completing a grid.

Stage 3

After listening, it may be appropriate to ask children to report back, express their opinions or relate the text to their own lives in a speaking activity using at least some of the language it contains.

Learning to speak

Speaking is a complex skill and the difficulty for children learning a foreign language should not be underestimated. Although children are good at imitating and may acquire better pronunciation than older learners, they are still developing language and discourse skills in their L1. Their age and level of social, cognitive and emotional development need to be taken into account when planning speaking activities in English.

Spoken interaction and spoken production

Speaking skills can be broadly divided into two areas: spoken interaction and spoken production. Spoken interaction refers to the ability to ask and answer questions and handle exchanges with others, whereas spoken production refers to the ability to produce language, for example, in a rhyme, a description or an account, such as retelling a story. It is important to develop children's competence in both these areas in order to build up confidence and lay the foundations for future learning.

Initially children will benefit from activities which require lots of repetition and which help them to memorize vocabulary and 'chunks' of language and acquire pronunciation in a natural way. Many such activities can be found in the sections on Vocabulary and grammar (Section 3), Games (Section 5) and Songs, rhymes and chants (Section 6). Much of the language children produce in the early stages of learning will be single words or short formulaic utterances, eg *I'm fine*. There may also be a tendency to mix languages, eg in the case of Spanish-speaking children, *Dáme el rubber* (give me the rubber), *Mira! El monkey está allí* (Look! The monkey's there). Rather than explicitly correcting language mistakes, it is best to respond to children's meaning and what they are trying

to communicate. As you do this, you can remodel or recast what they say, eg *Yes. You're right. The monkey's there!*

Very young children may be reluctant to speak at first, and it is important to give them time to listen and absorb the sounds of English before participating actively. Insisting on participation is likely to be counter-productive. The best strategy is usually to provide lots of opportunities for speaking activities in a very secure and non-threatening way, eg through choral repetition of action rhymes or choral counting games, and allow children to join in when they are ready.

In order for children with only minimal linguistic competence to start learning to communicate in English, it is important to establish simple classroom routines from the outset. These include, for example, greetings and goodbyes at the beginning and end of lessons, asking for permission, eg to go to the toilet, sharpen pencils, get crayons, etc and classroom language, eg *I don't understand. / Can you repeat that, please?* Even very young children can be taught the following three phrases formulaically: *I think …, Maybe … I don't know* and then be encouraged to use these regularly in class 'discussions', eg
T: (pointing to picture) *Who's behind the bush?*
P1: *I think it's the lion.* P2: *Maybe it's the elephant.*
P3: *I don't know.*

Frameworks for speaking activities

Whatever the children's age, it is important to provide frameworks for speaking activities which encourage them to use English for real purposes which they can relate to, rather than simply practise language for its own sake. As children become increasingly capable of interacting with each other in pairs and groups, it is also important to ensure that speaking activities are designed to foster active listening, turn-taking and respect for other people's opinions. None of these can be taken for granted because children are still developing these skills and attitudes as part of their general educational and personal development. Speaking activities which are personalized and offer choice tend to increase children's willingness to participate. Such activities give them 'ownership' of language, thus helping to make learning more memorable. Whenever possible, it is beneficial to establish frameworks where children are motivated to speak and feel that they have something they want to say.

In order for a speaking activity to be successful, it is important to set clear goals and establish what the outcome(s) of the activity will be. It is also important to ensure that the language demands are within the children's current level of competence and to prepare for, model, rehearse and demonstrate the language children will need to use before they begin. It may also be appropriate to introduce explicit rules to ensure that the activity is done in English, rather than in L1, and to elicit and talk about the reasons for this (See Section 10, Learning to learn).

Over time, through speaking activities which use different interaction patterns and provide opportunities for meaningful practice of a range of discourse types, children will develop confidence in their ability to produce English and to interact with others in class.

Pronunciation

Through exposure to English in the form of classroom language, instructions, games, stories, dialogues, conversations, rhymes, chants and songs, children develop familiarity with the sounds, rhythm and intonation patterns of English and imitate these features in a natural way. It is important to provide lots of models and to build up children's confidence through the acceptance of approximate pronunciation. This gives them time to acquire good habits in an unforced way. Insistence on correct pronunciation with very young children is likely to prove counter-productive.

With older children, in addition to an implicit, global approach to pronunciation, it is often appropriate to do activities designed to raise awareness of particular features of pronunciation that may be different from the children's own language. Pronunciation activities included in this section can be adapted to cater for particular difficulties that speakers of different languages may have. (See also Section 6, Rhymes, songs and chants, for further activities to improve pronunciation, and Section 2, Reading and writing activities, for ideas on developing awareness of sound–spelling correspondences in words.)

Reflection time

As you use the listening and speaking activities in this section with your classes, you may like to think about the following questions and use your responses to evaluate how things went and plan possible improvements for next time:

1 **Motivation:** Did the children want to listen/ speak during the activity? Why? / Why not?

2 **Purpose:** Was the purpose of the activity clear? Was it a purpose that the children could relate to?

3 **Preparation:** Were the language demands of the activity appropriate? Was there sufficient linguistic preparation and practice beforehand (if necessary) to enable the children to do the activity?

4 **Learning support:** What support did you give to help children understand and/or use language during the activity (eg pictures, actions, prompt words, a chart to fill in)? Was the learning support appropriate?

5 **Personalization:** Did the activity provide an opportunity for personalization? If so, how did this affect the children's response?

6 **Timing:** Was the activity a suitable length to sustain interest and involvement? Did it need to be timed?

1.1 Gym sequence

Level A1.1, A1.2   **Age** 4–10   **Organization** whole class

Aims To listen and respond to instructions; to focus attention and harness children's physical energy in a positive way.

Language focus imperatives, action words, parts of the body

Materials *Essential:* none / *Optional:* aerobic music

Procedure

1 Ask the children to stand up.
2 Give instructions for a short gym sequence in a rhythmic way and do the actions with the children in time with the music, if you use this, eg *Hands in the air. One, two! Touch your toes. One, two! Bend to the left. One, two! Bend to the right. One, two! Run on the spot. One, two! Turn around. One, two! And sit down. One, two! (Let's begin!)*

Comments and suggestions

- This activity works well as a routine for starting lessons. Change or add to the instructions regularly but always remember to demonstrate new actions first.
- Ask the children to put their chairs under their desks and move away from these before starting. This is important for safety reasons.
- Avoid actions like stretching arms out sideways in order to prevent physical contact between the children and possible disruption.
- Increase the level of challenge either by giving more complex instructions, eg *Put your left elbow to your right knee!* or by going faster, or by not modelling the actions yourself.
- With older children, you can ask pairs to prepare their own instructions for a gym sequence and take turns in different lessons to do these with the rest of the class.
- With younger children, keep the sequence short, introduce variations less frequently and avoid using 'right' and 'left'. Alternatively, you can simply say, eg *Do this! One, two! Do this! One, two!* in a rhythmic way and children copy your actions.
- This activity can also be used in conjunction with 10.3 in order to create a state of readiness for learning.

1.2 Listen and respond

Level A1.1, A1.2   **Age** 4–8   **Organization** whole class

Aims To listen and respond non-verbally to instructions; to develop concentration skills, confidence and physical coordination.

Language focus *In the examples:* imperatives and :
1.2b classroom objects
1.2c, 1.2e classroom objects, toys, any vocabulary on flashcards
1.2d classroom objects, prepositions of place
1.2f any vocabulary on flashcards, eg animals
Alternatives: any other familiar lexical set, eg parts of the body, food, colours, clothes

Materials *Essential:* classroom objects, (1.2f) flashcards / *Optional:* flashcards

Procedure

Use any one or a combination of the following procedures.

1.2a Do the actions

1 Give the children instructions, eg *Walk! Jump! Run! Skip! Hop!* Do the actions with the children at first.

2 Repeat the sequence regularly, eg as an opening or closing lesson routine. Introduce other new actions gradually to the sequence, eg *Fly! Walk on tiptoe! March!* Stop doing the actions yourself as children become familiar with the language and can respond confidently.

1.2b Show me

Say, eg *Show me your book / your pencil / your shoes* and hold up or point to the items with the children as they respond at first.

1.2c Bring me

1 Lay out classroom objects, toys or flashcards on a table away from you and the children.

2 Ask pairs of children to bring you the objects or flashcards in turn, eg *Bring me the red crayon, please! / Thank you.*

1.2d Put it here

1 Ask the children to hold up a crayon (or other small classroom object).

2 Say, eg *Put the crayon on your book / in your bag / under your desk* and children respond with you at first.

3 Speed up the instructions as children become more confident.

1.2e Take a photo

1 Ask the children to imagine they have a camera and demonstrate this.

2 Either stick flashcards on the walls around the classroom or use real objects or furniture.

3 Give instructions to pairs of children in turn, eg *Take a photo of the elephant, please!*

4 Children walk over to the flashcard of the elephant and pretend to take a picture. They can also say *Click!* each time they do this.

5 Encourage the rest of the class to clap and say, eg *Fantastic!* if they take a 'photo' of the object you say.

1.2f Jump to the elephant

1 Stick flashcards on different walls around the classroom.

2 Give instructions to pairs or groups of children in turn, eg *Jump to the elephant! / Hop to the tiger!*

3 Encourage the rest of the class to clap and say, eg *Hurray!* if children do the correct action and go to the correct flashcard.

Comments and suggestions

- Short activities such as the above give children lots of opportunities to listen to the teacher and respond non-verbally. This is non-threatening and builds up children's familiarity with listening to English in a natural way.

- You can vary the instructions to fit in with whatever you are teaching, eg *Touch your nose / eyes / mouth* for parts of the body; *Touch something blue / red / green* for colours; *Point to your trousers / shoes / shirt* for clothes; *Eat a(n) banana / apple / ice cream* for food. The instructions can also form part of simple action games (eg 5.9 Musical instructions).

- You can also increase the challenge by varying the type of instructions, eg *Jump three times! / Touch your nose! / Point to the window!* or by saying, eg *If you're wearing something blue, wave your arms! / If you're wearing something red, touch your toes!*

1.3 True or false?

Level All   **Age** 4–12   **Organization** whole class

Aims To listen and respond non-verbally or verbally to sentences which are true or false; to develop concentration and pay attention.

Language focus any, depending on the topic, story or unit of work, eg present simple, past simple, *can* (for ability), *there is/are*

Materials *Essential:* none / *Optional:* flashcards, poster or course book picture

Procedure

1 Decide on the non-verbal or verbal response you want the children to give in the activity and explain and demonstrate this. For example, non-verbal responses for true sentences could be for children to put their hands on their heads and for false sentences to fold their arms. Verbal responses could be to say *Yes!* or repeat the sentence for true sentences and to say *No!* or turn the sentence into a true one, for false sentences.

2 Say a series of true or false sentences based on the unit of work, topic or story that you are currently doing and children respond verbally or non-verbally in the way you have set up.

Comments and suggestions

- With very young children, this activity needs to be done with reference to real things, pictures or actions in the children's immediate environment, eg using flashcards *The duck is yellow / The horse is red.* With older children, sentences can be longer and need not necessarily refer to the immediate environment. For example, sentences may relate to topic or content-based work, eg *Mammals lay eggs / Bears can swim,* or to a story or other listening or reading text the children have done.

- You can vary the non-verbal responses in the activity depending on the age of the children, the space in your classroom, as well as the stage in the lesson and whether or not physical movement is appropriate. For example, in a more kinaesthetic version of the activity, you can ask children to jump three times for true sentences and turn round on the spot for false sentences.

- This activity gives you an opportunity to observe and evaluate informally which children respond confidently and appropriately each time, and which children wait and copy what their friends do, and who may need more individualized attention and help.

- The activity is also suitable to use for visual observation of a poster or picture in the course book, eg *There's a man driving a blue car.*

1.4 Mime what happens

Level All   **Age** 4–10   **Organization** whole class

Aims To listen to a sequence of events; to show understanding through mime; to supply missing language in the sequence.

Language focus *In the example:* present simple, clothes, places, actions, food, personal possessions
Alternatives: past simple, any other familiar vocabulary

Materials *Essential:* none

Procedure

1 Invent a simple sequence of events about something that happens to the children. Tell the events to the children and get them to respond by miming what happens. Do this with them at first, eg *One day it's very cold. You put on your coat, your gloves and your hat. You get your bicycle and you ride to the park. Suddenly you see a friend. You're very happy and you wave to your friend. You get off your bike. You put your bike on the grass and you and your friend play football together.*

You run, you kick the ball and, yes, you score a goal! Now you're very tired and very hot. You buy an enormous ice cream. Mmm, it's delicious! Suddenly you look at your watch. It's time to go home! You pick up your bicycle and wave goodbye to your friend. You ride your bicycle home.

2 Repeat the sequence. This time, if appropriate, do the mimes but leave gaps in the telling. Children do the mimes and also supply the words, eg T: *One day it's very* (mimes shivering) … PP: *cold!*

Comments and suggestions

- This activity can be graded depending on the language you use as well as whether you model the actions for children to copy.

- Through miming the events, children associate language and meaning kinaesthetically, which helps to make it memorable.

- With younger children, it is best not to include more than four to six short sentences to mime, as more than this is likely to be confusing, eg *One day you go for a walk in the jungle. You hear a noise. You look behind the tree. Oh, no! There's a lion! You run away as fast as you can. Phew! Now you're safe!* You also need to do the mimes each time you repeat the sequence with this age group.

- With older children, you can repeat the sequence, leaving more and more of the language for them to supply, until they are reconstructing the events independently. As a follow-up, you can ask them to write or complete a version of what happens or to prepare another similar sequence of events to tell the class in the same way.

1.5 Colour dictation

Level A1.1   **Age** 4–8   **Organization** individual, whole class

Aims To listen and colour a picture following instructions; to develop concentration skills; to name colours and/or describe a picture.

Language focus *be*, present simple, colours, familiar vocabulary

Materials *Essential:* crayons / *Optional:* a photocopy of any line drawing depicting known vocabulary (one for each child)

Procedure

1 Draw a simple picture on the board, eg as below, and ask the children to copy this, or give out photocopies of the picture.

2 Say sentences to describe the picture, eg *The house is purple.* Children colour the picture following your instructions.

3 Once the children have finished, either ask questions, eg *What colour is the house?* or get children to describe the picture, eg *The house is purple.*

Comments and suggestions

- If you draw a picture on the board for children to copy rather than use a ready-prepared picture, encourage the children to predict and guess what you are drawing as you do this.
- With younger children, using a ready-prepared picture is recommended, as copying one from the board will be too challenging and time-consuming.
- As you describe the picture, get the children to put only a dot of colour on each item. They then finish colouring at the end. This avoids the problem of children colouring at different speeds. It also helps you to manage the class if the children are sharing crayons.
- Alternatively, you can make the dictation collaborative by asking the children to suggest the colours. This also enables you to provide richer language input as you negotiate these, eg T: *The house is …* P1: *Orange!* P2: *Pink!* T: *O.K! Great! How many think it's orange? How many think it's pink?* (children raise their hands) *Fantastic! The house is orange. What a beautiful house! I'd like to live in an orange house! Would you like to live in an orange house?*
- The speaking part of the activity can be turned into a memory game by asking children to turn over the completed picture before describing it. Alternatively, if you colour the picture on the board differently from the instructions you have given or, if you prepare a copy of the same ready-prepared picture coloured differently, children can be asked to find the differences between this picture and their own.

1.6 Visualization

Level All **Age** 8–12 **Organization** whole class

Aims To listen to a description and create a picture in your mind; to develop the imagination; to settle the class and create a quiet, reflective mood.

Language focus *In the example:* present simple, present continuous, *can* (for ability), places, adjectives of description, adjectives of feeling
Alternatives: any familiar language and vocabulary

Materials *Essential:* none / *Optional:* a CD of slow, relaxing music

Procedure

1 If you have music, play this softly as a background to the activity.
2 Ask the children to put down their pens, relax and close their eyes. Ask them to try and imagine the scene as you describe it, eg *It's a beautiful, sunny day. You're at the seaside. The sun is shining brightly and the sea is deep blue-green. You're lying on a towel on the sand. Your whole body feels warm. You can feel the sand in your fingers – it's soft and warm. You can hear the sound and rhythm of the waves breaking on the beach – splash, splash, splash. You can hear the sounds of birds in the sky. In the distance you can hear some small children playing. Now a dog is barking and you can hear the engine of a small boat passing by.*
3 When you finish, give the children a few moments to come out of the fantasy you have created and back into the world of the classroom. If you like, you can ask questions about the visualization, eg *Where were you? What could you see/hear? How did you feel?*

Comments and suggestions

- This activity is not suitable for all classes – you need to have a good and trusting relationship with the group.
- It is important either not to include unfamiliar language or to make sure that any language is comprehensible, eg *Now a dog is barking … (Woof! Woof!)*
- It helps to modulate your voice softly and rhythmically and to speak quite slowly as you describe the scene you want the children to imagine.
- With younger children it is advisable to keep the visualization short.

- You need to plan when you do the activity carefully. The children are unlikely to be able to switch suddenly from a very lively activity to a quiet, reflective one and so you need to lead them to this gradually.
- As you do the activity, notice the different responses of the children. Although some may feel restless and find it hard to create pictures in their minds, you can tell that others can imagine the scene very vividly.

1.7 Sentence round

Level All   **Age** 4–12   **Organization** whole class

Aims To complete sentences following a given starter; to take turns; to develop confidence and self-esteem.

Language focus any, eg present simple, adjectives to describe feelings: *I like … / I feel happy when … / When I grow up, I want to …*

Materials *Essential:* a small object, eg coloured handkerchief, soft ball, toy, stone or puppet to pass round the circle

Procedure

1 Ask the children to sit in a circle.

2 Choose a sentence starter for them to complete which relates to the topic or language of the lesson and either say this or write it on the board.

3 Give one child the object to pass round the circle and invite them to complete the sentence with something which is true for them.

4 They then pass the object to the child next to them, who completes the sentence in a similar way, and so on round the circle.

Comments and suggestions

- This activity provides a framework for practising a particular language pattern in a personalized way.
- Through passing the object, a clear protocol is established for turn-taking and when to listen and when to speak.
- The repetition of the sentence starter provides repeated modelling for children who may be more hesitant about speaking. If you like, you can also build in a convention whereby children can say 'pass' the first time the object goes round the circle if they are not ready to contribute.
- With very young children, you may like to pass round a familiar puppet and ask the children to tell their sentences to the puppet rather than to the whole group. This is more intimate and may feel less threatening for some children. Alternatively, if you use a soft ball, you may find it works better to roll the ball to different children in the circle, who say a sentence and then roll the ball back to you each time, rather than passing it round the circle. This also keeps children alert as they do not know who you will roll the ball to each time.
- With older children, you may like to precede the sentence round with a pair work task in which children find out about their partner and use the sentence round to report, eg *When Elena grows up, she wants to be a famous ballerina.*
- See also, eg 7.8, 10.1 and 10.2 for other activities to develop children's confidence and self-esteem.

1.8 Favourites bar chart

Level A1.1, A1.2 / A2.1, A2.2   **Age** 6–10   **Organization** whole class

Aims To say your favourite thing in a particular category; to build up a bar chart on the board; to understand how to read a bar chart; to show interest and respect for other people's opinions.

Language focus *In the example:* sports, *be,* present simple, questions with *Who, What, How many, like,* numbers
Alternatives: animals, colours, food, fruit, school subjects, types of music, eg pop, rock, classical, jazz, rap, reggae, types of stories, eg animal stories, adventure stories, detective stories, ghost stories, fairy tales, science fiction

Materials *Essential:* pieces of paper or card to fit in the bar chart on the board (one for each child), blu-tac / *Optional:* large piece of paper or card

Procedure

1 Draw a line near the bottom of the board and divide this into six or however many sections you wish to include in the activity.

2 Write the names of the sports, or draw symbols, in each section, eg *basketball, football, tennis, karate, judo, swimming.*

3 Draw a vertical line and write numbers going up the board on the left side of the chart.

4 Give each child a piece of paper (the same size as the sections in the chart on the board) and ask them to write their name on this in large letters.

5 Ask individual children to say their favourite sport in turn, eg *My favourite sport is swimming* and to come and stick the card with their name in the appropriate place on the chart.

6 When all the name cards are in place, use the bar chart to talk about the class's favourite sports, eg *What's the class's favourite sport? Who likes karate? How many girls/boys like judo? What's David's favourite sport?*

5						
4						
3		Maria				
2	Isabel	David				
1	David	Alex	Jessica			
	basketball	football	tennis	karate	judo	swimming

Comments and suggestions

• This activity is useful in helping children understand how a bar chart works. Point to the numbers on the left of the chart and the name cards children have stuck in each section to demonstrate how to read the chart.

• As a follow-up, children can write or complete sentences about the chart, eg *In our class, the favourite sport is …. / … girls/boys like … .*

• If you wish to display the bar chart after the activity, build it up on a large piece of paper or card instead of the board. For best effect, the chart and the pieces of paper with children's names should be in contrasting colours.

• With older children, it may be appropriate to ask them to make a version of the bar chart using computers and PowerPoint (see 9.13).

1.9 Classroom shop

Level A1.1, A1.2, A2.1, A2.2 **Age** 6–10 **Organization** pairs, whole class

Aims To ask for and give things to people; to ask and say prices; to take turns; to use *Please* and *Thank you.*

Language focus *In the example:* present simple, *have got, can* (for requests), *How much …?*, shops, shopping, classroom objects, numbers, colours
Alternatives: I'd like …, clothes, pets, toys

Materials *Essential:* classroom objects, eg rulers, pens, scissors, pencil cases; pieces of paper to display prices (6–8 for each pair or group); paper money (eg 10 x 1 euro paper 'coins' for each child) / *Optional:* plastic toy money to use instead of paper money

Procedure

1 Divide the class into pairs or groups of four.

2 Ask each pair or group to choose six classroom objects from among their possessions to go into their classroom shop.

3 Ask the children to decide the price for each item, write the prices and make a display on their desks. (Make sure the children realize that the shop is only pretend and that they are not really going to sell their possessions!)

4 Elicit and practise language you want the children to use and demonstrate the activity with one pair, eg T: *Good morning.* P: *Good morning* T: *Have you got any rubbers?* P: *Yes, we have. Look.* T: *How much are the rubbers?* P: *Two euros.* T: *Can I have this rubber, please?* P: *Yes, of course. That's two euros, please.* T: *Here you are.* P: *Thank you.* T: *Goodbye.* P: *Goodbye.*

5 Ask the children individually to write a shopping list of three things they want to buy.

6 Give out paper money (the same amount to each child, eg 10 x 1 euro paper 'coins').

7 Divide the class in half and assign the role of 'shoppers' to one half and 'shopkeepers' to the other half.

8 Children visit the shops and buy three things.

9 At the end, ask the children to show and tell what they have got, eg *I've got a red pen, a green pencil sharpener and a rubber* and how much money they still have left, eg *I've got two euros.*

10 Children then change roles and repeat the activity.

Comments and suggestions

- This activity needs careful management. If you are concerned about having half the class as 'shoppers' at the same time, it is best to ask fewer children to take turns to visit the 'shops'.

- The currency for the classroom shop can either be the currency of the children's country or, eg American dollars, Australian or British pounds. With younger children, it is usually better to use the currency they are familiar with and, eg one and two euro coins only. With older children, it may be appropriate to use dollars or pounds, especially if they are likely to travel to these countries.

- After the activity, older children can compare dollars or pounds with their own currency and/ or use the internet to find out current conversion rates (see 9.20).

- This activity can be done in a similar way for a variety of different shops, eg clothes shop, pet shop, toy shop, grocers shop. For these, you will need to either prepare or download from the internet pictures of items to sell in the shops or use plastic fruit or real toys, etc.

1.10 Find a partner

Level A1.1, A1.2   **Age** 8–12   **Organization** whole class

Aims To find a partner by asking and giving personal information; to logically deduce who is your partner from the answers to your questions.

Language focus *What's your name? How old are you? Where are you from? I'm ...* countries, nationalities, cartoon characters

Materials *Essential*: a set of pairs of cards, one card for each child, with invented information; for a class of 24, you can make two each of the following cards:

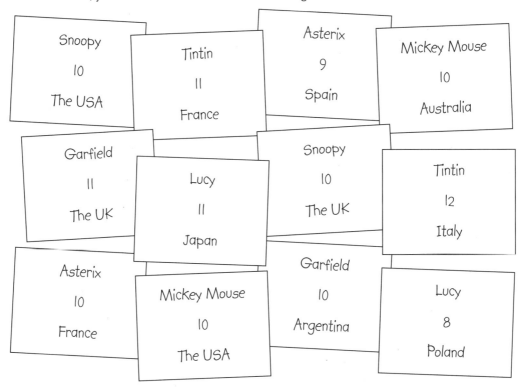

Procedure

1 Give out one card to each child.

2 Instruct them to look at the information on their card and to keep this a secret.

3 Tell them to imagine that this is their name, age and the country where they are from.

4 Explain that the object of the activity is to find a partner who has exactly the same identity as themselves.

5 Elicit the questions children will need to ask, ie *What's your name? / How old are you? / Where are you from?*

6 Demonstrate the activity by asking one or two children questions, eg T: *What's your name?* P: *I'm Asterix.* T: *Oh. Me too. How old are you?* P: *I'm ten.* T: *Oh, I'm nine. So we can't be partners.*

7 Ask the children to stand up and walk round the class taking turns to ask and answer questions until they find their partner.

8 As soon as they find their partner, ask the children to sit down together and write a short description of themselves, eg *My name is Snoopy. I'm ten years old and I'm American / from the USA.*

Comments and suggestions

- This activity can be made shorter or longer and more or less challenging, depending on how many pieces of information you include on each card. For example, you could just include names or you could add additional information, eg the month of their birthdays or their favourite food.

- If necessary, you can build in an additional rule to the activity which is that children should only answer questions if these are asked in English.

- As soon as children find their partner, it is important to give them a short task to do (eg as described in the procedure above) in order to settle them down and to ensure they don't disrupt others who are still doing the activity.

- If you are designing your own cards, you need to ensure that there are at least two pairs of cards with characters of the same name and only minimally different information.

- Instead of cartoon characters, you can also use the names of real film, pop or sports stars that the children know.

1.11 Three things about me

Level All   **Age** 8–12   **Organization** whole class (mingling) or groups

Aims To say things about yourself; to ask and find out about other people; to show interest and respect for the opinions of others.

Language focus *In the example: like + -ing*, sports and free-time activities
Alternatives: present simple, *can* (for ability), *want to*, *going to*, food, places, countries

Materials *Essential:* sticky paper notes, or small pieces of paper and paper clips (one for each child)

Procedure

1 Give a sticky paper note (or small piece of paper and clip) to each child.
2 Ask them to draw three small pictures to show what they like doing in their free time, eg a TV, a book, a football, and attach the paper to their fronts.
3 Explain and demonstrate that children should walk round the class, look at each others' drawings and talk about them, eg P1: *I like watching TV. Do you?* P2: *No, I don't. I like reading.* P3: *Me too.*
4 At the end, ask children to stand next to the person they've talked to who they have most in common with.
5 Ask a few pairs to report back to the class, eg *We both like playing football.*

Comments and suggestions

- This activity personalizes language and the pictures play an important role in providing a focus and prompt for children to speak.

- It is advisable to get the children to rehearse the language they are going to use before the activity, eg through choral repetition.

- It may be a good idea to set a time limit for both parts of the activity, eg drawing the pictures – two or three minutes, and mingling – five minutes.

- If the class is large, you may prefer the children to remain seated and do the activity in groups. Alternatively, if the children are seated in rows, you may ask them to just mingle with the children in their row.

- The activity can be used to practise a variety of different language structures and vocabulary, eg *I can play the piano. / I want to go to Peru. / I like chicken. / I'm going to the cinema.*

1.12 Describe and draw

Level All   **Age** 8–12   **Organization** whole class, pairs

Aims To draw and describe a picture; to listen and draw a picture from a description; to notice similarities and differences between pictures.

Language focus *In the example: there is/are*, present continuous, *have got*, actions, things in the park, prepositions of place, *on the left/right, at the top/bottom, in the centre*
Alternatives: any lexical set suitable to draw in a picture, eg furniture, parts of the body (people or animals)

Materials *Essential:* none / *Optional:* photocopies of two different pictures to describe and draw (one for each child)

Procedure

1 Ask the children to tell you things you can find in a park and write a list on the board, eg *tree, flower, bush, bench, pond, boat, kite, football, bike, skateboard, baby, child, man, woman, dog*.

2 Ask the children to draw two frames approximately 15x10cms with a ruler in their notebooks.

3 Ask them to choose six items from the board and secretly draw a picture of a park scene which contains these items in one of the frames. Give a time limit for this, eg five minutes.

4 When the children are ready, divide the class into pairs.

5 Explain that they should take turns to describe their picture to their partner and draw their partner's picture in the second frame.

6 Draw a frame on the board and demonstrate the activity by getting one child to draw what you describe, eg T: *There's a tree on the left. Two boys are playing football near the tree. On the right there's a pond. There's a boat on the pond. A child is flying a kite above the pond.*

7 Children take turns to describe and draw their pictures.

8 At the end, they compare their pictures, identify the similarities and differences and report back, eg *We've both got flowers in our pictures. / In my picture, there aren't any boys.*

Comments and suggestions

• This is a well-known activity which can also work well with children.

• It's advisable to familiarize children with phrases such as *on the left/right, at the top/bottom, in the centre* before the activity. It may also be helpful to label a frame on the board with these phrases for reference during the activity.

• It's important to insist that children draw simple pictures, using stick figures, and to set a time limit for drawing, as otherwise some children may draw elaborate pictures which are difficult to describe.

• Other contexts that work well for this activity are: drawing a room at home, eg a bedroom or living room, or drawing an imaginary animal, person or monster.

1.13 Photo of me

Level All   **Age** 8–12   **Organization** pairs, whole class

Aims To identify friends in photos; to describe what you were like when you were younger; to show interest in others; to develop self-esteem; to become aware of the way you change as you grow older.

Language focus *In the example:* be, have got, *present simple, parts of the body, adjectives to describe people, toys, favourites*
Alternatives: was/were, *past simple,* used to

Materials *Essential:* photos of the children when they were babies or toddlers (one photo of each child)

Procedure

1 During the previous week, ask all the children to bring in a photo of themselves when they were babies or toddlers.

2 Give each photo a number and stick them on the walls round the classroom.

3 Divide the class into pairs.

4 Ask the children to write the numbers in a list in their notebooks.

5 Ask them to go round the class together identifying who they think is in each photo, eg *I think it's … / Me too! / No, I think it's …*.

6 Ask the pairs to report back to the class who they think is in each photo. Ask *Why?* and encourage them to justify their answers, eg *She's got big eyes.*

7 Give each photo back to their owner as it is identified.

8 If children are A1 level, ask them to hold up the photo and tell the class one or two things about themselves, eg *In this photo I'm two years old. I've got my favourite teddy bear.* If children are A2 level or higher, ask, eg *What were you like when you were younger?* and children respond, eg *I was fat. / I had curly hair. / I liked milk. / I used to cry a lot. / My favourite toy was a yellow duck.*

9 Alternatively, divide the class into pairs and ask children to tell each other five things about when they were younger.

10 They then report back to the class and/or write a description of themselves or each other.

Comments and suggestions

- A few children may either forget to bring a photo or not have one. In this case, you can ask them to draw a picture of when they were a baby or toddler instead.

- Children usually find it very enjoyable looking at each others' photos and talking about when they were younger. Interest and curiosity in each others' past also helps develop self-esteem.

- This activity can also be done in conjunction with the rhyme 'When I was one' (see 6.14).

1.14 Fashion show

Level All   **Age** 8–10   **Organization** groups, whole class

Aims To prepare a fashion show; to describe what people are wearing.

Language focus present continuous, *have got,* clothes and accessories, colours

Materials *Essential:* clothes for the fashion show / *Optional:* dressing up clothes and accessories, eg handbags, scarves, hats, ties, fake jewellery; a camera or video camera

Procedure

1 In the previous lesson, ask the children to prepare and bring in (or wear) clothes from home for the fashion show. These can either be their own clothes or dressing-up clothes borrowed from members of their family.

2 As part of the preparation, ask children to be ready to describe themselves in the clothes they choose, eg *I'm wearing a long, purple skirt, a pink scarf and a white T-shirt. I've got a black handbag and a white hat.*

3 Divide the class into groups of 4–6 children.

4 Ask each group to decide the order for their show and who is going to present the 'models'. If there are any children who do not want to participate in the fashion show themselves, they can be asked to do the commentaries. Ask the children to prepare and write the commentaries for their fashion show in their groups, using a framework, eg *This is …. He/She's wearing … . He/She's got … .*

5 When the children are ready, move the desks, if necessary, to create a 'catwalk'.

6 Ask the groups to take turns to present their fashion shows to the rest of the class.

Comments and suggestions

• At higher levels, children can prepare more detailed commentaries with more complex vocabulary, eg *a striped/checked shirt, a v-neck/polo-neck jumper, a hat/cap/beret.*

• As the groups do their fashion shows, you can give a task to the rest of the class in order to focus their attention while they watch, eg *Find two things that are the same as your show* or *Be ready to say the clothes you like best.*

• You can also organize a class vote to find out which fashion show the children think is best (children can vote for any group apart from their own). However, it is best not to do this if you think it may lead to disappointment and loss of self-esteem.

• If you have a digital camera with a video function, you may like to video the 'shows' and download and watch them later with the sound down so children can reconstruct the commentaries. Alternatively, you can take photos of the children and they can subsequently use these to write descriptions and make a display of their 'show'.

1.15 My ideal bedroom

Level All   **Age** 9–12   **Organization** whole class, individual, pairs

Aims To plan, draw and describe your ideal bedroom; to ask and find out about other people's ideal bedroom; to compare ideal bedrooms.

Language focus furniture, prepositions of place, asking questions, *but*

Materials *Essential:* none / *Optional:* picture of a child's bedroom, A4 paper for each child

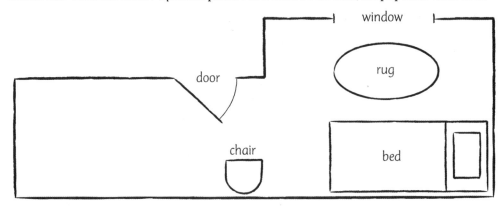

Procedure

1 Show children the picture of a child's bedroom if you have one.

2 Ask them to name bedroom furniture, eg *bed, table, desk, chair, rug, lamp, wardrobe, chest of drawers, mirror, shelves, bedside table, notice board* and write the words they suggest in a list on one side of the board. Remind them of others if necessary.

3 Draw a plan of a bedroom on the board and ask the children to copy this onto a page in their notebooks or give out sheets of plain A4 paper for them to do this.

4 Explain that you want them to design their ideal bedroom and to decide where each item of furniture should go on the plan.

5 Demonstrate this by drawing shapes and labelling them on the plan on the board.

6 Children work individually and design their bedrooms. Set a time limit, eg five minutes.

7 When they are ready, divide the children into pairs.

8 Without looking at each other's plans, get them to ask each other questions and find five differences, eg P1: *Where's your bed?* P2: *It's opposite the window.* P1: *Oh, my bed is near the door.*

9 At the end, children compare their plans and check the differences they have found.

10 Ask a few pairs to report to the class, eg *My wardrobe is opposite the window but David's wardrobe is next to the desk.*

Comments and suggestions

• Children frequently enjoy the 'design' side of this activity. However, it may be important to stress that the plan is 'ideal' and to be sensitive to the fact that, in real life, children's rooms may well be small and/or shared with siblings.

• At lower levels, the activity can be done with as few as six items of furniture and the prepositions *next to, near, opposite, between.*

• As a follow-up, children can be asked to draw and label plans of their real bedrooms at home. They can either take turns to describe these in the next lesson or write a short description.

• This activity can also be used for children to design, eg their ideal living room or their ideal garden.

1.16 Machines at home

Level All   **Age** 10–12   **Organization** individual, pairs, whole class

Aims To identify machines at home and who uses them; to ask and answer questions about machines members of your family use; to be aware of gender differences in machines that members of your family use.

Language focus present simple, questions and answers in third person, machines at home, members of the family, (adverbs of frequency, *because*)

Materials *Essential:* none

name	dishwasher	washing machine	telephone	computer	vacuum cleaner	iron
My mother	✓					

Procedure

1 Draw a simple grid on the board, as above, and ask the children to copy this.

2 Elicit the names of machines at home, eg *dishwasher, washing machine.*

3 Ask the children to write the words at the top of each column in the grid.

4 In the column on the left, ask the children to write members of their family, eg *My mother.*

5 Ask the children to think individually about who uses the machines in their family and to write ticks (✓) in the correct spaces in the grid.

6 Divide the class into pairs.

7 Children take turns to ask questions and find out about their partner's families, eg P1: *Does your father use the dishwasher?* P2: *Yes, he does. Does your sister use the iron?* P2: *No, she doesn't.*

8 At the end, ask some children to tell the class, eg *My mother uses the computer. / My father doesn't use the iron* and/or to write sentences about their families using the grid.

Comments and suggestions

• Try and find out machines children have at home and only use these in the activity.

• Show interest but make sure you never respond judgementally to things children tell you about their families.

• Children can also use adverbs of frequency as part of the activity, eg *Does your mother use the microwave? Yes, sometimes. / My brother never uses the iron. / My father often uses the computer.*

• As a follow-up, you may like to ask children why they think some people in their families use the machines and others don't, eg *My brother uses the microwave because he can't cook. / My father uses the vacuum cleaner because he likes cleaning the house.*

1.17 Listening grid

Level All   **Age** 9–12   **Organization** individual, whole class

Aims To listen to a dialogue or text for detail and complete a grid; to use the grid to reconstruct the information.

Language focus *In the example:* present simple, daily routines, times
Alternatives: any other suitable language and vocabulary

Materials *Essential:* a text or dialogue for children to listen to, eg from the children's course book, a prepared grid based on the text or dialogue (see example below) / *Optional:* cassette/CD and player

name	get up	have breakfast	go to school	have lunch	go home	have dinner	go to bed
Vanessa	7.30						
Jack							
Martha							

Procedure

1 Draw the grid you have prepared on the board and ask the children to copy it.

2 Explain that they should listen to the text you are going to read and note the times in the grid.

3 Give an example, eg *Vanessa gets up at half past seven* and write this in the table.

4 Play the cassette/CD or read the children the text yourself once or twice, eg *Vanessa gets up at half past seven. She has a shower and cleans her teeth and then she has breakfast at eight o'clock.*

Vanessa goes to school with her father at half past eight. She has lunch at half past twelve and she goes home on the bus at quarter to four. After school Vanessa does her homework and watches TV. She has dinner at seven o'clock with her mother and father. She goes to bed at half past nine.

5 Children note the times in the grid and compare and check their answers.

Comments and suggestions

- Listening grids provide a flexible means of checking comprehension of texts or dialogues about two or more people, places, animals or things. They are easy to prepare.
- The use of a grid provides an alternative to asking *Wh-* questions after listening. Instead you can say, eg *Tell me about Vanessa* and children reconstruct key information in the text using their completed grids.
- The use of a grid avoids children having to write complete answers and enables them to focus on listening, which is the target skill, rather than writing during the activity.
- The completed grid provides a framework and prompt for oral and/or written reconstruction following the activity.
- In many cases, all the activity requires is that children write ticks and/or crosses in the grid as they listen, eg in texts or dialogues about people's likes and dislikes or descriptions of different animals and features that they have or haven't got.

1.18 Follow the route

Level A1.2, A2.1, A2.2   **Age** 9–12   **Organization** pairs

Aim To give and follow directions on a simple plan or map.

Language focus imperatives, directions, places in a city or town, ordinal numbers

Materials *Essential:* none / *Optional:* photocopies of a plan or map (one for each child)

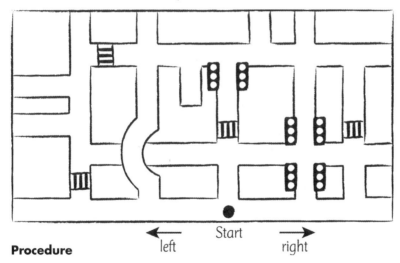

Start
←left   →right

Procedure

1 Divide the class into pairs.

2 Draw a simple plan or map on the board (see example above).

3 Ask the children to copy this and individually decide where their house is (or the supermarket, a lost puppy, treasure, a party, a concert etc, depending on the context you wish to use), and to draw an X in the place on the map, keeping this secret from their partner.

4 When the children are ready, explain that they should take turns to give each other directions and to draw the route to their partner's house (or other place) on their maps.

5 Mark the start position on the map on the board and draw arrows to show left and right.

6 Demonstrate the activity by giving one child directions, eg *Go straight on. Turn left. Go under the bridge. Turn first right.* and ask them to draw the route on the map on the board.

7 Once both children in each pair have had a turn giving directions, ask them to compare their maps and routes.

Comments and suggestions

- Make sure that the children have their maps the same way up as they do the activity so that there is no confusion between which is left and which is right when they give directions.

- This activity can be made less challenging if you do not add any additional elements to the map (children just say *Turn left/right. / Go straight on. / Stop.*) or more challenging if you do, eg *Turn right at the traffic lights. / Go under/past the bridge.*

- With higher levels and older children, the activity can also be done using enlarged copies or downloads of maps or plans from the internet and directions to real local places, eg tourist sites such as a castle or theme park. In this case, it may also be suitable to link the activity to planning an itinerary for a visitor (see 9.21) or a class outing (see 1.26).

1.19 Prize holiday course

Level All   **Age** 9–12   **Organization** individual, whole class (mingling)

Aims To ask about holiday plans; to deduce if someone has the same holiday plans as you.

Language focus *going to*, months, countries, holiday activities, sports (*because*, expressing opinions)

Materials *Essential:* none / *Optional:* photocopies of the table below (one for each child)

England	March	Rock climbing course
Scotland	August	Riding course
Ireland	December	Rowing course

Procedure

1 Ask the children to imagine that because they are so good at English they have won a holiday course in an English-speaking country.

2 Draw a table on the board as above.

3 Ask the children each to choose a country, a month and a course and note their choices on a piece of paper. Explain that they must keep this secret.

4 Ask children to go round the class asking questions to try and find someone who is going to do the same course, in the same country, at the same time as themselves.

5 Elicit and practise the questions before they begin, eg *Where are you going? When are you going? What are you going to do?*

6 Once children find one or more people who have chosen the same course in the same month and country as themselves, ask them to sit down together and write sentences about what they're going to do.

7 At the end, ask some pairs to report back.

Comments and suggestions

- The information in the table can be built up collaboratively, with the children suggesting options for countries, months and courses rather than you. This makes the activity more motivating, as it is then based on things the children really want to do.

- With older, higher level classes, instead of asking children to write sentences about where they're going, you can ask them to think of reasons for their choices and then report back to the class, eg P: *We're going to Ireland on a riding course in August.* T: *Why?* P: *We think there are beautiful horses in Ireland. / We think the weather will be better in August.*
- This can also be linked to using the internet to find out about real holiday courses (see 9.23).

1.20 Transport survey

Level All   **Age** 8–12   **Organization** groups, whole class

Aims To ask and find out how people come to school; to ask and find out how long the journey takes; (to compare journeys and means of transport).

Language focus *In the example:* present simple, questions with *How …?*, means of transport, journey times, preferences (comparative adjectives)
Alternatives: can, skills and activities; *have got,* pets, toys; *like,* food, fruit, vegetables

Materials *Essential:* none / *Optional:* photocopies of survey table (one for each child)

name	by bus	by car	by bus	by motor bike	walk (or on foot)	by train	🕐
Jo	✓						45 minutes

Procedure

1 Divide the class into groups of 4–6.

2 Draw the table on the board as above.

3 Ask the children to copy the table (or give them each a copy) and to write the names of the members of their group in the first column.

4 Elicit and practise questions children need to ask to complete the table.

5 Demonstrate the activity with one child, eg T: *How do you come to school, Jo?* P: *By bus.* T: *How long does it take?* P: *(About) 45 minutes.*

6 Children take turns to ask and answer questions in their groups and complete the table.

7 At the end, ask some children to report back to the class, eg *Jo comes to school by bus. It takes 45 minutes.* If appropriate, children can also compare journey times, eg *It's faster by car than by train. / It's slower by bike than by bus.*

Comments and suggestions

- With higher levels, you can ask children to say which means of transport they prefer and why, eg *I prefer cars. They're faster. / I prefer trains. You can read on a train.*
- With lower levels, you can omit the last column and the question about journey time.
- Children can use their completed tables to write sentences about the members of their group.
- This activity can be used as a lead-in to topic work on, for example, traffic, road safety, personal travel safety or air and noise pollution.
- Group and class surveys can be done on many topics, such as skills and activities children can do, pets or other things they have got, or food they like. (See also 9.13 for creating charts on computer to show the results.)

1.21 Find a friend who …

Level All   **Age** 10–12   **Organization** whole class

Aims To ask and answer questions giving personal information; to find and note the name of one person who answers 'yes' to each question.

Language focus *In the example:* present simple questions and answers, free-time activities, sports
Alternatives: any familiar language and vocabulary, eg *have got,* pets; past simple, free-time activities; *can* (for ability), sports, skills; *like + -ing; want to,* countries, jobs; present perfect, *ever*

Materials *Essential:* none / *Optional:* photocopies of a table to complete (one for each child)

Find a friend who …	name
… reads in bed at night.	
… has cereal for breakfast.	
… plays football on Saturday.	
… has piano lessons.	
… goes to bed at ten o'clock.	
… watches TV after school.	

Procedure

1 Prepare a table for children to complete (see above).

2 Write this on the board and ask the children to copy it into their notebooks, or give them each a photocopy.

3 Elicit the questions children will need to ask.

4 Explain and demonstrate that children should walk round the class, find a friend who answers 'Yes' to a question and write their names in the table. They should try to find a different friend for each question, eg T: *Do you read in bed at night?* P1: *No, I don't.* T: *Do you read in bed at night?* P2: *Yes, I do.*

5 Children sit down once their tables are complete.

6 Ask, eg *Who reads in bed at night?* and children reply with information they have collected.

Comments and suggestions

• This is a well-known activity which can also be used with children if it is not too long – no more than 6–10 items in the table.

• It is not usually suitable for younger children, as the mental operation of changing the statements in the table into questions can be confusing.

• If you have a large class, it may be best to get the children to mingle in rows, or in two halves, rather than the whole class together. This limits the amount of movement and helps to prevent over-excitement.

• In order to ensure children use English during the activity, you may like to build in a rule that they should only answer questions if these are asked in English.

• When children have completed their tables, it is important to set a further task to settle them and keep them engaged while others finish. This could be, for example, writing sentences from their tables or thinking of three more items they would like to find out about, eg *Find a friend who … goes to bed at midnight / … likes cowboy movies / … comes to school by bike.*

- Some examples of language you can use in variations of this activity are: *Find a friend who … has got a goldfish / … went to the cinema (last weekend) / … can do a handstand / … likes reading / … wants to be a doctor / … wants to go to Australia / … has been to London.*

1.22 Frisbee

Level All   **Age** 7–12   **Organization** pairs, whole class

Aims To say what you can use something for; to develop creative thinking skills; (to develop reference skills)

Language focus *can* (for possibility), any vocabulary children need

Materials *Essential:* frisbee or other object / *Optional:* picture dictionaries or bilingual learner dictionaries (class set)

Procedure

1 Show the children the object you have chosen for the activity, eg a frisbee.

2 Elicit or suggest one or two things you can do with a frisbee and demonstrate these, eg *You can use a frisbee as a plate. You can use a frisbee as a hat.*

3 Divide the class into pairs.

4 Ask them to see if they can think of ten more things to use a frisbee for and to write a list.

5 Explain that if they don't know the words in English, they should write them in their own language. Set a time limit for this, eg five minutes.

6 When the children are ready, go round the class getting one idea from each pair in turn, eg *You can use a frisbee as a shield.*

7 Count up the ideas as different pairs contribute.

8 Write words children say in L1 on the board.

9 At the end, ask the children to use bilingual or picture dictionaries with their partner to find two of these words each and then report back to the class.

10 As a follow-up, ask children to draw and label pictures of all the things that you can do with a frisbee.

Comments and suggestions

- By doing an activity like this, children are encouraged to think flexibly and to develop their imagination. They also feel a sense of achievement and 'ownership' of ideas and this helps to build self-esteem and make learning memorable as well as enjoyable.

- You may be surprised by how many creative ideas children have. An example by a seven-year-old child I once taught is 'You can use a frisbee as a swimming pool for ants'.

- Other everyday objects which are suitable to use for this activity are a ruler, a stone, a pot or a CD case.

Marco, age 7

1.23 Helping at home

Level All   **Age** 9–12   **Organization** individual, groups, whole class

Aims To reflect on ways in which you help at home; to ask and say ways in which you help at home; to complete a questionnaire in groups; to be aware of gender differences in ways boys and girls help at home.

Language focus *In the example:* present simple questions with *ever*, adverbs of frequency, jobs at home
Alternatives: activities and sports, food

Materials *Essential:* none / *Optional:* photocopies of the questionnaire (one for each child)

Do you ever ...	always	often	sometimes	never
... make your bed?				
... tidy your room?				
... lay the table?				
... clear the table?				
... put things in the dishwasher?				
... take the rubbish out?				
... water the plants?				

Procedure

1 Elicit ways in which it is possible to help at home, eg *make your bed, tidy your room.*
2 Write a questionnaire on the board (see example) and ask children to copy it into their notebooks, or give them each a photocopy.
3 Ask the children to complete the questionnaire for themselves by writing ticks in the appropriate boxes.
4 Divide the class into groups of four.
5 Explain and demonstrate that children should take turns to ask and answer the questions in their groups and write the initials of their friends in the appropriate boxes in the table, eg T: *Do you ever make your bed?* P: *Yes, often.* T: *Do you ever take the rubbish out?* P: *No, never.*
6 At the end, ask children in different groups to report back to the rest of the class, eg *Juan often lays the table. Pedro never lays the table. Ana and I sometimes lay the table.*
7 Ask the children to think about ways in which they could perhaps help more at home and listen to their ideas.

Comments and suggestions

• Before preparing the questionnaire, find out questions that are likely to be most relevant to the children, for example, if they don't have dishwashers at home, then it will be more appropriate to ask about washing the dishes or doing the drying up.
• The number of questions in the questionnaire dictates the length of the activity. It is usually best to restrict the number of questions to no more than 6–8 so that the activity is not too long.
• You may find it advisable to structure the activity so that children take turns to ask questions to each member of the group in turn.

- If you wish to make the activity easier, you can omit the adverbs of frequency and children simply answer *Yes, I do. / No, I don't.*
- With older, higher level children, it may be appropriate to discuss whether there is a difference in the way boys and girls help at home and the possible reasons for this.
- Activities based on simple questionnaires can also be used for other areas of personal habits, eg getting exercise (*Do you ever play a sport / walk to the shops?*) or eating healthily (*Do you ever eat fruit / drink milk?*). This can also be linked to content-based learning (see 8.13, 8.14, 8.19).
- Older children can also use computers to produce charts to show the results of questionnaires (see 9.13).

1.24 Agree or disagree?

Level A2.1, A2.2, B1.1, B1.2   **Age** 10–12   **Organization** individual, pairs, whole class

Aims To decide to what extent you agree or disagree with a number of statements; to listen to and express personal opinions; to show interest and respect for the point of view of others.

Language focus *In the example:* should, *expressing opinions,* because
Alternatives: must, ought to

Materials *Essential:* none / *Optional:* photocopies of the list of statements (one for each child)

1 Children should go to bed before 10 o'clock.	5 4 3 2 1
2 Children should have homework every day.	5 4 3 2 1
3 Children should do all schoolwork on computer.	5 4 3 2 1
4 Children should do sport every day.	5 4 3 2 1
5 Children should read one book every week.	5 4 3 2 1
6 Children should have more time to play.	5 4 3 2 1

Procedure

1 Explain that you recently read an article about children and you're interested to know the class's opinions about some of the views expressed.

2 Dictate six statements to the children or write these on the board and children copy them, or give them each a photocopy.

3 Write numbers 5 to 1 next to each statement and ask the children to do the same (see example).

4 Explain the key: 5 = strongly agree; 4 = agree; 3 = don't agree or disagree; 2 = don't agree; 1 = disagree strongly.

5 Ask the children to circle a number for each statement according to their personal opinion. Set a time limit for this, eg 2–3 minutes.

6 Divide the class into pairs.

7 Ask the children to take turns to tell their partner whether they agree or disagree with each statement and their reasons for this, eg *I don't agree children should have homework every day because they need time to do other things.*

8 Ask different pairs to report back to the class. Use their responses as the basis for a class discussion about each statement.

Comments and suggestions

- An activity like this encourages children to express, justify and defend their personal opinions. You may well be impressed by the maturity of their response!
- Give children time to try and express their views in English. It is usually best not to interrupt and correct mistakes but be ready to prompt, encourage, recast and/or extend contributions as appropriate.
- For a less challenging version of the activity, children can simply write a tick or a cross by each statement depending on whether they agree or disagree.
- This kind of activity is suitable to use in relation to any topic where there may be controversy and disagreement, such as class rules (eg *You must raise your hands to speak*) (see also 10.14) or healthy eating (eg *You ought to eat fresh fruit every day*) or as an introduction to content-based lessons to find out children's opinions and what they already know (eg *All bears hibernate in winter*).
- Older children can also use computers to produce charts to show the combined opinions of the whole class (see 9.13).

1.25 Questions galore

Level A2.1, A2.2, B.1.1, B1.2   **Age** 9–12   **Organization** whole class

Aims To listen to an account and ask relevant questions; to develop concentration skills and pay attention.

Language focus past simple, present simple, questions

Materials *Essential:* none

Procedure

1 Explain that you are going to spend about three minutes telling the class what you did at the weekend and that you want the children to interrupt you as much as possible by asking relevant questions.

2 Every time a child asks you a question, stop and answer before continuing again.

3 Keep a record on the board of the number of questions children ask you, eg T: *Last Saturday I went to see a friend … P: What's your friend's name? T: Jane. P: How old is she? T: About 25. P: Where does she live? T: In the country. I went to her house … P: What time did you go? T: At about half past ten. P: Did you walk? T: No, I didn't. I went by bus. P: How long did it take?*

4 At the end, count up the number of questions children have asked you and, if appropriate, praise the children for thinking of so many.

5 You may also like to review the different types of questions and encourage the children to notice the way they are formed.

Comments and suggestions

- Very often it is the teacher who asks all the questions in lessons rather than the children, so this activity is a refreshing way of reversing these roles.
- Children are generally interested in listening attentively to a real account of something you did. They also enjoy interrupting you in the activity since this is not what they are usually allowed to do.
- The activity is useful as a review of different question types. If you like, you can also turn it into a game with the class scoring two points for every correctly formed question they ask.

1.26 Making plans

Level A1.1, A2.1, A2.1, A2.2   **Age** 9–12   **Organization** individuals, pairs, whole class

Aims To plan a class outing in groups; to make and respond to suggestions; to compromise, if necessary, in order to agree a plan.

Language focus *In the example:* shall, suggestions (*Let's …, What about …ing?*), *want to …, like / don't like / love, places to visit*
Alternatives: I'd like to …, personal possessions (for birthday presents), items for a party

Materials *Essential:* none / *Optional:* leaflets of local places to visit and/or cinema and theatre listings or access to the internet

Our class outing
Morning:
Lunch:
Afternoon:
Dinner:
Evening:

Procedure

1 Ask the children to imagine that one day next week they can go on a class outing instead of coming to school.
2 Elicit some ideas of places to go, eg *safari park, water park, science museum, zoo, cinema, theme park, fun fair, zoo, shopping centre, cinema, theatre, concert.*
3 If you have leaflets of local places and/or cinema and theatre listings, show these to the children.
4 Ask the children each to think of three places they would like to go to (one in the morning, one in the afternoon and one in the evening) and where they would like to have lunch and dinner, eg pizza restaurant, hamburger restaurant, and to note their ideas.
5 If you like, write a frame on the board for children to copy and use (see example).
6 Divide the class into pairs.
7 Explain that the children should take turns to make and respond to suggestions with their partner and plan their day. Set a time limit for this, eg five minutes.
8 Demonstrate this with one child, eg T: *What shall we do in the morning?* P: *Let's go to the science museum.* T: *Oh, no. I don't like science. What about going to the safari park?* P: *Great idea! I love animals.*
9 When the children are ready with their plans, invite different pairs to make suggestions for the day out to the whole class and note the plans which everyone agrees on in the frame on the board.

Comments and suggestions

• You may like to consider putting pairs together in groups of four to discuss and agree plans before bringing the whole class together. This has the advantage of providing more opportunity to practise the language. On the other hand, children may get restless and start using L1 if the activity goes on too long.

- This activity can be developed into a project on local places to visit, in which children use the internet to find out, for example, opening times, cost of entry, and to identify things they most want to see. (See also 9.21 for a related activity.) It can also be linked to giving directions (see 1.18).

- If it is feasible to subsequently organize a real class outing to one of the places children have suggested, this can be very motivating.

- This activity can also be used in the context of planning a class party and/or a collective present to give to a teacher or friend.

1.27 Camping weekend

Level A2.1, A2.2, B1.1   **Age** 9–12   **Organization** whole class, pairs

Aims To decide and agree on eight items you need for a camping weekend; to list the items in order of importance; to explain and give reasons for your choices.

Language focus *In the example: need, because, may/might, suggestions (Let's …, What about …?),* camping items
Alternatives: will

Materials *Essential:* none / *Optional:* photocopies of a list of camping items (one for each child)

Things to take camping
- rucksack
- sleeping bag
- mobile phone
- camping stove
- saucepan
- tin opener
- torch
- matches
- penknife
- spoon and fork
- watch
- plasters
- insect repellent
- compass
- towel
- radio

Procedure

1 Ask the children to imagine that it is a cold and rainy weekend in spring and that they are going to go camping by a lake in the mountains with a group of friends. Explain that they have got a tent, warm clothes and tins of food.

2 Ask the children to suggest what else might be useful and write a list on the board (see example), or give them each a photocopy.

3 Divide the class into pairs.

4 Explain that the children can only take eight items with them.

5 Ask them to work with their partner and write a list of the eight things they decide to take, in order of importance. Alternatively, ask them to tick eight things on the list you have given them and then number them in order of importance.

6 Demonstrate the activity with one child or pair, eg T: *What do we need?* P: *I think we need a sleeping bag.* T: *Why?* P: *Because it may be cold.* T: *Yes, you're right.*

7 At the end, ask the pairs to report back to the class and give reasons, eg T: *Who thinks you need a mobile phone?* P: *Isabel and me.* T: *Why?* P: *Because we may need to phone the police.*

Comments and suggestions

- This activity appeals to children's imagination. Some children may feel very strongly about which items to take and the reasons for these. You need to be ready to prompt and/or help with language to explain these, if necessary. However, it is usually best not to do this too quickly and to give children an opportunity to experiment in getting their meaning across independently if they can.

- Activities in which children are asked to prioritize or rank things in order of importance usually generate lots of discussion. Any kind of adventure situation works well for this, eg a week in the jungle, on a raft at sea, in the Arctic, or on a desert island.

Pronunciation activities

1.28 Tongue twisters

Level All   **Age** 8–12   **Organization** whole class, pairs

Aim To practise saying a particular sound in a tongue twister; to raise awareness of how particular sounds are formed; to improve pronunciation skills.

Language focus any, depending on the tongue twister

Materials *Essential:* none / *Optional:* stop watch

Procedure

1 Draw the children's attention to the particular sound to be practised in the tongue twister and demonstrate how it is made. For example, in the case of /s/ followed by a consonant, hold your index finger to your mouth and make a hissing noise like a snake.

2 Repeat, but this time turn the hissing noise into a word, eg *Sssssss...snake!* Do this several times with different words the children know followed by a consonant, eg *school, spider, Spain, star.* Demonstrate that there is no vowel sound before 's' at the beginning of words.

3 Say the tongue twister you have prepared slowly, eg *Stupid Steve stole sixty scary spiders from a school in Spain* and get the children to repeat it with you. If you like, write it on the board.

4 Get the children to say the tongue twister again three times, going faster and faster each time.

5 Divide the class into pairs.

6 Ask the children to see how many times they can say the tongue twister with their partner in one minute. If you have a stop watch, use it to time the activity.

7 Ask the children to report back how many times they managed to say the tongue twister.

8 You can also ask them to tell you any tongue twisters they know in their own language.

Comments and suggestions

- Tongue twisters provide an enjoyable way of practising individual sounds that children may find difficult depending on their L1. (This one is particularly suitable for Spanish speakers.) You need to be aware and find out which sounds these are in order to maximize the usefulness of the activity.

- Some other examples of tongue twisters to practise sounds children may find difficult are:
  /h/ *Happy Hurry helps at home in the holidays.*
  /b/ and /v/ *Brian is brilliant at basketball. Vanessa is very good at volleyball too.*
  /l/ and /r/ *Lovely Lucy likes lonely Luke. Rich Roland rides a red racing bike.*
  /s/ and /ʃ/ *Sue sells seashells at the seaside. Sheila sells shoes at a shop in the city.*
  In cases where there are two sentences and contrasting sounds in the tongue twister, children can take turns to say one sentence each when they time themselves in pairs.

1.29 Sort the sounds

Level All   **Age** 8–12   **Organization** whole class

Aim To practise discriminating between two or more sounds; to raise awareness of the differences between sounds; to raise awareness of the correspondence between sounds and spelling; to improve pronunciation skills.

Language focus any plural nouns

Materials *Essential:* none / *Optional:* copies of outlines to write the words in (one for each child)

Procedure

1 Decide on the contrasting sounds you want to focus on, eg /s/ as in *elephants* and /z/ as in *birds*.

2 Explain and demonstrate that if you say a word with /s/, children should repeat the word and hold out an arm like the trunk of an elephant. If you say a word with /z/, they should repeat the word and pretend to fly like a bird.

3 Say different plural words in random order and children respond by repeating the words and doing the actions. Examples of words you can use are: *bananas, shops, dogs, cats, sweets, tomatoes, leaves, books, plants, bears, cars, bikes, boats, flowers.*

Comments and suggestions

• The words you use in the activity should be known to the children. It is usually best to have no more than 20 words.

• Other examples of contrasting sounds suitable to use in this activity are, eg /ɪ/ and /iː/ as in *chicken* and *cheese* and /ʃ/, /tʃ/ and /dʒ/ as in *sugar, chocolate* and *jam*.

• As a follow-up to the activity, it may be suitable to draw two outline shapes on the board which suggest the sounds you have practised, for example shapes of a chicken and a wedge of cheese, and ask the children to copy these. Dictate the words to the children and they write them in the shapes according to the sounds. You can then ask them what they notice about the spelling of the words with the same sound. For example, they will notice that /ɪ/ in eg *fish, chicken* and *chips* is written with an 'i', whereas /iː/ in eg *cheese, ice cream, green* and *meat* may be written either with 'ee' or 'ea'.

1.30 Clap the stress!

Level All   **Age** 8–12   **Organization** whole class

Aims To practise word (or sentence) stress; to raise awareness of the importance of stress in pronouncing English intelligibly; to improve pronunciation skills.

Language focus any, depending on the words or sentences chosen

Materials *Essential:* none / *Optional:* a percussion instrument

Procedure

1 Draw two sets of circles on the board to reflect the word stress patterns you wish to practise, eg 1 Ooo   2 oOo.

2 Clap the rhythm for each one (or use a drum or other percussion instrument) and get the children to join in clapping loudly on the stressed syllable, and softly on the other two.

3 Explain that words with more than one syllable have the stress on different syllables and that people understand us more easily if we say the stress correctly. You may like to demonstrate this by saying a word in the children's own language with the wrong stress which they may find difficult to understand.

4 Elicit or give two examples of words which have the stress patterns you want to practise, eg 1 Ooo *elephant*   2 oOo *banana* and get the children to clap the rhythm and say the words.

5 Divide the class in half and assign one stress pattern to each half.

6 Explain that you are going to say a series of words and that the children should repeat the word and clap the rhythm if it has their stress pattern. Examples of words you can use are: *telephone, tomato, hamburger, Saturday, December, computer, cinema, grandfather, pyjamas.*

7 Children can then change roles and repeat the activity with different words.

8 At the end, ask the children to write a list of the words in their notebooks and mark the stress.

Comments and suggestions

• The words you use in the activity should be familiar to the children.

• Other word stress patterns you may wish to practise are, eg two syllable words with patterns Oo as in button or oO as in report.

• Children can also repeat and clap the stress in sentences or questions you say, eg *Where's the ball? / It's time* for *lunch.* or in rhymes and chants (see Section 6).

• Through clapping the rhythm of word and sentence stress, children develop awareness of this feature of pronunciation. With older children, it may also be appropriate to draw their attention to how stress patterns in English may be different from their own language.

1.31 Weak forms /ə/

Level All   **Age** 10–12   **Organization** whole class, pairs

Aims To raise awareness of the existence of weak forms in connected speech; to notice and produce weak forms appropriately in their own speech; to improve pronunciation skills.

Language focus *In the example:* present simple, *have got,* personal information
Alternatives: any familiar language and vocabulary

Materials *Essential:* none

Procedures

1 Demonstrate the difference between weak forms and strong forms in *a, and, to* and *at* by saying contrasting pairs of phrases or sentences, eg
I've got a (/eɪ/) sister. / I've got a (/ə/) sister.
Fish and (/ænd/) chips. / Fish and (/ən/) chips.
I'm going to (/tuː/) the shops. / I'm going to (/tə/) the shops.
I learn English at (/æt/) school. / I learn English at (/ət/) school.

2 Explain that when we speak naturally, we usually say these words and many others like them, eg *an, but, for, the, of,* in their weak forms and the vowel sound then becomes /ə/. Draw this symbol on the board.

3 Explain that you're going to tell the children something about yourself and ask them to try and notice the way you use weak forms. Say, eg *My name's Susana and (/ənd/) I live in Valencia. I work at (/ət/) St. John's school. I've got a (/ə/) dog and (/ənd/) I like listening to (/tə/) music.*

4 Ask the children to help you reconstruct the text and write it on the board.

5 Say the text again. This time pause after each sentence and ask the children to identify the words with /ə/. Invite individual children to draw the symbol above these words on the board.

6 As a follow-up, ask children to write a similar short text about themselves and to practise saying it naturally, using weak forms.

Comments and suggestions

• Raising children's awareness of weak forms helps them to pronounce English naturally and also helps them to produce sentence stress patterns correctly. However you need to be careful that because the focus of the activity is on weak forms, children don't over-emphasize these when they speak.

• As further practice in recognizing weak forms, you can play any listening text in the course book you are using and ask children to say *Stop!* when they hear any weak forms.

Section 2 **Reading and writing**

Reading and writing are two sides of the same coin. The more children read, the better writers they are likely to become. This is generally held to be the case as much in L1 as when children learn a second or foreign language.

Learning to read

Many children are growing up in an increasingly print-dominated world where, although they may learn to click on a computer mouse before they learn to turn the pages of a book, reading is a vital skill. As children grow older, reading competence in English is essential to pass exams and to succeed at secondary school and beyond. Through learning to read in English, children develop positive attitudes, strong motivation and a sense of achievement. Reading also reinforces and extends what children learn orally. Reading in English provides an opportunity to build on and transfer skills from and to L1. For all these reasons, it is arguable that it would be doing children a disservice not to lay solid foundations in early foreign language literacy at primary school.

When to start reading

One of the main debates is not about whether children should learn to read and write in English, but when it is most beneficial to start. The answer is neither clear-cut nor conclusive and depends on the context and a range of factors, such as the children's L1, and whether this shares the Roman script, the children's existing literacy skills in L1, how much English they already know, and their own interest and enthusiasm for learning to read. With very young children, it may quite often be this latter factor which drives the process, as for example, when pre-reading children notice that instead of writing 'Very good', you write something else, such as 'Excellent', on their work, or when beginning readers respond enthusiastically to using a word card bank as 'important and serious' learning. The usual approach in most foreign language programmes, however, is that reading and writing in English are introduced gradually after basic literacy has been established in L1 (and possibly also L2, if the children are growing up in a bilingual environment).

What is involved in reading

Reading competence involves constructing meaning and making sense of written text. It requires the complex interaction of knowledge and skills at multiple levels. These include, for example, the recognition of shapes of letters of the alphabet, grapho-phonemic correspondences and the direction of text. They also include sight recognition of common, high frequency vocabulary and morphemes, the recognition of syntactic patterns and word order within sentences, and an understanding of the structure and organization of texts. When children read in English, they need to learn to make use of visual, phonological and semantic cues in an integrated way and to relate these to their previous knowledge and experience of the world, the topic and the genre in order to construct coherent personal meaning. To enable children to become competent readers in English, they need practice in developing their knowledge and skills in all these areas.

How to approach teaching reading

As a start, it is a good idea to ensure that the children's classroom is a literate, print rich environment in English. This can include, for example, labelling classroom furniture, creating a weather and date chart, making a birthday calendar and making a chart of key instructions, eg *Listen, Read, Draw,* with symbols to show what they mean. It can also include a display of pictures of famous people, story or course book characters with speech bubbles for key classroom language, eg *Can you repeat that, please? I've finished, I don't understand* and a notice board where you and the children can write messages, eg *Please remember to bring a photo on Monday.*

In developing initial reading skills in a foreign language, it is beneficial to read aloud regularly with the children (see 2.7 Shared reading) while they follow the pictures and/or the text in a story or big book. This provides an implicit, global opportunity for children to become familiar with conventions of print and text. It also enables you to show and share your own pleasure and enthusiasm for reading, which is likely to be catching, and to model the processes and strategies involved.

When teaching children to read themselves, it is best to base this initially on language that is already familiar orally/aurally and to use a combination of whole-word sight recognition, as in activity 2.3, and phonics, as in activity 2.1. The potential for using phonics in a foreign language context, however, is often limited, given children's lack of vocabulary in English. Care also needs to be taken that children are not sounding out letters and words in a meaningless way. The use of phonics is usually most effective when embedded in a context such as a rhyme or chant (see Section 6).

Whether at word, sentence or text level, reading activities should be meaningful and create a reason and purpose for reading which practise one or more sub-skills. These include de-coding written language, skimming a text for global understanding, scanning a text for specific information, inferring implicit meaning in a text and understanding the writer's intention. As children move up through primary, it is important to expose them to an increasingly wider range of text types or genres and to develop their awareness of different purposes for reading and strategies to use (see 2.32).

As with developing listening skills, many reading activities can be usefully staged into *before, while* and *after* reading. If children are not yet confident readers, it is particularly important to create interest and motivation before reading, as they can easily feel daunted by chunks of text. After reading, it is often suitable to lead into an activity in which children write, using the text they have read as a starting point or guide.

As well as developing intensive reading skills, it is also important to develop extensive reading for pleasure, either through the use of class readers and/or a school or class library. By encouraging children to write book reviews of what they read (see 2.20) children can build up a personalized record of their reading and also be encouraged to develop critical reading skills.

While there are no definitive conclusions from research on how reading in a foreign language should be taught to children, by providing opportunities to develop skills at letter, word, sentence and text level, creating frameworks for children to read for meaning in purposeful ways, modelling your own enthusiasm and the processes and strategies involved, encouraging personal, divergent responses, and raising

reading awareness of genres and strategies, as and when appropriate, children will develop into increasingly competent readers by the end of primary school.

From reading to writing

Reading provides a scaffold for learning to write and it is frequently appropriate to teach reading and writing in an integrated way, both in the initial stages and when children have more developed skills.

Initial writing

In the initial stages of learning to write, young children need to develop hand–eye coordination and fine motor skills, and the effort and concentration which goes into forming letters and words is a challenge in itself. The amount of time children need to spend on the mechanics of forming letters and words in English lessons also depends on the writing system used in their L1.

The emphasis in initial writing is to support and consolidate oral/aural work, through, for example, reinforcing the understanding and spelling of familiar vocabulary items and sentence patterns. However, even at this early stage, it is important that writing activities are made meaningful and cognitively engaging rather than mechanical (see 2.4 and 2.5) and that children are given opportunities for personalization and choice in what they write (see 2.17 and 2.19).

As children progress, they can be introduced to writing short texts, which may either be based on a model (see 2.11) or structured by a series of questions or prompts (see 2.27). Through providing frameworks which guide children's writing and lead to successful outcomes, children develop confidence and enthusiasm for writing, as well as an increasing ability to incorporate linguistic features typical of writing, such as the use of conjunctions, and to structure and organize texts.

How to approach teaching writing

When setting up writing activities, it is important to create motivating and meaningful contexts, a reason and purpose for writing and also to ensure that the children have a sense of audience and who they are writing for. There also needs to be careful preparation to equip children with the language they need to express and order their ideas in an appropriate way. Before children write independently, it is also often helpful to model the processes and strategies involved in creating a text with the class together (see 2.8 Shared writing).

During the writing process, it is important to encourage children to be responsible for checking and correcting their own work (see also Section 10 Learning to learn) and, as they get older, to be willing to draft, edit and revise their written work, and to understand the value of this. By regularly displaying children's written work or publishing this in class books, you can convey that you value their efforts. This also encourages children to take pride in the presentation of their work, and take care over things such as legibility and accuracy, as well as develop an interest in, and respect for, the work of others.

During the primary years, as children become more confident writers, it is important to give them experience of different genres and areas of writing in addition to initial writing. These include collaborative writing, a dynamic process in which children's ideas are shaped through working with others and the final product is a joint effort (see 2.18, 2.22, 2.31), functional writing such as invitations (eg 2.24) and reports (eg 2.25), personal writing in which children record their experiences, attitudes and feelings (eg 2.19), poetry writing, which gives children the opportunity to explore the power of words and play with the rhythms and patterns of language (eg 2.28–2.31) and imaginative writing (eg 2.18, and see also Section 4 on Storytelling), which takes children beyond real experiences and into a world of invention.

Feedback and correction

When giving feedback and correcting written work, particularly in more challenging and/or personalized areas of writing, it is important to respond to children's meaning, and not just to spelling and grammatical mistakes. A positive comment on the content, eg *What a lovely poem! I can almost feel I'm at the seaside!*, plus, with older children, possibly also focused correction of a target aspect of language, eg verb forms or use of prepositions, is far more likely to make your feedback memorable and motivating, than correcting every single mistake. Through conveying that you are interested in what

children have to say and value their attempts to communicate what they mean, children will leave primary school with the confidence and enthusiasm to develop into more skilled writers in future.

Reflection time

As you use the reading and writing activities in this section with your classes, you may like to think about the following questions and use your responses to evaluate how things went and plan possible improvements for next time:

1 **Skills:** What sub-skills of reading and/or writing was the activity aiming to improve? Was it effective? Why? / Why not?

2 **Meaning:** Was the activity meaningful for the children? In what way? How did this influence their response?

3 **Control:** How controlled was the activity? Did the children need more or less guidance to be able to work independently?

4 **Reasons for reading/writing:** Were these made clear to the children? Were they relevant? In the case of writing, did the children have a sense of who they were writing for?

5 **Modelling strategies:** Was there an opportunity for you to explicitly model reading and/or writing strategies and processes with the children? What impact did this have?

6 **Feedback and correction:** How did you give children feedback on their written work? Did you respond to their meaning as well as their language? Do you think the feedback will motivate the children to want to write in future?

2.1 Letters in the air

Level A.1.1   **Age** 4–8   **Organization** whole class

Aims To recognize the shapes of letters; to draw letters with your index finger; to relate letters and sounds; to develop motor skills.

Language focus Letters of the alphabet, familiar vocabulary

Materials *Essential:* flashcards or pictures of familiar vocabulary

Procedure

1 Show the children a picture or flashcard of a familiar vocabulary item, eg *banana* and children say the word.
2 Say, eg *Banana starts with 'b' (/biː/). It's 'b' (/b/) for 'banana'. Can you draw a 'b' like this?*
3 Stand with your back to the children, hold out your arm to the right and draw a big 'b' in the air with your finger.
4 Get the children to do the same.
5 Repeat the procedure with other familiar vocabulary, eg *apple, ball, car, doll, elephant, fish.*
6 Stick the pictures or flashcards on the board.
7 Secretly choose one and write the initial letter in the air. Children identify the letter you draw and say the word.
8 Repeat once or twice, then ask individual children to take turns to do the same while the rest of the class looks and identifies the letters and words.
9 Write the initial letters for all the words in jumbled order on the board.
10 Invite individual children to draw matching lines from the letters to the corresponding pictures or flashcards on the board.
11 Ask the children if they can think of other words they know which start with each letter and sound you have worked on, eg *alligator, bear, cat, dog, egg, frog.*

Comments and suggestions

• Use either upper or lower case letters in the activity depending on what you have previously taught the children and/or the letters they are most familiar with in L1 (if their language uses the same script as English).

• With older children, instead of drawing letters in the air, you can ask a child to the front of the class and draw the letters on their back. In this case, children work in pairs during the first part of the activity and take turns to draw the initial letters on each other's backs. The second part of the activity can then be a guessing game in pairs.

• As a follow-up, you can make a classroom display of the letters you have worked on, with pictures of vocabulary items the children know. In later lessons, you can then repeat the activity with different letters and vocabulary items and change the display regularly to reflect these. If appropriate, you can also include the words for each vocabulary item in the display in order to encourage whole-word sight recognition.

2.2 Plasticine letters

Level A1.1   **Age** 4–8   **Organization** individual, whole class

Aims To make letters of the alphabet out of plasticine; to identify the shapes of letters from touch; to memorize the shapes of letters; to develop motor skills.

Language focus Letters of the alphabet

Materials *Essential:* a strip of plasticine for each child, a blindfold / *Optional:* alphabet flashcards or frieze

Procedure

1 Write the alphabet in large letters on the board or display the alphabet flashcards or frieze.

2 Children say the alphabet with you.

3 Demonstrate how to make letters out of plasticine by rolling it into a strip and making the shape of a letter.

4 Give out plasticine to each child.

5 Ask the children to use the plasticine to make the shape of any letter of their choice or, for example, a letter which is included in their first name. Encourage the children to use the letters on the board, alphabet frieze or flashcards as a guide.

6 When the children are ready, get them to trace over their plasticine letter with their fingers in the same way that the letter is written and to say the letter.

7 They can also repeat the procedure with other letters made by their friends.

8 Collect all the plasticine letters and arrange them in a row on your desk.

9 Ask individual children to the front of the class in turn. Blindfold them and ask them to try and identify one or two of the letters by touch alone.

10 If appropriate, get the rest of the class to clap and say, eg *Fantastic!* if they do this correctly.

Comments and suggestions

- With younger children, it may be more appropriate to give them an outline shape of a letter on paper or card and ask them to stick bits of plasticine onto the shape of the letter instead.

- Older children can also use plasticine to make whole words. In this case the activity can be used for revision, eg *Make one of the clothes words we learnt last week,* or as part of a unit of work, e.g *Make a word for one food you like in blue plasticine and one food you don't like in red plasticine.* Children can then read each others' words.

- Through using plasticine children are encouraged to attend closely to the shape of individual letters. As well as developing motor skills and hand–eye coordination, the activity makes forming letters and words both memorable and enjoyable.

2.3 Word shapes

Level A1.1   **Age** 6–8   **Organization** whole class, individual

Aims To recognize the shapes of familiar words; to match words and shapes; to copy and write familiar words; to develop motor skills.

Language focus *In the example:* colours
Alternatives: any familiar vocabulary

Materials *Essential:* none / *Optional:* coloured pens, crayons, photocopies of jumbled words and shapes (one for each child) (they are in the correct order below)

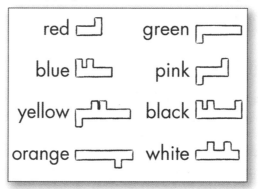

Procedure

1 Ask the children to name colours they know and write the words on the board.

2 Draw the shape of one of the words, eg *red*, and ask the children to say which colour it corresponds to.

3 Ask a child to draw a matching line from the shape to the word 'red' on the board, and if appropriate to write the word 'red' inside the shape, or you can do this. If you have coloured pens, use a red pen to do this.

4 Draw the children's attention to the way that the 'r' and the 'e' are the same height in the word and the stalk on the 'd' is higher.

5 Repeat the procedure for all the colours.

6 If you have prepared photocopies with jumbled colour words and shapes, give these out to the children.

7 Ask them to work individually and use crayons or coloured pens to match the shapes and words and to write the colour words inside each shape.

8 Children then compare their completed sheets with a friend and read the colour words together.

Comments and suggestions

- This activity helps to develop sight recognition of whole words which are a familiar part of children's vocabulary. It also draws children's attention to the importance of reproducing stalks and tails of letters above and below the line in their own writing.

- Children enjoy the puzzle element and close visual observation involved in matching words and shapes.

- With older children, the activity can be a guessing game in pairs. Children take turns to draw the shape of a word from a specific lexical set they have learnt, eg pets. Their partner guesses the word and then spells and writes it to show how it corresponds to the shape.

2.4 Word sequences

Level A1.1   **Age** 6–9   **Organization** whole class, individual, pairs

Aims To logically deduce the pattern in word sequences; to practise writing familiar words; to write a word sequence for a partner to complete.

Language focus *In the example:* clothes
Alternatives: any other familiar vocabulary

Materials *Essential:* none

Procedure

1 Write a sequence of familiar words on the board following a 1,2,1,2 pattern, eg
   boots, shoes, boots, shoes, boots, _____ , _____ .

2 Read the sequence rhythmically. Encourage the children to join in and supply the last two missing words.

3 Repeat the procedure with other word sequences from the same lexical set, eg
   hat, T-shirt, coat, hat, T-shirt, _____ , _____ (following a 1,2,3,1,2,3 pattern) or
   trousers, jumper, jumper, trousers, jumper, _____ , _____ (following a 1,2,2,1,2,2 pattern) or
   shirt, shirt, socks, shirt, shirt, _____ , _____ (following a 1,1,2,1,1,2 pattern).

4 Ask the children to copy and complete the word sequences in their books.

5 Check the answers by asking the children to read the word sequences.

6 Ask them to invent and write the first five words of one or two more sequences using familiar

vocabulary from the same lexical set. They can either follow any of the patterns you have introduced or they can create a new pattern.

7 Get them to check the spelling of words before they begin, eg by looking in their course book.

8 When they are ready, children exchange their books with a partner and read and complete each other's word sequences.

9 They then return the books to the original owner, who checks that the sequences have been completed correctly.

Comments and suggestions

• This activity gives children practice in copying and writing familiar words. The logical deductive element involved in working out what comes next in the sequence ensures that they are also cognitively engaged.

• Through reading the word sequences aloud in a rhythmic way, children are helped to predict what comes next. The use of rhythm while reading also helps children to memorize the written form of the words.

2.5 Copy and classify

Level A1.1, A1.2   **Age** 6–10   **Organization** whole class, individual

Aims To copy and classify familiar words into categories.

Language focus *In the example:* food, fruit and vegetables
Alternatives: any language, eg animals, sports, free-time activities

Materials *Essential:* none

Procedure

1 Ask the children to tell you food words they know and write these on the board, eg *egg, tomato, hamburger, chicken, sausage, cheese, apple, banana, lettuce, ham, pear, orange.*

2 Draw two columns on the board and write headings, eg 'Food from animals' / 'Food from trees or plants' at the top of each one.

3 Ask the children to copy the headings into their notebooks and to copy all the food words on the board into the correct column.

4 At the end, children check their answers in pairs and then with the whole class.

Comments and suggestions

• This activity provides practice in copying and writing at word level but also challenges children to think by asking them to classify the words. This helps to transform a potentially mechanical copying activity into a cognitively engaging and meaningful one.

• A range of other vocabulary and categories can be used in the activity, eg *Food that is good / bad for you, Fruit / Vegetables, Animals that are mammals / reptiles, Sports that use / don't use a ball, Free-time activities that are / aren't good exercise.*

• Children can also be asked to copy and classify words in a personalized way, eg *Food I like / don't like, Animals I think are scary / not scary.* This can lead into a speaking activity in which children ask questions and exchange their views.

2.6 Alphabet cards

Level A1.1, A1.2   **Age** 6–10   **Organization** pairs, whole class

Aims To practise spelling and making familiar words and/or sentences using alphabet cards.

Language focus *In the example:* the alphabet, parts of the body
Alternatives: any familiar language and vocabulary

Materials *Essential:* sets of the alphabet cards below in envelopes (one for each pair) /
Optional: sets of plastic letters in bags

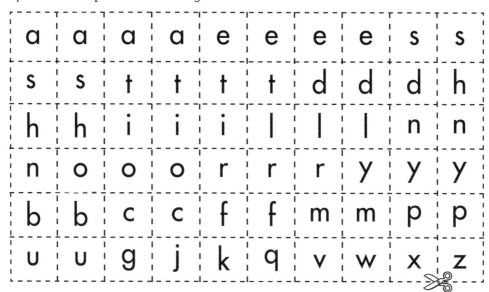

a	a	a	a	e	e	e	e	s	s
s	s	t	t	t	t	d	d	d	h
h	h	i	i	i	l	l	l	n	n
n	o	o	o	r	r	r	y	y	y
b	b	c	c	f	f	m	m	p	p
u	u	g	j	k	q	v	w	x	z

Procedure

1 Divide the class into pairs.

2 Give each pair a set of the alphabet cards above.

3 Ask the children to use the alphabet cards to make as many words as they can from a particular lexical set, eg parts of the body. Set a time limit, eg five minutes.

4 At the end, ask each pair to say and spell one of the words they have made in turn.

5 If other pairs have the same word, they turn their cards or letters for this word face down, so that the same word doesn't get reported back repeatedly.

6 Keep a score of how many words the children collectively manage to make.

7 Be ready to remind them of any words which are part of the lexical set that they may have forgotten.

Comments and suggestions

• Sets of alphabet cards can be made by writing letters in a grid on an A4 sheet of paper, photocopying the sheet for as many sets as you want and then cutting out the letters and storing them in envelopes. For each set of alphabet cards, you need more of certain letters to reflect how frequently they are used, eg four each of 'a', 'e', 's', 't', three each of 'd', 'h', 'i', 'l', 'n', 'o', 'r', 'y'; two each of 'b','c', 'f', 'm', 'p', 'u' and one each of the rest: 'g', 'j', 'k', 'q', 'v', 'w', 'x', 'z'.

• Children can cut out and make the sets of alphabet cards themselves before doing the activity. It is a good idea to give each set of alphabet cards a number and to ask the children to write this on the back of every card in their set and on the envelope used to store the cards. This means that if any alphabet cards fall on the floor or get mislaid, it is possible to identify immediately which set they belong to.

• Alphabet cards can be used for a variety of activities which do not take up much time. It can be useful to keep the sets to hand, either for use whenever there are a few spare minutes in a lesson or for fast finishers (eg *How many words can you make that we've used in today's lesson?*).

• Here are three examples of other activities you can do using alphabet cards.

a) Dictate words related to the topic, story or unit of work (or invite individual children to do this) and children use the alphabet cards to make the words you say as fast as they can.

b) **Alphabet bingo:** Children choose 6–8 alphabet cards, lay them out on their desks and turn them over as you say the letters. The first child to turn over all the letters says *Bingo!* and is the winner.

c) **Anagrams:** In pairs, children make anagrams of three words related to the topic, story or unit of work using the alphabet cards. They then exchange places with another pair and move the alphabet cards to turn the anagrams into words.

- The physical manipulation of the alphabet cards supports children's initial reading and writing skills and helps to make accurate spelling enjoyable and memorable.

2.7 Shared reading

Level All   **Age** 4–12   **Organization** whole class

Aims To read a text aloud with the children in order to model reading strategies; to build up understanding of the content and textual features in a shared and collaborative way.

Language focus any

Materials *Essential:* any text, eg letter, factual text, story, picture book, big book, graded reader, text in the course book

Procedure

1 Prepare for reading the text by, for example, discussing the topic, eliciting what the children already know, encouraging prediction and, possibly also, pre-teaching essential vocabulary whose meaning cannot be inferred from the context.

2 Read the text aloud with the children. Children either listen and look at pictures only or follow the text as you read. Encourage participation and ask questions to build up children's understanding of the language and the content of the text, the way that it is organized and any particular features of the genre, such as the formulaic openings and endings of a letter or story, or features of the language, eg the use of repetition, alliteration or onomatopoeia (children don't need to use these terms) that you wish them to notice.

3 Be ready to pause, go back and reread bits of the text again as often as necessary in order to clarify children's understanding and to model reading strategies that help them to decode and make sense of the text.

4 Ask questions that help children relate the text both to their own experience and lives, as well as to other similar texts that they may have read.

5 Encourage them to form their own personal views and responses to the text and think about their reasons for these.

6 With older children and higher levels, it may also be appropriate to guide their thinking about such things as the audience, style and structure of the text, as well as the writer's intentions and inferred meanings.

Comments and suggestions

- Reading aloud with children can have enormous benefits. These include modelling basic skills such as decoding spelling and sound patterns, and phrasing text in order to construct language and meaning from print on a page.

- The concept of shared reading implies that you read *with* the children rather than *to* the children. In other words, you and the children interact and work together in order to investigate, analyse, reflect, reason and develop understandings based on the text. The fact that the reading is 'shared' enables you to explicitly model out loud cognitive strategies and processes which the children will be able to internalize and subsequently make use of in their own independent reading.

- In order for shared reading to be successful, it is important to think carefully about the kinds of questions you will ask to build confidence and help children construct meaning from the text. There needs to be a balance between questions to check and establish basic comprehension and higher order, open questions which lead to analysis, reflection and a deeper level of understanding and learning. Depending on the age and level of the children, it may be appropriate or necessary to ask some of these questions in L1.

- It is not usually advisable to ask children to read aloud to the rest of the class. Other children either tend to lose interest quickly or else cannot easily hear or understand what is being read. If you do want children to practise reading aloud, it is best to get children to do this in pairs ('paired reading') using a text that is already familiar, or to find time for children to take turns to read to you individually, while the rest of the class is engaged in other work.

2.8 Shared writing

Level all   **Age** 5–12   **Organization** whole class

Aims To create a text with children in order to model writing strategies; to draft, edit and write contributions in a shared and collaborative way.

Language focus *In the example:* be, present simple, adjectives to describe animals, *have got*
Alternatives: any language and vocabulary or text type

Materials *Essential:* none / *Optional:* a picture, poster or DVD to use as a stimulus to writing

Procedure

1 Prepare for the writing activity by creating interest and using a stimulus to prompt ideas, eg a picture or poster, a letter (which the children are going to reply to), a related text, an extract from a DVD.

2 Set a goal for the activity. For example, with younger children doing a topic of work on bears and responding to a poster: *Let's write a description of the grizzly bear together. What can you tell me about the grizzly bear?*

3 Use the children's contributions to build up a text and write this on the board, eg P1: *Is big.* (sic) T: *Yes. That's right. So what can we write? The grizzly bear …* P2: *is big.* T: (writes) *Good. And anything else?* (using gesture to show height) P3: *Tall.* T: *Very good. So what can we write?* P4: *The grizzly bear is big and tall.* T: (writes) *Great. What about the grizzly bear's colour? Shall we write about that?* P5: *Yes! Brown!* T: *OK. And what's this?* P6: *Fur.* T: *Well done. So what can we write?*

4 At the end, get the children to read the description you have constructed together and ask them to copy it into their notebooks (with younger children this may be one or two sentences only), eg *The grizzly bear is big and tall. It has got brown fur. The grizzly bear has got a big head and small eyes. It has got sharp teeth and sharp claws. The grizzly bear likes swimming. It eats fish. It also eats fruit and berries from trees.*

5 As a follow-up, older children can write a description of another bear, eg a giant panda or polar bear, either individually or in pairs, using the text you have constructed together as a guide and model.

Comments and suggestions

- As with shared reading, shared writing enables you to model cognitive strategies and processes which the children will be able to internalize and subsequently make use of in their own independent writing.

- Shared writing is a technique that can be used with all ages and levels of primary. With very young children just beginning to write, it helps develop fine motor skills and is motivating in the way that it involves children in contributing to and creating what they write themselves, rather than mechanical copying. With older children, the technique is particularly useful to use when you are introducing them to a new writing genre, eg a story, a report, a letter, a recipe, a poem, and you can demonstrate and model specific language features and conventions with the whole class before children work more independently.

- Through the technique of shared writing, children have a permanent record in their notebooks of a written text that they can refer to as a model and guide in their own writing. In this way, shared writing provides an invaluable scaffold or support in developing children's skills and confidence as autonomous writers.

2.9 Secret code

Level A1.1, A1.2, A2.1, A2.2   **Age** 8–12   **Organization** whole class, pairs

Aims To develop familiarity with the alphabet; to encode and decode messages using a secret code; to practise reading coordinates in a grid.

Language focus *In the example:* the alphabet, present simple, prepositions of place
Alternatives: numbers, present simple (describing people)

Materials *Essential:* none / *Optional:* pictures of the 'gang' and 'jewels'

Procedure

1 Create a context for the activity, eg *A very dangerous gang has stolen the Queen's crown jewels in London. The police have intercepted an internet message in secret code saying where the jewels are.* If you have pictures to show the 'gang' and the jewels, stick these on the board.

2 Check children understand the context.

3 Draw a grid on the board to show how the secret code works:

	A	**E**	**I**	**O**	**U**
P	a	g	m	s	y
T	b	h	n	t	z
G	c	i	o	u	
S	d	j	p	v	
M	e	k	q	w	
B	f	l	r	x	

4 Explain and demonstrate this by showing that PI = m, GA = c, PO = s, etc. Write a word in code on the board, eg MI GO MA MA TI and ask the children to work it out using the code (the word is 'queen').

5 Divide the class into pairs.

6 Write the 'intercepted internet message' in upper case letters on the board and ask the children to work it out and write the message as fast as they can:
    TO TE MA / SE MA MO MA BE PO / PA BI MA / GE TI / PA / PO PI PA BE BE / BI MA SA / TA PA PE / GE TI / PA / MO TE GE TO MA / SO PA TI / GO TI SA MA BI / PA / TO BI MA MA / GE TI / TO TE MA / GA PA BI / SI PA BI ME.

7 Check the answers by asking children to tell you where the jewels are and to read the complete message: *The jewels are in a small red bag in a white van under a tree in the car park.*

8 Explain that the police open the white van in the car park but, instead of the jewels, they find another message.

9 Ask the pairs to work together and invent and write the message saying where the jewels are now. Set a time limit, eg five minutes.

10 When the pairs are ready, ask them to exchange and work out each other's messages.

Comments and suggestions

- Reading and writing messages in secret code is generally very appealing to children – and you may be surprised how fast they work!
- Depending on the age of the children, you can increase or decrease the level of cognitive challenge in the way the code works. An example of a simpler code is A = 1, B = 2, C = 3, etc. A more complex code is one where A = n, B = o etc and conversely N = a, O = b, etc.
- An alternative version of the activity is to have a description of a person, eg spy, robber, in secret code and children work out the message and match the description to a picture.
- Instead of using an invented code, you can teach older children the phonemic alphabet and use this as a 'secret code'. Children generally find this both challenging and enjoyable, especially learning new shapes of letters such as /ʊ/ and /ŋ/. This also has the added benefit of being useful in the long-term for learning how to pronounce new words. However, it is only likely to be suitable for children who come from a language background that shares the same alphabet as English and who are already confident speakers.

2.10 Date puzzle

Level A1.1, A1.2   **Age** 8–12   **Organization** individual, pairs, whole class

Aims To read a series of sentences and identify the date in a puzzle.

Language focus *In the example:* days, months, ordinal numbers, prepositions of time, *be, have got*
Alternatives: adjectives to describe people, clothes

Materials *Essential:* none / *Optional:* pages from a year calendar

Procedure

1 Create a context for doing the puzzle, eg to find out the date of someone's birthday (yours or a story character's), the date of a party or school outing (real or pretend), the date of a secret meeting (eg between spies, story characters).

2 Draw the calendar below on the board and ask the children to copy this.

MAY

Sun	Mon	Tue	Wed	Thu	Fri	Sat
						1
2	3	4	5	6	7	8
9	10	11	12	13	14	15
16	17	18	19	20	21	22
23	24	25	26	27	28	29
30	31					

3 Draw children's attention to the short form of writing the days and pre-teach 'odd' (1, 3, 5, 7, etc) and 'even' (2, 4, 6, 8, etc) numbers.

4 Divide the class into pairs.

5 Write the puzzle sentences below on the board.

1 The date isn't on a Friday.
2 The date is after the 15th.
3 The date is an even number.
4 The date hasn't got a two in it.
5 The date isn't on a Sunday.

6 Explain that children should read the sentences and cross off the dates on the calendar in order to find the date as fast as they can.

7 Check the answer (Tuesday 18th).

8 With older children, if you have a year calendar available, give the page for one month to each pair.

9 Ask the children to work with their partner and write five sentences to create a similar puzzle for a date of their choice using the month of the calendar they have got. Explain that they should order and structure the sentences the same way as the original puzzle, eg 1 *The date isn't on a …* 2 *The date is before/after the …* 3 *The date is an even/odd number.*

10 When the children are ready, ask them to exchange their puzzles and work out the dates.

Comments and suggestions

- The logical-deductive nature of this puzzle makes reading and writing at sentence level purposeful, challenging and enjoyable.

- With younger children you will need to work through one puzzle with the whole class first in order to model the thinking process out loud, eg *The date isn't on a Friday. So let's cross off all the Fridays like this.*

- The cognitive demands of solving and creating a puzzle are likely to appeal to some children more than others. By organizing them in pairs, children can help each other and talk through the steps to solve the puzzle. This also ensures that the activity is not threatening.

- With pictures of people or a group photo, you can create similar reading puzzles for finding a mystery person, eg *The person hasn't got long hair. The person isn't wearing jeans.*

2.11 Riddle time

Level A1.1, A1.2, A2.1, A2.2   **Age** 7–12   **Organization** pairs, whole class

Aims To create and write riddles; to read and solve the riddles.

Language focus *In the example:* colours, present simple, *have got*, animals
Alternatives: present simple, jobs, food, everyday objects, *It's made of …, You use it to …*

Materials *Essential:* A4 paper (one sheet for each child), crayons, paper clips (two for each child) or blu-tac (a small amount for each child)

Procedure

1 Say one or two riddles orally and ask children to guess the animal, eg *It's white. It lives in the Arctic. It's got fur and fat to keep warm. It eats fish, meat and plants.* (A polar bear.)

2 Divide the class into pairs.

3 Ask each pair to choose two animals and to write a riddle about each one in their notebooks. If appropriate, write a skeleton framework for this on the board, eg *It's _____ . It lives in _____ . It's got _____ . It eats _____ .*

4 When the children are ready, give an A4 sheet to each child. Demonstrate folding this into thirds.

5 Ask the children in each pair to write one of the riddles they have prepared in the top inside third of the A4 sheet, and to draw a picture of the animal and write the name in the middle third.

6 They should then fold up the bottom third of the paper to cover the picture and either put two paper clips (one on each side) or stick the corners and middle down with small pieces of sticky-tac to ensure that the picture is not visible.

7 When the children are ready, circulate the riddles round the class. Children read and solve each riddle with their partner and then look at the picture to see if they are right.

8 If you like, ask them to keep a score of how many riddles they solve correctly and report back at the end.

9 The riddles can then be displayed for children to read again at their leisure.

Comments and suggestions

- In this activity, children are writing for an audience (other children in the class) with a clear purpose in mind (to invent a riddle – usually as challenging as possible! – for other children to do). This takes the focus off practising writing for its own sake and makes the activity engaging and enjoyable.

- The use of A4 paper for the riddles and the process of drafting and rewriting, which forms part of the activity, encourage children to take care in the presentation of their work. You may need to set a time limit, however, to ensure children do not spend too long drawing pictures to go with their riddles.

- Other examples of lexical areas which are suitable for riddles are jobs, eg *She wears a white coat. She works in a hospital. She helps people.* (a doctor); food, eg *It's white or brown. It comes from an animal. It gives you protein.* (an egg); everyday objects, eg *It's made of metal. You use it to cut food.* (a knife)

2.12 Reading grid

Level All   **Age** 9–12   **Organization** individual, whole class

Aims To read a text for detail and complete a grid; to use the grid to reconstruct or exchange the information.

Language focus *In the example:* be, there is/are, present simple, questions, adjectives to describe places, cities
Alternatives: any other language and vocabulary, eg animals, *can* (for ability), action words

Materials *Essential:* text(s) for children to read, eg from the course book, junior reference book, magazine, reader or the internet, a prepared grid based on the text(s) (see example on the next page) / *Optional:* photos or pictures to illustrate the texts

	London	New York	Tokyo
location	South of England, on the River Thames		
population	12 million		
main language	English		
places to visit	Big Ben, Buckingham Palace, London Eye		

Procedure

1 Draw the grid you have prepared on the board and ask the children to copy this.

2 Explain and demonstrate that children should read the text(s) and note the answers in the grid. An example of a short text for the grid above is: *London is in the south of England. It is on the River Thames. The population of London is about twelve million. The main language is English. There are many famous places to visit in London. Some of the most popular places are Big Ben, Buckingham Palace and the London Eye.*

3 When children have completed the grid, elicit the questions they need to ask for each piece of information, eg for location: *Where's …?*

4 Children then check the answers by asking and saying the information they have noted in the grid, either in pairs or with the whole class.

Comments and suggestions

- As with listening grids (see 1.17), reading grids provide a flexible means of checking comprehension of texts and are easy to prepare.

- The use of a grid can provide an alternative to asking *Wh-* questions after reading. Instead you can say, eg *Tell me about London* and children reconstruct key information using their completed grids.

- The use of a reading grid avoids children having to write complete sentences and enables them to focus on extracting specific information from a reading text, which is the target skill.

- The use of a reading grid can provide the basis for an oral information gap activity, for example, if you ask the children to read about one city each and then exchange the information in groups of three.

- Reading grids can be used as the basis of internet websearch activities (see Section 9).

- You can also prepare simple reading grids at sentence rather than text level. In this case, children write ticks and/or crosses in the grid as in the example below.

		dog	cat	hamster	bird	turtle	fish
✓ = Yes	It can … jump	✓					
✗ = No	… run	✓					
? = I don't Know	… fly	✗					
	… climb	✗					
	… swim	✓					

2.13 Guess and find out

Level All   **Age** 8–12   **Organization** pairs, whole class, individual

Aims To motivate children to read; to predict or guess whether statements are true or false; to check your predictions.

Language focus *In the example:* weights and measures, present simple, *can* (for possibility), superlative adjectives, explaining and justifying opinions, *because*
Alternatives: any familiar language and vocabulary, eg *was/were*, past simple, dates, famous historical figures

Materials *Essential:* texts for children to read, eg from the course book, junior reference book, magazine, reader or the internet / *Optional:* photocopies of true/false statements based on the text (one for each pair), a photo or picture to illustrate the text

Procedure

1 Divide the class into pairs.

2 Introduce the topic and show the children a picture if you have one. *Either* give out the true/false statements *or* dictate these *or* write them on the board. For example, for a text on blue whales, these could be:

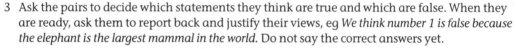

1 The blue whale is the largest mammal in the world.
2 A baby whale is five metres long when it is born.
3 An adult blue whale can weigh more than 100 tons.
4 The blue whale can stay under water for an hour.
5 The blue whale has sharp teeth.
6 The blue whale eats big fish.

3 Ask the pairs to decide which statements they think are true and which are false. When they are ready, ask them to report back and justify their views, eg *We think number 1 is false because the elephant is the largest mammal in the world.* Do not say the correct answers yet.

4 After a brief class discussion about all the statements, children read the text to find out how many answers they got right.

The blue whale is the largest mammal in the world. When it is born, a baby whale is about seven metres long and weighs nearly two tons. For about six months it feeds on its mother's milk. By the time it is fully grown, the blue whale can be thirty metres long and weigh 130 tons.

It can stay under water for about an hour before it comes to the surface to breathe. The blue whale has no teeth and is harmless to other fish. It eats very small sea creatures. In spring and summer it eats four tons of food a day.

5 At the end, check the answers (1 T 2 F 3 T 4 T 5 F 6 F). Ask the children if there are any facts about the blue whale that they find surprising and listen to their response.

Comments and suggestions

- By guessing or predicting whether statements are true or false, children are motivated to read the text and find out whether or not they are right.
- The true/false statements and class discussion prepare the children for language they will read in the text and help to ensure that the reading activity is focused and purposeful.
- This activity works well with a wide range of topics, eg biographical texts about famous people and/or historical figures, eg Mozart, Isaac Newton, or descriptions of natural phenomena, eg volcanoes, icebergs. It is also suitable to use as the basis of a websearch activity (see Section 9).

2.14 Read and order

Level A1.2, A2.1, A2.2   **Age** 8–12   **Organization** pairs, whole class

Aims To read and order instructions to make a recipe; to show interest in a recipe from another country and culture.

Language focus *In the example:* cooking vocabulary, imperatives, weights and measures, sequencers (*first, next, then, after that, finally*)
Alternatives: present simple, daily routines

Materials *Essential:* none / *Optional:* copies of vanilla fudge recipe with the instructions in jumbled order (one for each child), either picture(s) or real items for the recipe, vanilla fudge

Procedure

1 Pre-teach vocabulary for cooking instructions, eg nouns: *bowl, saucepan, tin, spoon;* verbs: *stir, boil, beat, cut, add, pour.*

2 Explain that children are going to learn how to make a sweet called 'vanilla fudge', that is popular with children in Britain.

3 Either give out the photocopies or write the ingredients on the board (see step 6 below).

4 Elicit or explain that g= grams and ml=millilitres.

5 Divide the class into pairs.

6 If you are not using photocopies, write the instructions to make the recipe in jumbled order on the board (they are in the correct order below):

Vanilla fudge	Put the butter, sugar and milk in a saucepan. **1**
	Boil the butter, sugar and milk for 30 minutes. Stir with
Ingredients	a spoon.
500 g brown sugar	Take the saucepan off the heat. Add vanilla essence.
60 g butter	Beat the mixture until it is thick and creamy.
275 ml milk	Pour the mixture into a tin and leave it to cool.
vanilla essence	Cut the fudge into squares and eat it – mmm, delicious!

7 Ask the children to read and order the instructions with their partner. Write 1 by the first instruction as an example. If the children have photocopies, ask them to number the instructions in order.

8 When they are ready, ask the children to report back, using sequencers, eg *First put the butter … Next boil the butter … Then take the saucepan … After that …* (repeat *Then …, After that …* alternately until)*… Finally cut the fudge …*

9 If you have brought some vanilla fudge to class, it may be appropriate to give the children a little piece each to try (but see also comment in second bullet point below).

10 Ask the children if they like the fudge and encourage them to compare it with recipes for typical sweets in their country.

11 If you like, explain that they can also make chocolate, nut or raisin fudge in the same way by adding these to the recipe instead of vanilla essence.

Comments and suggestions

- Make the point that cooking can be dangerous and that children should never attempt to make fudge on their own unless there is an adult willing to help.

- Before doing any activity which involves tasting food or drink, you need to check if children have allergy problems. If there is any doubt about this, omit this stage of the activity.

- With older, higher level children, you can ask them to write recipes for their own favourite sweets, cakes or biscuits, using the vanilla fudge recipe as a guide. They may also like to make the recipes at home (with parental or adult help) and bring the results into class for others to try (if this is suitable given the proviso above). The children's recipes can be illustrated and displayed or made into a class recipe book. Alternatively, the recipes can be produced in an electronic format including scanned digital photos of the results (see Section 9).

- This activity is also appropriate to use in other contexts, such as describing daily routines, e.g. *First she has a shower. Next she has breakfast.*

2.15 Pairs dictation

Level All   **Age** 8–12   **Organization** pairs

Aims To read, dictate and write missing words in a text; to collaborate and take turns with a partner; to use communication strategies appropriately.

Language focus *In the example:* present simple, *can* (for ability), *penguins*, continents
Alternatives: any familiar language and vocabulary

Materials *Essential:* photocopies of the same text, eg from the course book, junior reference book, magazine, reader or the internet, with different words missing (A and B versions) (one copy of A and B for each pair)

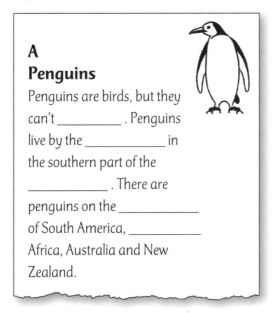

A
Penguins
Penguins are birds, but they
can't _____ . Penguins
live by the _____ in
the southern part of the
_____ . There are
penguins on the _____
of South America, _____
Africa, Australia and New
Zealand.

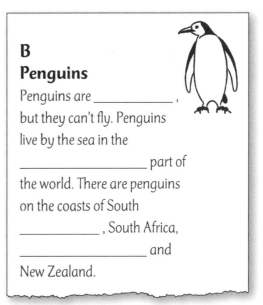

B
Penguins
Penguins are _____ ,
but they can't fly. Penguins
live by the sea in the
_____ part of
the world. There are penguins
on the coasts of South
_____ , South Africa,
_____ and
New Zealand.

Procedure

1 Divide the class into pairs of A and B.

2 Give each child their respective version of the text and explain that they should keep this secret. Explain that although their texts are the same, different words are missing.

3 Demonstrate that children should take turns to read the text and dictate the missing words to their partner (Child A starts). Point out that they can ask their partner any questions they like in order to do this, eg *Can you repeat that please? How do you spell 'southern'?*

4 When they have finished, children compare and check their texts are the same.

Comments and suggestions

• Pairs dictation gives children an opportunity to read aloud in a non-threatening context and motivates them to do this in a clear and intelligible way. The activity also encourages turn-taking and active listening.

• Since the main focus of attention is on dictating and writing the missing words, it is usually a good idea to follow up a pairs dictation with a further activity to ensure understanding of the whole text.

2.16 Wall dictation

Level All   **Age** 8–12   **Organization** groups

Aims To read, dictate and write missing words in a text; to collaborate and take turns in groups; to use communication strategies appropriately.

Language focus *In the example:* be, have got, present simple, dinosaurs, parts of the body, adjectives of size
Alternatives: any familiar language and vocabulary, eg past simple

Materials *Essential:* short texts on coloured card (one for each group) (NB the names of the dinosaurs in brackets on the example below are for reference only; they should not appear on the texts.) / *Optional:* pictures which match the texts

---

1 This dinosaur has got a big body and is very long. It has got a very long neck and a very long tail. It has got a small head and small eyes. It has got small teeth. This dinosaur has got big legs and feet like an elephant. It eats plants. (Diplodocus)

---

2 This dinosaur is very big and tall. It has got a big head and very long, sharp teeth. This dinosaur has got a short neck and a big body. It has also got a big tail. This dinosaur has got two long legs and two very short legs. It eats meat. It is very dangerous. (Tyrannosaurus Rex)

---

3 This dinosaur has got a big body and a big head. It has got two long horns and one short horn. It has got small eyes and a big mouth. This dinosaur has got a frill on its neck. It has got four short legs and a tail. It is very strong. It eats plants. (Triceratops)

---

4 This dinosaur has got a small head and small eyes. It has got a big body and a big tail. It has got lots of spikes on its back and its tail. This dinosaur has got four short fat legs and big feet. It can't run very fast. It eats plants. (Stegosaurus).

Procedure

1 Divide the class into groups of 4–6.

2 Assign a coloured card with a text to each group.

3 Stick the cards on the classroom walls away from where the groups are sitting.

4 Explain that the objective of the activity is for the groups to get the text from the card on the wall into their notebooks as fast as they can. Explain and demonstrate that one person from each group should go to their text, read and remember one or more sentences and then go back and dictate it to the rest of the group. Point out that the rest of the group can ask any questions they like, eg *Can you repeat that please? How do you spell 'spike'?*

5 Whenever you say *Change!* the person who is dictating must immediately sit down and another member of the group takes over.

6 While they are dictating, children leave a gap in the text in their notebooks which they can complete later. Once they have finished, ask the groups to take their text off the wall, compare it to what they have written and correct any spelling or other mistakes. If you have pictures which match the texts, stick these on the board. Ask the groups to read their text again and identify the description they have got. (**Answers:** 1 C 2 A 3 D 4 B)

Comments and suggestions

• The dinosaur dictations can be done using either the present or past tense, eg *This dinosaur had a big body and was very long,* whichever is most suitable. As a follow-up, children can work in different groups and play a guessing game, eg *Has your dinosaur got horns? / Did your dinosaur have horns?*

• Wall dictations integrate listening, speaking, reading and writing skills and help develop children's memory. They also provide a framework for encouraging children to collaborate, listen to each other and take turns.

• Children generally enjoy the physical movement during the activity. However, for safety reasons you need to ensure that there is nothing to trip over and that children do not run.

• It is usually a good idea to have different texts for each group so that they cannot listen in and copy each other. The texts can either be related to the same topic, as with dinosaurs, or they can be separate paragraphs from a longer text or story. In this case, children from different groups can then work together to decide on the best order of their paragraphs to make the complete text.

2.17 A special photo

Level All   **Age** 7–12   **Organization** whole class, individual, pairs

Aims To describe a special photo; to say why the photo is special.

Language focus *In the example: be,* present simple, present continuous, members of the family, clothes, adjectives to describe people, feelings, *because*
Alternatives: past continuous, past simple

Materials *Essential:* you and each child bring a special photo to class

Procedure

1 Write the following prompt questions on the board: *Who is in the photo? Where are you/they? What are you/they wearing? Why do you like the photo?*

2 Show the children your photo. Build up a description in response to the prompt questions and write this on the board, eg *This is a photo of my mother, my father, my sister and me. We are in the garden. My mother is wearing blue trousers. My father is wearing a red shirt. My sister is wearing green shorts. I'm wearing a yellow skirt. I like this photo because we're happy.*

3 Children then work individually and write a description of their special photo by answering the prompt questions and using the description of your photo as a guide.

4 At the end, divide the class into pairs and children show each other their photos and read their descriptions. These can then be displayed or made into a class album.

Comments and suggestions

- Children enjoy the personalization of this activity and the use of prompt questions helps them to organize and structure their writing.

- With older children and higher levels, you can adjust the prompt questions to make the activity more challenging, eg

  Who took the photo? (context)
  Why/Where/When did he/she take the photo?
  What were the people wearing/doing? (description)
  How were they feeling?
  Why is the photo special for you? (personalization)

  An example of a description of a photo using these prompts is: *My father took this photo at my grandmother's 70th birthday party last August. My grandmother was wearing a blue dress. She was opening her presents. My cousin and brother were helping her. My dog was playing with the paper and barking. Everyone was laughing and feeling very happy. This photo is special for me because it was a great party.*

- The opportunity to show and describe special photos in class helps children feel good about themselves and boosts their self-esteem.

2.18 It happened yesterday!

Level A2.1, A2.2, B1.1, B1.2   **Age** 10–12   **Organization** groups, individual, whole class

Aims To create dialogues and write about an imaginary event; to collaborate and take turns in groups; to show willingness to draft, revise and edit written work; to develop imagination.

Language focus *In the example:* past simple, actions, everyday activities, sequencing words
Alternatives: past continuous, conjunctions

Materials *Essential:* sets of past tense verb cards with two or three blank cards (one set for each group)

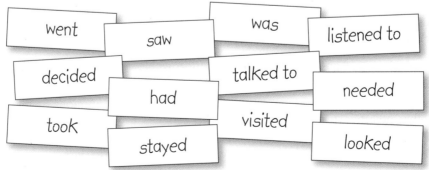

Procedure

1 Divide the class into groups of four.

2 Ask the children to imagine that yesterday they didn't come to school and something extraordinary happened.

3 Give a set of verb cards to each group. Ask one child in each group to give out the verb cards (2–3 for each child) and to put the blank cards on the desk.

4 Explain and demonstrate that the children should take turns to say a sentence using one of their verb cards and build up an imaginary account of what happened yesterday. If a child wants to use a different verb from the ones they have got, they should write this on one of the blank cards.

5 As children do the activity, demonstrate that they should lay out the verb cards they use for each sentence on the desk in order, eg *Yesterday we <u>decided</u> to go to the centre of town. We <u>saw</u> a brilliant film. We <u>went</u> to a restaurant. We <u>talked</u> to a man and a woman. The man and woman <u>looked</u> very nervous. They <u>had</u> a million dollars in cash. They <u>needed</u> to escape from the police. We <u>listened</u> to their story. They <u>wanted</u> to give us the money. The police <u>arrived</u>. The police <u>arrested</u> the man and woman. The police <u>took</u> the man and woman away. We <u>went</u> home.*

6 Once the children have finished, ask them to write the sentences they have built up, using the verb cards laid out on the table as a prompt. Ask them to look for ways of combining sentences and/or using additional words to make their account more interesting, eg *Yesterday we decided to go to the centre of town and we saw a brilliant film. After the film, we went to a restaurant where we talked to a man and a woman.*

7 Children can also add more verbs and more detail to their accounts, eg *The man was tall with a black beard and the woman had long, red hair and was very beautiful.*

8 When children have finished revising their accounts, ask them to write out (and also possibly illustrate) a final version.

9 Children then take turns to read each others' accounts and/or these can be displayed.

Comments and suggestions

• Through collaborating in groups and using the past tense verb cards as support, the process of creating an imaginative narrative text is made feasible and enjoyable.

• Before asking children to revise and improve their accounts in groups, it may be best to take one group's account and explicitly model this process with the whole class. Alternatively, you may like to elicit or suggest conjunctions which are likely to be useful, eg *and, so, but, because, next, then, after,* before they begin.

• To make the activity more challenging, you can write the verb cards in the infinitive and children transform these into past simple or past continuous as they create their accounts, eg *We were listening to the man and woman's story when the police arrived.*

2.19 My diary

Level All   **Age** 6–12   **Organization** whole class, individual

Aims To write (and draw pictures to illustrate) a personal diary; to take pleasure in writing about personal activities and events; to develop self-awareness (eg about what you do in free time or food you eat).

Language focus dates, days of the week, times, past simple, free-time activities, food, meals

Materials *Essential:* none / *Optional:* special notebooks to be used as diaries or hand-made books (see 7.14a) (one for each child)

Procedure

1 Children *either* use their school notebooks *or* special notebooks *or* make a diary.

2 Explain the purpose of the diary. This may be open for children to record whatever they like about each day, or it may be more structured as part of a unit of work, for example to write what they did in their free time, or to record the food they ate, every day for a week.

3 Establish when you expect the children to write their diaries, for example in the last ten minutes of class time, and elicit or give an example of a diary entry, eg *Monday 2nd February: I had my piano lesson at 5 o'clock. I did my homework. I had dinner at 7 o'clock. I watched TV for two hours. At 9.30 I went to bed. / Wednesday 4th June: For breakfast I had cereal and milk. For a snack in the morning I had a banana. For lunch I had pizza and an apple. For a snack in the afternoon I had three biscuits. For dinner I had soup and a yogurt.*

4 If you like, children can also illustrate their diaries with drawings or photos.

Comments and suggestions

- If children are writing diaries for a specified period and objective, at the end ask questions, eg *How many people … watched TV every day? / … ate fruit every day?* and use the children's responses as the basis of a class discussion about personal routines and habits.

- If the children are writing an open-format diary in an ongoing way, give them an opportunity to show you this from time to time, but do not insist. When you read children's personal diaries, be sure to respond to their meaning, eg *What a great day!* or *I'm sorry you had a headache on Tuesday. I hope you're better now* rather than correct them for spelling or grammatical mistakes. Be aware also that children's diaries may contain information that you need to act on, for example, if a child writes about being bullied.

- Keeping a personal diary in English gives children a sense of satisfaction and boosts their self-esteem. Responsibility for choosing what to write gives children 'ownership' of language and makes the activity motivating and enjoyable. This also often has a positive impact on children's care and pride in their work, with diaries often beautifully illustrated and presented.

- With younger children who are just beginning to write, it may be suitable for them to keep a weekend diary. In this case, children tell you one or two activities they did after every weekend and you write sentences in their diary, eg *I went swimming. I had lunch with my Granny.* Children copy the sentences you write and draw a picture to illustrate what they did.

2.20 Book review

Level All   **Age** 6–12   **Organization** whole class, individual

Aims To write about a book you have read; to describe it and say what you like and dislike about the book; (to say if you would recommend the book to someone else, to give reasons for your opinions).

Language focus present simple, (adjectives to describe people, places, clothes or animals, adverbs of manner, *would*)

Materials *Essential:* none / *Optional:* photocopies of a book review form (one for each child) or A4 paper for children to write their reviews (and draw pictures)

Procedure

1 Briefly discuss the book or books that children have recently read or that you have read to them. Ask questions as appropriate about the pictures, characters, setting, plot, genre, etc.

2 Encourage children to say what they like and/or dislike about the book and to give reasons.

3 Give out the book review form you have prepared or write it on the board for the children to copy. See the next page for two examples of forms for different ages and levels.

   NB you will need to include more space for children to write than is shown here.

4 Ask the children to work individually on their reviews.

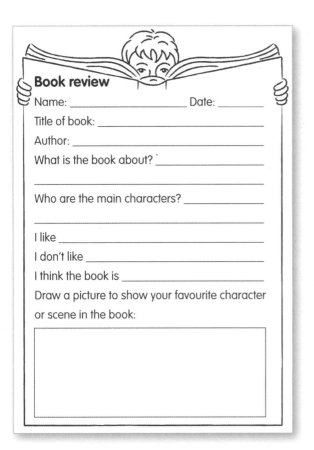

Book review

Name: _____ Date: _____

Title of book: _____

Author: _____

What is the book about? _____

_____

Who are the main characters? _____

_____

I like _____

I don't like _____

I think the book is _____

Draw a picture to show your favourite character
or scene in the book:

```



```

Book review

Name: _____ Date: _____

Title of book: _____

Author: _____

What kind of book is it? _____

Describe the setting: _____

Describe the main characters: _____

_____

Was the plot interesting? Why? / Why not?

_____

Did the author use humour, suspense, mystery or

surprise? How? _____

_____

What did you like / dislike about the book?

_____

Would you recommend the book to your friends?

Why? / Why not? _____

_____

5 At the end, ask children to exchange and read each others' reviews.

Comments and suggestions

- By writing reviews of books they read, children are encouraged to develop critical reading skills and also to become better writers.

- If children keep their book reviews together in a folder or file (paper or electronic), over time they build up a permanent record of what they have read in English. If children are using portfolios, they may also like to include book reviews they write as part of their dossier.

2.21 Speech bubbles

Level A1.1, A1.2, A2.1, A2.2   **Age** 7–12   **Organization** whole class, pairs

Aims To read and match speech bubbles to people in a poster; to write and act out a dialogue.

Language focus any language children know which is suitable for direct speech, eg greetings, requests, offers, questions; food or other vocabulary relevant to the picture you have chosen

Materials *Essential:* a poster including lots of people (eg one that accompanies a course book), two or three prepared pairs of speech bubbles (see next page), empty pairs of speech bubbles (two for each pair of children) / *Optional:* magazine pictures showing two or more people, or cartoon strip stories

Procedure

1 Show the children the poster you have chosen for the activity.

2 Ask questions about the poster, eg *Where are they? What are they doing? What's he/she eating?*

3 Show the children the pairs of speech bubbles you have prepared and read them out in turn, eg *Do you want a sandwich? Yes, please. / Is the fish good? No, it's horrible. / Can I try your milkshake? No, you can't.*

4 Ask the children to imagine who in the poster is saying each speech bubble. Invite children to the front of the class to stick the speech bubbles by the appropriate characters.

5 Divide the class into pairs.

6 Give each pair two more empty speech bubbles (or children can make these). Ask them to choose two characters in the poster and invent and write an exchange between them on the cut-out speech bubbles.

7 When the children are ready, invite them to take turns to stick their speech bubbles by the characters on the poster and read them to the class.

8 If appropriate, you can then ask the pairs to extend the speech bubble exchange and write a dialogue of about 8–12 lines between the characters on the poster they have chosen.

9 When they are ready, the pairs can take turns to act out their dialogues to the class.

Comments and suggestions

- This activity gives children practice in writing direct speech in an enjoyable, and often humorous, way. It also encourages them to observe detail and expressions in pictures of people.

- Posters are often available as part of children's course books. However, if you don't have a poster, you can use photos of people from old magazines or download these from the internet.

- An alternative is to use comics or jokes. In this case, you need to blank out the text in some or all of the speech bubbles. Children then work in pairs and (re-)invent and write the text.

2.22 Consequences

Level All   **Age** 9–12   **Organization** whole class, groups

Aims To write sentences in order to construct 'stories' following a set pattern; to collaborate and take turns in groups.

Language focus *In the example:* past simple, places
Alternatives: present simple, *be, have got,* clothes, colours, numbers, parts of the body

Materials *Essential:* A4 paper (one sheet for each child)

Procedure

1 Give a sheet of paper to each child. Explain that children are going to write a simple story together, following a set pattern. Write this pattern on the board:

   (name of a boy / man) met
   (name of a girl / woman)
   in (place)
   He said to her:
   She said to him:
   And the consequence was …

   Check the children understand the meaning of 'consequence', ie result.

2 Give an example of a story following the pattern, using the names of either famous people or storybook characters or real people the children know, eg *Harry Potter met Little Red Riding Hood in the disco. He said to her, 'I like chocolate.' She said to him, 'Go away!' And the consequence was they went to live on Mars.*

3 Explain and demonstrate that children should write the first line only.

4 They should then fold the paper down so that no-one can see what they have written and pass it on to the next person.

5 That person should then write the second line, fold down the paper and pass it on in the same way until the story is completed.

6 At the end, divide the class into groups.

7 Ask the children in each group to unfold the papers they have got, read the stories in turn and choose the best or funniest one.

8 When they are ready, ask one child from each group to read the story they have chosen to the rest of the class.

9 At the end, ask the class to decide or vote which story they think is overall best.

Comments and suggestions

• Children enjoy the secrecy of folding down the paper after each line and the nonsensical, often humorous, stories which are created.

• As the linguistic demands are limited and follow a pattern, the activity is suitable to use at elementary level. It can also be done in the present tense if this is more appropriate.

• Instead of a story, children can, for example, invent the name of an animal and write a description following a set pattern, eg name / size / colour / ears / eyes / legs / tail.

- An alternative version of consequences involves children drawing pictures (hat and head / chest and arms / waist and legs / feet, shoes) and inventing a monster or person. In groups, children then choose the picture they like best, invent a name and write a description. They then show the picture and read the description to the rest of the class, who listen and decide which one is best.

2.23 A work of art

Level All   **Age** 6–12   **Organization** whole class, pairs

Aims To describe a work of art; to express personal opinions; to read and match works of art and descriptions; to show interest and respect for the opinions of others; to develop visual literacy and awareness.

Language focus *In the example: can* (for ability), *there is/are,* colours, adjectives to describe people and feelings, places, opinions
Alternatives: looks like

Materials *Essential:* a reproduction of a work of art, postcards of a selection of works of art (one for each pair), paper to write the descriptions on

Procedure

1 Show the children the work of art you have selected for the activity. Either elicit or tell the children the name of the artist and title of the painting.

2 Ask the children to describe what they can see in the painting. Elicit what they like or don't like about it and the reasons for this.

3 Build up a description of the work of art with the whole class and write this on the board. Use a framework to do this, eg *In the picture I can see … .There's also … . I like the …. I think the picture is … .*

4 Divide the class into pairs.

5 Give a postcard of another work of art and a piece of paper to each pair. Ask them to write a description of it in the same way.

6 When they are ready, collect in the postcards and descriptions.

7 Give each postcard a number and each description a letter and stick them in jumbled order on the classroom walls.

8 Ask the children to walk round the classroom with their partner, read the descriptions and match them to the works of art.

9 At the end, check the answers and invite the children to say which work of art they like best.

Comments and suggestions

- This activity encourages children to develop visual literacy through noticing detail and interpreting meaning in paintings.

- With younger children, it may be better to choose paintings which are realistic and uncluttered and they can simply write, eg *I can see … a blue horse, a girl in a red dress,* or to choose abstract paintings and they write the colours and/or shapes, eg *I can see red, purple, blue and black. / I can see a red, green and yellow circle.*

- With older children, you can choose paintings with more detail or abstract paintings and children can write, eg *It looks like …. / It makes me feel ….* It may also be appropriate for children to write about materials, eg water colour, and techniques, eg collage, that the artist uses.

- If children are doing a project on a particular artist, eg Picasso, you can select postcards from different artistic periods of his life and use the activity as an introduction to discussing and comparing these.

- If appropriate, children can also paint a picture in the style of a particular artist as a follow-up to this activity.

2.24 Party invitations

Level A1.1, A1.2   **Age** 7–10   **Organization** whole class, individual

Aims To identify information to include in a party invitation; to write and respond to a party invitation.

Language focus prepositions, days, dates, times, *please, thank you, I'd love to come / I'm sorry I can't come*

Materials *Essential:* none / *Optional:* A4 coloured card (cut in quarters) to use for the invitations (one for each child)

Procedure

1 Establish possible contexts for party invitations, eg a birthday party, class party, fancy-dress party, beach party, Christmas or carnival party.

2 Ask the children what information you need to include in a party invitation, eg who it's for, what kind of party, the day, date, place, time and who the invitation is from, plus possibly also special instructions about what to wear or bring.

3 Create a framework for the invitation on the board, eliciting or establishing the prepositions that it would be appropriate to use for each piece of information.

Party Invitation

To: _____

Please come to _____ party

on: _____

at: _____

from: _____ to: _____

From: _____

Please bring / wear _____

---

4 Give an example of a completed invitation, eg *To David / Please come to my birthday party / on Saturday 2nd June / at my house / from 5 o'clock to 8 o'clock. / from Michael / Please wear fancy dress.*

5 Assign who each child in the class should write their invitation to (as far as possible, pair children who like each other but who are sitting far away from each other).

6 Either give out the coloured card or children can write the invitation in their notebooks.

7   Ask them to decide what kind of party they are going to have, invent the information about the time and date, etc and write an invitation to the child they have been assigned.

8   Ask two children to act as 'postboy' and 'postgirl' and deliver all the invitations.

9   Children read the invitations and then write a reply following a framework, eg *Dear Michael, Thank you for the invitation to your _____ party on _____ . I'd love to come. / I'm sorry I can't come. From David.*

10 The 'postboys' and 'postgirls' deliver the replies and children read them.

11 At the end, count up how many children accepted the invitations they were sent.

Comments and suggestions

- Although children will want to choose who to write their invitations to, it is best if you decide, in order to avoid a situation where some children get lots of invitations and others get none.

- Children enjoy writing and receiving instant replies to their invitations through the 'postboys' and 'postgirls'. Having an immediate audience also makes the activity purposeful.

- Whenever there's an opportunity, you can use the first part of the activity for real invitations, eg for children to invite their parents to come to an end of term show.

2.25 Interview and report

Level All   **Age** 7–12   **Organization** pairs, individual

Aims To prepare and write questions for an interview; to carry out an interview; to ask for personal information; to use the information from the interview to write a report.

Language focus present simple, questions, personal information, jobs, daily routines
Alternatives: past simple, *was/were*

Materials *Essential:* none

Procedure

1   Ask the children to decide who they are going to interview, eg another teacher, member of staff, family member, neighbour or other adult friend. Point out that whoever they interview should speak English!

2   Divide the class into pairs.

3   Ask the children to prepare 6–10 questions for their interview together, eg *Where do you live? What's your job? What time do you start work? How do you go to work?*

4   Children then interview the person they have chosen using these questions. They can either do this in pairs if, for example, you have arranged for them to interview colleagues in break time, or individually, if they are going to interview someone at home.

5   Children then write up their interviews into a report, eg *Mrs Scott lives in Rome. She's a teacher. She goes to work by bus.*

6   If you like, children can illustrate their reports with a photo or picture of the person they have interviewed. These can then be displayed.

Comments and suggestions

- This activity provides practice in writing questions for a real purpose and introduces children to the genre of report writing. Children also have an opportunity to communicate in English outside the classroom.

- Interviews can be conducted on a range of different topics, eg to find out food and leisure habits, to find out favourites in a number of different categories, or to find out opinions about particular issues. The activity is also suitable to use to practise the past simple tense, for example, in interviews to find out what people *did* and *liked* etc when they were younger or when they were at school.

2.26 Mind maps for writing

Level All   **Age** 9–12   **Organization** whole class

Aims To prepare for writing a text by creating a mind map; to collaborate to produce a text.

Language focus *In the example:* tigers, present simple, adjectives to describe an animal, parts of the body, comparatives, superlatives
Alternatives: any familiar language or vocabulary

Materials *Essential:* a pre-prepared mind map / *Optional:* a picture or photo to introduce the topic of the text, a large piece of paper to write the mind map and/or text on

Procedure

1. Write the topic of the text in the centre of the board or paper, eg *Tigers* and show the children a picture if you have one.

2. Say, eg *Let's write a description of tigers. What kinds of things do we want to include?* Use the children's suggestions to establish the main categories and write these around the heading.

3. Continue in the same way, asking the children to suggest things to include in the description for each category and add them to the mind map. Use the mind map you have pre-prepared for your own reference and to guide the children's ideas, if they get stuck, but do not stick to this rigidly.

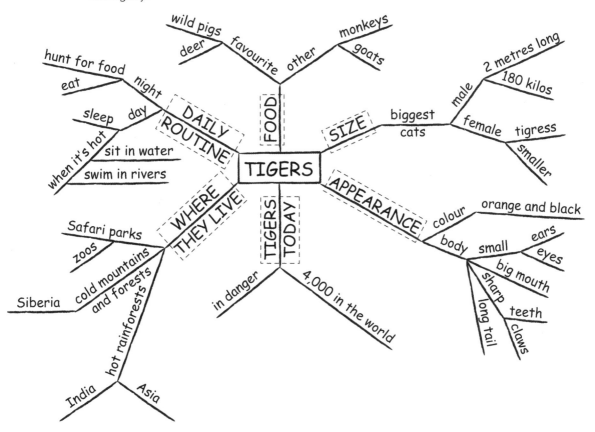

4. Once the mind map is finished, use it to build up a text collaboratively with the children. Either write the text on the board or on paper as the children suggest sentences, or ask children to take turns to be the 'class secretary' and do this. An example of a text built up with children using the mind map of tigers is as follows:

> Tigers are the biggest cats in the world. A male tiger is two metres long and weighs 180 kilos. The female tiger is a tigress. It is smaller than the male.
>
> Tigers are orange and black. They have got small ears and small eyes. They have got a big mouth and sharp, pointed teeth. They have got sharp claws and a long tail.
>
> Tigers live in India and Asia in hot rainforests. They also live in Siberia in cold mountains and forests with snow. There are also tigers in zoos and safari parks.
>
> Tigers sleep in the day. When it's hot, they sit in water or swim in rivers. At night they hunt for food. The tiger's favourite food is wild pig and deer. They also eat monkeys and goats.
>
> Tigers are animals in danger. There are only 4,000 tigers in the world today.

5 As a follow-up, children can construct a similar mind map in pairs for a different animal in danger and then write a text independently based on this.

Comments and suggestions

- The use of mind maps based on the work of Tony Buzan (see p.320 for reference) introduces children to a way of organizing and planning their written work which they may find helpful. Be aware, however, that mind maps tend to appeal strongly to some children and much less so to others.

- Mind maps are particularly useful for planning texts such as descriptions, which do not develop in a linear or chronological way.

- As you build up a text from the mind map with children, talk about the language, eg *Do you think we should write 'They' or 'Tigers' here? Which sounds best? Why?* By explicitly modelling the processes involved in constructing a text, you help children become aware of these when they write independently.

- See also Section 10 for using mind maps to help children learn grammar (10.10) and to identify how they like to work (10.18).

2.27 Structured paragraphs

Level A1.1, A1.2, A2.1, A2.2   **Age** 8–12   **Organization** pairs

Aims To read and find the answers to a series of questions; to use the answers to write structured paragraphs.

Language focus unusual mini-beasts, present simple, *be, have got,* colours, parts of the body, adjectives to describe unusual mini-beasts, adjectives of size
Alternatives: any language or vocabulary, depending on the topic and text

Materials *Essential:* copies of texts or reference books containing the answers to the questions (one for each pair) / *Optional:* photos or pictures to illustrate the topic, access to the internet

Procedure

1 Divide the class into pairs.

2 Announce the topic, eg unusual mini-beasts, and write a list of questions on the board that you want each pair to answer for one unusual mini-beast, eg:

> What colour is it?
>
> How big is it?
>
> What special features has it got?
>
> How many years does it live?
>
> Where does it live?
>
> What does it eat?
>
> Is it dangerous?

2 Assign an unusual mini-beast to each pair, eg tarantula, whip scorpion, shield bug, rag worm.

3 Give out the texts or reference books. Children work with their partner and find the answers to the questions.

4 They then write two paragraphs about their mini-beast following the order of the questions, eg *The whip scorpion is black. It is six centimetres long and has a long, thin tail. It lives for about one year. The whip scorpion lives in Asia and South America. It eats insects, cockroaches, frogs and toads. It isn't dangerous.*

5 If the texts or books are illustrated, children can also draw a picture of their mini-beast. They can then either circulate and read each others' descriptions or tell each other about their mini-beasts.

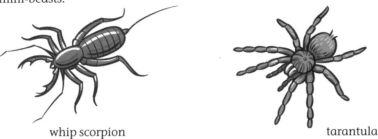

whip scorpion   tarantula

Comments and suggestions

- This activity is particularly suitable to use in order to grade the task if the texts you have available are above the children's reading level. The questions you prepare should require the children to scan the text for specific key information, but not to read or understand it in detail.

- In order to cater for different abilities within the class, you may like to have available a framework for writing the paragraphs on card, which you can give to children who need more support, eg *The X is … (colour). It is … (size). It has got … (special features). It lives for … (number of months/years). The X lives in … (name of country/continent). It eats … (food). It is / isn't dangerous.*

- This activity can be done as an internet websearch activity using a suitable pre-selected site in a similar way to a mini-quest (see 9.24). It can also be linked to other content-based work on the topic of bugs (see 8.6).

2.28 Shaped poems

Level All   **Age** 7–12   **Organization** whole class, pairs

Aims To write sentences to describe something; to create a shaped poem.

Language focus *be*, *have got*, present simple, adjectives to describe, eg trees or plants, animals, objects, fruit or vegetables

Materials *Essential:* an example of a shaped poem / *Optional:* paper or card (one piece for each child)

Procedure

1 Tell the children that they are going to write a shaped poem. Explain what you mean by this, ie a poem which is written and laid out in the shape of a picture of what it describes. Show and read the children the shaped poem you have prepared, eg *Sunflowers are yellow, Sunflowers are tall, Sunflowers are beautiful, Sunflowers follow the sun, Sunflowers have got seeds, Sunflower seeds are delicious.*

2 Ask the children to suggest ideas of things for a shaped poem, eg a tree, a banana, an apple, a snake.

3 Divide the class into pairs.

4 Ask the children to choose the subject of their shaped poem and to write six sentences to describe it in their notebooks.

5 Monitor and get the children to check and correct their work before moving on to the next stage.

6 If you have paper or card, give this out to the children and ask them to draw a picture and write their sentences to make a shaped poem. Both children in each pair should make an individual version of the shaped poem based on the sentences they have prepared.

7 When they have finished, children circulate and read each others' poems. These can also be displayed or made into a class book.

Comments and suggestions

• Shaped poems practise descriptive writing at sentence level and allow children to be creative with minimum linguistic competence. Drawing a picture also helps to make language memorable.

2.29 Five senses poems

Level All   **Age** 8–12   **Organization** whole class, pairs

Aims To create and write a poem based on the five senses; to develop the ability to visualize and imagine a place.

Language focus *can* (for possibility), the five senses, the seaside, adjectives of description
Alternatives: countryside, weather

Materials *Essential:* none

Procedure

1 Draw a simple web on the board.

2 Write *The seaside* in the centre and the verbs *see, hear, smell, taste* and *touch* arranged around this.

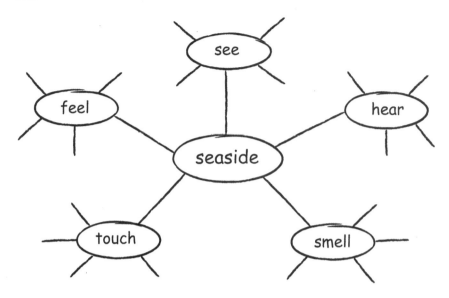

3 Ask the children to suggest things they can see, hear, smell, taste and touch at the seaside. Add these to the web. Use this as an opportunity to revise or introduce vocabulary related to the seaside.

4 Either use the web created on the board to build up a poem with the whole class, or divide the class into pairs and, after eliciting or suggesting one or two example lines, get the children to write a poem based on the web with their partner. An example of a poem using this technique is as follows:

At the seaside
I can see blue sea and grey sky
I can hear the wind and the waves
I can smell the sea
I can taste the salt
And I can touch the soft, yellow sand.

5 Once the children are ready, invite a few pairs to read their poems to the class.

6 Children can also illustrate their poems and these can then be displayed or made into a class book.

Comments and suggestions

• This activity encourages children to visualize and imagine a place using the five senses as a prompt for ideas.

• The five senses determines the number of lines in the poem and provides a framework which makes writing a poem accessible.

• This activity can form part of a unit of work on places or holidays. In this case, you may like to give children the choice of writing a poem about the countryside instead. It can also be linked to other work on the senses (see, eg 8.11).

2.30 Object poems

Level A2.1, A2.2, B1.1 **Age** 9–12 **Organization** whole class, pairs

Aims To observe, touch and examine an object closely; to answer questions in order to describe the object; to use the answers to create, write and edit a poem about the object.

Language focus present simple, feelings, adjectives to describe objects, *like a …*

Materials *Essential:* objects for the activity, eg shells, conkers, pebbles, feathers (one for each pair) / *Optional:* photocopies of the question sheet (one for each pair)

Procedure

1 Show the children the object you have chosen for the activity, eg a shell.

2 Either give out the question sheet you have prepared or write the questions on the board.

What is it? _____

Where do you find it? _____

What size and shape is it? _____

What colour is it? _____

How does it feel when you touch it? _____

What other words describe it? _____

What does it make you think of? _____

What does it make you feel? _____

---

3 Divide the class into pairs.

4 Give each pair a shell to examine closely and ask them to write answers to the questions.

5 Once the children are ready, get them to write their answers in the form of a poem.

6 Once they have written a draft, encourage them to cut, add or change words in order to improve their poems. An example of a poem using this technique is as follows:

A shell
On the wet sand
Like a small plate
White and pink
Smooth and shiny
I think of the sea
I feel happy

Comments and suggestions

• The questions provide a scaffold which helps children structure the poem.

• This activity allows for personal, divergent responses and can be realized at different levels, as the two examples of poems about conkers written by eleven-year-old boys following a similar question sheet show:

```
Conker
From a Chestnut tree
In Autumn
On the ground
Round and brown
Hard and shiny
The winter is coming
I feel cold and sad
```

```
In a cold winter
A butterfly
Sits on a conker
And falls down the tree
It bounces
And the prickly shell opens
It's brown and light
And it seems like a brain broken
```

César and Javier   Eduardo and Rafael

2.31 Feelings poem

Level All   **Age** 10–12   **Organization** individual, groups, whole class

Aims To express personal feelings; to create and write a poem collaboratively; to show willingness to draft, redraft and edit written work.

Language focus present simple, adjectives of feeling

Materials *Essential:* different starter lines written on card, eg *I feel happy / sad / angry / frightened when ...* (one for each group), strips of paper (one for each child)

Procedure

1 Divide the class into groups of 4–6.

2 Give each group, or let them choose, a starter line.

3 Give each child a strip of paper and get them each to complete the sentence with something which is true for them in relation to the feeling on their starter card, eg *I feel happy when ... I play football with my friends.*

4 Children read and compare their sentences in their groups and arrange them in order, to make a poem. At this point, explain that they can add words, cut words or change the sentences in order to improve their poems.

5 Once the children are ready, ask them to think about how their poems will end. In order to help them, you may like to suggest that they write a final sentence starting with 'But' which contrasts with previous ideas in the poem. An example of a poem using this technique is as follows:

   I feel happy when ...
   I go to the park on my bike
   My friends come to my house
   I play on my Mum's computer
   I stay up late and watch TV.
   But I feel sad when
   It's time to go to bed
   And the end of another day.

6 At the end, invite the groups to read their poems to the rest of the class.

7 The children can then write out and illustrate their poems. These can either be displayed or made into a class book.

Comments and suggestions

- This activity is suitable at elementary level since, individually, the children are only required to write one sentence.
- If children have not done an activity like this before, it is best to model the procedure by creating a poem with the whole class first.
- Be prepared for the fact that the children will probably need to use L1 when revising and editing their poems in groups, as it is likely to be beyond their productive level to do this in English.
- Notice the way children read their poems. As these are something they have created, they are likely to do this with special care.
- Use the poems to make a class book or wall display, thereby showing that you value the children's efforts and promoting self-esteem.

2.32 Text types

Level A2.2, B1.1, B1.2   **Age** 10–12   **Organization** whole class, pairs

Aims To develop awareness of different text types; to notice features which help identify different text types

Language focus names of text types, giving reasons with *because*

Materials *Essential:* examples of different text types, eg poem, menu, newspaper article, recipe, instruction manual, letter, greeting card, postcard, advertisement, comic, joke, diary, timetable, numbered for the activity / *Optional:* bilingual dictionaries (one for each pair)

Procedure

1 Ask the children if it's important to be able to read in English and if so, why, and listen to their ideas.
2 Divide the class into pairs.
3 Ask the children to write a list of things people read, eg text messages, emails, web pages, newspapers. If they don't know the words in English, they can either use a simple bilingual dictionary or note their ideas in L1. Set a time limit, eg five minutes.
4 Ask the children to report back and recast their ideas in English if necessary. Write a list of the text types they suggest on the board and add any additional ones.
5 Pass the numbered texts round the class to each pair in turn and ask the children to identify the text types.
6 At the end, check the answers and encourage the children to say why, eg *We think number 1 is a poem because the lines are short. We think number 2 is a menu because it's got the names of food and prices.*
7 At the end, discuss different purposes for reading, eg *We read a menu to see if there is something we want to eat. We read a manual to find out how a new camera works.* Discuss the way this influences the strategies we use for reading.

Comments and suggestions

- An awareness of text types helps children to understand that there are different purposes for reading and different strategies which they can use.
- In this activity you can use authentic texts which are beyond the children's reading level, since all they are required to do is identify the types of texts.

Section 3 Vocabulary and grammar

Vocabulary and grammar are closely interrelated in children's early language learning, both in L1 and in a second or foreign language. Young children initially learn chunks of language, which combine vocabulary and grammatical patterns, in a holistic, unanalysed way. As they grow older, they develop the ability to relate vocabulary to networks of meanings and to notice and analyse language forms and functions more explicitly. Whether they are learning holistically when younger, or developing more conscious language awareness and powers of analysis as they grow older, it is vital to give children plenty of opportunities to memorize, practise, recycle and extend their vocabulary and grammar in meaningful contexts throughout the primary years.

Learning vocabulary

Children often measure their own language learning progress in terms of 'how many words they know'. Learning vocabulary can be one of the most significant and satisfying outcomes in the first years of English lessons. It boosts children's confidence and self-esteem. It also lays the foundations for leading children into using grammatical structures, which initially present a greater learning challenge, in more extended and creative ways.

Words and concepts

Although initial vocabulary learning in a foreign language appears straightforward, with an apparent one-to-one correspondence between words and the objects or concepts that these refer to, it is in reality a very complex process, which develops gradually in a cyclical way over time.

As part of the process of learning vocabulary, children need to learn the form of the word, that is, the way the word sounds and is spelt, and the way it changes grammatically, eg when used in the plural. They also need to understand the meaning and the way that this relates to other concepts and words, eg the way a word like *tiny* relates to other words to describe size, such as *big* and *small*. In addition to this, children need to be able to recall the word whenever they need it and, in the longer term, to gradually extend

their understanding of its use. This includes, for example, the different ways it can be combined grammatically with other elements in sentences or discourse, the way it collocates with other words, eg we can talk about a *tall building* or a *tall person* but not a *tall mountain* (we need to use *high* instead), the connotations that it may have, eg to refer to someone as *very clever* may imply that they are cheeky as well, and an awareness of style and register and whether it is appropriate to use in formal or informal situations. With older children, it may also be appropriate for them to identify the grammatical properties of words and use metalanguage, eg noun, adjective, verb, to describe this as well. In addition to this, children's learning of vocabulary may be compounded by cultural factors and expectations, eg their concept of a 'pie' to eat may be very different from an English or American pie. It will also be influenced by their L1 background and their ongoing stage of cognitive, social and psychological development, where they are still in the process of acquiring concepts and vocabulary which they bring to their understanding of English in a continually evolving way.

The importance of recycling

Children often appear to learn vocabulary easily, 'like little sponges', as the saying goes. However, in the same way that sponges lose water, children also forget vocabulary very easily too, unless they are given regular opportunities to use it, and to deepen and extend their understanding of how it relates and connects to other language they know. Given this, it is essential to recycle vocabulary regularly and systematically at all levels and ages in primary school.

Through regular recycling, children can be given opportunities to meet the same vocabulary, embedded in different contexts, language and activity types, again and again. This not only improves their recall and develops memory processes, but also extends their understanding and associations of vocabulary in an ever expanding network of meanings and use. Through using vocabulary in a variety of social, experiential and personalized ways, children develop 'ownership' of language and this also leads to new learning.

In addition to the vocabulary activities in this section, there are many examples of other activity types, such as games, rhymes, songs, stories, drama, art and craft, which provide opportunities to recycle vocabulary in a range of meaningful and creative ways. These are described in different sections of this book.

Vocabulary practice

With younger children, it is most appropriate to teach concrete vocabulary items which relate to the 'here and now' of their immediate environment and personal experience. As children grow older, they gradually become able to deal with more abstract concepts and vocabulary removed from their immediate surroundings. When practising vocabulary, it is important to provide opportunities to help children:

- associate words and meanings and develop their recall of vocabulary (see 3.1, 3.2)
- think about the properties and meanings of words (see 3.4)
- improve their recognition and spelling of vocabulary (see 3.5, 3.6)
- reinforce connections between words (see 3.7)
- personalize vocabulary learning (see 3.8, 3.15)
- develop strategies for inferring meaning (see 3.10)
- develop strategies for conveying the meaning of unfamiliar words (see 3.11)
- collaborate and interact with others (see 3.3, 3.14).

Children also need to be encouraged to develop independent and individualized learning skills and strategies that will help them to enrich and extend their vocabulary, to organize and record vocabulary in systematic and logical ways, and to reflect on and evaluate their own learning in an increasingly autonomous way (see Section 10, Learning to learn).

Learning grammar

In order to lay the foundations for understanding and learning aspects of grammar, it is above all important to give children exposure to language in meaningful contexts which engage them in practising and using English for purposes which they can relate to and enjoy.

Initial stages

With young children, initial learning of grammatical patterns is implicit, based on formulaic sequences and unanalysed chunks of language met in the context of, eg lesson routines, songs, rhymes, stories and games. As a result of acquiring chunks of language, children develop a sense of achievement and become increasingly willing to participate in classroom activities in English. As they grow in confidence, they also begin to transfer chunks to new contexts and to use them creatively. Two examples of this are a child spontaneously transferring the chunk *Too much noise!* from the song 'The wheels on the bus' to the classroom, and a child asking *Can I go the colour please?* (sic) to request permission to colour a collectively produced mural, by using part of a chunk of classroom language for asking to go the toilet. The holistic learning of language chunks plays an important role in fostering children's enthusiasm for learning English. It also provides them with a potentially rich, internal language resource as they grow older and are encouraged, or expected, to pay attention to grammatical features and apply more explicit analytical skills to the way they learn.

Understanding how English works

One of the key issues and challenges during the primary years is when and how to move beyond the implicit teaching–learning of language chunks, and to develop children's awareness and explicit understanding of aspects of grammar. This will enable children to begin to systematize their knowledge and potentially enrich and extend the creative ways in which they are able to use language. In terms of age, it is unlikely to be appropriate before somewhere between the ages of 8–10. It depends on factors such as the educational and cultural context, children's cognitive maturity and conceptual readiness, their level and the number of hours spent studying English (it is best if they already have basic skills), as well as the approach used in teaching their first language. This may include explicit analysis of parts of speech and the use of metalanguage which can usefully be transferred to the learning of English. In terms of how it is done, it is vital to find child-friendly, 'hands on' ways which naturally develop children's interest and curiosity in how English 'works' and to use these from time to time as an integral part of building up their understanding of language meaning and developing language use.

Language awareness

One way to explicitly develop children's language awareness is by encouraging them to notice particular language patterns or features of grammatical forms and, if appropriate, to compare and contrast these with other patterns and forms and/or with their own language. Through stimulating children to show interest and ask questions about how English works as a system, and encouraging them to observe and pay attention to this, children are helped to develop metacognitive awareness. This means becoming more self-knowledgeable and aware of the processes involved in their own learning (see also Section 10, Learning to learn). The provision of opportunities to notice features and/or regularities in grammatical patterns can also be particularly helpful for children who have a more logical–deductive kind of intelligence and who may feel more engaged when treating language as a kind of logical 'puzzle', and also more secure knowing that there are 'rules' that they can apply.

Awareness-raising or noticing activities with children need to provide concrete means of drawing their attention to abstract concepts in ways which involve active participation and cognitive engagement. These can take a variety of forms and include, for example:

- using analogy or metaphor (see 3.16)
- relating parts of speech to colours (see 3.17)
- manipulating word cards (see 3.17, 3.18)
- using mime, movement and gesture (see 3.19 and 3.28)
- using logical deduction (see 3.20, 3.21, 3.23, 3.26)
- classifying skills (see 3.22).

It is important to stress, however, that noticing activities by themselves do not by any means ensure that children can automatically apply whatever they notice to their own language performance. For this reason, therefore, noticing activities need to be accompanied by lots of practice over time.

The kinds of practice activities that children most benefit from include both controlled opportunities to manipulate grammatical forms in order to express specific meanings within supported frameworks (see 3.13, 3.15, 3.21, 3.27; see also Sections 1 and 6), and more open-ended opportunities to experiment, negotiate meaning and express and communicate what they want to say (see 3.4, 3.11, 3.24; see also Sections 1, 4 and 5). As with learning vocabulary, regular recycling of grammatical patterns and forms is also essential.

Metalanguage

In addition to developing language awareness and providing for frequent, varied opportunities for contextualized, meaningful practice, with older children it may also be helpful to gradually introduce them to grammatical metalanguage. This is usually best done as it arises naturally following meaning-based work on stories or other texts, and is especially relevant if children are also learning metalinguistic terms in their first language. In this case, it may be appropriate, for example, to organize a colour-coded classroom display of grammatical categories, such as nouns, adjectives, verbs, and regularly update this with words the children are learning in each category (as suggested in 3.17), or do other activities (see 3.30) in order to familiarize them with grammatical terms and concepts in a creative and enjoyable way.

The potential value of beginning to learn metalanguage to describe and analyse language towards the end of primary school does not replace the importance of practice and needs to be assessed in each context. If it is considered worthwhile, however, it can contribute significantly to children's developing metacognitive awareness and also play an important role in helping to prepare children for the transition to secondary school where the approach to learning is likely to be more explicitly grammar-based.

Teaching and learning in primary school is predominantly concerned with developing basic skills and confidence in using English. Raising children's language awareness and explicitly focusing their attention on aspects of the language system in appropriate age-related ways can help to complement and enhance this process. It can also lay solid foundations for the years of study still to come. As with other areas, it is also important to encourage children to develop independent learning strategies to support their learning of grammar (see Section 10, Learning to learn).

Reflection time

As you use the vocabulary and grammar activities in this section with your classes, you may like to think about the following questions and use your responses to evaluate how things went and plan possible improvements for next time:

1 **Concept / meaning:** Was the concept and/or meaning of the language in the activity clear to the children? How was this achieved?

2 **Memory / recall:** Were the children able to memorize and recall the vocabulary and/or language pattern(s) practised during the activity? What helped them to do this?

3 **Practice:** What kind of practice did the activity provide? How was this complemented and/or extended by other activities during the lesson and in subsequent lessons?

4 **Recycling:** In what way(s) did the activity recycle language and extend children's learning? How could the language be usefully recycled again?

5 **Noticing / awareness raising:** What impact did noticing an aspect of language have on children's interest, motivation and ability to use language?

6 **Thinking skills:** What kinds of thinking skills did children need to use during the activity? How did this influence their response?

3.1 Learn with a puppet

Level A1.1   **Age** 4–6   **Organization** whole class

Aims To recognize, practise and memorize vocabulary and/or short chunks of language by responding to a puppet; to create an affective atmosphere which encourages active participation.

Language focus any lexical set and/or short chunk of language

Materials *Essential:* a puppet, real objects or flashcards / *Optional:* a bag for objects or flashcards (see 3.1d), music (see 3.1f)

Procedure

Use any one or a combination of the following procedures:

3.1a Follow the puppet's instructions

1 Lay out the flashcards or objects on the floor or stick them on the board.

2 Use the puppet to say, eg *Touch the banana … Maria and Daniel.*

3 Children listen and do what the puppet says.

3.1b Repeat what the puppet says

1 Use the puppet to say vocabulary or short sentences which the children are familiar with, varying the pitch, volume and pace, eg *The giraffe is tall. / The lion is fierce.*

2 Children listen and repeat what the puppet says in the same way.

3.1c Correct the puppet

1 Ask questions and get the puppet to give the wrong answers or to say sentences with the wrong information, eg *The ball is blue.*

2 Children listen and correct the puppet in chorus, eg *No, …!* (naming the puppet) *Green!*

3.1d Guess what the puppet's thinking about

1 Put 3–6 flashcards on the floor or board. Use mime to convey that the puppet is thinking about one of them. Encourage children to guess which one.

2 Make the puppet shake its head and say *No* and then nod and say, eg *Yes, brilliant!* when a child guesses correctly.

3.1e Guess what's in the puppet's bag

1 Put several different objects or flashcards in a bag. Make the puppet hold up the bag. Children take turns to guess what's in the bag, eg *Elephant!*

2 The puppet nods or shakes its head and says *Yes* or *No.* Whenever the puppet says *Yes*, take the relevant toy or flashcard out of the bag. Children clap and say *Yes! Elephant! Hurray!*

3.1f Pass the puppet

1 Children sit in a circle.

2 Play music and children pass the puppet round the circle.

3 Whenever you pause the music, the child who has the puppet tells the puppet something about themselves using language you want them to practise, eg *I like biscuits.*

Comments and suggestions

- The use of a class puppet helps to create a positive affective climate which encourages participation in English and makes very young children feel secure. A familiar puppet provides a friendly, funny, helpful presence which the children can relate to in a direct and spontaneous way. The puppet brings fantasy, magic and humour into the classroom and helps to make learning natural and part of real events.

- You may have a puppet as part of the children's course book. If not, any soft toy, felt puppet, or puppet you make yourself, eg from an old sock or kitchen glove, can serve the purpose just as well.

- In addition to procedures such as the above, a class puppet is useful to mark the beginning and ends of lessons with greetings and goodbyes, to give feedback and praise, and to manage the class in a positive way, eg *Quiet now everyone! … (puppet's name) is asleep!*

3.2 Flashcard vocabulary activities

Level A1.1, A1.2, A2.1, A2.2   **Age** 6–10   **Organization** whole class

Aims To recognize, practise and memorize vocabulary through associating words, meanings and pictures.

Language focus any lexical set or combination of lexical sets

Materials *Essential:* flashcards for one or more lexical sets / *Optional:* word cards to match the flashcards

Procedure

Use any one or more of the following procedures:

3.2a Flashcard instructions

1 Stick a set of flashcards on the walls around the classroom.
2 Divide the class into groups.
3 Give each group instructions in turn, eg *Group 1 – walk to the elephant. Group 2 – jump to the lion.*

3.2b Flashcard groups

1 Divide the class into groups. Assign each group a flashcard, eg 'apple' – this is their name.
2 Give instructions, eg *Apples, touch your nose! Carrots, put your hands on your head!* Children listen and follow the instructions for their group.

3.2c Missing flashcard

1 Stick a set of flashcards on the board. Children say the words.
2 Ask the children to close their eyes. Remove one of the flashcards. Children open their eyes and name the missing flashcard.

3.2d Magic eyes

1 Stick a set of flashcards in a row on the board. Children say or repeat the words.
2 Remove the flashcards one by one. Point to where they were and children repeat the names as if they were still there.

3.2e Lip reading

Stick a set of flashcards on the board. Choose one flashcard and mouth the word silently. Children read your lips and say the word.

3.2f Repeat if it's true

Stick a set of flashcards on the board. Point to one of the flashcards and say the word. If you have said the correct word, children repeat it. If not, they fold their arms and stay silent. This activity can be made more challenging if you say sentences, eg *It's a blue car.*

3.2g Flashcard chain

1 Stand or sit in a circle with the children.

2 Pass a flashcard to the child on your left and ask, eg *Do you like …?* or *What's this?*

3 The child answers, then asks the question and passes the flashcard to the next child, and so on round the circle.

4 Introduce other flashcards in the same way until all the flashcards in the set have passed round the circle.

Comments and suggestions

• Short activities using flashcards familiarize children with vocabulary which has been previously introduced. They aid memorization through the association of visual images and words, and help pronunciation by giving children frequent opportunities to listen to and say new words.

• Children can also match word cards to the flashcards on the board if it is appropriate to familiarize them with the written forms of new words as part of the procedure.

3.3 Kim's game

Level A1.1, A1.2, A2.1, A2.2   **Age** 8–12   **Organization** groups

Aims To observe, memorize and recall vocabulary in a picture or word list; to arrange the words in order of the alphabet or classify them; to work collaboratively in groups.

Language focus *In the example:* animals
Alternatives: any lexical set, eg food

Materials *Essential:* real objects, flashcards, a poster or word list for children to memorize, small pieces of paper / *Optional:* A4 envelopes

Procedure

1 Divide the class into groups.

2 Give out small pieces of paper to each group (enough to write each word in the activity on a separate piece of paper) or children prepare these.

3 Give the children one minute to look in silence and memorize a set of real objects, flashcards, details in a poster or a word list. For example, a list of animals could be: *horse, snake, penguin, whale, butterfly, kangaroo, gorilla, dolphin, parrot, koala, chimpanzee, crocodile, polar bear, zebra.*

4 After a minute, remove the word list. Children work in their groups and write the words they can remember on the pieces of paper.

5 When they are ready, *either* children arrange the words in alphabetical order on their desks *or* you can write the sentences below on the board and children classify the animals (two for each sentence):
 1 They are mammals and live in the sea.
 2 They can fly.
 3 They eat grass.
 4 They live in Australia.
 5 They like eating fish.
 6 They are reptiles.
 7 They are like people.

6 At the end, find out how many words the children remembered and check the answers to the activity they have done. (Alphabetical order: butterfly, chimpanzee, crocodile, dolphin, gorilla, horse, kangaroo, koala, parrot, penguin, polar bear, snake, whale, zebra. Classifying: 1 whale, dolphin 2 butterfly, parrot 3 horse, zebra 4 kangaroo, koala 5 penguin, polar bear 6 snake, crocodile 7 gorilla, chimpanzee)

Comments and suggestions

- The name 'Kim's game' is from the novel, *Kim*, by Rudyard Kipling, in which Kim and others are trained to memorize objects. In the traditional version, there are twenty small objects on a tray which, after one minute, is covered with a cloth and participants recall as many as they can.

- In this version, in addition to memorizing the vocabulary, children do a further activity, such as arranging the words in alphabetical order or classifying them. In the case of the former, this encourages children to think about spelling and develop reference skills through arranging the words in alphabetical order. In the case of the latter, children read sentences which encourage them to think about meaning and relate the vocabulary to their knowledge of the world in a classifying activity.

- If you have A4 envelopes, instead of writing the sentences on the board, you can write one sentence on each envelope and stick them on different walls around the classroom. Children then classify the words by putting the pieces of paper into the correct envelopes. If you do this, it helps to ask each group to write the words in a different colour in order to be able to check answers easily at the end of the activity.

- An alternative example of this version of Kim's game is with food vocabulary, eg *cheese, tomato, sausage, bread, chicken, milk, pasta, rice, carrot, banana, tuna fish, rice.* After recalling the words, children classify them into four food groups: meat and fish, fruit and vegetables, cereals, and dairy products.

- If children memorize a written list of words, it may be appropriate to focus on spelling when checking the answers. If children memorize the vocabulary from pictures, however, you may decide it is more important that they recall the words rather than focus on spelling accuracy.

3.4 Odd one out

Level All   **Age** 6–12   **Organization** whole class, pairs

Aims To think about the meanings and properties of words; to identify a vocabulary item in a sequence that is different; to say why it is different.

Language focus any familiar vocabulary; *be, have got,* present simple, *(because)*

Materials *Essential:* none / *Optional:* flashcards or pictures

Procedure

1 Write a sequence of four words on the board, eg *apple, carrot, banana, strawberry.*

2 Ask the children to identify the odd one out and say why, eg *Carrot – (because) it's a vegetable.*

3 With older children, ask them to look again and think of other possible answers, eg *Banana – (because) it grows in hot countries / (because) it's the only one without double letters. Apple – (because) it starts with a vowel.* Point out that there isn't only one correct answer.

4 Divide the class into pairs.

5 Write several different word sequences on the board, eg *butterfly, beetle, spider, grasshopper / turtle, mouse, rabbit, bat.*

6 Ask the children to decide with their partner which is the odd word out in each sequence and why.

7 At the end, ask the pairs to report back and count up all the possible answers and reasons for the odd one out in each sequence.

Comments and suggestions

- This activity encourages children to think about the meaning of words and relate this to their knowledge of the world. You may be surprised by how many possible answers and reasons children come up with, for example, for the animal sequence above, *Mouse – (because) it's part of a computer.*

- With younger children, it is likely to be more appropriate to do the activity with one word in each sequence that is obviously different, eg *hat, coat, ball, T-shirt* and children identify the word.
- The activity can also be used with older children as a grammar-awareness activity, eg *red, small, hat, old* where 'hat' is the odd one out because it is a noun and all the others are adjectives.

.5 Word search

Level All   **Age** 8–12   **Organization** individual

Aims To prepare and do a word search puzzle; to improve recognition and spelling of familiar vocabulary.

Language focus any familiar vocabulary

Materials *Essential:* none / *Optional:* photocopies of a grid of squares (10 x 10) (one for each child)

Procedure

1 Explain that the children are going to make a word search puzzle for someone else in the class to do.
2 *Either* give out photocopies of the grids *or* ask the children to use a ruler to draw a grid of 10 x 10 squares (1cm for each square) in their notebooks.
3 *Either* specify the number of words and lexical set that children should 'hide' in the grid, eg eight clothes words *or* leave this more open, eg *Hide ten words we've learnt this term!*
4 Explain and demonstrate that children can hide the words horizontally, vertically or diagonally and that some letters may form part of more than one word.
5 If they are unsure of spelling, ask them to check this, eg by looking in their course books, before they begin. Set a time limit for preparing the word search, eg 5–10 minutes.
6 When the children are ready, collect in the grids and redistribute them. Children do each others' puzzles by circling or colouring the squares of the words they find. Again, you may like to set a time limit for this, eg five minutes.
7 At the end, children return the grids to their owners, who check whether all the words in their puzzle have been found.

Comments and suggestions

- Children generally want to prepare word searches for their peers which are as challenging as possible! This provides a strong motivation and purpose for reviewing vocabulary they have learnt.
- A shorter, simpler alternative to a word search is a 'word snake'. Children 'hide' between 4–6 words in the snake and then take turns to find each others' words in the same way. Word snakes are suitable for younger children. If possible it is best to give them a copy of the snake, divided into sections for each letter, for them to complete.

- As neither word searches nor word snakes focus on meaning or use of vocabulary, you need to ensure that you combine them or follow up with other activities that do. For example, children can draw pictures and match these to the words in the puzzles or play a guessing game to discover the hidden words.

3.6 Key word crossword

Level All   **Age** 8–12   **Organization** pairs

Aims To prepare and do a simple crossword; to review spelling of familiar vocabulary; to think in a logical-deductive way.

Language focus *In the example:* jobs, present simple, *(It must be …)*
Alternatives: any familiar vocabulary, eg food

Materials *Essential:* none / *Optional:* A4 sheets of paper (one for each pair)

Procedure

1 Divide the class into pairs.

2 Explain that they are going to design and write a crossword for another pair to do. Either specify the type of crossword, eg job crossword, food crossword, or leave it open for the children to use any vocabulary they know.

3 Explain that the children should choose a key word for their crossword and write this vertically. They should then make the crossword by writing other words horizontally, numbering the squares and writing clues. Demonstrate what you mean by building up part of a crossword with the class on the board.

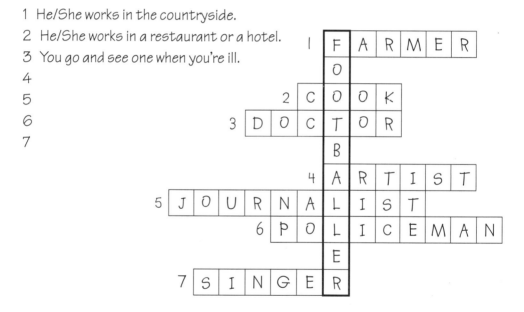

1 He/She works in the countryside.
2 He/She works in a restaurant or a hotel.
3 You go and see one when you're ill.
4
5
6
7

4 Children prepare and write clues for a crossword with their partner. You may like to ask them to do this in draft form in their notebooks first and then give out A4 paper for the final version. Set a time limit for this, eg 10–15 minutes.

5 When they are ready, children exchange and do each others' crosswords to find the key word.

6 At the end, they return the crosswords to the original owners, who check the answers.

Comments and suggestions

• The format of this crossword, with one vertical key word, makes it practical and feasible for children to prepare themselves.

• Through preparing and reading clues, children are encouraged to think about the meaning of words and to deduce the answers in a logical way. If appropriate, you can set the activity up so that children practise using *It must be …* as they do each others' puzzles.

3.7 Sort into sets

Level All   **Age** 4–12   **Organization** pairs

Aims To sort and classify vocabulary into sets; to aid memory and reinforce connections between words.

Language focus *In the example:* rooms and furniture, present simple
Alternatives: any familiar vocabulary

Materials *Essential:* sets of small picture or word cards (one for each pair)

Procedure

1 Divide the class into pairs.

2 Give out a set of cards to each pair, eg a set of cards for rooms and furniture might include:
   bed, shower, cooker, TV, sofa, fridge, toilet, chest of drawers, wardrobe, armchair, dishwasher, bath.
   Alternatively children can cut out and make the cards before the activity.

3 Ask the children to sort the cards according to the rooms at home where you usually find them (bedroom, kitchen, bathroom, living room).

4 At the end, children compare their answers and report back, either by naming the items in each room or saying, eg *The bed goes in the bedroom.*

5 If you like, you can then ask them to think of one more item that goes in each room, eg *a lamp in the bedroom, a table in the kitchen, a rug in the living room, a basin in the bathroom.*

Comments and suggestions

• Very young children can sort pictures into sets of different colours, eg red, blue, yellow and green things, or sets of animals, eg wild animals and farm animals. The physical manipulation of the cards helps to develop visual observation and classifying skills in a concrete, hands-on way.

• With older children, you can make the task more challenging and creative by asking them to categorize cards in any way they like. For example, for rooms and furniture, children might choose to classify the items according to whether or not they use electricity, or whether or not they are essential in a home.

• With older children, this activity can also be used for familiarizing children with grammatical categories, eg nouns, adjectives, verbs, using language taken from a familiar text.

3.8 Venn diagrams

Level All   **Age** 8–12   **Organization** whole class, individual/pairs

Aims To classify known vocabulary in a lexical set using a graphic organizer; to compare and report back on the way the items have been classified.

Language focus *In the example:* clothes, present simple
Alternatives: any familiar vocabulary, eg animals, food, furniture

Materials *Essential:* none / *Optional:* photocopies of a Venn diagram (one for each child)

Procedure

1 Ask the children to tell you all the words they know in a familiar lexical set, eg clothes.

2 Write the words on the board or ask individual children to take turns to do this.

3 Draw a Venn diagram on the board as on page 96. Label the circles 'summer' and 'winter'.

4 Ask the children to copy this or give out the photocopies of a Venn diagram.

5 Either divide the class into pairs or children can do the activity individually.

6 Children should write the names of clothes they wear in summer in the circle on the left

and clothes they wear in winter in the circle on the right. In the space where the two circles overlap, children should write the names of clothes they wear in both summer and winter.

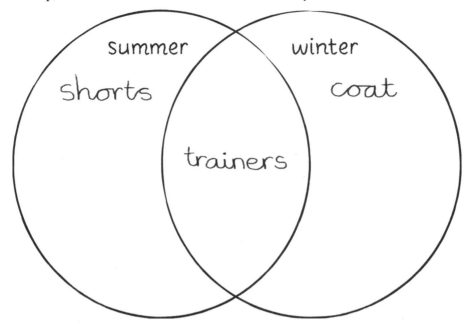

7   If the children are not familiar with Venn diagrams, model the thinking process before they begin, to enable them to do the task successfully, eg *I wear shorts when it's hot. It's hot in summer. So shorts go here. I wear a coat when it's cold. It's cold in winter. So coat goes here. I wear trainers when it's hot and when it's cold. In summer and in winter. So trainers go here.*

8   At the end, ask them to report back and compare the way they have classified the vocabulary.

9   Children can also use dictionaries to find three more words to add to the Venn diagram.

Comments and suggestions

- Be ready for children to classify the vocabulary in different, personalized ways and encourage them to justify their answers, eg *I wear shorts in summer and in winter. In winter I wear shorts for gym.*

- With younger children, it may be appropriate to ask them to draw (or copy) pictures of the vocabulary as well as write the words. This will also turn the Venn diagram into a useful record of vocabulary learnt.

- Venn diagrams provide opportunities for children to think about vocabulary in a meaningful way. Other examples of suitable lexical sets for children to classify include animals (eg whether they eat meat/fish, fruit/vegetables or both), food (eg whether it contains salt, sugar or both), furniture (eg whether it's in the living room, the bedroom or both).

3.9 Vocabulary swap

Level All   **Age** 8–12   **Organization** groups, whole class

Aims To recall and practise saying four items of vocabulary from different lexical sets in a rhythmic way; to 'teach' the items to friends.

Language focus *In the example:* jobs, transport, school subjects, food
Alternatives: any vocabulary items from familiar lexical sets

Materials *Essential:* vocabulary swap cards (one for each child – see step 1; for a class of 24, make six each of the following cards)

Jobs

teacher   artist

fire fighter   vet

Transport

bus   motorbike

helicopter   plane

School subjects

maths   history

music   science

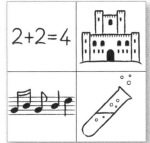

Food

biscuit   sandwich

crisps   cake

Procedure

1 Divide the class into four groups. Give all the children in each group the same vocabulary card from one of the sets.

2 Ask the children if they can recall the vocabulary on their card and get them to say the words as in a rhythmic chant. Spend a little time with each group separately to practise this.

3 When all the groups are ready, explain that they should stand up and take turns to 'teach' their words to someone who has a different card by saying the words rhythmically and getting the other person to repeat them.

4 As soon as the children have 'learnt' each other's words, they swap cards. They then find someone else with a different card and repeat the procedure.

5 The activity finishes when the children have swapped their cards three times and practised saying all the words.

6 At the end, you may like to collect in the cards and ask the children to recall all the vocabulary.

Comments and suggestions

• This activity is a useful way of recalling and memorizing vocabulary from different lexical sets. Through 'teaching' and 'learning' the words in a rhythmic way in order to swap the cards, repetition practice is made purposeful, memorable and enjoyable.

• If you prefer, children can remain seated in groups during the activity. In this case, each member of the group should have a different card.

3.10 Nonsense words

Level A2.1, A2.2 , B1.1, B1.2   **Age** 10–12   **Organization** whole class, pairs

Aims To infer the meaning of words from the context; to develop awareness of strategies to use when deducing the meaning of unfamiliar words.

Language focus any language or vocabulary

Materials *Essential:* none / *Optional:* photocopies of sentences containing nonsense words (one for each child)

Procedure

1 Write a sentence on the board including familiar language and a nonsense word, eg *The glooper has got short legs and a long tail.*

2 Ask the children what they think a *glooper* is. They will probably say an animal, possibly a bird. Ask how they know, and listen to their response, eg *It's got a tail.* Point out that looking at other words in the same sentence (or paragraph) is a good strategy to use when working out the meaning of unfamiliar words. Elicit or point out that looking at the form of words can help too, for example we know that a *glooper* is a thing (or a noun) because of the word *the* in front of it and also because of *-er* at the end (as in *singer* or *robber*).

3 Divide the class into pairs.

4 *Either* write 6–8 sentences with nonsense words on the board *or* give a photocopy to each pair.

5 Ask the children to work out the meaning of all the nonsense words. If children are familiar with metalanguage, you can also ask them to identify the parts of speech of each nonsense word. Some examples of the kinds of sentences you can use are: *I was so pillatch that I went to sleep.* (*tired* or *exhausted*, adjective) / *She didn't hear the alarm clock and glicked very late.* (*got up* or *arrived* – need to read more to confirm – past simple verb) / *I didn't want to go to school so I walked very zibly.* (*slowly* or *reluctantly*, adverb) / *She was very rich but not very jaffrey.* (*clever* or *happy* or *beautiful* – need to read more to find out – adjective).

6 As a follow-up, encourage children to apply strategies for guessing the meanings of words in context when you next use a shared reading text in class.

Comments and suggestions

- Children generally enjoy the puzzle element in deducing the meaning of nonsense words from the context. The activity also raises children's awareness that just because they haven't come across a word before, it doesn't automatically mean that they can't understand it. This is important for boosting confidence and self-esteem. It is also useful training for children's own independent reading and will help them if they are required to do exams.

3.11 Definitions

Level A2.2, B1.1, B1.2   **Age** 10–12   **Organization** whole class, groups

Aims To define what you mean without saying the word; to develop communication strategies for conveying the meaning of vocabulary you don't know.

Language focus present simple, relative pronouns, *It's a person (who) / place (where) / animal/ thing (which) …*, any familiar vocabulary

Materials *Essential:* word cards (1–3 for each child). The word cards should be a mixture of people, places, animals and things that are familiar to the children and possible for them to define (see below for examples).

Procedure

1 Explain that the purpose of the activity is to define a person, place, animal or thing without saying the word.

2 Elicit and establish that children can say, eg *It's a person who … / It's a place where … It's an animal which … / It's a thing which (you use to) …*

3 Do several examples with the whole class and children guess the word, eg *It's a person who helps sick animals.* (vet) *It's a place where people stay on holiday.* (hotel) *It's a bird with big eyes which hunts at night.* (owl) *It's a thing which you use to cut paper.* (scissors)

4 Give 1–3 word cards to each child. Ask them to secretly prepare a definition for each one without using the word.

5 When they are ready, divide the class into groups. Children take turns to say their definitions and guess the words.

Comments and suggestions

- Draw the children's attention to the fact that it is very useful to be able to define what you mean if you don't know the word for something. Using mime or gesture can also help to convey what you mean.
- Through learning to use general purpose words such as *thing, place, person,* children develop strategies which help them become more effective communicators without needing necessarily to resort to L1.

3.12 Categories

Level All   **Age** 8–12   **Organization** groups, whole class

Aims To recall vocabulary from different lexical sets at speed; to collaborate in groups.

Language focus any familiar lexical sets

Materials *Essential:* none / *Optional:* stopwatch or timer

Procedure

1 Divide the class into groups.

2 Say the name of a lexical set, eg *food.* Use a stopwatch or timer if you have one. Give the children three minutes to work with their group and write a list of as many food words as they can think of.

3 After three minutes, ask each group to say one of their words in turn while the rest of the class listens. If another group has the same word, then everyone crosses it off their list.

4 When the children have finished reading their lists, count up the number of words the class has thought of collectively in that category and write this and the words which only one group had, if there are any, on the board.

5 Repeat the procedure with several other categories and lexical sets, eg clothes, animals, sports. At the end, use the scores on the board to identify the lexical set in which the class knows most words and to identify the words that fewest people know.

6 Follow with an activity such as Magic eyes (3.2d) to help more children remember these words too.

Comments and suggestions

- This activity gives children practice in retrieving words from memory at speed. Through working in groups, children are encouraged to listen to and value each other as a learning resource.
- For a more challenging version of the activity, draw and label four columns on the board, eg food, clothes, animals, sports. Say a letter of the alphabet. Children have three minutes to think of as many words as possible in each category beginning with the letter you say. They then report back in the same way. Repeat several times with different letters. Choose letters which begin several words the children are likely to know in each category, and avoid letters which are difficult, eg K, Y, J, Z.

3.13 Secret letter

Level A1.2, A2.1, A2.2, B1.1, B1.2   **Age** 9–12   **Organization** whole class, groups

Aims To practise asking and answering questions using a particular language pattern; to think about the spelling of familiar vocabulary in order to deduce a secret letter.

Language focus *In the example: like* – questions and short answers, any familiar vocabulary
Alternatives: have got, present simple statements, *but*

Materials *Essential:* none

Procedure

1 Explain that you are going to secretly choose a letter of the alphabet and children should ask you questions to find out what it is, eg if you choose 'a': P1: *Do you like cake?* T: *Yes, I do.* P2: *Do you like biscuits?* T: *No, I don't.* P3: *Do you like apples?* T: *Yes, I do.* P4: *Do you like coffee?* T: *No, I don't.* (You only like the things that have the letter 'a'.)

2 The child who finds out the secret letter comes to the front of the class and has the next turn.

3 Repeat the procedure with the whole class several times.

4 Divide the class into groups.

5 Children take turns to choose a secret letter and repeat the activity in their groups.

Comments and suggestions

- This activity provides repetition practice of a single language pattern which is made purposeful through trying to deduce the secret letter. It also encourages children to think about the spelling of words they know.

- The activity can be used to practise a range of different structures and vocabulary, eg (again with the letter 'a') P: *Have you got a ball?* T: *Yes, I have.* P: *Have you got a book?* T: *No, I haven't* or P: *Are you tired?* T: *No, I'm not.* P: *Are you angry?* T: *Yes, I am.* Alternatively, instead of asking and answering questions, children can make statements, eg *I like ham but I don't like chicken.*

- With older children, instead of explaining that there is a secret letter, you may like to turn the activity into a lateral thinking puzzle in which children work out the criteria you are using for the things you like and don't like, eg *I like apples but I don't like pears. I love swimming and I love running but I hate walking.* If you tell the children a few statements about yourself as above each lesson, the activity may well continue over a week or more, with children suggesting a range of imaginative theories to explain what you like and don't like. Once individual children realize the criteria (in this case, you only like things that are spelt with double letters), tell them to keep it a secret and to contribute saying things with you to the rest of the class, eg *I like green but I don't like red.* Once about half the class has guessed, give lots of clues in order to share the 'secret' with everyone and bring the activity to a close.

3.14 Word tennis

Level All   **Age** 6–12   **Organization** pairs

Aims To recall words in a lexical set (or according to other criteria); to take turns and collaborate with a partner.

Language focus any familiar lexical set, eg local places
Alternatives: the alphabet, days of the week, months of the year, adjectives (opposites), infinitive and past tense verb forms

Materials *Essential:* none

Procedure

1 Divide the class into pairs.

2 Ask the children to turn their chairs so that they are facing their partner.

3 Explain and demonstrate that the children are going to play a game of word tennis. The child who starts pretends to serve the ball and says a word in a lexical set that you specify, eg local places. Their partner then pretends to hit the ball back and says another word, and so on, eg *cinema / park / library / supermarket / hospital / zoo / bank*, until the children can't think of any more words.

4 Tell the pairs to keep a score of how many words they include in their 'rally' and ask them to report back at the end.

Comments and suggestions

- This is a short activity which is useful for revising vocabulary that has been previously introduced, eg as a warmer at the start of lessons. By pretending to play tennis, children are encouraged to take turns with their partner and keep up a rhythm in recalling and saying vocabulary they know.

- For safety reasons, you need to ensure that children do not pretend to hit the ball in a way that might accidentally hurt others. If you are concerned about this, word 'table tennis' with smaller racquet strokes may be more appropriate.

- Word tennis can be used for, eg recalling the alphabet, days of the week or months of the year. With older, higher level children it can also be used for opposites, eg *big – small, fast – slow* or for remembering the past forms of irregular verbs, eg *go – went, see – saw.*

3.15 Sentence chains

Level All   **Age** 8–12   **Organization** groups

Aims To listen, recall and repeat what other people say; to take turns and collaborate in groups.

Language focus *In the example: want to be*, jobs and professions
Alternatives: any familiar language structure or lexical set, eg present simple, food; past simple, everyday activities; *I'd like …*, toys

Materials *Essential:* none

Procedure

1 Divide the class into groups of 4–6.

2 Explain and demonstrate that one child should say a sentence about what they want to be or do when they grow up, eg *I want to be a doctor.* The next child should repeat the sentence and then add one of their own, eg *Jane* (or *She*) *wants to be a doctor and I want to be a journalist,* and so on round the group.

3 If a child can't remember a sentence, they say *Help!* and other members of the group remind them of the sentence. Ask the children to try and make their 'chains' as long as they can.

4 At the end, ask the groups to report back and/or get one or two groups to demonstrate their chains to the rest of the class, who listen to find out how many jobs that they want to do are the same.

Comments and suggestions

- This activity provides simple, personalized practice of a language pattern and familiar vocabulary. It also develops memory and encourages children to listen to what each other says.

- In the traditional version of this activity, if children can't remember a sentence, they are out. By introducing the technique of saying *Help!*, children are encouraged to work collaboratively and participate throughout.

- This activity can be used to practise any relevant structure and vocabulary, for example, food you like: *I like bananas. / She likes bananas and I like hamburgers;* what you did at the weekend: *I went to the cinema. / He went to the cinema and I went to the park;* or what you'd like for your birthday: *I'd like a bicycle. / She'd like a bicycle and I'd like a football.*
- Instead of 'sentence chains' children can also make word chains following the same procedure. In this case, the next word in the chain starts with the same letter (or with younger children, it can be the same sound) as the last sound in the previous word, eg *elephant – tarantula – armadillo – owl – lion ... Help!*

3.16 Horse and cart

Level A1.1, A1.2, A2.1, A2.2   **Age** 9–12   **Organization** whole class

Aims To notice how word order changes in affirmative sentences, negative sentences and questions.

Language focus *In the example:* present continuous, *has got*
Alternatives: present simple, past simple

Materials *Essential:* none / *Optional:* word and picture cards
(one set, large enough for the class to see)

Sally   is   riding   a   bicycle.

Procedure

1 Write a relevant sentence from language children have been practising on the board, or use word cards, eg *Sally is riding a bicycle.* Underline 'is' or stick the picture card of the horse above this word.

2 Explain that the horse is the auxiliary verb 'is'. Ask the children where the horse needs to go to make a question. Elicit or explain that in order to make a question, you need to ride the horse to the start of the sentence (and add a question mark). Show this by moving the word and picture cards or rubbing out and rewriting the words: *Is Sally riding a bicycle?*

3 Elicit or explain that to answer affirmatively, you ride the horse back: *Yes, she is (riding a bicycle).* To answer negatively, or make a negative statement, you need to ride the horse back and collect the cart ('not'): *No, Sally is not riding a bicycle. / Sally is not riding a bicycle.* You can then show how the horse and cart are linked by making the contracted form: *Sally isn't riding a bicycle.*

4 If appropriate, repeat with other sentences, eg *David has got a sister. / Mary can sing.* and ask individual children to move the horse and cart on the board to make questions and negative statements in the same way.

Comments and suggestions

- This activity is a visual, hands-on way of encouraging children to notice patterns in word order and the image of the horse and cart helps to make this memorable. Remember though that children will need lots of practice to enable them to incorporate these patterns naturally or automatically into their own speech.
- If the image of a horse and cart is too rural for your teaching context, then you can use the image of a car and trailer instead.

3.17 Colour-coded grammar cards

Level A1.2, A2.1, A2.2   **Age** 9–12   **Organization** whole class

Aims To associate parts of speech with colours; to notice and generate language patterns; to ask for personal information; (to introduce and/or familiarize children with useful metalanguage).

Language focus *In the example:* Wh- questions, present simple, prepositions of time, personal information, daily routines
Alternatives: any familiar language pattern

Materials *Essential:* colour-coded grammar cards (one set, large enough for the class to see). For the example activity, you need 25 colour-coded cards (red for *Wh*-questions, orange for auxiliaries, yellow for subject pronouns, green for verbs (include 'get up' on one card), blue for prepositions, purple for nouns, black for question marks) to make the following questions:

Where do you live?
When does she get up?
What does he have for breakfast?
How do they go to school?

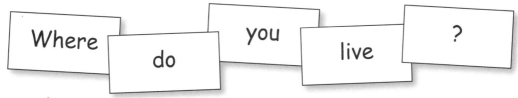

Procedure

1 Stick the colour-coded grammar cards in jumbled order on the board.

2 Ask a pair of children to come and choose any cards they like and arrange them to make a question, eg *When do you have breakfast? / Where do you go to school?*

3 Repeat the procedure with several different pairs. Ask the children what they notice about the order of colours in the questions, ie that it's always red, orange, yellow, green at the start, and then sometimes blue and purple as well. If appropriate, introduce or use metalanguage when talking about the colours and parts of speech.

4 Ask the children to help you make four questions using all the cards on the board. Stick the words in columns according to the colours as you do this. Point out that the colours in the questions follow the order of colours in a rainbow. Use this to help the children remember the order, eg orange always comes before green in a rainbow.

5 Either elicit other questions that children can make following the same pattern or divide the class into pairs and set a time limit, eg five minutes, for them to do this.

6 At the end, ask the children to report back. Examples of questions following a similar pattern are: *Where do you have lunch? When does she have gym? What do they do after school?*

Comments and suggestions

- You can use an activity like this *either* as a follow-up to a speaking activity in which children use the same language pattern *or* as revision and a reminder before leading into a speaking activity. In either case, it is important to remember that although awareness of how to form *Wh*- questions may help children learn, it does not replace the need for meaningful, contextualized practice for children to be able to use them in their own speech.

- Colour-coded grammar cards can be used to help children notice a variety of different language patterns and aspects of grammar, eg word order of adjectives and nouns, pronoun replacement, the use of conjunctions to link sentences and add or contrast ideas. It is usually best to only focus on one structure or language pattern at any one time.

- As a follow-up to work on stories or other texts, you can use the same colour-code system to get children to notice and underline or circle words in the grammatical category you wish to focus on.
- You may also like to keep a colour-coded display of parts of speech, using the same colours as the grammar cards, on the classroom noticeboard. The different parts of speech can be displayed inside stars, circles, fish, flowers, monsters, etc and referred to during lessons as appropriate.

3.18 Sentence scramble

Level All   **Age** 10–12 (6–8)   **Organization** pairs

Aims To order words to make sentences by manipulating word cards; to develop awareness of word order in sentences.

Language focus *In the example:* conditional sentences with *if*, everyday activities
Alternatives: any familiar language pattern or structure

Materials *Essential:* sets of word and punctuation cards to make sentences in separate numbered envelopes (one for each pair), eg *If it rains at break time, we'll stay in the classroom. / If Miss Anna is ill, we won't have English. / If we play well, we'll win the football match. / If we don't have homework, I'll watch TV.*

Procedure

1 Recycle the language structure which is the focus of the activity by asking, eg *What'll happen if it rains at break time? / What'll you do if you don't have homework?* and elicit qualifying statements from the children using *if*, eg *If it rains at break time, we'll play on the computers.*

2 Ask the children to write a list of numbers, eg 1–8 (depending on how many sets of word cards you have prepared) in their notebooks.

3 Divide the class into pairs.

4 Give each pair a numbered envelope containing word cards. Children work with their partner and arrange the cards from the envelope on their desk to make a sentence. They write the sentence next to the corresponding number in their notebooks.

5 They then exchange envelopes with another pair, and so on, until they have completed sentences next to each number in their notebooks.

6 At the end, check the answers and draw the children's attention to the forms of the verbs and the position of the comma in each sentence.

Comments and suggestions

- This activity provides for physical, hands-on experimentation with word order in sentences and helps to familiarize children with particular language patterns in an enjoyable way.
- At the end of the activity, children have a permanent record of correctly written sentences in their notebooks which can be used as a model or guide in subsequent work.

- This activity is also suitable to use with younger children and lower levels to order short, simple sentences relating to language they have practised or to a story, eg *The giraffe is tall. The lion is fierce.* If you are using a puppet, you can use this to mix up the words (silly puppet!) and children order them.

3.19 Physical line-up

Level A1.1, A1.2   **Age** 8–10   **Organization** groups, whole class

Aims To stand in a line to show word order in sentences; to develop awareness of word order and contracted forms; to collaborate in groups.

Language focus any familiar language which includes verbs with contracted forms, eg *there is/are, have got, be,* present continuous, present simple

Materials *Essential:* sets of word cards (large enough for the class to see) to make short sentences (one for each group), eg *We are very hungry. He has got a ball. There is a monkey. It is sunny and hot. They are running home. He does not like bananas.*

Procedure

1 Divide the class into groups of four. Give a set of word cards to each group.

2 Ask the children to take one card each (or two if there are five cards) and stand in a line to make a sentence.

3 Explain and demonstrate that if they have any words in their sentences that we usually contract when we speak (e.g. *I* + *am*, *we* + *are*), then the children with these cards should link arms.

4 Once they are ready ask each group to hold up their word cards and show their sentence to the rest of the class.

5 The rest of the class checks if children are linking arms correctly and everyone says the sentence together, first in the full form and then using the contracted form.

6 You may also like to write the contracted forms on the board to ensure children are aware how these are written.

Comments and suggestions

- This activity uses kinaesthetic learning to help children make the connection between full and contracted forms of auxiliary verbs. In subsequent lessons, if appropriate, you can refer to linking arms to remind and encourage children to use contracted forms when they speak.

- It is important to use sentences in the activity which are meaningful to the children in some way and relate to language they have practised or a story they have heard or read.

3.20 Grammar detective

Level All   **Age** 9–12   **Organization** pairs, whole class

Aims To logically deduce a language rule from given input or data; to develop an interest in and awareness of language patterns and rules.

Language focus *In the example:* determiners *(a/an)*
Alternatives: any grammar point where there is a regular pattern to 'discover', eg formation of comparative and superlative adjectives

Materials *Essential:* none / *Optional:* photocopies of input/data for the activity (see step 2; one for each child)

Procedure

1 Explain to the children that they are going to be 'grammar detectives' and discover a rule in English.

2 *Either* give out the photocopies *or* write on the board in jumbled order a range of familiar vocabulary including *a* or *an*, eg *a banana, an orange, an elephant, a lion, an apple, a coat, a shirt, an umbrella, a cake, an ice cream, a spider, an ant, an egg, a tomato.*

3 Divide the class into pairs.

4 Ask the children to work with their partner and see if they can discover the rule about when we use *a* before words and when we use *an.*

5 At the end, ask the children to report back and, if appropriate, introduce or use the words 'vowel' and 'consonant', eg *We use 'a' before words (or nouns) that begin with a consonant and 'an' before words (or nouns) that begin with a vowel.*

6 Explain and demonstrate that we do this because it's easier to say. If you like, ask the children to identify the five English vowels (a, e, i, o, u) from the words on the sheet or the board.

Comments and suggestions

- By 'discovering' the rule themselves, rather than being told, children are much more likely to remember to use and apply it in their own work.

- This principle holds for any regular language pattern or rule, eg for the formation of selected comparative adjectives, children can be given a sheet with a range of examples, eg *tall – taller, short – shorter, ugly – uglier, pretty – prettier, dangerous – more dangerous, beautiful – more beautiful* and deduce how the comparatives are formed.

3.21 Monster adjectives

Level A1.1, A1.2, A2.1, A2.2   **Age** 9–12   **Organization** whole class, pairs

Aims To notice and become aware of the order of adjectives before nouns; to ask and answer questions to practise the order of adjectives before nouns.

Language focus adjectives of size, numbers, colours, parts of the body, *have*, questions

Materials *Essential:* none

Procedure

1 Ask the children to imagine a monster. Write the following table on the board:

three	big	red	eyes
six	small	yellow	ears
nine	tiny	purple	feet

2 Ask the children to secretly choose one word from each column to describe a feature of their monster, eg *three, tiny, yellow eyes / six, big, red feet* and to note the words they choose in their notebooks.

3 Demonstrate the activity by getting the children to ask you up to six questions to find out the special feature of your monster, eg *Does your monster have nine, small, purple ears?* If they don't guess after six questions, tell them the special feature, eg *My monster has nine, big, yellow ears.*

4 Divide the class into pairs.

5 Children take turns to ask their partner six questions and guess the special feature of their partner's monster in the same way.

6 At the end, ask the children to look at the adjectives in each column and identify the order of adjectives before nouns, ie number – size (or other descriptive adjective, eg *hairy*) – colour.

7 If appropriate, you may also like to ask the children how this order of adjectives compares to their L1 and whether this makes it easier or more difficult to remember the order in English.

Comments and suggestions

• This activity encourages children to explicitly notice a feature of grammar that they may have practised implicitly (most probably with two, rather than three, adjectives).

• Through inviting comparison with L1, children are encouraged to become aware of similarities and differences between the two languages, which may affect the way they learn.

3.22 Sort the plurals

Level A1.2, A2.1   **Age** 9–12   **Organization** whole class, pairs

Aims To classify regular plural nouns according to the spelling; to be aware of differences in the pronunciation of plural nouns; to become aware that irregular plural nouns are exceptions that need to be learnt

Language focus regular and irregular plural nouns

Materials *Essential:* none

Procedure

1 Explain and demonstrate the following rules on the board, eliciting as much as you can from the children:

– to make a regular word plural you add -s, eg *boys, girls*
– if a word ends in -ch, -o, -s, -sh or -x, eg *lunch, potato, class, bush* or *box*, you add -es
– if a word ends in -y after a consonant, eg *baby*, you delete the -y and add -ies
– some words are irregular and you need to learn the plural, eg *children*.

2 Draw the table below on the board and ask the children to copy it.

s	es	ies	irregular

3 Divide the class into pairs.

4 Say and write singular words the children know on the board.

5 Ask the children to work with their partner, decide the plural form of the word you say and write it in the correct column in the table.

6 Check the answers and ask the children to think of three more words to go in each column. Some examples of words you can use are: *bus, friend, car, banana, potato, dog, cat, beach, fox, glass, child, man, woman, story, table, foot, city, pen, day, tooth, shirt, mouse, country, bike, tomato, person, tree, flower, lady, prince, princess.*

7 Draw the children's attention to the differences in pronunciation of regular plural nouns, ie /s/ after /p/, /t/, /k/, /f/, /θ/ eg *shirts, bikes;* /ɪz/ after /s/, /z/, /ks/, /ʃ/, /tʃ/, /ɪ/, eg *buses, stories* and /z/ after other sounds, eg *pens, tables,* and encourage children to practise saying the words.

Comments and suggestions

• In this activity, children work deductively from a given set of rules. The activity develops classifying skills and increases children's awareness of spelling.

• When introducing new vocabulary in subsequent lessons, you can refer children back to the table by asking them how to make the plural form of a new word, if it is regular, and adding it to the irregular column in their tables, if it isn't.

3.23 Beep!

Level All   **Age** 9–12   **Organization** whole class, pairs

Aims To deduce a missing grammatical word; to notice different situations in which it is appropriate to use it.

Language focus *In the example: have got*
Alternatives: modal verbs, eg *can, must*

Materials *Essential:* none

Procedure

1 Dictate a set of six sentences containing a target point of grammar, eg *have got.* As you dictate each sentence, say *beep!* instead of *got* and explain that children should leave a gap when they hear this word, eg *I've beep a computer. Mary's beep two brothers. Ron's beep a cat. Jane and Dave have beep brown eyes. Leo's beep blue trousers. Sue's beep long hair.* Personalize the sentences by making them refer to children in the class.

2 In pairs, children identify the missing word and identify the situations in which it is appropriate to use it, eg to talk about possessions, family, pets, clothes and to describe people.

Comments and suggestions

• Children enjoy the puzzle aspect of deducing the missing word and the activity helps them notice the range of situations in which it is appropriate to use the target grammatical form.

• Other modal verbs which are suitable to use in this activity include eg *can* with sentences to show ability, permission, possibility, making a request or asking someone to do something and *must* with sentences to show obligation and deduction.

• By dictating the sentences, children have a record of sentences in which it is appropriate to use the target grammar in their notebooks at the end of the activity.

3.24 It looks like …

Level A2.2, B1.1   **Age** 9–12   **Organization** whole class, pairs

Aims To deduce what things are like using verbs of sensation; to use creative thinking skills; to practise using *like* as a preposition, rather than a verb; (to use the five senses).

Language focus *It looks like / sounds like / feels like / smells like / tastes like*

Materials *Essential:* 'mystery' pictures (see next page) / *Optional:* small objects, eg a key, a rubber, a ring; a recording of sounds, eg a tap running, something being fried, a car engine; small pieces of food, eg different types of fruit; reproductions of abstract art, eg on postcards.

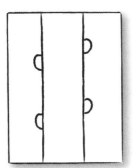  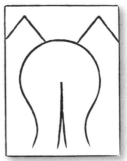 

Procedure

1 *Either* have ready copies of the pictures large enough for the whole class to see *or* be ready to draw these on the board.

2 Divide the class into pairs.

3 Show or draw the first picture. Ask *What does this picture look like?* Give the children a few moments to confer with their partners and then listen to their ideas, eg *It looks like a train track. / It looks like birds sitting on electricity wire. / It looks like a koala climbing a tree.* Be ready to help with vocabulary to enable the children to express their ideas if necessary.

4 After listening to all the suggestions, ask the children which one they like best. Show or draw the remaining pictures and ask children to say what they are like in the same way, eg *It looks like … a giraffe passing a window / an elephant walking towards mountains / the jaws of a shark.*

5 If you have a recording of sounds, repeat the procedure above, playing the sounds in turn and asking *What does this sound like? It sounds like …*

6 If you have small objects, ask children to the front of the class in turn, give them an object to feel behind their backs and ask *What does this feel like? It feels like …*

7 Children can also take turns to give each other small objects and say what they feel like in pairs.

8 If you have small pieces of fruit, ask children to the front of the class in turn, get them to close their eyes and ask, eg *What does this smell like? It smells like …* and, if appropriate, *What does this taste like? It tastes like …* (but see comment below).

Comments and suggestions

- Children enjoy using all their senses and thinking creatively in this activity. Through interpreting the pictures, sounds etc, the concept of *look/sound/feel/taste/smell like …* is clearly conveyed.

- Remember to check about food allergies before asking children to taste food and, if there is any doubt, avoid doing this part of the activity.

- As an alternative in the first part of the activity, you can use reproductions of abstract art, eg on postcards, and children say what they think the pictures look like.

- As a follow-up to the first part of the activity, children can copy the pictures and write sentences about each one. Alternatively, they can draw their own pictures for others to interpret.

3.25 Stop!

Level A1.1, A1.2, A2.1, A2.2, B1.1   **Age** 9–12   **Organization** whole class, pairs
Aims To listen and notice a target point of grammar
Language focus any target point of grammar, eg past simple verbs
Materials *Essential:* a text to read / *Optional:* photocopies of the text (one for each child)
Procedure

1 After doing comprehension work and/or getting children's personal responses to a text, either from the course book or another source, eg an information book, the internet or a story, explain that you are going to read the text to the children again. Ask them to call *Stop!* every time they hear a target point of grammar which you want them to notice, eg past tense verb forms.

2 Read slowly at first, signalling with a pause and your voice, if necessary, when the children should call *Stop!* Speed up as they become familiar with the activity.

Comments and suggestions

- If appropriate, you may like to ask children to note down the verbs every time they call *Stop!* These can then be used as prompts in a follow-up activity in which children reconstruct the text.

- If you're concerned about noise levels when children call out *Stop!*, alternatively you can ask them to write STOP! on a piece of paper before the activity and hold it up silently when they hear the verbs instead.

3.26 Discover the question

Level A2.1, A2.2, B1.1   **Age** 10–12   **Organization** whole class
Aims To guess or deduce a question from given answers.

Language focus *In the example:* past simple, statements and questions
Alternatives: present simple, statements and questions in any tense

Materials *Essential:* none
Procedure

1 Ask two children to come and sit at the front of the class with their back to the board and facing the other children.

2 Write a question on the board, eg *What did you do last weekend?* without the two children at the front seeing it.

3 Ask the rest of the class to think about a sentence to say in answer to the question. The children at the front then point to and name several children who tell them their answers, eg *I did my homework. / I went to the park. / I watched TV. / I read a comic.*

4 After listening to the answers, the children at the front try to guess the question on the board. Be ready to prompt with a word or two if necessary.

5 Repeat the procedure several times with different children and questions.

Comments and suggestions

- In this activity children are encouraged to actively listen out for 'grammar' as this is the key to guessing the question correctly.

- The questions you use in the activity can be graded in difficulty to suit the level of the children, eg *How do you come to school? What's your favourite food? Where are you going on holiday?*

3.27 Sentence machine

Level All   **Age** 9–12   **Organization** pairs, whole class

Aims To make sentences following a pattern based on a substitution table; to familiarize children with the format of substitution tables.

Language focus *In the example: have got*, adjectives of description, colours, parts of the body
Alternatives: any target language structure and vocabulary

Materials *Essential:* none / *Optional:* photocopies of the sentence machine (one for each pair)

Procedure

1   Divide the class into pairs.

2   Either draw a simple sentence machine on the board or give a photocopy to each pair.

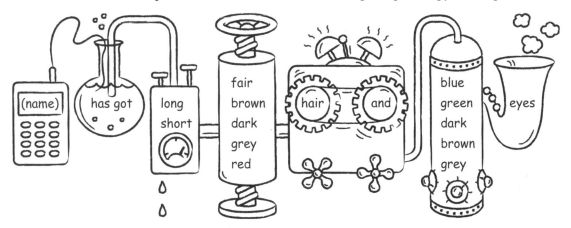

3   Demonstrate how the 'sentence machine' works by describing someone in the class, eg *Sandra has got short brown hair and blue eyes.*

4   Ask the children to use the 'machine' to write as many sentences as possible to describe people they know, eg other children in the class, within a time limit, eg five minutes.

5   At the end, ask children to take turns to read out one of their sentences describing someone in the class, using *he* or *she* instead of the name. Other children listen and identify who it is.

Comments and suggestions

•   As children progress and get older, they are likely to come across substitution tables, either in their course book or other materials. 'Sentence machines' familiarize children with the format of substitution tables and allow them to generate sentences following a pattern in a safe and non-threatening way.

•   When creating 'sentence machines' for your classes, you need to ensure that the sentences generated are meaningful to the children in some way, eg by referring to a story, to factual information or to real life (as in the example above).

3.28 Mime the grammar

Level A1.2, A2.1, A2.2   **Age** 8–12   **Organization** whole class

Aims To mime and make guesses; to take turns and collaborate as a group; to reflect on the language used.

Language focus *In the example:* adverbs, imperatives
Alternative: present continuous, everyday actions

Materials *Essential:* none

Procedure

1 Ask two children to come to the front of the class and stand facing the board with their hands over their ears.

2 Whisper or mouth an adverb to the rest of the class, eg *happily*. Mime what it means yourself and check that everybody understands.

3 Ask the two children by the board to turn round. Explain and demonstrate that they should take turns to give the class instructions, eg *Stand up!* and that the class should respond in the manner of the adverb.

4 After giving two or three instructions each, the pair should confer and try to guess the adverb. When they guess correctly, write the adverb on the board. Be ready to help if necessary.

5 Repeat the procedure several times with different pairs of children and different adverbs. Examples of adverbs you can use are: *sadly, angrily, quickly, slowly, nervously, fiercely, carefully.*

6 At the end, establish that adverbs tell us how people do things. Ask the children what they notice about all the words on the board (that they end in *-ly*).

Comments and suggestions

• Children enjoy the physical movement and guessing element in this activity. Through mime the concept of adverbs of manner to describe how people do things is made very clear.

• Another example of a grammar point which lends itself to mime is the present continuous tense. Ask two children to the front of the class and whisper an action to them, eg *You're playing tennis.* The children then mime what you say to the rest of the class who guess the action. As with adverbs, through the use of mime the concept of the present continuous to describe things happening now is made very clear. At the end, you can also get the children to notice the form of the verb.

3.29 The longest sentence

Level A2.1, A2.2, B1.1   **Age** 10–12   **Organization** groups

Aims To raise awareness of how to write well-formed sentences; to practise using, eg conjunctions, sequencers and relative pronouns; to take turns in an orderly way.

Language focus past simple, conjunctions, sequencers, relative pronouns
Alternatives: any language, eg present simple

Materials *Essential:* chalk or board pens

Procedure

1 Draw a line down the middle of the board. Write a starter word, eg *Yesterday* on the left side of each half of the board at a height the children can reach.

2 Divide the class into two groups.

3 Explain that the groups should each write one sentence on the board, beginning with the starter word, and make it as long as they can. Each child can only write one word and must then pass the pen or chalk to the next person in the group. Set a time limit, eg 3–4 minutes.

4 As the children add words to their sentence, rub out any which are not grammatically correct. The next child then has a chance to add a word which is acceptable.

5 When the time is up, let the child at the board add one or two words to finish the sentence.

6 Read both sentences and count the words to see which one is longest. Draw the children's attention to the words they used that helped them to construct their sentence, eg conjunctions, sequencers and relative pronouns.

Comments and suggestions

• In the interest of making their sentences as long as possible, this activity encourages children to try out using grammar words that they usually tend to avoid in their own writing.

- You may find that you need to create a rule of silence during the activity in order to avoid some children calling out and trying to dictate words to other members of their group.
- Depending on the sentences produced, it may be suitable for children to work together and continue constructing the text and turn it into a story.

3.30 Metalanguage poems

Level All   **Age** 9–12   **Organization** pairs

Aims To develop familiarity with useful metalanguage; to produce simple poems following a pattern.

Language focus *In the example:* wild animals, adjectives of description, metalanguage
Alternatives: any language and vocabulary following a grammatical pattern which uses familiar metalanguage

Materials *Essential:* none

Procedure

1 Write a pattern for the poem on the board, eg

   Adjective – noun
   Adjective – noun
   Adjective – noun
   Verb

2 Within a topic you are doing, eg wild animals, show how the pattern can be followed to make a simple poem, eg

   Big lion
   Hungry lion
   Fierce lion
   Run!

3 Divide the class into pairs. Children work together and write their own poems about a different wild animal following the same pattern.

4 At the end, ask different pairs to read their poems to the class.

Comments and suggestions

- Many children are taught metalanguage when they learn their first language and can usefully transfer this knowledge to English.
- As well as being enjoyable, this activity encourages children to apply their understanding of metalanguage in a purposeful way.
- The patterns for children to follow to create poems can be adjusted to suit different levels. Two more examples of patterns to use are:

Noun	*Crocodile*
Adjective and adjective	*Green and scary*
Verb and adverb	*Snap suddenly*

   or, at a higher level, with children who are more familiar with metalanguage:

Article – noun – verb	*The elephant walks*
Adjective and adjective	*Heavy and noisy*
Adjective and adjective	*Big and grey*
Article – noun – verb	*The elephant walks*
Pronoun – auxiliary + verb + -ing, verb + -ing	*He's coming, coming*
Free choice	*Hurray!*

Section 4 **Storytelling and drama**

Storytelling and drama share a number of features which make it natural to integrate them during lessons. Both build on children's innate capacity for fantasy and imaginative play, and even very young children can differentiate between the conventions of a story or drama and real life. Through stories and drama, children develop understanding of themselves and the world around them. The distance afforded by characters and events which are not real also helps children to explore significant issues which are relevant to their daily lives, in a way that is safe and enjoyable.

In storytelling and drama, the usual norms of time, place and identity are temporarily suspended as, for example, in a story which spans a hundred years yet takes three minutes to tell, or a drama activity which transforms the classroom into a 'jungle' and all the children in it to 'hungry lions'. Storytelling and drama are above all shared, communal classroom events which engage children's interest, attention and imagination and develop their language skills in a holistic way. They also appeal to children with different intelligences and learning styles and provide a framework for fostering social skills and attitudes, such as active listening, collaborating, turn taking and respect for others, in a positive way.

Learning through stories

Most children start school familiar with stories and narrative conventions in L1 and quickly transfer this familiarity into a willingness to listen to and participate in stories in English. Stories provide a natural, relevant and enjoyable context for exposure to language and an opportunity to familiarize children with the sounds, rhythm and intonation of English. The discovery and construction of meaning is supported through things such as visuals, mime, gesture, voice and characterization, and children also develop learning strategies and thinking skills, such as predicting, hypothesizing, guessing and inferring meaning. Stories help young children to develop concentration skills and also aspects of emotional intelligence, such as empathy and relating to other people. Stories also provide a springboard for a wide range of activities which develop language, thinking skills, positive attitudes and citizenship, as well as appreciation of other cultures, or understanding of content from other areas of the curriculum. As children increasingly develop their ability to understand, retell, act out and/or create their own stories in English, this also has a positive effect on their motivation, confidence and self-esteem.

There are various possible approaches to using stories in class. These range from occasional use of stories to supplement a topic or structure-based course book, to using a story-based course book, and possibly supplementing this with additional stories as well, to basing the whole language programme and syllabus on a selection of stories which the children study over a period of time, eg two or three stories per term.

Choosing stories

Stories can be selected from a range of sources, including graded readers, story websites on the internet or picture books originally written for children whose first language is English. Whatever the source, the most important thing is that the story you choose is suitable for the children it is intended for. You need to check that the content is relevant, interesting, appealing and memorable and, if the story is illustrated, that the visuals are clear and attractive and will support children's understanding. The language level of the story also needs to be appropriate and to fit in at least partially with your syllabus. Other features, such as whether the discourse pattern of the story is repetitive, cumulative or includes a rhythmic refrain (and therefore promotes participation, aids memory and practises a particular language pattern) will also influence your choice. Over time, it is important to vary the kinds of stories you use, including, for example, traditional stories or, with older children, spoof or modern versions of these, fables or stories with a moral, myths, legends, funny stories, rhyming stories, stories with flaps or pop-ups, biographical stories, stories which help children understand their own feelings, stories from other cultures and stories which are linked to content from other areas of the curriculum.

Telling stories

Before telling a story to children for the first time, it is usually advisable to practise how you are going to do this, including for example, mime or actions you plan to use to convey meaning, the way you are going to use your voice, eg for different characters or to create surprise or suspense, and the places you are going to pause or ask questions to encourage the children to show their understanding or predict what's going to happen next. When you tell the story, you need to make sure that everyone can see and hear you and, if you are using a picture book, hold this up and show each illustration slowly round the group. With younger children it is usually best if they can sit on the floor in a semi-circle near you and you may also like to introduce the story with a rhyme to settle the children before you begin (see 6.1). As you tell the story, it is a good idea to maintain frequent eye-contact with the children, in order to help them stay focused and attentive. You also need to give them time to think, look, comment, ask or respond to questions and, if appropriate, encourage them to join in with you as you tell the story. At the end, it is important to invite a personal response, eg by asking children if they like the story, or have had similar experiences or feelings to the characters in the story, and be ready to recast or extend their contributions in English as necessary. Above all, it is important to show and share your own enjoyment of the story – it's catching!

Planning story-based lessons

As with other listening and reading activities (see introductions to Sections 1 and 2), it can be helpful to plan story-based lessons following the three stages of *before, while* and *after*. If you decide to use a story in an extended way over several lessons, then this is likely to be a cyclical process which starts by creating interest, motivation and attention in the story and predicting what it is about (see 4.1–3), followed by an initial telling of the story, related activities and follow-up. The cycle can then be extended through a combination of retelling(s) of the story in a variety of ways (see 4.4), interspersed with a series of appropriately selected activities (see 4.4–31) that lead children from an initial, global understanding of the story to using more and more of the language it contains. In some cases, the storytelling cycle may lead to children producing their own versions of the story (see 4.14) or dramatizing some aspect of it in a role play (see 4.28, 4.31).

With older children, as part of their understanding of storytelling, it is also important to develop their awareness of how stories are constructed and to give them opportunities to create stories themselves (see 4.13, 4.15).

As part of activities in the storytelling cycle, and in order to enrich and enhance children's learning, it is often appropriate to integrate storytelling with drama.

Learning through drama

Drama provides opportunities for multi-sensory, kinaesthetic responses to stories and engages children in 'learning by doing' at a number of different levels. At a basic level, through listening and responding to storytelling (see 4.4) and doing short, introductory drama activities (see 4.19–23), children use mime, sounds, gestures and imitation to show their understanding and to make connections between language and corporal expression. This helps young children associate actions, words and meanings and memorize key language in a natural and enjoyable way. As children become familiar with the story, more extended drama activities provide opportunities for recycling the language it contains through retelling or acting out, either by the children themselves or by the children using puppets (see 4.24–26). In these activities, the use of drama provides a focus and support for children to use (some) language from the story in an independent way and also contributes to building up their confidence and self-esteem. At a more sophisticated level, the use of drama techniques such as hot seating (see 4.27), role play (see 4.28) or thought tunnel (see 4.30) provides opportunities for children to go beyond the story and explore the issues, problems or moral dilemmas that it contains. This not only provides opportunities for children to use language they know beyond the story script within a clearly defined framework but also encourages them to develop critical and creative thinking skills and to work with others in a collaborative way.

In addition to classroom drama, it may sometimes be suitable to use a story the children have specially enjoyed as the basis of a class play. The preparation of a class production for an audience of parents and others is different from other classroom drama activities in this section, which put the emphasis on using drama as part of a process of personalized learning. However, preparing and performing a class play can also have enormous benefits for children's language development, confidence and self-esteem and prove extremely worthwhile and rewarding (see 4.32).

Managing drama activities

Drama activities with children can be 'risky' in terms of classroom management and need to be handled carefully and sensitively. It is usually advisable to introduce drama gradually, in activities which are short and where you use techniques such as 'freeze' or shaking maracas (see 4.19) to control the action. In addition to general points about classroom management (see Introduction pp.11–14), it is vital to show yourself willing to participate in classroom drama and to model the kinds of responses you expect from the children. Although it is important to give children encouraging feedback after doing a drama activity, it is best not to look at them (too) directly during the activity, as this may unwittingly convey an impression that you are judging them. This can be off-putting to some children, who will be drawn in naturally as long as they do not feel under pressure. If you regularly use story-related drama activities with your classes, over time you may be surprised at the increasingly confident and mature way in which children respond.

Although the drama activities described in this section relate to storytelling, see also Games (Section 5), Songs, rhymes and chants (Section 6) and Content-based learning (Section 8) for additional activities using drama.

Reflection time

As you use the storytelling and drama activities in this section with your classes, you may like to think about the following questions and use your responses to evaluate how things went and plan possible improvements for next time:

1 **Interest:** Did the story engage the children's curiosity, interest and attention? Why? / Why not? If so, how was this sustained?

2 **Participation:** Did the children participate actively? What factors encouraged – or discouraged – this?

3 **Creative thinking:** How did the children respond to activities which invited a creative or imaginative response? Did this affect the way they used language? If so, how?

4 **Kinaesthetic learning:** How did the children respond to activities involving mime and movement? In what ways did such activities seem to help or detract from the children's learning? What were the reasons for this, do you think?

5 **Collaboration:** Did the children collaborate and work well together? What factors influenced this?

6 **Enjoyment:** Did the children enjoy the story and related activities? Why? / Why not? What effect did this have on their motivation, confidence and self-esteem?

4.1 Words in the story

Level All   **Age** 4–12   **Organization** whole class

Aims To predict a story from key words; to create interest and attention in listening to the story; to listen and compare the story with predictions.

Language focus *In the example:* vocabulary from the story, present simple, making predictions with *perhaps, maybe*
Alternatives: past simple

Materials *Essential:* a copy of the story / *Optional:* flashcards or pictures of key vocabulary

Procedure

1. Introduce and write a selection of key vocabulary from the story on the board. For example, for a story about the mythical sea creature, the Kraken, you could use the words: *monster, sea, island, sailors, boat, fire.* If you like, draw pictures or use flashcards to illustrate the words.

2. Ask the children to predict what they think happens in the story based on the vocabulary on the board, and listen to their suggestions, eg *I think some sailors are in a boat. / There are big waves in the sea. / The sailors fall in the sea. / They nearly drown. / I think they swim to an island. / Perhaps there is a monster on the island. / Maybe the monster breathes fire.* Be ready to help the children express their ideas and encourage them to be as imaginative as possible.

3. Then say *Let's listen to the story and find out!* Read or tell the story once. Get the children to compare what happens with their predictions.

4. Follow with further work on the story as appropriate (see 4.4–18).

The Kraken

There was once an enormous sea monster called the Kraken. The Kraken was more than two kilometres long. It had an enormous head, big eyes and hundreds of tentacles.

The Kraken was a peaceful, quiet monster and it usually lived at the bottom of the sea. But it sometimes swam to the surface and stayed there for eight or ten years. Then trees and plants grew on the Kraken and it looked like an island in the sea.

One day a boat sailed near the island. The sailors decided to stop and explore. They took lots of food and drink with them and rowed to the island on a small boat.

The sailors climbed on to the island and had a party. They ate lots of food and told stories. They sang songs and they danced. At night it was very cold and they lit a big fire.

Suddenly, there were big waves and the whole island began to move and shake. The sailors shouted for help. Was it an earthquake? No, it was the Kraken.

The Kraken was no longer a peaceful, quiet monster. It was a fierce and furious monster. The Kraken was angry with the sailors because the fire hurt its back.

The Kraken made a loud noise. It threw the sailors into the sea and they all drowned. Then the Kraken dived down to the bottom of the sea and disappeared. No-one ever saw the Kraken again.

Comments and suggestions

- This prediction activity encourages children to develop their imaginations and express their ideas freely through hypothesizing what the story is about. In some cases, you may find that the children's suggestions are more imaginative than the story you propose to tell!

- Children are usually very motivated to find out if their predictions are correct. This creates a reason for listening to the story attentively. It also provides an initial activity to check global comprehension by comparing the children's predictions with what happens in the story at the end.

- With younger children, it may be appropriate to use fewer words, eg *princess, tower, witch, prince* (see story in 4.7) and for children to use L1 instead of English to predict what happens in the story.
- An alternative version of this activity is to give children the title of the story, eg *The enormous sea monster* or *The princess in the tower* and ask them to predict words in the story. They then listen and compare their predictions and the story in the same way.

4.2 Picture the story

Level All   **Age** 4–12   **Organization** whole class, (pairs)

Aims To describe a picture from a story; to predict what happens in the story before and after the moment in the picture; to create interest and attention in listening to a story; to listen and compare the story with your predictions.

Language focus *In the example:* present continuous, past simple, *there is/are,* making predictions with *perhaps, maybe, going to*
Alternatives: present perfect, past simple

Materials *Essential:* a picture depicting a moment in a story (eg an enlarged copy of the picture from *The Boys and the Bear* below, adapted from Aesop's fable)

Procedure

1 Show children the picture and ask them to describe it in detail. Use this as an opportunity to pre-teach vocabulary in the story if necessary.

2 Explain that the picture is part of a story. Ask the children to predict what they think happens in the story before and after the moment in the picture. Ask questions to stimulate their ideas, eg *Why is the boy lying on the ground? Is he dead? Did the bear kill the boy? What is the bear going to do? Why is the boy in the tree? Did he escape from the bear? How? What is the boy in the tree going to do?*

3 Once the children have elaborated their ideas about the story, say *Let's listen and find out!* Read or tell the story once.

4 Get the children to compare what happens in the story with their predictions.

5 Ask them what they think is the moral of the story (eg *a true friend never abandons you in danger*).

6 Follow with further work on the story as appropriate (see 4.4–18).

The boys and the bear

One day two boys, David and Alex, were going for a walk in the forest. Suddenly they saw a big, brown bear coming towards them. David ran away quickly and climbed a tree. But Alex didn't have time to run away.

The bear came nearer. Alex was terrified. He lay down on the ground, held his breath and pretended to be dead. The bear looked uncertain. It walked up to the boy lying on the ground and touched him with its paw. Alex didn't move. Then the bear walked round sniffing the boy's body but still Alex still didn't move.

Finally the bear put its mouth near the boy's ear and sniffed several times. It then walked away into the forest. Alex waited until the bear disappeared and then stood up. He was shaking with fear.

David climbed down from the tree. He asked Alex what the bear said to him before it walked into the forest. Alex looked at David slowly and replied, 'The bear said to be careful of friends who abandon you when you are in danger.'

Comments and suggestions

- This activity develops children's imagination and ability to interpret a picture. It also creates a motivating purpose for listening to the story.
- Instead of the whole story, you may like to tell the children the first three paragraphs only. Children work together in pairs and invent and write their own endings. The pairs can then take turns to read their endings to the class and vote for the one they like best.
- With younger children, it may be appropriate to use a picture from a story that is already familiar to them in L1, eg a picture of the wolf 'grandmother' sitting in bed from Little Red Riding Hood. This activates children's knowledge of the story (in L1) and prepares and motivates them to listen to it in English.

4.3 Picture book covers

Level All   **Age** 4–12   **Organization** whole class

Aims To use the front and back covers of a picture book to engage children's interest and attention in a story; to develop visual literacy; to predict a story from the cover.

Language focus *In the example: can* (for possibility, ability), *have got, big/little*, adjectives of feeling, animals, making predictions with *perhaps, maybe*
Alternatives: any language, depending on the picture book chosen

Materials *Essential:* a copy of the story book (eg *Monkey Puzzle*, as below) / *Optional:* a big-book version of the story, if available

Procedure

1 Show the children the book cover and read the title of the story. Explain the meaning of *puzzle* if necessary.

2 Ask the children to say what they can see in the picture, eg *I can see a monkey / a butterfly / three red flowers*. Introduce any new vocabulary if necessary.

3 Ask further questions *Where's the monkey?* (in the jungle) *Is the monkey big or little?* (little) *Is the monkey happy?* (No) *How's he feeling, do you think?* (eg sad, lonely, worried, lost) *Why?* Listen to the children's ideas, recasting and/or extending them as appropriate, eg *Perhaps the little monkey hasn't got any friends. / I think the little monkey can't find his way home. / Maybe the little monkey can't swing in the trees.*

4 Point to the picture of the monkey and butterfly, and use mime and gesture to convey meaning as you tell children the reason by reading the blurb on the back cover: *'I've lost my mum!' 'Hush, little monkey, don't you cry. I'll help you find her,' said Butterfly. But somehow Butterfly keeps getting it wrong. Will Monkey ever find his mum?*

5 Ask the children to predict the answer and how they think the butterfly keeps getting it wrong. (**Answer:** by finding the wrong mum.)

6 Then ask them to predict which animals Monkey and Butterfly meet in the jungle on their quest to find little monkey's mum. (**Answer:** elephant, snake, spider, parrot, frog, bat.) Use this to lead into reading the story to the children, pausing to encourage them to guess the animals and compare them with their predictions as you turn each page.

7 Follow with further work on the story as appropriate (eg 4.17, 4.20–24, 4.27, 4.28, 4.31).

Comments and suggestions

- Children's picture books, such as the example used here, are often beautifully illustrated and can have a magical effect in engaging children's interest and attention in listening to stories in English.

- Through exploiting the front and back cover of a picture book before reading the story, children are encouraged to develop close visual observation and prediction skills. Over time, they also become more discerning about identifying picture books they would like to read independently (eg when choosing books to take home from a class library).

- Although the language of some picture books is likely be beyond the productive level of the children, features such as a repetitive discourse pattern, rhythm and rhyme, and appealing illustrations make them immediately comprehensible. In subsequent work, however, it may only be suitable to focus on selected aspects of language in the story for the children to produce themselves.

- With older children, appropriately selected picture books may also be appropriate to use as a transition or 'bridge' into reading longer books with fewer illustrations. Examples of this are the *Clarice Bean* stories by Lauren Child (Orchard Books), a collection of humorous and insightful stories about self-identity and family relationships from the point of view of a modern, opinionated pre-teenage girl.

4.4 Storytelling many ways

Level A1.1, A1.2   **Age** 4–8   **Organization** whole class

Aims To encourage children to engage and participate in a picture book story in a variety of ways; to show understanding, eg through mime.

Language focus *In the example:* animals *(elephant, giraffe, lion, camel, snake, monkey, frog, puppy)*, adjectives *(big, tall, fierce, grumpy, scary, naughty, jumpy, scary)*, past simple
Alternatives: any language, depending on the story

Materials *Essential:* a copy of the story book, eg *Dear Zoo* by Rod Campbell / *Optional:* a big-book version of the story, if available (4.4f); small picture cards of the animals in the story (one set for each child) (4.4g); sticky paper notes

Procedure

When (re-)telling a picture book story, eg *Dear Zoo*, to children over a series of lessons, you can vary the way you do it by using any combination of the following procedures:

4.4a Initial storytelling

1 Tell the story to the children using mime and gesture to convey the meaning of *wrote, sent back, fierce, grumpy* in the repeated pattern on each page: *I wrote to the zoo to send me a pet. They sent me a …. He was too (fierce/grumpy, etc) so I sent him back.*

2 Ask the children to guess the animal in the box before lifting the flap on each page.

4.4b Respond with gestures

Tell the story and encourage children to join in with gestures to show understanding of *wrote* (pretend to write in the air) and *sent back* (make dismissive gestures, as if shooing each animal away, using the back of your hand) on each page. Children also join in naming the animal in each box.

4.4c Mime the words

Tell the story and encourage children to mime the adjective for each animal (*fierce, grumpy* etc) with you.

4.4d Lift the flaps

Tell the story and invite different individual children to lift the flap and say, eg *It's a lion!* on each page.

4.4e Correct the animal

Tell the story naming the wrong animals and children correct you, eg T: *They sent me a giraffe.* PP: *No, a lion!*

4.4f Hold up picture cards

Tell the story and children hold up a picture card of the animal which corresponds to each page.

4.4g Sticky paper notes

Cover key words, eg the adjectives on each page, with sticky paper notes. Tell the story, pause before each adjective and children supply the words.

4.4h Remember the story

Tell the story and ask at the end of each page *What animal is next? What colour is the box?* before turning the page to check if the children have remembered correctly and continuing the story.

Comments and suggestions

- Although young children love listening to stories again and again, it is important to vary the ways in which you retell a story in a classroom context in order to keep the children actively participating and engaged.

- Through repeated telling of a story over a series of lessons, children are drawn into using more and more of the language it contains in a natural and spontaneous way. By the end, you will probably find that some children know the whole story off by heart!

- Although a story such as *Dear Zoo* contains the past simple tense, the children will have no problem understanding this in the context of the story. However, the language you actively encourage children to remember and produce is likely to be the names of the animals and adjectives and does not need to focus on the past simple.

- If you use a story such as *Dear Zoo* as part of a unit of work, you can combine retelling the story with a range of other activities, eg flashcard games with the animals (see 3.2), a memory game based on the colours of the boxes, word puzzles (see 3.5), drama (see 4.19–21), simple story-related writing activities (see 4.17), songs, rhymes and chants (see 6.23), as well as making a story mobile (see 7.2) and learning about one or more animal (see 2.8).

4.5 Finger stories

Level A1.1   **Age** 4–6   **Organization** whole class

Aims To listen and follow a story doing the actions with your fingers; to develop concentration skills; to develop physical coordination.

Language focus *In the example:* present simple, greetings, *house, hill, up, down, door, knock, open, close*
Alternatives: any language, depending on the story

Materials *Essential:* a copy of the story, eg *Mr Wiggle and Mr Waggle* (traditional story, see below)

Procedure

1 Arrange the children in a circle round you.

2 Hold up your right thumb, wiggle it around, and say *This is Mr Wiggle.* Hold up your left thumb, wiggle it around, and say *This is Mr Waggle.*

3 Tell the story, doing the actions with your hands every time you say POP!

4 Repeat, encouraging the children to join in doing the actions and telling the story with you.

Mr Wiggle and Mr Waggle

This is the story of Mr Wiggle	*(show right thumb and wiggle it around)*
and Mr Waggle	*(show left thumb and wiggle it around)*.
Mr Wiggle lives in a little house here	*(open right hand, lay thumb on palm of hand and close fingers over it)*.
Mr Waggle lives in a little house here	*(open left hand, lay thumb on palm of hand and close fingers over it)*.

One day, Mr Wiggle thinks, 'I'd like to visit Mr Waggle.'

So he opens his door – POP!	*(open fingers of right hand)*
goes out of his house – POP!	*(put up thumb)*
and closes his door – POP!	*(close fingers again)*
He goes up the hill and down the hill and up the hill	
and down the hill	*(move your thumb up and down)*
and knock, knock, knock!	*(knock on your left fist)*
No reply! Knock, knock, knock!	*(repeat)*
No reply! So Mr Wiggle goes up the hill and down	
the hill and up the hill and down the hill,	*(retrace with your thumb)*
opens the door of his house – POP!	*(open your hands)*
goes into his house – POP!	*(lay finger on palm)*
and closes his door – POP!	*(close your fingers)*

The next day, Mr Waggle thinks , 'I'd like to visit Mr Wiggle.'   *(repeat the process with your left hand)*

The next day, Mr Wiggle still thinks, 'I'd like to visit Mr Waggle.'
And Mr Waggle still thinks, 'I'd like to visit Mr Wiggle.'

So they open their doors – POP!	*(open both hands)*
go out of their houses – POP!	*(put both thumbs up)*
and go up the hill and down the hill and up the hill	
and down the hill.	*(move both thumbs up and down towards each other and stop)*
'Hello, Mr Wiggle.' 'Hello, Mr Waggle.'	*(move thumbs)*
'How are you today?' 'I'm fine.'	
'And how are you today?' 'I'm fine.'	
'Goodbye, Mr Wiggle.' 'Goodbye, Mr Waggle.'	
And they go up the hill and down the hill and up	
the hill and down the hill.	*(retrace steps with thumbs)*
They open their doors – POP!	*(fingers out)*
go into their houses – POP!	*(put thumbs on palms)*
and close their doors – POP!	*(close fingers)*
And that's the end of the story.	

Comments and suggestions

- Children are usually fascinated by the finger movements and concentrate very hard to follow them as you tell the story. They will need (and probably ask!) to hear the story many times before they can do the movements and join in telling the story with you confidently. Over time, however, they may well learn most, or all, of the story off by heart in a completely natural and spontaneous way.

- This story can be very useful to settle children down and focus their attention if they have become over-excited. Children's absorption in moving their hands and manipulating their fingers as you tell the story provides a focus for listening and generally has a calming effect.

- As a variation of the technique, you can easily invent other little stories which involve finger movements and fit in with your teaching theme, eg two little caterpillars who live on a leaf, get hungry and go looking for food, or two fish who live behind rocks and swim over the waves to see each other.

4.6 Respond to the word!

Level All   **Age** 4–12   **Organization** whole class, groups

Aims To be reminded of a story through listening attentively and responding to specific words; to develop concentration skills; (to scan a text for key words).

Language focus *In the example: ant, grasshopper, work, play, food*
Alternatives: any key words in the story chosen

Materials *Essential:* a copy of the story for you, eg *The ant and the grasshopper* , a version of Aesop's fable / *Optional:* a copy of the story for each child

---

The ant and the grasshopper

One summer day, there was an ant and a grasshopper in a field. The ant worked very hard collecting food for winter and the grasshopper played. The ant said, 'Grasshopper, why do you play all the time? You should work and collect food for winter like me.' The grasshopper laughed and said, 'I don't like work. It's much more fun to play. I can work and collect food tomorrow.'

Every day of summer was the same. The ant worked and worked collecting food for the winter. The grasshopper played and played. He didn't collect any food.

Soon it was winter. There was snow in the field and it was very cold. The grasshopper went to see the ant and said, 'Hello, ant. I'm hungry and it's cold. Please share your food with me.' The ant said, 'No, grasshopper. Sorry. You had a chance to work and collect food in the summer. But you only played. I collected food for myself. I don't have any food for you.' The grasshopper walked away sadly and thought, 'Oh, dear. What a fool I am! In the summer I played and played. Why didn't I work like the ant? Where can I find food now?'

Procedure

1 Use this activity to remind children of a story they have already listened to once. Select key words that are repeated several times in the story, eg *ant, grasshopper, work, play, food.*

2 Divide the children into five groups and assign one word to each group. Teach the children to respond to the words they have been assigned in the following way:

in response to *ant* children should say: *busy, busy, busy*
in response to *grasshopper*: *hop, hop, hop*
in response to *food*: *yum, yum, yum*
in response to *play* or *played*: *hee, hee, hee*
in response to *work* or *worked*: *sigh, sigh, sigh.*

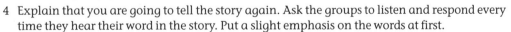

3 Say, *Ant! / Food!* etc in random order and practise getting the children to respond in chorus with their group quickly and rhythmically.

4 Explain that you are going to tell the story again. Ask the groups to listen and respond every time they hear their word in the story. Put a slight emphasis on the words at first.

5 Ask the children how many times they think they heard their word in the story and listen to their response. Either tell the children the answer or, with older children, if you have copies of the story, ask them to scan the text to find and underline their words and then count them to check the answer (*grasshopper* 8; *ant* 8; *food* 10; *work* 8; *play* 8). This can then act as a lead-in to further detailed comprehension work on the story.

Comments and suggestions

- This activity is an enjoyable way of retelling a story. As children respond to the key language by saying their three words in a rhythmic way, the effect can be dramatic as well as humorous.
- As a variation, children can respond to key words or names of characters in the story with mimes or actions instead of verbal responses. When retelling *Little Red Riding Hood*, for example, the children can be divided into three groups: for *wolf* they make a pouncing action, for *Little Red Riding Hood* they pretend to hold a basket and skip on the spot, and for *Granny* they pretend to knit.

4.7 Story sequence

Level All   **Age** 6–12   **Organization** groups

Aims To read and order a familiar story; to practise reading and retelling the story; to collaborate in a group; (to write and draw pictures to illustrate the story).

Language focus *In the example:* past simple, *princess, prince, witch, tower, forest*
Alternatives: any language, depending on the story chosen

Materials *Essential:* strips of card, each with a sentence from the story (one set for each group) (see example below, based on a traditional song) / *Optional:* paper for children to write and illustrate the story

> Once upon a time there was a beautiful princess. ✂
>
> She lived in a tall, dark tower.
>
> One day a wicked witch cast a spell.
>
> The princess fell asleep for a hundred years.
>
> A big forest with very tall trees grew around the tower.
>
> One day a handsome prince came riding by.
>
> He cut the trees down with his sword.
>
> He climbed the tower and took the princess by the hand.
>
> The prince and the princess lived happily ever after.

Procedure

Use this activity to consolidate a story that children are familiar with either orally/aurally or through a song (see 6.24 for the song that accompanies this example).

1 Divide the class into groups of four. Give a set of sentences (in jumbled order) to each group.

2 Children arrange the sentences in the order of the story on their desks.

3 Check the answers by inviting individual children from different groups to take turns to read the sentences in order.

4 Ask one child in each group to collect and shuffle the sentences and distribute them randomly to each member of the group (2–3 sentences for each child). Explain and demonstrate that the children should not show each other their sentences. The child who has the sentence *Once upon a time …* should begin reading the story clearly to the rest of the group. The child who has the second sentence should then read that sentence, and so on until the group has read the whole story.

5 They then reshuffle the strips of card, redistribute the sentences and repeat the procedure. The aim is to take turns to read the story as a group as seamlessly and fluidly as possible.

Comments and suggestions

- This activity develops sequencing skills and gives children practice in reading aloud in a collaborative, non-threatening way. It also fosters active listening and turn-taking. Children usually exert healthy pressure on each other to ensure that the whole group reads the story in a seamless way.

- As a follow-up, you may like to join the groups in order to form bigger groups of eight (children do not need to move). Either assign, or children choose, one (or two) sentence(s) of the story to write out and illustrate on a sheet of paper. Children can then organize their sheets in order to make a book of the story. This can be stapled together (or see 7.14 for simple ideas for making books).

- If appropriate, you may like to draw the children's attention to the phrases *Once upon a time … and … happily ever after*, which traditionally mark the beginning and end of fairy stories.

- You may also feel it is important to draw children's attention to the gender stereotyping in this archetypal fairy story (see also 6.24 for suggestions for acting out the song).

- With older children, picture books such as *Princess Smartypants* or *Prince Cinders* (Puffin Picture Books), which parody traditional fairy tales in an amusing way and encourage children to explore issues such as gender stereotyping, are likely to be more suitable to use than this traditional version.

4.8 Story whispers

Level All   **Age** 6–12   **Organization** teams

Aims To listen and whisper sentences that tell a story; to read and order sentences to tell the story; to collaborate as part of a team.

Language focus any, depending on the story

Materials *Essential:* two copies of the story (one for each team); two photocopies of the same text with the sentences cut into strips, eg as for *The princess in the tower* above (one for each team)

Procedure

Use this activity for a story which is not familiar to the children but which does not contain new language.

1. Divide the class into two teams. Get each team to stand or sit in a line.

2. Stick a copy of the story on the wall at the back of each line.

3. Place a set of cut-up sentences which tell the story in jumbled order at the front of each line (far enough away so that the children cannot read the sentences from where they are standing or sitting).

4. Explain and demonstrate that the child at the back of each line reads the first sentence of the story and then whispers it to the next child in the line. That child whispers it to the next child, and so on down the line, until it gets to the child at the front. This child then selects the correct sentence from the cut-up strips, and places it in order on the desk. They then go to the back of the line to read the next sentence of the story and start the process again.

5. Once the teams have arranged all the sentences in order, ask one child from each team to bring the story text to the front of the class to check that they have done this correctly.

6. When everyone is seated, either ask general comprehension questions about the story and encourage the children to recall as much as they can and/or do further activities based on the story, eg 4.9 or 4.10.

Comments and suggestions

- This activity promotes active listening and children are naturally motivated to make their pronunciation as clear as possible so their team finishes first.
- As an alternative, the activity can also be done by teams of children sitting in rows going across the class. As children do not need to stand up or move about, this is likely to be easier to manage. However, you will need more photocopies of the material (as many as there are rows) and it will be the same child who starts the whispering and orders the sentences in each row. The activity will also be shorter, as the first child in each team can start whispering the next sentence as soon as the previous one has got to, say, the third child in the row.

4.9 That's not right!

Level All   **Age** 4–12   **Organization** whole class

Aims To listen to the retelling of a story; to identify and correct mistakes or things which are different in the story.

Language focus *In the example:* past simple, negative and affirmative statements
Alternatives: any, depending on the story

Materials *Essential:* a copy of the story for you, eg from a picture book, course book or children's reader / *Optional:* photocopies of the story including mistakes (one for each child)

Procedure

Use this activity to retell any familiar story to the children.

1 Explain to the children that you are going to tell them a story and say the title, eg *Cinderella*. Pretend that you can't remember the story very well. Ask the children to help you by saying *That's not right!* and correcting you every time they hear a mistake, eg T: *Cinderella lived with two horrible brothers* … PP: *That's not right! Cinderella didn't live with two horrible brothers. She lived with two horrible sisters!* Depending on the age and level of the class, children can either say full sentences or simply correct the mistake, eg *That's not right! Horrible sisters!*

2 At the end, ask the children to think back and count up how many mistakes you made. Be ready to tell them the answer.

3 Alternatively, if you have prepared a written version of the story including the mistakes, give this out to the children. Ask them to read the story again and count and underline all the mistakes.

4 They can then write out a correct version of the story.

Comments and suggestions

- This activity encourages children to concentrate and listen attentively. They also usually enjoy the role reversal involved in saying *That's not right!* and correcting your 'mistakes'.
- With older children and higher levels, as a follow-up or for homework, you can ask them to choose another fairy tale and write a version of it deliberately including about ten mistakes. In subsequent lessons, children can then take turns to read their fairy tales to the class and correct them in the same way.

4.10 Whistling story

Level All   **Age** 6–12   **Organization** whole class, pairs

Aims To listen to a story and supply missing words and phrases; to retell (a shorter version of) the story.

Language focus any, depending on the story

Materials *Essential:* a copy of the story for you (eg from a picture book, course book or children's reader)

Procedure

Use this activity to remind children of a story they have previously worked on in class or read independently.

1 Retell the story to the children but, instead of saying key vocabulary, whistle and children supply the missing words, eg T: *Robinson Crusoe was a* (whistle)… PP: *sailor.* T: *One day there was a terrible* (whistle) … PP: *storm.* T: *Robinson Crusoe swam to a small, tropical* (whistle)… PP: *island.*

2 Depending on the length of the story, repeat the procedure, this time whistling for longer and leaving more of the story for the children to complete, eg T: *Robinson Crusoe* (longer whistle)… PP: *was a sailor.* T: *One day* (longer whistle)… PP: *there was a terrible storm.* T: *Robinson Crusoe* (longer whistle) … PP: *swam to a small, tropical island.*

3 Divide the class into pairs.

4 Children reconstruct and retell the whole story with their partner.

5 When they are ready, ask one or two pairs to retell the story to the class.

Comments and suggestions

- This activity builds up children's ability to recall and retell a short story.
- If you can't whistle, either you can pause and use gesture or say a nonsense word, eg *Bleep!* to indicate that children should supply the next bit of the story.
- Depending on the age and level of the children, you may also like to ask children to write a short version of the story after they have reconstructed it orally.

4.11 Story circle

Level All   **Age** 6–12   **Organization** whole class

Aims *Either* to listen and retell a familiar story in turns (A2.1+) *and/or* to express your views and opinions about a story; to collaborate and take turns; to respect and value other people's opinions

Language focus any, depending on the story; opinions, *like / don't like, favourite*

Materials *Essential:* a soft ball, scarf or bean bag to pass round the circle / *Optional:* small pictures which tell the story (one set)

Procedure

1 Ask the children to sit in a circle.

2 Explain that the aim of the activity is for children to take turns to retell a familiar story, eg *The Three Bears,* by passing the ball, scarf or bean bag (depending on the object you have chosen) round the circle. If children get stuck, they can say *Pass!* and give the object to the next person in the circle. They can only speak if they have got the object.

3 Give the object to one (confident) child in the circle and invite them to start the story, eg *Once upon a time, there was a family of bears.* This child then passes the object to the child on their left, who adds a sentence, eg *There was Mummy Bear, Daddy Bear and Baby Bear* and so on round the circle until the end of the story.

4 As children tell the story, be ready to prompt and help if necessary by asking questions, eg T: *Where did the bears live?* P: *The bears lived in a house in the forest* or by providing sentence starters, eg T: *One day* … P: *… Mummy Bear cooked porridge for breakfast.*

5 When children have finished telling the story, explain that they should pass the object round the circle again. This time choose a sentence starter for them to express their opinions about the story, eg *I think the story is … / I like … but I don't like … / My favourite part of the story is when ….* Children take turns to pass the object round the circle again, expressing and listening to each others' opinions about the story.

Comments and suggestions

- It is important not to underestimate the challenge of retelling a story in a story circle and this part of the activity is likely to be suitable only for higher level, more confident children. If you have a set of small pictures which tell the story, it can help if you distribute these in the order of the story to individual children or pairs round the circle and they then use these as a visual prompt for their contribution to the story.

- The second part of the activity can be done with all ages and levels using very simple language to express opinions about the story, eg *I like the gorilla. / I think the story is funny.*

- With older, more confident children, it may be appropriate to use a story circle to get the children to invent their own story or retell one they have previously prepared (see 4.13 and 4.14). In this case, you may need to provide an opening line for the story, eg *It was a cold, dark and windy night. / There was once an ogre who lived in a cave.*

- As an alternative to children contributing in order round the circle, it may be more appropriate to invite children to volunteer to speak when they're ready.

4.12 Character in the round

Level A1.1, A1.2, A2.1, A2.2   **Age** 6–10   **Organization** whole class, pairs

Aims To draw a picture and make notes on a character in a story; to use the notes to describe the character.

Language focus *In the example:* present simple, *have got,* clothes, colours, adjectives to describe people
Alternatives: any language related to the character and story; past simple

Materials *Essential:* none / *Optional:* photocopies of the circle diagram on A4 sheets (one for each child).

Procedure

Use this activity to develop character profiles from stories you have previously read or told the children.

1 Draw a circle diagram on the board and divide it into segments as above. Check that children understand the meaning of the words in the segments.

2 Draw a picture of one of the characters from the story, eg Robin Hood, in the inner circle.

3 Elicit the children's ideas and build up a profile of Robin Hood by making notes in the segments of the outer circle, eg for physical description: *young, handsome, brown hair, brown eyes, green cap, green shirt, brown trousers, brown boots, bow and arrow;* for character: *strong, brave, daring, intelligent, generous, kind;* for action in the story: *steals money from rich people, gives money to poor people, falls in love with Marion, helps King Richard.*

4 Divide the class into pairs.

5 *Either* ask the children to copy the circle diagram on the board onto an empty page in their notebooks *or* give out photocopies of these.

6 Children then choose (or you can assign them) another character from the same story, eg Prince John, King Richard, the Sheriff of Nottingham, Maid Marion, Little John, Friar Tuck, and build up a profile with their partner in the same way.

7 Ask children to take turns to present and describe their character to the rest of the class, using the notes they have made. The 'character in the round' sheets can then be displayed.

Comments and suggestions

- This activity encourages children to think about different aspects of story characters and to develop their ability to describe them.

- With older children, you may like to ask them to use the notes they have made in order to write one or two paragraphs describing their character. In this case, it may be appropriate to write a description of one character with the whole class first, eg Robin Hood, using the notes on the board and a shared writing approach (see 2.8) to prepare the children for this.

- With younger children, it is unlikely to be appropriate to divide the outer circle into three segments and children can simply note key features to describe their character (but not the actions in the story) anywhere in the circle.

4.13 Story stepping stones

Level A2.1, A2.2, B1.1   **Age** 9–12   **Organization** pairs, whole class

Aims To identify key episodes in a story; to use the key episodes to reconstruct the story; to write a flow chart to show how the story is constructed; to develop awareness of how stories are constructed.

Language focus *In the example: was/were,* past simple
Alternatives: any, depending on the story

Materials *Essential:* a copy of the story for you (eg *The Kraken* in 4.1) / *Optional:* photocopies of the story (one for each child)

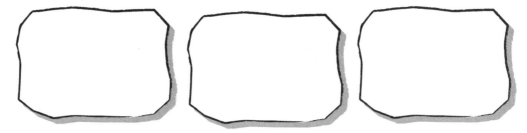

Procedure

Use this activity with a story that is familiar to the children, eg the story of the Kraken in 4.1.

1   Draw a series of stepping stones on the board as on the previous page and ask the children to copy these into their notebooks. (For the story of the Kraken, draw nine stepping stones.) Explain that each 'stepping stone' represents a key episode in the story.

2   Divide the class into pairs.

3   Ask the children to identify the key episodes in the story and to write one on each stepping stone. Give an example of what you mean, eg on the first stepping stone, the children could write, eg *The Kraken lived at the bottom of the sea.*

4   *Either* tell the story again *or* give out photocopies of the story. Children work with their partner, identify the key episodes and write one on each stepping stone.

5   When they are ready, ask them to share and compare their answers. Be ready to accept variation in the number and detail of episodes children have noted on their 'stepping stones' and write an agreed version on the board, eg (following the example sentence) 2 *The Kraken swam to the surface.* / 3 *The Kraken looked like an island.* / 4 *Some sailors rowed to the island.* / 5 *The sailors had a party.* / 6 *The sailors lit a big fire.* / 7 *The Kraken threw the sailors into the sea.* / 8 *The sailors drowned.* / 9 *The Kraken disappeared.*

6   Ask the children to identify which 'stepping stone' sets the scene of the story (1), which 'stepping stones' describe events leading to the conflict (2–5), which 'stepping stone' describes the conflict (6), which 'stepping stone' describes the event following the conflict (7), and which 'stepping stones' describe the resolution (8–9).

7   Use coloured pens or chalk to group the 'stepping stones' for each stage of the story together and write a flow chart of the way the story is constructed on the board. Ask children to copy this and point out that it may be helpful for them to follow when writing their own stories.

Comments and suggestions

- This activity introduces children explicitly to the concept of narrative structure. Once they are aware of this, children often become interested in identifying similar patterns in other stories. It can also have a positive impact on their own writing.

- As a follow-up to this activity, it may be appropriate to ask children to research another mythical creature, eg Pegasus or Cyclops, either using reference books or the internet, and construct and write a story in pairs using the flow chart and following similar 'stepping stones'.

4.14 Parallel story

Level All   **Age** 7–12   **Organization** pairs

Aims To develop awareness that people perceive the world in different ways; to develop interest in stories from other cultures; to create a parallel version of a story.

Language focus *In the example:* present simple, *Wh-* questions, *like* (for comparison), ordinal numbers (to 5), vocabulary from the story
Alternatives: past simple, any other language, depending on the story

Materials *Essential:* copies of the story (one for each pair) / *Optional:* a picture of an elephant

The blind children and the elephant

In a village in India there are six blind children. The children are great friends. They often talk and play together.

One day a man brings an elephant to the village. All the people are happy and excited. The six blind children are puzzled.

'What is an elephant?' asks one.

'I don't know,' says another. 'Let's go and find out.'

The children find the man and the elephant under some trees.

'What is an elephant? Please tell us,' they ask the man.

'Come here and touch the elephant,' says the man. 'And then you can find out.'

The first child touches the elephant's trunk.

'Aha,' he says. 'An elephant is like a snake.'

The second child touches the elephant's tusk.

'Aha,' he says. 'An elephant is like a stick.'

The third child touches the elephant's ear.

'Aha,' he says. 'An elephant is like a big leaf.'

The fourth child touches the elephant's leg.

'Aha,' he says. 'An elephant is like a tree.'

The fifth child touches the elephant's body.

'Aha,' he says. 'An elephant is like a wall.'

The sixth child touches the elephant's tail.

'Aha,' he says. 'An elephant is like a rope.'

Then the children argue.

'An elephant is like a snake.'

'No, it isn't. It's like a stick.'

'You're wrong. I think the elephant is like a big leaf.'

'No, it's like a tree.'

'No, it isn't. It's like a wall.'

'Like a wall? No! An elephant is like a rope!'

The man smiles. He looks at the elephant and then he talks to the children. Can you guess what he says?

'Listen. An elephant has got a trunk like a snake, tusks like sticks, ears like big leaves, legs like trees, a body like a wall and a tail like a rope. You are all right!'

Procedure

1 Hold up the picture of an elephant if you have one and ask *What is an elephant?* Listen to the children's responses, eg *It's a very big animal. It's grey. It's got big ears.* and pre-teach the words *trunk* and *tusk* if necessary.

2 Explain that you are going to tell the children a traditional story from India about six blind children. Tell them you want them to listen and to answer the question *How do the blind children find out about the elephant? Do they agree?*

3 Tell the story up to the last paragraph and check the answers. (They find out by touching the elephant. No, they don't agree.)

4 Encourage the children to guess what the man says and then tell them the last bit of the story.

5 Ask detailed questions about the story, eg *What does the first child touch?* (The elephant's trunk.) *What does he think?* (It's like a snake.) Make sure the children understand that *like a* means 'similar to' and contrast this with the meaning of *I like elephants* to avoid confusion.

6 Ask: *Do you like the story? What can we learn from the story?* and listen to the children's response.

7 Divide the class into pairs. Give out copies of the story.

8 Ask them to write a parallel version about 2–3 blind children and a different animal in a different country. Elicit or give an example before the children begin, eg *A lion in a village in Africa. The first child touches the lion's whiskers. A lion is like a hair brush. The second child touches the lion's mane. A lion is like a teddy bear.* Children invent and write their parallel versions of the story in pairs using the original as a model.

9 Children can then tell or read each others' stories and these can be illustrated and displayed or made into books (see 7.14 for ideas).

Comments and suggestions

- This activity provides a framework for writing a story which is highly supported and at the same time allows children to think creatively. It is most suitable to use with stories which have a clear structure and repeated pattern.

- With younger children, there are many simple picture book stories which lend themselves to this technique. One example is *Mr Wolf's Week* (Colin Hawkins, Picture Lions) which can lead to children creating a story with the following pattern: *Monday is hot. Mr Rabbit puts on his red shorts and walks on the beach. Tuesday is wet. Mr Rabbit puts on his ...* etc.

4.15 Build a story

Level A2.1, A2.2, B1.1   **Age** 10–12   **Organization** pairs, whole class

Aims To create a story in response to questions; to develop imagination; to collaborate with others

Language focus *In the example:* present simple, present continuous, *have got,* adjectives to describe people, clothes, actions, weather, time
Alternatives: past simple, any familiar language

Materials *Essential:* none

Procedure

Use this activity as preparation and lead-in to children writing a story.

1 Divide the class into pairs.

2 Explain that the children are going to create a story with their partner in response to questions and that you will give them time (eg 3–5 minutes) to prepare and note their answers to each question before continuing.

3 Ask a series of questions, as below. Elicit possible answers to one or two of the questions as an example before starting, eg *There's a bank robber and a dancer in the story. The bank robber is tall. He's got dark hair and he's wearing glasses. The dancer is short and very beautiful. She's got long red hair.* Pause between each question to give the children time to prepare their answers. Questions you can ask are:
Who is in the story? (two characters) What are they like?
Where does the story happen? What is the place like?
What is the weather like? What time of day is it?
What do the characters want?
What is the problem?
What happens? (think of up to three events)
How does the story end?

4 At the end of the activity, invite different pairs to tell the stories they have prepared to the rest of the class.

Comments and suggestions

- This activity helps children to share and structure their ideas for writing a story. Once they have the basic content and a plan in place, this frees them up to concentrate more on the language they will use.

- As a follow-up to this activity, you can ask the children to write a draft version of their stories, either in class or for homework. Children can then be encouraged to revise and edit these in subsequent lessons with a view to, for example, writing a suitable opening and ending to the story, organizing paragraphs, adding or changing words to make to the language more interesting, using pronominal reference and connecting sentences and ideas in relevant ways. The final versions of the stories can then be illustrated and displayed or made into books (see 7.14).

4.16 Film of the story

Level A1.2, A2.1, A2.2, B1.1   **Age** 9–12   **Organization** whole class, groups

Aims To plan to make a film or DVD of a traditional or well-known story; to develop imagination; to collaborate as a group.

Language focus *going to,* film vocabulary, eg *star, title, location,* countries, vocabulary related to the story chosen

Materials *Essential:* none / *Optional:* photocopies of film worksheets (one for each child)

Title of story:	Changes to story:
Title of film:	
Main characters:	Location:

Procedure

1 Tell the children that a famous film company is planning to produce new, up-to-date versions of traditional stories as films and they are looking for ideas.

2 Elicit things the children need to think about, eg the title, the stars, the location, possible changes to the story, and introduce vocabulary for this as necessary.

3 *Either* write the form above on the board and ask the children to copy this *or* give out photocopies, if you have prepared these.

4 Divide the class into groups of 3–5 children.

5 Ask each group to think of a traditional or well-known story that they are all familiar with to make into a film and to complete the information on their worksheets for the story they choose. Before they begin, elicit or give a few examples of possible stories, and show them how to complete the work sheet for a story all the children know, eg

Title of story: *Cinderella*
Title of film: *'Love at midnight'*
Main characters: *Cinderella, the Prince, the two sisters*
Changes to the story: *The prince is going to marry Cinderella and then fall in love with one of the sisters.*
Location: *Dracula's castle in Rumania*

Encourage the children to be as imaginative and inventive as possible in their preparation. Set a time limit for this, eg 15 minutes.

6 When the children are ready, ask each group to take turns to present their ideas to the class, eg *We're going to make …* (name of story) *into a film. The title is going to be … The location is going to be … … is going to star as …* Encourage everyone to clap at the end of each presentation.

7 At the end, ask the children which film they think is going to be most popular and why, and listen to their views.

Comments and suggestions

- This activity encourages children to think about stories in the context of another medium which they find appealing. The outcomes are often humorous and imaginative and children usually enjoy 'casting' their favourite real-life stars (whether from the world of pop, sport or cinema) in major roles in their invented films.

- As an extension to the activity, children can also plan other things for their film, eg the music and costumes. The activity can also be linked to recording a short dialogue about their film using the video function of a digital camera (see 9.5).

4.17 Story-related writing

Level All   **Age** 6–12   **Organization** individual / pairs

Aims To practise writing related to a story in a meaningful context; to think about the story from different points of view; to develop awareness of different writing genres.

Language focus *any,* depending on the story and activity

Materials *Essential:* none / *Optional:* a model, gap-fill text, questions or other prompts for the activity chosen (copies for each child or pair)

Procedure

As part of extended work on a story, you may like to choose one or more relevant activities from those outlined below to practise writing. Where appropriate, children can also illustrate their work. In each case, you can either use a shared writing approach (see 2.8) or prepare a model, gap-fill text, questions or other prompts for the children to follow.

4.17a Invitation

Children write the invitation in stories which include a party or wedding, eg the invitation to the ball in Cinderella (see 4.9, 4.27) or to the wedding in Robin Hood (see 4.12). They can also write a letter to accept the invitation (see also 2.24).

4.17b Letter

Children write a letter from the point of view of one of the story characters, eg a letter from Baby Bear to Goldilocks inviting her to come and play at his house (see also 4.22, 4.28), or a letter to the zoo asking for an animal (which they also draw) from *Dear Zoo* (see 4.4, 4.19).

4.17c Postcard

Children write a postcard from a story character to their family, eg Beauty can write a postcard to her father from the house of the Beast in the traditional story, or Alex can write a postcard home recounting the incident with the bear (see 4.2).

4.17d E-mail

Children can send an e-mail to a character in the story, eg to the wolf in *Little Red Riding Hood*, telling him how bad he is and not to follow or eat people in future (see also 4.23, 4.24).

4.17e Wanted poster

Children draw a picture of a character who is missing or wanted in a story, eg a poster describing Goldilocks, missing after she runs away from the bears' house.

4.17f Diary

Children write a diary from the point of view of a character in the story, eg the diary of Hansel or Gretel from the traditional story, when they are prisoners in the witch's house.

4.17g Newspaper report

Children write the story in the form of an article for a newspaper, eg for the Kraken (see 4.1), 'Sailors drown in sea monster drama'.

Comments and suggestions

- Stories can provide a communicative context for practising writing which may motivate otherwise reluctant writers.
- In the case of letters, e-mails and postcards, you can extend the activity by getting children to exchange their work in pairs and write replies.
- Story-related writing can also be displayed as part of a collage of work on each story the children do.

4.18 My opinion of the story

Level All   **Age** 6–12   **Organization** individual, whole class

Aims To express personal opinions about the story; to develop critical thinking skills; to share opinions; to respect other people's opinions.

Language focus opinions, *like /don't like, favourite,* adjectives to express opinions, eg *funny, boring, exciting,* vocabulary from the story

Materials *Essential:* none / *Optional:* photocopies of 'My opinion of the story' forms (one for each child) or A4 paper for children to write their opinions (and draw pictures) on

My opinion of the story	My opinion of the story
Name:	Name: ....
Date:	Date: ....
Title of the story:	Title of the story: ....
😊 I like the story.	I think the story is ....
😐 The story is OK.	....
☹ I don't like the story.	My favourite character is ....
My favourite character is: [box]	because ....
My favourite scene is: [box]	I like the part when ....
	I don't like the part when ....
	I think the ending of the story is ....

Procedure

Use this activity once the children have completed work on a story.

1 Explain that you want the children to think about their personal opinions of the story they have read. *Either* give out photocopies of the form you have prepared *or* write this on the board and ask the children to copy it. See above for two examples of forms for different ages and levels.

2 Check the children understand the form. With older children, it may also be appropriate to elicit possible adjectives they can use to describe the story and ending before they begin, eg *funny, exciting, scary, sad, interesting, boring.*

3 Ask the children to work individually and write their opinions and, in the case of younger children, draw pictures.

4 At the end, organize a brief class discussion and encourage the children to exchange and listen to each others' opinions.

Comments and suggestions

- By writing their personal opinions of stories, children are encouraged to develop critical thinking skills and confidence in expressing their views.
- With young children in particular, you may need to make it clear that there are no right answers and that you value their ability to think about their own opinions independently of others.
- If children keep their 'My opinion of the story' forms together in a folder or file, over time they build up a permanent record of stories they know. If children are using portfolios, they may also like to include their story opinions as part of their dossier.

4.19 Freeze!

Level A1.1   **Age** 4–6   **Organization** whole class

Aims To move round the classroom pretending to be a story character; to freeze in position at a given signal; to practise self-discipline and self-control.

Language focus *In the example:* be, animals, adjectives (from *Dear Zoo*, see 4.4)
Alternatives: any, depending on the story

Materials *Essential:* none / *Optional:* maracas or a tambourine

Procedure

Use this activity once children are familiar with the story (see 4.4).

1 Ask the children to stand up. Say, eg *You're lions! You're fierce!* Get the children to walk round the classroom pretending to be fierce lions. If you have maracas or a tambourine, make a soft noise with this as children do their mimes.

2 Stop the noise suddenly and/or say *Freeze!* Demonstrate that the children should freeze in positions showing that they are fierce lions. Walk round commenting positively on the children's mimes, eg *What a fierce lion! You look very scary. I hope you're not hungry.*

3 Repeat the procedure with different animals and adjectives from *Dear Zoo* (see 4.4).

Comments and suggestions

- Young children love pretending to be animals and the physical movement and mime helps to make the names of the animals and the adjectives associated with each one in the story memorable.
- The use of the 'freeze' technique helps you to manage the activity in a positive way. As soon as you feel the children becoming over-excited in their mimes, you can say *Freeze!* and immediately bring the situation under control again.
- As part of the activity, you may like to tell the children that they must not touch or bump into anyone as they walk around in character during the activity. This helps to prevent any lion fights (!) and also encourages the youngest children, who will tend to cluster together, to share and negotiate the space.

4.20 Sound collage

Level All   **Age** 4–12   **Organization** whole class

Aims To listen and create a dramatic atmosphere related to a story through sounds; to collaborate as a group; to practise self-discipline and self-control.

Language focus *any*, depending on the context

Materials *Essential:* none / *Optional:* maracas

Procedure

Use this activity *either* to introduce a story or as a transition between telling a story and acting it out. For example, if you are using a story which takes place in the rainforest, eg *Monkey Puzzle* (see 4.3), you can get the children to create a sound collage of the rainforest in the following way.

1 Ask the children to close their eyes and imagine the noises in the rainforest. Talk them through this softly, making sure that the language you use is comprehensible, eg *It's very hot and you can hear the rain – pitter, patter, pitter, patter. The wind is gently blowing through the trees – rustle, rustle, rustle, rustle. There is water in a stream splashing over the rocks – trickle, trickle, splash, splash. Insects are buzzing in the undergrowth – buzz, buzz, buzz – and birds are hooting in the trees.*

2 Explain to the children that in just a moment, you are going to ask them to make noises from the rainforest; the noise they choose should be loud enough for children around them to hear but not so loud that they can't hear other people's noises.

3 Give a cue to start the activity by saying, eg *Let's go to the rainforest now!* and softly shaking maracas, if you have these. Children start making their rainforest noises.

4 After a minute or so, stop shaking the maracas and say, eg *Let's leave the rainforest now!* Children stop making their noises and open their eyes. Give positive feedback (if deserved) on the atmosphere created.

Comments and suggestions

• Sound collage is a very powerful drama activity and you may be surprised at how convincingly the atmosphere of a rainforest is created. In order to work successfully, however, it is vital that children respect the convention of not making any noises apart from the ones in the drama. If you model taking the activity seriously, then the chances are that they will too.

• An alternative version of the activity is that instead of making sounds, children repeat words associated with the context in a whisper. For example, in a sound collage of the countryside different children could whisper the words *trees / birds / bees / flowers / sky / butterfly* etc. If children keep their eyes open during the sound collage, you or a child can pretend to be a character in the story and walk round the class. Children make their noises louder as you walk near them and softer as you move away.

• Simple, short drama activities like sound collages help children practise the kind of self-discipline and self-control needed for successful classroom drama and prepare them for doing longer, more complex activities as they become accustomed to using drama techniques.

4.21 Follow my leader

Level All **Age** 4–12 **Organization** whole class

Aims To listen and create a dramatic atmosphere related to a story through movement; to collaborate as a group; to practise self-discipline and self-control.

Language focus any, depending on the context

Materials *Essential:* none / *Optional:* a hat or scarf, music

Procedure

Use this activity in a similar way to 4.19.

1 If, for example, you are using the story *Monkey Puzzle,* show the children the front cover (see 4.3) and say, eg *Let's go to the rainforest and find the little monkey!*

2 Ask the children to stand up. Explain that they should follow you to the rainforest and copy your movements as closely as possible. Ask the children to either stand by their desks and do the actions on the spot or make a line behind you and move round the class.

3 Mime going through the rainforest to look for the little monkey and give a commentary to accompany your actions, eg *Let's walk along slowly and carefully, round the rock, under the branch of the tree and jump over the stream. Stop! Ssh! Oh, no! Listen! Sssssssss. I think it's a snake – look up in the tree. Quick! Let's go this way! Now look – I can see a tiger. Let's crouch down low. Make yourself very small – as small as you can.* End the mime by saying, eg *And look, here's the little monkey, sad and alone in the branch of the tree.*

Comments and suggestions

- As well as creating the atmosphere of a rainforest, this activity gives children an opportunity to listen to rich language input which is made comprehensible through mime. As with 4.19, it also practises the self-discipline and self-control needed for classroom drama.

- It is easier to manage the activity if children mime on the spot rather than move round the classroom, when they are likely to move at a different pace and may bump into each other. With very young children, it may be best to do the activity in a circle so that children can easily copy your movements (which will need to be simpler than those above) and you can monitor their response.

- A variation of this activity is to invite a child to be the leader and ask them to wear the leader's hat or scarf, if you have one. You may also like to play music to evoke the context or theme. Ask the rest of the class to stand in a line behind the leader. Set the context or theme, eg *You're walking along by the sea collecting shells!* Children follow the leader round the class, following his or her movements exactly. When you say *Change leader* the child at the front gives the hat or scarf to the next child in the line, making them the leader, and then goes to the back of the line. The mime continues, or you can change the context, with everyone following the movements of the new leader.

4.22 Copycats

Level All   **Age** 6–12   **Organization** pairs

Aims To mime a character and/or event in a story; to closely observe and copy a partner's movements; to collaborate in pairs.

Language focus present continuous, any vocabulary from the story

Materials *Essential:* none

Procedure

Use this activity once children are familiar with a story and possibly as a lead-in to a more elaborate drama activity, such as a role play (see 4.28).

1 Divide the class into pairs (A and B). Ask the children to stand side by side with their partner.

2 Explain that Child A should mime a character and/or event in the story that you say, and Child B should copy their partner's mime as closely as possible. Give an example, eg *Goldilocks is trying Baby Bear's porridge.* Demonstrate the mime yourself and encourage Child A in each pair to mime the character, actions and facial expressions as convincingly and with as much detail as they can, for their partner to copy. Get the children to change roles after each mime.

3 Give positive feedback to pairs who work well. Examples of other sentences you can use for *The Three Bears* story are: *Mummy Bear is making Porridge. / Daddy Bear is walking in the woods. / Baby Bear is playing in the woods. / Goldilocks is going into the three bears' house. / Goldilocks is trying Daddy Bear's chair.*

Comments and suggestions

- This activity focuses children's attention on specific characters and/or events in a story and encourages them to do mimes which are detailed and thoughtful.

- Miming events provides a useful way of recycling language from the story and helps to make this memorable. The 'copycat' technique also encourages children to work together cooperatively.

4.23 Story statues

Level All   **Age** 6–12   **Organization** pairs

Aims To create a 'statue' of a character at a specific moment in the story; to look at and identify other statues; to collaborate in pairs.

Language focus *be, Wh-* questions, present continuous, opinions, vocabulary from the story

Materials *Essential:* none

Procedure

1 Ask a child to the front of the class. Explain that you are going to make them into a 'statue' of a character in the story. Move the child into position so that they are standing smiling and slightly leaning over, as if they have got a basket on one arm and with the other arm taking something out of the basket to give to someone. Get the child to 'freeze' like a statue.

2 Ask the rest of the class to guess, eg T: *Who's this?* P: *I think it's Little Red Riding Hood.* T: *What's she doing?* P: *She's giving a present to her 'grandmother'.*

3 Divide the class into pairs (A and B).

4 Tell the children to choose another character and moment from the story and ask the Child As to make the Child Bs into a sculpture in the same way.

5 When the children are ready, ask the Child As to look at all the sculptures and guess the character and what they are doing.

6 Children then change roles and repeat the procedure.

Comments and suggestions

- This activity serves a similar purpose to 4.22 above. In choosing a character and specific moment in the story for their 'statues', it also encourages children to recall the story in detail.

4.24 Still images

Level All   **Age** 6–12   **Organization** groups, whole class

Aims To mime specific scenes from a story in still images; to use the still images to reconstruct and retell the story; to collaborate in groups.

Language focus present simple and any other language, depending on the story

Materials *Essential:* none / *Optional:* strips of paper with key scenes from the story (one for each group)

Procedure

1 Ask the children to think of the key scenes in the story and write a list of these on the board. For example, for *Little Red Riding Hood* (LRRH) these could be: *LRRH and her mother prepare the basket to take to her Granny. / LRRH meets the wolf in the forest. / The wolf goes to Granny's house. / The wolf eats Granny. / The wolf dresses up as Granny. / LRRH talks to her 'Granny' in bed. / The wolf attacks LRRH. / The woodcutter arrives to rescue LRRH and Granny just in time.*

2 Divide the class into groups of 3–4.

3 Assign a scene from the story to each group. Ask them to prepare a still image to depict their scene. Explain and demonstrate that, as well as the characters, children can mime being objects as part of their still image, eg trees in the forest. Set a time limit, eg 1–2 minutes, for children to prepare their scene.

4 When they are ready, explain that you are going to tell the story 'reading' the still images they have prepared.

5 Pretend that you have got a big book and explain that each group should show the still image of the scene they have prepared in the order of the story, as you mime turning over the pages and tell the story. For example, the first group shows their scene as you say: *Once upon a time there was a little girl who lived with her mother in a house in the forest. One day her mother said, 'Let's prepare a basket of food for you to take to Granny.' Little Red Riding Hood and her mother put some cake, bread, jam, biscuits and honey into the basket. Little Red Riding Hood said goodbye to her mother and set off.*

6 Mime turning the page of the imaginary big book, which is a signal for the first group to unfreeze and the second group to show their scene.

7 Continue in the same way till the end of the story.

8 Repeat the procedure, this time getting the children who are not showing their scene to join in or take turns telling the story with you.

Comments and suggestions

• This activity engages the children in actively reconstructing and retelling a familiar story. However, it also requires careful management and the 'freeze' control technique is very useful as children present their still images from the story.

• An alternative version of the activity is to give each group a strip of paper with a 'still image' to prepare. When they are ready, the groups take turns to present their still images in random order. The rest of the class identifies what's happening in each one and at the end orders them chronologically to tell the story.

4.25 Number story

Level A1.1, A1.2   **Age** 4–6   **Organization** whole class

Aims To listen to and act out a story with numbers; to practise counting; to develop physical coordination.

Language focus *In the example:* numbers, language from the story
Alternatives: language from any counting song or rhyme as a basis for the story (see 6.21 for examples)

Materials *Essential:* none / *Optional:* pictures of a Mummy duck and five baby ducks (see also 7.4 for a craft idea to practise counting)

Procedure

1 Introduce Mummy duck and the baby ducks either by holding up pictures, if you have prepared these, or drawing on the board.

2 Encourage the children to count the baby ducks with you. Say, eg *Mummy duck and the baby ducks like swimming in the pond* (draw this on the board). *Let's pretend to be ducks and walk to the pond!* Hold your head up like a duck and put your arms by your sides with your hands turned out as 'wings'. Walk along with your feet turned out and rolling from side to side as if you are a duck!

3 Get the children to do the same and follow you in a line round the classroom pretending to be ducks. Every few steps, stop, look round and say *Quack! Quack!* and get the children to join in.

4 Ask the children to sit down and tell them a story about the ducks based on the song *Five little ducks* (see 6.21). Remove the pictures of the baby ducks, or rub them off the board, as they disappear in the story, and bring them all back at the end: *One day five little ducks went swimming on the pond. Mummy duck was worried: Quack! Quack! Please come back! But only four little ducks came back. One, two, three, four. Poor Mummy duck, what bad luck! The next day four little ducks …* etc until: *The next day one little duck went swimming on the pond. Mummy duck was very, very worried: Quack! Quack! Please come back! And look! Five little ducks came back. One, two, three, four, five. Happy Mummy duck, what good luck!*

5 Choose six children to stand up and assign them the roles of Mummy duck and the five baby ducks. Tell the story again. Get the children to act it out, pretending to be ducks and walking away from and back to 'Mummy duck' as you tell the story. Be ready to gently prompt and move the 'ducks' in the right direction if necessary.

6 Encourage the whole class to join in counting the ducks with you each time and saying the two rhythmic refrains in the story: *Quack! Quack! Please come back!* and *Poor Mummy duck! What bad luck!*

7 Repeat the procedure with six different children.

Comments and suggestions

- The idea of telling children a simple story based on a traditional, counting song like *Five Little Ducks* can be applied to many different counting songs (see 6.21 for examples). The story can also prepare children for learning to sing the song. Through integrating stories and songs, and combining them with physical movement and drama, learning is made appealing and enjoyable.

- Repetitive refrains in stories for young children are often what they learn and remember most easily. Some of the language from these refrains, eg *Please come back!* and *What bad/good luck!* is also easily transferable to real life and can contribute to developing children's everyday classroom language in English.

- When acting out the story with very young children who are still in the process of developing spatial awareness, you may need to provide very close guidance as to when and where they should 'swim' and 'come back' to.

- When assigning roles, it may be a good idea to give the role of Mummy (or Daddy) duck to a child whose confidence you need to boost, as although s/he is the 'star' of the story, they don't need to move but just flap their 'wings' and look worried (and happy at the end).

4.26 Act out a story with puppets

Level A1.1, A1.2, A2.1, A2.2   **Age** 4–10   **Organization** pairs or groups (depending on the number of characters and structure of the story)

Aims To listen and act out a story with puppets; to manipulate puppets appropriately according to the story; to focus attention and develop concentration skills.

Language focus any, depending on the story

Materials *Essential:* puppets for characters in the story (see 7.12 for ideas for making puppets); a version of the story for acting out (one copy for your reference if this is different from the original story) / *Optional:* Cuisenaire rods or classroom objects to use instead of puppets, eg ruler, glue stick, pencil case

Procedure

Use this activity once the children are familiar with the story and confident about using key language it contains.

1 Get the children to make puppets prior to doing the activity (see 7.12). Alternatively, give out Cuisenaire rods or get the children to use classroom objects instead of puppets, for example, if you use the story *The Gruffalo*, a pencil case held vertically for the gruffalo, a rubber for the mouse.

2 Divide the class into groups of five. Assign a role to each child or let the children decide this in their groups. In the case of *The Gruffalo*, for example, children work in groups of five and the roles are gruffalo, fox, mouse, owl and snake.

3 Act out the story with the whole class, using different voices for the characters, and getting the children to move their puppets on their desks as they speak.

4 Get the children in each group to change roles and repeat the procedure. If the children are confident, ask them to act out the story independently in their groups.

Comments and suggestions

- For many children, using a puppet to act out a story makes them feel secure (as they can 'hide' behind the puppet) and therefore more willing to participate.

- The use of puppets provides a framework for turn-taking and the physical manipulation of the puppets during the story provides a focus for children to work together and stay attentive and engaged.

- Stories which are most suitable for acting out with puppets are ones which contain direct speech and repetitive discourse patterns. It also helps if there are short rhythmic refrains, such as, in the example of *The Gruffalo* story: *Ho! Ho! Ho! There is no gruffalo!*

- For stories like *The Gruffalo*, where the language of the original story may be beyond the children's productive competence, you will need to prepare a suitable version for the children to act out before doing the activity.

- As a follow-up to acting out a story with puppets, children can act out the story themselves, eg wearing character headbands or masks (see 7.13). You may also wish to turn the story into a class play (see 4.32) to perform for parents and carers and/or another class.

4.27 Hot seating

Level A2.1, A2.2, B1.1   **Age** 8–12   **Organization** whole class

Aims To ask relevant questions to someone playing the role of a character in the story; to think in more depth about a character and story, eg by considering moral issues

Language focus present simple, past simple, questions, any other language relevant to the story

Materials *Essential:* none

Procedure

Use this activity once children are familiar with the story and possibly as preparation for a role play (see 4.28).

1 Put an empty chair at the front of the class (the 'hot seat').

2 Ask the children what they know and think about the character in story you are planning to focus on, eg one of Cinderella's step-sisters. Explain that in just a moment they will have a chance to meet the character. Elicit the children's ideas and help them prepare questions they would like to ask, eg *Why were you horrible to Cinderella? Why didn't you clean the house? Are you jealous of Cinderella?* If appropriate, ask children to note the questions and/or write them on the board.

3 Explain to the children that as soon as you sit in the 'hot seat', you will become Cinderella's step-sister and you will stay as Cinderella's step-sister until you stand up again.

4 Start the activity by sitting down and, for example, looking a bit irritated and saying you haven't got much time and that the children had better ask their questions straight away. As children ask the questions they have prepared, respond in role as appropriate, depending on the children's level and age, and as far as possible in a way that encourages them to ask more questions and to express their opinions about the step-sister's behaviour towards Cinderella.

5 Stop the activity when the children run out of questions by saying, for example, that you're in a hurry now and must go. Stand up from the chair and become a teacher again!

6 Ask the children what they thought of Cinderella's step-sister and listen to their response. If you ask about her as though you weren't there at the time, children will readily enter into the fictional pretence and be willing to tell you what she was like and what she said.

Comments and suggestions

• In this activity, you play a central role which clearly models for the children the dramatic convention of taking on a different identity and role. There is no need for you to change your accent or voice; more important is to convey the attitude, opinions and personality of the character you are playing.

• As children become accustomed to the technique, it may be appropriate for them to try sitting in the 'hot seat' themselves. However, the challenge of this should not be underestimated and it is likely to need considerable guidance and preparation in terms of both content and language, even with older children and at higher levels.

• If you sense the children running out of questions when you are in the 'hot seat', it is a good idea to be ready to ask them some of your own, eg *What do you think I should do to help Cinderella now?*

4.28 Story role play

Level All   **Age** 6–12   **Organization** pairs or groups (depending on the role play)

Aims To prepare and do a role play between two or more characters in a story; to think and act creatively in relation to story characters and situations; to collaborate in pairs or groups.

Language focus *In the example:* greetings, be, have got, want to, like / don't like, family, activities
Alternatives: any, depending on the characters, story and role play

Materials *Essential:* none / *Optional:* puppets, role cards for each character, props

Procedure

1 Decide on the characters, situation and language of the role play children are going to do, eg 'A week after the story, Baby Bear invites Goldilocks round to play at his house' (see also 4.17).

2 Prepare children to do the role play by building up a possible dialogue with the whole class. Either do this by taking the part of one of the characters yourself and getting children to respond as the other character, or by asking the children to make suggestions for what both characters say. Encourage children to use any language they know in the role play and be ready to prompt or remind them of this if necessary, eg *Have you got a pet? Do you like music? Do you want to play on the computer? Are you hungry? Would you like a sandwich?*

3 If appropriate, you can also write question stems on the board for the children to use as prompts during the role play, eg *Have you got …? Do you like …?*

4 Divide the class into pairs and either assign or get the children to choose their roles.

5 Children act out the role play with their partner.

6 Children can then either change roles and repeat the role play and/or you can ask a few individual pairs to act out their role play to the class.

Comments and suggestions

- Story role plays give children an opportunity to use language in a freer way within a clearly defined context. Although children may be hesitant at first, as they grow accustomed to the technique they become increasingly willing to experiment in using language in creative ways to express their meanings. They also develop in confidence and self-esteem.

- With younger children, role plays are likely to be very short, eg 1–2 minutes. If pair work is not suitable, you can invite different children to take turns to do the role play to the whole class instead. Other children listen and clap at the end. You can also ask them questions about the content of each role play, eg *Does Baby Bear like football?*

- With older children and higher levels, you can vary the way you prepare for role plays, for example by using role cards. Children can use these as the basis for preparing what they will say in the role play in pairs. They then do the role play with a different partner who has prepared the other role. For example, a role play based on a visit by the wolf to Little Red Riding Hood's mother after the story could have the following role cards:

> 1 You are Little Red Riding Hood's mother. You are very angry with the wolf. Your daughter is scared to walk in the forest. Granny is scared to live alone. You also want money to pay for damage to Granny's house and clothes.

> 2 You are the wolf. You don't want to go to prison. You must say sorry to Little Red Riding Hood's mother. You pretend to be nice. In fact you are planning to eat Little Red Riding Hood's mother. You do not have any money. You refuse to pay for damage to Granny's house and clothes.

4.29 Story party

Level All   **Age** 8–12   **Organization** individual, whole class (mingling)

Aims To ask for and give personal information in the role of a story character; to develop confidence in turn-taking and using familiar language.

Language focus greetings, present simple, personal information, *like / don't like*, questions, opinions

Materials *Essential:* story character cards (one for each child), eg Gruffalo, Goldilocks, Robinson Crusoe

Procedure

Use this activity once children are familiar with lots of story characters, eg from the course book, picture books, graded readers or other sources.

1 Explain that the children are going to go to a 'party' in the role of a story character and meet different characters from other stories.

2 Give a story character card to each child and demonstrate and explain that they must keep this secret.

3 Ask them to invent and note some personal information for their character, eg their age, where they live, their family, sports or other things they like or don't like. Set a time limit for this, eg five minutes.

4 When they are ready, ask the children to stand up and go to the 'party' in role (without their notes) and try and meet and find out about as many characters as possible. Elicit the kinds of questions children will need to ask, eg *What's your name? Where do you live?* and demonstrate the activity with one or two children at the front of the class before they begin.

5 Stop the activity after the children have 'met' three or four other characters.

6 Ask individual children to take turns to report back on a character they met at the party and use this to establish all the characters who were there.

Comments and suggestions

- This activity can be made longer or shorter depending on the information you ask the children to exchange and find out at the 'party'. At the simplest level, children can just find out each others' names.

- If you feel it is necessary, you can say that the story characters only speak English and build in a rule that children should not say who they are or exchange information unless they are asked in English.

- If you do not want the children to walk round the classroom, they can remain seated and do the activity in pairs or groups.

4.30 Thought tunnel

Level All   **Age** 6–12   **Organization** whole class

Aims To make statements expressing opinions about a character and/or what they should do in the context of a story; to collectively explore issues or problems of a character in the story.

Language focus opinions, suggestions, *should*
Alternatives: any language related to the story

Materials *Essential:* none

Procedure

1 Ask the children to stand in two lines facing each other and to raise their arms high with the tips of their fingers touching to make the thought tunnel.

2 Choose a child to take on the role of the character who is to go through the thought tunnel.

3 Ask the rest of the class each to prepare a sentence either giving an opinion about the character, eg *You are a very bad wolf!* or suggesting what the character should do, eg (to Cinderella) *Why don't you run away?*

4 Ask the child who is the character to walk slowly through the thought tunnel in role. Get the children on either side of the thought tunnel to alternately say their sentence to the child as they pass by.

5 At the end, ask the child who has walked through the thought tunnel to comment briefly on the opinions and/or advice they heard.

Comments and suggestions

- This activity provides a controlled dramatic context for encouraging children to express opinions about characters and to think about problems and issues in the story. Although individually children only say one sentence, the collective outcome can be very rich.

- An alternative way of using a thought tunnel is for children to voice the internal thoughts in the mind of the character who is going through the tunnel. This is particularly appropriate to use to explore the feelings of a character at a moment of conflict or crisis in the story, eg for Cinderella, *I hate my sisters. I'm so tired. All I do is work. I love beautiful clothes. I want to go to the ball.*

- See also 10.2 for a version of this activity to develop children's confidence and self-esteem.

4.31 Bystander

Level A1.2, A2.1   **Age** 8–12   **Organization** whole class, pairs

Aims To retell a story or part of a story from the point of view of a bystander; to recycle language from the story.

Language focus *In the example:* present simple, parts of the body, adjectives of size, adjectives to describe animals
Alternatives: any, depending on the story

Materials *Essential:* picture of a 'bystander', eg in picture book of the story

Procedure

1   Create a context for a bystander to recount the story. For example, with the story of *The Gruffalo* (see 4.26) a description of the gruffalo could be recounted by a bird who had been sitting on a branch and watching everything.

2   Elicit the children's ideas for how the conversation might go, eg Bird: *Guess what? There's a gruffalo in the wood.* Friend: *A gruffalo? There's no such thing as a gruffalo.* Bird: *Oh, yes, there is.* Friend: *What's a gruffalo like?* Bird: *It's very big. It's brown and it's got big, orange eyes …*

3   Divide the class into pairs.

4   Children take turns to act out being a bystander in the story and recounting a description of the gruffalo to a friend. Encourage them to use their voices and facial expressions to convey their surprise and amazement about the gruffalo as they listen and recount the story.

5   If appropriate, you can also ask the children to write their conversations.

Comments and suggestions

• This activity provides a context for recycling language from a story in a way which lifts the children's voices and intonation since they are pretending to recount the story to somebody hearing it for the first time. This also helps to prepare them for recounting personal stories in an interesting way in real life.

• If you also teach children expressions such as *Guess what? / Can you believe this?* this helps them to make their bystander accounts of stories sound more spontaneous and natural.

4.32 Class play

Level All   **Age** 6–12   **Organization** whole class

Aims To prepare and act a class play over time based on a familiar story; to collaborate with others; to develop memory skills; to develop confidence and self-esteem.

Language focus *In the example:* language from the traditional story of *The Three Little Pigs*
Alternatives: any, depending on the play and story

Materials *Essential:* copies of the play (one for each child) (see example below) / *Optional:* simple props (eg headbands, see 7.13), costumes

Procedure

1   The preparation of a class play is best when it develops naturally out of a story that children have done lots of previous work on (see earlier activities in this section) and particularly enjoyed. This example is an adaptation of a traditional story.

2   Once roles are assigned, it is usually advisable to organize rehearsals over at least 3–4 weeks of lessons, practising different scenes with different children on different days for short periods, eg 5–10 minutes, either after more formal work has been completed, or while children not in the scene are engaged in other activities related to the play, eg making programmes or writing invitations (see 2.24).

3   As the day of performance gets near, you will probably need to devote at least two whole lessons to practise the whole performance including music, songs, costumes and props, in the place where the play is to be performed, if this is different from the children's classroom.

The Three Little Pigs

Scene 1

Narrator 1: Once upon a time, there were three little pigs. They lived with their mother.

Mother pig: Little pigs, you are big now. You must go.

Pig 1: Goodbye, Mummy.

Mother pig: Goodbye, little pig.

Pig 2: Goodbye, Mummy.

Mother pig: Goodbye, little pig.

Pig 3: Goodbye, Mummy.

Mother pig: Goodbye, little pig.

Everyone sings and dances:

We're off to build a beautiful, new house now
We're off to build a beautiful, new house now
We're off to build a house
A beautiful, new house
We're off to build a beautiful new house now.

(Sing to traditional tune 'If you're happy and you know it, clap your hands' and do a skipping dance.)

Scene 2

Pig 1: Hello, Mr Man. Please give me straw to build my house.

Man 1: Here you are, little pig.

Pig 1: Thank you. Goodbye.

Man 1: Goodbye.

Pig 2: Hello, Mr Man. Please give me sticks to build my house.

Man 2: Here you are, little pig.

Pig 2: Thank you. Goodbye.

Man 2: Goodbye.

Pig 3: Hello, Mr Man. Please give me bricks to build my house.

Man 3: Here you are, little pig.

Pig 3: Thank you. Goodbye.

Man 3: Goodbye.

Narrator 1: So the first little pig built his house of straw.

Narrator 2: And the second little pig built his house of sticks.

Narrator 3: And the third little pig built his house of bricks.

Scene 3

Narrator 1: One day the first little pig heard a knock at the door. It was the big, bad wolf.

Wolf: Little pig, little pig, let me in.

Pig 1: No! No! Not by the hair on my chinny chin chin I'll not let you in!

Wolf: Then I'll huff and I'll puff and I'll blow your house in.

Narrator 2: So the wolf huffed and he puffed and he blew the house in.

Narrator 3: And the first little big ran to his brother's house.

Everyone sings and dances:

Ha, ha, ha, hee, hee, hee
We're not afraid of the big, bad wolf
Ha, ha, ha, hee, hee, hee
We're not afraid of the big, bad wolf.

(Sing to traditional tune of 'Little, brown jug'.)

Scene 4

Narrator 1: One day the second little pig heard a knock at the door. It was the big, bad wolf.

Wolf: Little pig, little pig, let me in.

Pig 2: No! No! Not by the hair on my chinny chin chin I'll not let you in!

Wolf: Then I'll huff and I'll puff and I'll blow your house in.

Narrator 2: So the wolf huffed and he puffed and he blew the house in.

Narrator 3: And the first little big and the second little pig ran to their brother's house.

Everyone sings and dances:

Ha, ha, ha, hee, hee, hee
We're not afraid of the big, bad wolf
Ha, ha, ha, hee, hee, hee
We're not afraid of the big, bad wolf.

(Sing to traditional tune of 'Little, brown jug'.)

Scene 5

Narrator 1: One day the third little pig heard a knock at the door. It was the big, bad wolf.

Wolf: Little pig, little pig, let me in.

Pig 3: No! No! Not by the hair on my chinny chin chin I'll not let you in!

Wolf: Then I'll huff and I'll puff and I'll blow your house in.

Narrator 2: So the wolf huffed and he puffed and he huffed and he puffed…

Narrator 3: But he couldn't blow the house in.

Narrator 1: All was quiet.

Pig 1: He's gone.

Pig 2: No, he's coming.

Pig 3: Quick! I've got some water. Let's put it under the chimney.

Pig 1: Here he comes!

Pig 2: I can see his foot.

Pig 3: I can see his body.

Pig 1: I can see his head.

Narrator 2: The big, bad wolf fell into the pot.

Narrator 3: The big, bad wolf ran far, far away.

Narrator 1: The three little pigs never saw the big, bad wolf again.

Narrator 3: And they lived happily ever after.

Everyone sings and dances:

Ha, ha, ha, hee, hee, hee
We're not afraid of the big, bad wolf
Ha, ha, ha, hee, hee, hee
We're not afraid of the big, bad wolf.

(Sing to traditional tune of 'Little, brown jug'.)

THE END

Comments and suggestions

- If, for religious reasons, it is not suitable to use a play based on the traditional story of *The Three Little Pigs,* then you can easily change this to, eg three little lambs or three little goats instead.

- When adapting a story into a play for younger age groups, it is usually a good idea to include short songs, rhymes and dance routines if possible. This adds variety and interest to the performance and also helps children to remember their lines.

- When assigning roles, it is important to ensure that every child has a part and that these are more or less evenly distributed. In *The Three Little Pigs* play, for example, depending on the size of the class, different children can play the parts of the pigs and the narrators in each scene.

- You will probably also need to do some judicious casting, eg to ensure that shy children have a role which does not feel threatening. This can sometimes be tricky and needs to be planned carefully and handled sensitively. In *The Three Little Pigs* play, for example, some children may only join in the songs and dances done by everyone, and yet still be made to feel that they have a significant role.

- It is a good idea to give children their own copy of the play and either highlight their lines or get them to do this. Children will usually memorize their part in a short play naturally as part of rehearsals. It may nevertheless be a good idea to allow the narrators to keep copies of the play during the performance, even if they know their parts – just in case, in order to keep things on track.

- Through rehearsals and the process of preparing a play, children are exposed to and acquire a lot of language outside their normal syllabus in a spontaneous and natural way. For example, children quickly understand the phrases you use to direct them, eg *Try and speak a bit louder please! Look up! Show me you're very, very frightened of the wolf!* and even begin to use parts of these, eg *Louder!* as part of their own productive repertoire.

- In addition to rehearsals, children can also do a craft activity and make piggy noses and headbands to wear in the play (see 7.13).

- Although the challenge of preparing a play with young children should not be underestimated, it is also extremely rewarding. After all the excitement and nerves on the day, you can almost see the children grow in confidence and self-esteem as a result of their performance (however low-key and modest) and the parental pride that this usually invokes. In the longer term, doing a class play can also have an extremely bonding effect on the class as a group – and they may well ask to do a play based on every story you do from now on!

- If you wish to prepare a performance for parents with children in the 4–6 age range, it is usually advisable to base this on singing and acting out a selection of songs and rhymes (see Section 6 for ideas), rather than a play, which may put too much emphasis on individual performance.

Section 5 **Games**

Games are the stuff of life in the primary classroom. As well as providing stimulation, variety, interest and motivation, they help to promote positive attitudes towards learning English. They also encourage active participation and boost children's confidence and self-esteem. Far from being peripheral or used on an occasional basis, games are an essential, integral part of children's language learning. At the same time, however, the use of games comes with a 'health warning', especially with large classes or in contexts where children are not used to playing games to learn in other subjects. In order to have the intended language benefits and achieve desired learning outcomes, games need to be selected, set up and managed with great care.

Characteristics of games

Games share many characteristics of other primary classroom activities. They may be multi-sensory and involve movement. They may develop a range of different social, cognitive and language skills. They may be played using a variety of different interaction patterns. Games also have specific outcomes and goals, for example, to remain in the game as long as you can, or to reach the last square of a board game first. The fact that the goals of many games are non-linguistic engages children naturally in using English as a vehicle to achieve the goal, rather than practising language for its own sake.

Games are above all enjoyable and fun, and this is both the source of their appeal and what makes them potentially hard to manage, especially if children do not perceive them as part of 'real work'. Games also have rules which need to be adhered to if they are to function successfully. From the point of view of classroom management, this is a major advantage, since children are usually much more willing to adhere to rules that are an intrinsic part of a game, rather than other kinds of rules.

In addition to rules, another defining characteristic of games is the existence of some kind of contest. This may be either a contest between the players, in which case the game is competitive, or a contest between the players and the goal, in which case the game is cooperative.

Different games may also contain a different balance between skill, eg whether the player is able to answer the question in the game correctly, and luck, eg whether they throw a two or a six on the dice. This balance between skill and luck influences the process and outcome of games. It may also be an important factor to consider when selecting games which homogenize rather than accentuate the different abilities of individual children.

Although competitive games are not suitable for very young children, you need to weigh up carefully the pros and cons of using them in the later primary years. It is certainly the case that healthy competition between children can be very motivating. Competition is also an undeniable fact of real life and, as part of their overall personal and social development, children need to recognize that 'a game is only a game' and learn to be 'good losers'. At the same time, however, competitive games tend to bring out the worst in children and can lead to over-excitement, or even aggression, and this may make them difficult to manage, especially if you have a large class. You also need to consider the behaviour implications of competitive games if, for example, as part of the rules children are eliminated or 'out' of the game. If children are excluded and no longer involved in a game, it will not be very surprising if they become bored or disruptive and seek attention in other ways. With competitive games, there is also the danger of always having the same 'winners' and 'losers' and the consequent negative impact that this is likely to have on some children's motivation, confidence and self-esteem.

Selecting and adapting games

When selecting and/or adapting games to use in class, it is frequently possible to address the potential drawbacks of competitive games by making a small shift in the rules to turn what is potentially a competitive game into a cooperative one. In musical or action games, where children are traditionally made 'out', you can introduce a system of 'lives' instead and end the game before any child has lost all their 'lives' in order to maintain the participation of everyone till the end. In memory games, where children repeat and add to what others have said, you can, for example, introduce a rule whereby, instead of being eliminated, children can call on others to 'help'. At the end, you can then count up how many things they have remembered collaboratively. Another solution for some games is to organize them so that children are cooperating within groups or teams, at the same time as competing against other groups or teams, in order to win. This kind of organization keeps a motivating, competitive edge to the game but defuses the potential problem of competition between individual children. It also allows you to place an emphasis on the value of the process of participation and collaboration between children during the game, rather than winning as such.

Learning through games

Young children have a natural tendency to express themselves and find out about their world through play and this can provide positive foundations for learning a foreign language too. Through games and directed play (as opposed to free play), children can be given initial opportunities to recognize and respond to language non-verbally. They can also produce chunks of language, in contexts which require enjoyable repetition and which draw them into using English in a natural and spontaneous way. With very young children, the use of games and directed play provides a familiar context for encountering new language, and acts as a bridge between home and school in much the same way as storytelling (see Section 4) and learning rhymes, songs and chants (see Section 6).

Games and directed play allow for holistic learning and the integrated physical, social, emotional and cognitive development of young children. As well as developing language skills, games and directed play help to develop young children's social skills, such as showing willingness to cooperate and take turns, listening to others and learning to follow and respect the rules of a game. In games which involve actions or movement, they also help to develop physical coordination and psychomotor skills, while other games develop skills such as children's visual-spatial awareness, creative thinking or numeracy. In addition to this, games and directed play allow for divergent responses and also have an important role in developing young children's concentration and memory skills, as well as their ability to associate language and meaning with actions, pictures, objects and sounds.

Given that very young children are still egocentric and have only recently embarked on the whole process of socialization at school, the most suitable games for language lessons tend to be ones which the whole class play together (although an exception to this is if you have an 'English corner' in the classroom where there are also games available for independent play). With young children, you need to lead and direct games, especially at first, demonstrating and modelling the processes and responses involved in a very explicit way. As children develop familiarity and confidence in playing the game, however, they can increasingly lead or take over more of the game themselves, while you continue to supervise but play a less directing role.

As children move up through primary school, it is unrealistic to expect them to be willing or able to interact and play games in English in pairs and groups without training them. The use of simple games such as, for example, picture card games (see 5.12), guessing games (see 5.17) or board games (see 5.28, 5.29) provides frameworks which encourage children to practise interacting and taking turns in ways which are purposeful and also involve other cognitive skills, such as strategic thinking, visual observation, memorization and logical deduction. The regular use of such games also helps children to build up and transfer the interactive skills they are developing to everyday communication in the classroom.

In order for children to understand the language learning value of games and recognize that these are 'real work', it is important to explicitly state the reasons for playing specific games, for example, when setting lesson objectives, eg *We're going to play a guessing game in order to practise asking and answering questions about food*, and to encourage children to reflect on these themselves when reviewing learning, eg *Why did we play the guessing game?* This can be either in L1 or English (see Section 10 Learning to learn). If children are aware of the reasons for playing games, they are much more likely to make an effort to use English when working independently in pairs and groups and to recognize the learning benefits of this.

There are many different types of games included in this section. In addition to the games mentioned above, these include, for example, name games (5.1), mime and drama games (5.2, 5.5), feely bag games (5.4), playground games (5.10, 5.11), games for getting into pairs or groups (5.7), musical games (5.9), spelling games (5.15), word games (5.14, 5.16), team games (5.16, 5.20, 5.26), revision games (5.19, 5.20), dice games (5.21) and drawing games (5.27). As children become more confident in using English and cooperating with others, you can continually extend and add to the repertoire of games you regularly use in class. These can include games which make a range of different language and/or cognitive demands, eg reading coordinates in a grid (5.23). If appropriate, you can also involve children in designing and creating their own games for others to play (see 5.30).

Tips for playing games

When setting up games in class, it may be useful to refer to the general points about classroom management (see Introduction pp.12–15). Some other general tips for playing games with children are as follows:

- Go for simplicity! It's often the simplest games that 'work' the best, especially in large classes.

- Make sure that all the children are involved all the time (even if not directly).

- Make sure you know how the game works yourself before getting the children to play it!

- Give clearly staged instructions and demonstrate and/or model playing the game. Play with the whole class first.

- Teach children interactive language for playing the game, if appropriate, eg *It's my/your turn* and encourage them to use it.

- Be fair and firm about enforcing rules (children expect and want this).

- If children are playing the game independently, circulate and monitor. At the same time, however, give children space to experiment and to show that they can play the game responsibly on their own.

- Stop the game while the children are still 'on task' and before they begin to lose interest.

- Familiarize the children with the names of games you play regularly to reduce the need for instructions.

- Keep favourite games, or games children have made themselves, at hand for independent play by fast finishers, or for whenever there are a few minutes to spare in the lesson.

Reflection time

As you use the games in this section with your classes, you may like to think about the following questions and use your responses to evaluate how things went and plan possible improvements for next time.

1 **Setting up the game:** Were the rules and goals of the game clear to the children? Did they understand what to do? If yes, how did you achieve this? If no, how could you make this clearer next time?

2 **Interaction pattern:** How did the children play the game – in pairs, groups, teams or the whole class together? How did this affect their motivation, involvement and language performance?

3 **Competition vs cooperation:** Was the game competitive, cooperative or a mixture of both? How did this effect the children's response?

4 **Classroom management:** Were you able to manage the game positively and effectively? What helped – or hindered – you to do this? Are there any changes you would make next time?

5 **Appeal of the game:** In what way(s) did the game appeal to the children? Can you learn from this for planning other activities?

6 **Language and learning benefits:** What were the apparent language and learning benefits of playing the game? How do these compare with other types of classroom activities you use?

5.1 Name games

Level All   **Age** 4–12   **Organization** whole class

Aims To introduce yourself and say your name; to give personal information; to create a positive socio-affective learning climate with a new class.

Language focus Greetings, *I'm … / My name's …*, personal information

Materials *Essential:* none / *Optional:* a soft ball, a puppet

Procedure

Use one or more of the following games when you start teaching a new class, to give the children an opportunity to introduce themselves and you an opportunity to learn their names.

5.1a Roll the ball (age 4–6)

Children sit in a circle on the floor. Say your name: *I'm …* . Roll the ball to any child in the circle. Encourage them to say their name in the same way and roll the ball back to you. Repeat with different children in random order until everyone has said their name.

5.1b Say hello to the puppet (age 4–6)

Children sit in a circle on the floor. Move the puppet towards one child and say *Hello. I'm …* . Encourage the child to respond *Hello, …* (naming the puppet). *I'm …* . Repeat with different children in random order until everyone has said hello to the puppet.

5.1c Silly puppet (age 4–6)

Pretend the puppet has a bad memory and needs help to remember the children's names. Children supply the names and say *Silly puppet!* eg T: *Hello, um, um um …* . P: *David! Silly …!* (naming the puppet)

5.1d Clap the names (age 4–8)

Children sit in a circle or stay at their desks. Clap twice using a strong, even rhythm and say *I'm …* . Clap twice again and the next child says *I'm …* , keeping the rhythm. Continue round the class, getting the children to alternately clap twice and say their names in a rhythmic way until everyone has introduced themselves.

5.1e Throw the ball (age 8–12)

Children stand in a circle. Say *I'm …. What's your name?* and throw the ball to a child. That child then says their name, asks the question and throws the ball to another child, and so on, until everyone has introduced themselves. If children already know each other, miss out asking the question.

5.1f Introductions chain (age 8–12)

Children stand or sit in a circle. Say, eg *My name's … and I like … (dogs)*. Accompany this with a mime, eg pretending to stroke a dog. The child next to you says *This is … and she likes dogs.* (everyone joins in repeating the mime) *I'm … and I like football.* (and adds a mime of their own, eg kicking a ball). Continue in the same way round the circle, getting the children to repeat the sentences and mimes until everyone has introduced themselves. If a child can't remember what others have said, they say *Help!* rather than go out of the game and other children respond. If you have a large class, children can do the activity in two or three groups.

Comments and suggestions

- Learning first names as soon as possible is a golden rule for any teaching, and with children it is particularly important for creating a positive socio-affective climate and managing the class effectively.

- In many situations, children will already know each others' names and you will be the only person not familiar with these. If this is the case, avoid activities which artificially get the children to ask each other their names when they already know the answer.

- In addition to name games, see also ideas for a name rap (6.3) and making name cards (7.1) and children's portraits (9.1) to help you remember children's names when you start teaching a class for the first time.

5.2 Abracadabra!

Level A1.1   **Age** 4–6   **Organization** whole class

Aims To show understanding through mime and physical response; to develop physical coordination.

Language focus *In the example:* animals, numbers 1–3, *be*
Alternatives: present continuous, food, actions

Materials *Essential:* none / *Optional:* improvized magic wand, eg ruler; witch puppet or hat

Procedure

1 Teach the children simple mimes to go with a familiar lexical set such as animals. For example, for *frog* children jump, for *cat* children make ears with their hands, for *duck* children make a beak with their hands.

2 Hold up the witch puppet or put on the witch's hat, if you have one, or wave your 'magic wand'. Explain that you're the witch and you're going to make spells to change the children into different animals. Say the following in a rhythmic way.

    Abracadabra! Listen to me!
    You're a …(frog/cat/duck)!
    One! Two! Three!

3 As you name the animal in line 2, turn away from the children and pretend to close your eyes as you count to three. Explain and demonstrate that children should mime the animal you name as you do this. As soon as you get to three, open your eyes and turn round suddenly. Look at the class and say, eg *Fantastic! The witch's magic works! What a lot of lovely frogs!*

4 Explain that every time the spell works perfectly, ie all the children respond by doing the mime you say, the class scores a point.

5 Say different spells, speeding up the time you give children to respond as they become familiar with the game.

6 Keep a score of the class's points on the board and count them up at the end.

Comments and suggestions

- Very young children love the element of 'magic' in this game. The more surprised and amazed you make your response at their ability to change into different animals and that the 'spell' has 'worked', the more enthusiastic their participation will be!

- Once the children are familiar with the game, you can ask individual children to take turns to come and be the witch, or the witch's helper, and say the rhyme with you and/or name the animal in line 2.

- This game can also be used with the present continuous and actions, eg *You're swimming!* or food, eg *You're eating a banana!*

5.3 Pass the secret!

Level A1.1, A1.2 **Age** 4–6 **Organization** whole class

Aims To listen to and whisper instructions (or words); to show understanding by responding to instructions (or words); to take turns following a prescribed order.

Language focus *In the example:* imperatives, actions
Alternatives: any familiar vocabulary, adjectives of feeling (eg *happy, sad, angry, scared*), numbers

Materials *Essential:* none / *Optional:* puppet, flashcards or objects, keys (or other object)

Procedure

1 Get the children to sit in a circle.

2 If you have a puppet, use it to whisper a secret instruction to one child, eg *Jump to the door!* Explain and demonstrate that the child should whisper the instruction to the child next to them clockwise, and so on round the circle. If you like, use the puppet to emphasize that the instruction should be kept as secret as possible until it gets to the last child in the circle.

3 The last child then says the instruction out loud and does the action. The puppet and all the other children clap and say eg *Hurray!* or *Fantastic!* if they do this correctly.

4 Repeat several times, starting with different children and using different instructions.

Comments and suggestions

- This game encourages children to listen attentively, speak (whisper) clearly and take turns in an orderly way. The two alternative versions below also develop physical coordination and concentration skills.

- Instead of instructions, the puppet can whisper a secret word to a child in the circle. In this case, stick flashcards of familiar vocabulary items on the board or arrange objects on your desk before the game. Children whisper one of the words, eg *Umbrella!* round the circle. The last child says the word and finds the flashcard on the board or object on your desk.

- An alternative version of the game to practise adjectives of feeling is 'Pass the feeling'. In this game, bring your hand down over your face as if it is a mask, give a big smile and say *I'm happy*. Mime passing the 'mask' to the child next to you, who pretends to put it on, makes a sad face and says *I'm sad*, and so on round the circle, either using just *happy/sad* or any other adjectives of feeling they know.

- An alternative version of the game to practise counting is 'Pass the keys' (or any other object you have available). In this game, children clap and count rhythmically to five, emphasizing the beat on the count of one, and passing the keys from child to child around the circle every time they say 'one', eg <u>One</u>, *two, three, four, five.* <u>One</u>, *two, three, four, five.*

5.4 Feely bag games

Level A1.1, A1.2, A2.1 **Age** 4–10 **Organization** whole class

Aims To guess what's in a bag; to identify objects from touch; to focus children's attention on a central point.

Language focus opinions, *Is there …? Have you got …?,* classroom objects, adjectives to describe size, texture and shape, materials, *made of,* any familiar vocabulary

Materials *Essential:* a feely bag (ie non-transparent drawstring bag, eg shoe bag or bread bag), items to put in the bag

Procedure

Use a feely bag to play one or more of the following games with the whole class.

5.4a Identify the objects

1 Put either cardboard silhouettes, toys, plastic food or real objects in a bag.

2 Children take turns to put their hand in the bag, feel one of the objects and guess what it is, eg *I think it's a banana!* Ask the rest of the class, *Do you think he/she's right?* before the child takes the object out of the bag to check.

3 Encourage everyone to clap and say, eg *Fantastic!* if they have identified the object correctly.

5.4b Guess what's in the bag

1 Before playing the game, choose 8–10 familiar objects and put them in the feely bag without the children seeing.

2 Show the children the bag and shake it up and down. Explain that they have got twenty guesses to find out what's in it, eg *Is there a rubber in the bag?*

3 Keep a record of the number of questions asked on the board.

4 When the children guess an object correctly, take it out of the bag. The children win if they find out all the contents in fewer than twenty guesses.

5.4c Find an object which ...

1 Before playing the game, choose 8–10 objects of different shapes, sizes and textures, eg a coin, stone, button, feather, piece of felt, piece of cotton wool, and put them in the feely bag without the children seeing.

2 Give children instructions in turn by saying, eg *Find an object which is round, hard and made of metal.* Children identify the object you have described by touch alone and say what they think it is, eg *a coin.* They then take it out of the bag to check.

Comments and suggestions

- A feely bag is a very useful basic resource to have to hand in primary teaching and children enjoy guessing and identifying objects by touch in short games such as the above.

- As individual children put their hand in the feely bag to guess or find an object, you need to use strategies to keep the rest of the class engaged, eg as described in 5.4a above.

- Feely bags can also be used in games where children have to choose a card at random or, for example, for collecting class votes.

- With younger children, a feely bag may also be the same bag where the class puppet lives, if you use one. As part of opening and closing lesson routines, children can call for the puppet to come out of the bag at the start of lessons and say goodbye when the puppet goes back into the bag at the end.

5.5 Jumping beans

Level A1.1   **Age** 5–7   **Organization** whole class

Aims To listen and respond with actions; to develop physical coordination; to let off physical energy; to cooperate with others.

Language focus beans (eg *jumping, runner, jelly, baked, coffee, broad, string*)

Materials *Essential:* none / *Optional:* examples or pictures of different types of beans

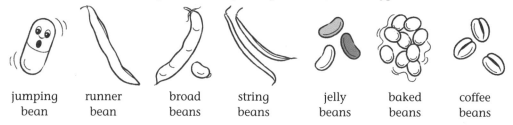

| jumping bean | runner bean | broad beans | string beans | jelly beans | baked beans | coffee beans |

Procedure

1 Show the children examples or pictures of different kinds of beans, if you have these, or draw some beans on the board. If you like, ask the children *Are you full of beans?* and use mime to convey that this means 'Are you full of energy?' If the children say yes, say *Then let's play jumping beans!*

2 Ask the children to stand up and demonstrate the following actions for the game: for 'jumping beans' children should jump up and down; for 'runner beans' they should run on the spot; for 'jelly beans' they should pretend to shiver; for 'baked beans' they should cuddle together in groups (the exact number doesn't matter); for 'broad beans' they should hold out their arms to make themselves look broad; for 'string beans' they should hold hands with others and stand in a line (again the exact number doesn't matter); for 'coffee beans' they should pretend to drink a cup of coffee.

3 Call out the names of the different kinds of beans in random order and children respond by doing the actions. Be ready to do these with the children at first.

4 Repeat and either increase the speed and/or stop doing the actions yourself as the children respond more confidently.

Comments and suggestions

- Children love the physical movement in this game and will often ask to play it again and again! It can also be very useful to use if you sense children need to let off physical energy or you wish to change the pace and mood of a lesson, eg after they have worked quietly completing an activity sheet.

- In order to manage the game positively, it may be useful to use the 'freeze' control technique (see 4.19). You can also introduce 'sleepy beans' as the final instruction in the game, to which children respond by lying down and pretending to go to sleep. This settles the children before moving on to the next activity.

- With younger children, it is advisable not to introduce all the beans and actions at once. If you play the game on repeated occasions, you can start by teaching them the actions for, eg three beans, and then add a new one each time you play.

- This activity can also be linked to growing a bean seed in 8.8.

5.6 Hopscotch

Level A1.1 **Age** 4–6 **Organization** whole class

Aims To practise counting; to identify familiar objects and vocabulary; to develop physical coordination; to develop confidence in participating in a game in English.

Language focus numbers 1–8, action words, *jump, hop,* any familiar vocabulary

Materials *Essential:* tape or chalk, objects, picture cards or flashcards, a bean bag or other soft item to throw (not a ball)

Procedure

1 Use chalk or tape to make hopscotch squares (approximately 50 cms x 40 cms) in a row on the floor. Number the squares 1–8.

2 Place a familiar object or flashcard in the top left corner of each square.

3 Explain and demonstrate that children should take turns to throw the bean bag onto one of the squares.

They then hop (on the single squares) and jump, landing on both feet (onto the double squares) to number 8 and back down again to the square where the bean bag has landed. They then name the flashcard or object on the square, eg *It's a teddy bear!*, pick up the bean bag and hop or jump out of the hopscotch squares.

4 As each child has a turn, the rest of the class watch. They count the squares in chorus with you as the child goes up the hopscotch eg *One, two, three, four* and chant eg *Hop, Jump*, (depending on the square), *Stop!* (while the child picks up the bean bag and names the object or flashcard) and *Out!* as they jump out of the last square on the way back. If you like, you can encourage the children to clap and say, eg *Fantastic!* after every turn.

Comments and suggestions

• This is an adaptation of a traditional game which children may already know. Through counting the squares and chanting, children are drawn into using language naturally as they participate in watching and playing the game.

• With very young children, it is better to play with fewer hopscotch squares, eg four, in a straight line. Children jump from square to square rather than hop.

• If you have space in the classroom to leave the hopscotch squares set up, you can play the game regularly using different vocabulary or have a routine over a few weeks whereby two or three children have a turn to play at the end of each lesson.

5.7 Get into groups!

Level All   **Age** 5–12   **Organization** whole class

Aims To listen and follow instructions to make groups; to move to music.

Language focus *In the examples:* numbers (5.7a), colours, *have got* (5.7b)
Alternatives: any familiar vocabulary

Materials *Essential:* none / *Optional:* dance music, different coloured sticky paper notes, small picture cards of vocabulary from different lexical sets

Procedure

Use either of the following games to get the children to form groups.

5.7a Five in a hug

1 Demonstrate the meaning of *hug*. Ask the children to stand up and tip-toe around the classroom space as quietly as they can without touching anyone else. When you say, eg *Five in a hug!* explain and demonstrate that children should form groups of five as fast as they can by standing in a circle with their arms round each other.

2 Repeat several times calling different numbers.

3 At the end, call the number of the size groups you want for the next activity, eg *Four in a hug!* (or *Two in a hug!* if you want pairs).

4 As an option, if you have music, children can dance before you pause and call the number each time.

5.7b Colours together

1 Before the game, prepare sets of different coloured sticky paper notes for the size and number of groups you want, eg for a class of twenty to get into groups of four, you need five sets of four sticky paper notes of different colours, eg yellow, pink, blue, orange, green.

2 Give a sticky paper note to each child and get them to stick it on their chest.

3 When all the children are ready, ask them to stand up and get into groups of the same colour. Encourage them to say, eg *I've got pink!* / *Me too!* as they do this.

4 In the next activity, you can refer to the groups by their colours, eg the pink group, the yellow group.

Comments and suggestions

- Short games such as the above provide variety in the way you get the children to form groups (or pairs). In 5.7a, groups are formed randomly, whereas in 5.7b, you can predetermine the composition of the groups by deciding which children to give different coloured stickers to. If you wish, for example, to mix ability levels or avoid putting certain children together, then a game such as 5.7b will be more suitable.

- Alternative versions to 5.7b include giving the children either small picture cards with vocabulary from different familiar lexical sets, eg animals, food, or small pieces of paper with different numbers. Children then form groups depending on the picture card or number they have got.

- A similar game to form pairs with older children and higher levels is to give out pairs of word cards, either with words that go together, eg *salt/pepper, fish/chips, cat/mouse* or opposites, eg *big/small, high/low, long/short,* and children form pairs depending on the word they have got.

5.8 Fox and rabbits

Level A1.1   **Age** 4–7   **Organization** whole class

Aims To practise repeating familiar vocabulary and a simple language chunk rhythmically in chorus; to develop physical coordination.

Language focus *In the example:* present continuous, *fox, rabbit, Hurry!*
Alternatives: any other animal vocabulary, eg *wolf/hen, cat/mouse* and suitable chunks, eg *Quick! Quick! The cat can't catch you!*

Materials *Essential:* none / *Optional:* a sock or handkerchief

Procedure

1 Get the children to sit in a circle making sure there is plenty of room to walk round behind them.

2 Walk round the circle tapping each child gently on the head and saying *Rabbit!* as you pass. Encourage the children to join in, repeating the word with you.

3 After about six children, tap the next child on the head and say *Fox!* Demonstrate and explain that the child who you name as 'fox' should stand up and walk as fast as possible after you round the circle until you get back to their place and sit down. As you walk fast round the circle away from the 'fox', say, eg *Hurry! Hurry! The fox is coming* and repeat this in a rhythmic way, encouraging all the children to join in.

4 The child who is the fox then has the next turn walking round the circle and naming the rabbits and fox with everyone participating in the same way. Repeat the game several times.

Comments and suggestions

- This game provides a natural context for choral repetition and promotes active participation by all the children.

- For safety reasons, it is advisable to insist on children walking, rather than running, after each other round the circle.

- An alternative version of the game can be played with a sock or handkerchief. As you walk round the circle, put the sock or handkerchief behind one child. Get that child to stand up, pick up the sock and walk after you round the circle until you get back to their place and sit down. As you walk round the circle, say rhythmically, eg *Hurry, Jenny! Hurry, Jenny!* and get the children to join in. The child with the sock then has the next turn walking round the circle.

5.9 Musical instructions

Level A1.1, A1.2   **Age** 4–10   **Organization** whole class

Aims To listen and move to music and respond to instructions as fast as you can; to follow and respect the rules of the game; (to develop awareness that participating in a game is more important than winning).

Language focus *In the example:* imperatives, parts of the body, colours
Alternatives: be, jobs, present continuous, actions, *have got* or any other suitable language

Materials *Essential:* a lively music CD

Procedure

1 Ask the children to stand up and move to a space in the classroom without furniture.
2 Play the CD and encourage the children to dance.
3 Pause the music and give an instruction, eg *Touch your toes! / Touch something blue!* The last one or two children to follow the instruction are out. They then help you either to give instructions and/or to identify which children should be out each time.
4 The last child still in the game is the winner.

Comments and suggestions

- This game allows for non-verbal responses to language. It is easy to organize and frequently a favourite, particularly with younger children.

- It is up to you to decide whether it is appropriate to make the game competitive or not. Although children need to learn not to mind losing in a game, you also need to consider the potentially disruptive effect of children who are 'out' and no longer involved. With younger children, it is usually best to let everyone continue participating whether they are last to follow the instruction you give or not. Alternatively, you can introduce a system of, eg three 'lives' and ensure that no-one has lost all their lives by the time the game ends.

- In addition to the basic procedure above, you can also use the following variations:

   Musical statues: when you pause the music, say, eg *You're a painter!* or *You're playing a computer game!* Children respond by 'freezing' in a mime to show what you say.

   Musical bumps: when you pause the music, say, eg *Everybody who has got blues eyes!* Those children sit on the floor as fast as they can.

5.10 Big, brown bears

Level A1.1   **Age** 4–7   **Organization** whole class

Aims To listen and respond to language in a playground game; to follow and respect the rules of a game; to use English as a natural vehicle for play.

Language focus *be,* numbers, *big*
Alternatives: any other animals and adjectives, eg *fierce, hungry lion*

Materials *Essential:* none

Procedure

Play this game in the playground or gym.

1 Divide the children into four groups.
2 Ask each group to stand in a different corner of the play area. Choose one child to be the big, brown bear. Get the bear to say *I'm a big, brown bear. One ... two ... three!*
3 As soon as the bear says ... *three!* all the children must run and change corners, and the bear tries to catch them.
4 The first child to be caught becomes the bear in the next round of the game.

5 Alternatively, any children caught become bears so that, with each round of the game, there are more and more bears and fewer children to catch. In this case, the last child to be caught by bears is the winner.

Comments and suggestions

- This game involves children playing in English outside the context of the classroom. Once children are familiar with the game, you may find that they choose to play it independently in break times. This gives them a sense of 'ownership' of language as well as a sense of achievement.

- You can increase the language children use in the game as appropriate, eg the bears can count up to ten and say *I'm a big, brown bear. I'm very hungry. And I'm going hunting now ...* and the children can say, eg *Please don't catch me, bear!* as they run away each time.

- If you like, you may wish to make the point that wild animals such as bears are dangerous and that it is important to keep a safe distance from them in real life, eg when visiting a zoo or safari park.

5.11 Can I cross your river, Mr Crocodile?

Level A1.2, A2.1, A2.2   **Age** 7–10   **Organization** whole class

Aims To ask permission and respond according to the reply in a playground game; to follow and respect the rules of a game.

Language focus *can* (for permission), *if,* present continuous, *have got,* clothes, parts of the body, colours

Materials *Essential:* chalk or tape to mark the 'river banks'

Procedure

Play this game in the playground or gym.

1 Use tape or chalk to mark the boundaries of the 'river' (5–10 metres apart).

2 Either choose a (confident) child to be the crocodile or take this role yourself.

3 Get the other children to stand on one of the banks of the river and to ask you in chorus *Can I cross your river, Mr (or Miss/Mrs) Crocodile?* Mime looking crafty and thoughtful and then answer, eg *Yes, if you're wearing something red! / Yes, if you've got curly hair!*

4 Explain and demonstrate that children who fit the description should say *Thank you, Mr (or Miss/Mrs) Crocodile!* and try and run across the river without you catching them.

5 Any children who are caught become crocodiles and help you think up answers in the following turns. The last child to be caught is the winner and becomes the crocodile in the next round of the game.

Comments and suggestions

- As with 5.10, this game involves children playing in English outside the classroom and using language in a natural, motivating and enjoyable way.

- The language demands of the activity can be adjusted to suit the children, eg it may only be appropriate to play the game using one structure and lexical set eg *... if you're wearing blue shoes.*

- Although children are unlikely to have formally come across *if* or conditional sentences, they usually have no problem either understanding or using the word *if* in the context of the game. If necessary, you can give a quick translation at the start of the game.

5.12 Picture card games

Level A1.1 **Age** 5–8 **Organization** pairs, whole class

Aims To identify vocabulary on picture cards; to ask and answer questions; to listen to others; to manipulate picture cards; to move to music (5.12h); to take turns.

Language focus any vocabulary depending on the cards and
5.12a *can* (for ability), *Hurray*
5.12b *Can I have ...?*
5.12c *Where's the ...? hot, cold (warm, cool, freezing)*
5.12d, 5.12h *have got*
5.12e *Where's the ...?*

Materials *Essential:* sets of 6–8 vocabulary picture cards (one set for each child, apart from 5.12c and 5.12h where you only need one set) / *Optional:* music (see 5.12h)

Procedure

Either get children to cut out the picture cards, if these are included in their course book, or give these out. Use one or more of the following card games to practise specific language and vocabulary as appropriate.

5.12a Hurray!

1 Divide the class into pairs.

2 Explain and demonstrate that the children should put their cards face down in a pile.

3 They turn over their cards at the same time and say, eg *I can see the ... tomato!* As soon as they turn over matching pictures, they say *Hurray!* and take that pair of cards out of the game.

4 After turning over all their cards, they reshuffle them and start again.

5 The game ends when there are no more cards left.

5.12b Can I have ...?

1 Divide the class into pairs.

2 Ask each child to secretly choose four cards from their set of picture cards and hold them in a fan so their partner can't see the pictures.

3 Explain and demonstrate that Child A should ask, eg *Can I have the lion, please?* If Child B doesn't have the card of the lion, they say *No. Sorry. (I haven't got the lion)*. If they do have the card of the lion, they say *Here you are!* and give it to Child A, who says *Thank you* and puts it on the table.

4 Child B then has the next turn asking a question. The game ends when the children have discovered all of each other's cards.

5.12c Hot, hot, hot!

1 Play with the whole class. Ask two children to wait outside the classroom door for a moment.

2 While they are outside the door, stick one of the vocabulary cards somewhere in the classroom, where it is 'hidden' but nevertheless visible without moving anything. Involve the rest of the class in helping you to do this.

3 Ask the two children back into the classroom and everyone asks, eg *Where's the elephant?* The two children look for the vocabulary card of the elephant and the rest of the class helps by saying *Hot! Hot! Hot!* if the children move near to where the card is hidden and *Cold! Cold! Cold!* if they move away.

4 When they find the card, the two children say, eg *Here's the elephant!* and everyone claps and says *Hurray!*

5 Repeat several times with different children. If appropriate, you can also introduce the words *warm, cool* and *freezing*, using mime to convey the differences, into the game as well.

5.12d Memory

1 Divide the class into pairs.

2 Explain and demonstrate that children should lay out two sets of vocabulary cards in random order face down on the desk.

3 Child A turns over one of the cards and names what's in the picture, eg *Ball!* or says a sentence, eg *I've got a ball!* They then turn over another card and repeat the procedure. If the two cards are the same, Child A keeps them. If they are not the same, Child A puts them back face down exactly where they were.

4 Child B then has the next turn. The child with most cards at the end of the game is the winner.

5.12e Find the card

1 Divide the class into pairs.

2 Explain and demonstrate that Child A should lay out their cards face down on the desk and ask Child B, eg *Where's the car?* Child B points to a card and says, eg *(I think) it's here!*

3 Child A turns the card over and says *Yes, (you're right!)* if it is the car, or *No, (you're wrong!)* if it isn't.

4 As soon as Child B guesses correctly and the car is found, they have the next turn.

5.12f Arrange the cards

1 Either play with the whole class, with you giving instructions and/or children play in pairs with a screen, eg an open book, between them. Child A lays their cards in a row and then gives instructions, eg *cheese, ham, chicken* to their partner to order their cards in the same way.

2 At the end, children check that their cards are in the same order and then change roles.

5.12g The puppet says…

1 Play with the whole class. Ask the children to lay their set of picture cards face up on the desk.

2 Hold up the puppet and say, eg *The puppet* (or use its name) *says: Show me the apple, please!* Children hold up the corresponding card. If you don't say 'please', children fold their arms and do nothing. Speed up the game as children respond more confidently. If you like, use a system of 'lives' if children respond wrongly, but don't make them out of the game.

5.12h Musical cards

1 Play with the whole class. Children stand or sit in a circle.

2 Give out the vocabulary cards from one set to different children in the circle.

3 Play any music and children pass the cards clockwise round the circle.

4 Pause the music. Children with the vocabulary cards hold them up and name what's on their card in turn, eg *Giraffe!* or say a sentence, eg *I've got the giraffe!*

5 At the end, everyone claps and says, eg *Fantastic!*

6 Repeat several times either with the same or different cards.

5.12i Picture card bingo

1 Play with the whole class.

2 Ask children to choose 4–6 cards (from a set of eight) and lay them face up on their desks.

3 Call out the words in random order (keeping a record of words you call). Children turn their cards over when they hear the words.

4 The first child to say *Bingo!* wins but it is usually best to continue playing until everyone has turned over their cards.

Comments and suggestions

• Picture cards are frequently included in children's course books. They are very useful for short games which practise specific language and vocabulary and get children used to taking turns and working in pairs.

- In addition to the games above, you can also use picture cards to get children to show listening comprehension, eg by holding up the correct card when they hear it in a story or song, and for games to get the children into pairs or groups (see 5.7).

5.13 The last word

Level All   **Age** 8–12   **Organization** pairs

Aims To practise saying the days of the week (and/or months of the year) in sequence; to logically deduce how to say the 'last word'; to take turns in pairs.

Language focus days of the week (and/or months of the year)
Alternatives: any poem, rhyme or text containing familiar language, about 8–12 sentences long

Materials *Essential:* none / *Optional:* photocopies of the selected text (one for each pair)

Procedure

1 Divide the class into pairs.

2 Explain and demonstrate that children should take turns to say the days of the week. They can say one or two days at a time. The winner is the child who says the 'last word' ie 'Sunday', eg P1: *Monday* P2: *Tuesday, Wednesday* P1: *Thursday* P2: *Friday* P1: *Saturday, Sunday.*

3 Give the children time to play three or four rounds of the game with their partner, alternating who starts each time. The child who says 'Sunday' most times in each pair is the winner.

4 If appropriate, children can repeat the game with the months of the year. In this game, they can say up to three months at a time, and the winner each time is the child who says 'December'.

Comments and suggestions

- This game provides lots of repetition practice of the days of the week or months of the year, which is made cognitively challenging by deducing how many words to say in order to be left with the 'last word' and win.

- This game can also be used to provide practice in reading a rhyme, poem or short text which is familiar to the children. In this case, children work in pairs and take turns to read one or two lines or sentences of the text. The winner is the child who says the 'last sentence' or 'last line' each time rather than the 'last word'.

5.14 The grid game

Level All   **Age** 6–12   **Organization** teams

Aims To identify words from initial letters and clues or questions; to collaborate as part of a team.

Language focus affirmative statements in the present simple or past simple, *Wh-* questions, letters of the alphabet

Materials *Essential:* clues or questions to match the letters in the grid / *Optional:* flashcards

Procedure

1 Divide the class into two teams and assign either circles or crosses to each one.

2 Draw a grid of letters on the board, eg

r	h	j
s	m	t
a	l	d

3 Ask a child in one team to choose a letter, eg 'm' and either give a clue or ask a question to the other members of the team, for them to guess the word, eg *It's a type of animal. It's got warm blood.* or *What's the name of a warm-blooded animal?* (**Answer:** mammal)

4 Give the team a few moments to confer before answering. If the team guesses the word correctly, they 'win' the square and you draw a circle or cross, depending on which they have been assigned, to show this. The next team then has a turn in the same way.

5 The first team to win three squares in a row are the winners.

Comments and suggestions

- This game can be made easier or more challenging depending on the level of language in the clues or questions.

- With younger children, instead of letters you can stick flashcards face down in the spaces in the grid. In order to win a turn, children in each team take turns to name what's on the flashcard they choose.

- This game is useful as a revision activity. It can also be used for general knowledge, either in the present or past tense, eg (P) *It's the capital of France* (Paris); (S) *Who wrote 'Hamlet'?* (Shakespeare); or as part of content-based learning, eg (c) *a stage in the life of a butterfly* (chrysalis or cocoon).

- Once they are familiar with the game, older children can be asked to prepare their own versions in pairs. They can then take turns to play this with the rest of the class. This provides purposeful and enjoyable writing practice and also gives the children an opportunity to manage an activity independently of you.

5.15 The hungry crocodile

Level All   **Age** 6–12   **Organization** whole class

Aims To recognize and practise saying letters of the alphabet; to guess and/or deduce a known word from the spelling.

Language focus any known vocabulary, letters of the alphabet

Materials *Essential:* none

Procedure

1 Draw a simple picture of a hungry crocodile and eight stepping stones on the board.

2 Think of a word the children know and draw a dash for each letter.

3 Ask the children to take turns to guess the letters. If the letters they suggest are correct, write them in the spaces. If not, rub out the stick figure and draw it again on the next stepping stone, moving nearer the crocodile each time.

4 Keep a record of all the letters suggested on the board.

5 The children win if they guess the word before the stick figure is eaten by the crocodile. The first child to say the word has the next turn.

Comments and suggestions

- This game is a variation of the traditional game of 'hangman'. As well as familiarizing children with letters of the alphabet and the spelling of known words, the game can be useful either to introduce the topic of a lesson or as a quick revision filler if you have a few minutes extra time at the end.

- Once older children are familiar with the game, they can also play it independently in pairs.

5.16 Alphabet race

Level A1.2, B1.1, B1.2   **Age** 8–12   **Organization** teams

Aims To recall vocabulary and spelling at speed; to collaborate as part of a team.

Language focus familiar vocabulary, letters of the alphabet

Materials *Essential:* none

Procedure

1 Divide the class into two teams. Number the children in each team and explain that this is the order in which they should come to the board.

2 Draw a line down the centre of the board to separate the space for each team.

3 Explain that the object of the game is for each team to write a word on the board for each letter of the alphabet in order as fast as they can.

4 All books must be closed during the game and the teams are not allowed to write the same words for any letter. This means if one team has already written the word *apple* for A, then the other team must think of another word, eg *animal*. If the teams can't think of a word for a letter, they write 'Pass'.

5 There can only be one child at the board from each team at a time and the next child can only go once the previous child is sitting down again. It is up to you whether to write the letters of the alphabet across the top of the board before the game to ensure that children follow the order correctly.

6 Start the game by saying, eg *Number ones. Are you ready? Go!*

7 Stop the game as soon as one team gets to the end of the alphabet.

8 Score the game by counting the number of 'passes' for each team (for the team who hasn't finished, these also include all the letters still outstanding) and deduct points for spelling mistakes. The team with the most correctly spelt words is the winner.

Comments and suggestions

- This game is useful for revising vocabulary and spelling. Children also find it motivating and enjoyable. However, they may also tend to get over-excited. If this is the case, you will need to settle them with a quieter activity following the game, eg copying their team's alphabet of words into their notebooks.

- As a follow-up, it may be appropriate to get children to make and illustrate an alphabet frieze or book (see 9.2).

5.17 Guessing games

Level All   **Age** 4–12   **Organization** whole class, groups or pairs

Aims To ask and answer questions; to mime an action (5.17b); to make logical deductions; to listen to others; to take turns.

Language focus see below:
5.17a any vocabulary, depending on the flashcards, *What's this? Is it a ...? Yes it is. / No, it isn't.*
5.17b present continuous (questions and short answers)
5.17c, 5.17d present simple, *have got*, (questions and short answers)
5.17e *have got*, describing people
5.17f present simple (1st person questions)
5.17g any lexical set, questions with present simple and *be*
5.17h prepositions of place

Materials *Essential:* flashcards (5.17a); a bag, small pieces of paper (5.17c); sticky labels (5.17f); a poster or a large picture, eg in course book (5.17h) / *Optional:* mime cards (5.17b); word cards (5.17g)

Procedure

Use one or more of the following guessing games to practise specific language and vocabulary as appropriate.

5.17a Guess the flashcard (age 4–8)

1 Place 6–8 flashcards of familiar items face down in a pile.

2 Pick up the first flashcard card and hold it so that children can't see the picture. Ask *What's this?* and children guess, eg P: *Is it a banana?* T: *No, it isn't.* P: *Is it a pencil case?* T: *Yes, it is.*

3 If children guess the flashcard before asking six questions, they score a point; if not, you score a point.

4 At the end of the game, count up the points to decide the winner.

5.17b Guess the mime

1 Ask a child to the front of the class. Whisper an action for them to mime, eg playing a computer game. Other children watch and guess, eg P2: *Are you writing an email?* P1: *No, I'm not.* P2: *Are you playing a computer game?* P1: *Yes, I am.*

2 The child who guesses correctly has the next turn.

3 If you prepare mime cards with suggestions for mimes, eg *eating a banana, cleaning your teeth,* children can also play the game in groups.

5.17c Guess the name (age 7–10)

1 Ask the children to write their names on a small piece of paper.

2 Collect the names and mix them up in a bag. Invite a child to take one of the names out of the bag and to keep this secret.

3 Other children ask up to six questions to find out who it is, eg *Is it a boy/girl? Has he/she got brown hair? Does he/she play the piano? Has he/she got a brother? Does he/she like football? Is it ...?*

4 The child who guesses correctly has the next turn.

5.17d Animal, object or person (age 8–12)

1 Choose the name of an animal, object or person. Explain that children can ask you twenty yes/no questions to find out what it is, eg P1: *Is it a person?* T: *No, it isn't.* P2: *Is it an animal?* T: *Yes, it is.* P3: *Does it live on a farm?* T: *No, it doesn't.* P4: *Does it live in the rainforest?* T: *Yes, it does.*

2 The child who guesses correctly has the next turn.

3 After one or two rounds with the whole class, children can then play the game again in groups.

5.17e Guess the star (age 8–12)

1 Think of a famous star the children know, eg singer, TV personality, movie star or sports star. Describe him/her to the class, eg *He isn't very tall. He's got brown hair and brown eyes. He plays football. He's from Brazil.* Children ask *Is it …?* and guess who it is.

2 The child who guesses correctly has the next turn.

5.17f Guess the job (age 8–12)

1 Write the names of jobs, eg *teacher, waiter, hairdresser, doctor, vet* on sticky labels (enough for one job per child).

2 Attach one label to the back of each child so they do not know which job they have got.

3 Demonstrate that children should walk round the class taking turns to ask and answer questions in order to find out their job, eg *Do I work in a school? Do I wear a uniform? Do I help people? Do I like animals?*

5.17g Guess the word (age 8–12)

1 Choose a word within a topic the children are doing, eg food (*ice cream*) and children ask questions to guess what it is, eg *Is it a vegetable? Is it salty? Do you eat it for lunch?*

2 The first child to guess the word has the next turn.

3 If you prepare word cards, eg *apple, hamburger,* children can also play the game in groups.

5.17h Guess the place (age 6–10)

1 Children look at a poster or a large picture in the course book. Ask them to imagine there is a mouse or spider hidden somewhere in the picture or poster.

2 Ask *Where's the spider/mouse?* and encourage children to ask questions to find out, eg *Is it under the table? Is it in the bag?* The child who guesses correctly has the next turn.

Comments and suggestions

• Guessing games are easy to set up and can be very useful in providing short, contextualized practice of specific language patterns and vocabulary.

• In the case of 5.17e, it may be advisable to ask children to write 3–4 sentences describing the famous star they choose before playing the game.

• In the case of 5.17f, if you do not want the children to walk about, you can play the game as in 5.17b or 5.17c. In this case, you will need to write the jobs on cards and the children take turns to take a card while others ask questions to find out the job.

• If children play guessing games in groups, as suggested for 5.17d, it is a good idea to ask them to note the animal, object or person they choose before playing in order to ensure they aren't tempted to change this during the course of the game. See also 7.11 for a craft activity and similar game which avoids this being necessary.

5.18 Birthday line

Level All   **Age** 9–12   **Organization** whole class

Aims To ask and answer questions about the month (and date) of your birthday; to stand in a line showing the order of class birthdays from January to December; to collaborate with others as a team.

Language focus Wh- questions, *be,* months of the year, (ordinal numbers – dates)

Materials *Essential:* none / *Optional:* stop watch or timer

Procedure

1 Ask the children to stand in a line. Explain that one end of the classroom is 'January' and the other end is 'December'.

2 Explain that the object of the game is for the children to rearrange themselves in the line according to the order of their birthdays, from January to December, as fast as they can and, if you have a stop watch or timer, before this rings.

3 Demonstrate that in order to do this they need to ask and say the month of their birthday to the children standing next to them in the line, eg P1: *When's your birthday?* P2: *It's in May.* They then move up or down the line depending on how the answer relates to the month of their own birthday. Set a time limit for the activity, eg between 5–10 minutes, depending on the size of the class.

4 If the class can arrange themselves in a line before the timer rings, they win. At the end, check that children are standing in the correct order by getting each child to say, eg *My birthday is in January*, and so on down the line.

Comments and suggestions

• This game involves the whole class working collaboratively towards a common goal. Don't be surprised, however, if in their speed to make the line, children don't repeat the question *When's your birthday?* every time but just say the month. This is totally natural and English speakers would do the same.

• If you want to make the activity more challenging, you can ask children to arrange themselves not only by the months of their birthdays but also by the dates. In this case instead of replying *It's in May,* they will say *It's on the 25th of May* and arrange themselves in order within each month as well as for the whole year.

• With older children, line games can also be used in other contexts, for example, to get the children to arrange themselves in order of how much they know about a topic, eg technology from 'a lot' to 'a little', or how much they like something, eg a DVD or school subject from 'very much' to 'not at all'. In both these cases, however, it is important that the children understand that you are interested in their opinions and are not being judgmental abut the way they respond.

5.19 Forfeits!

Level All   **Age** 8–12   **Organization** pairs, whole class

Aims To recall familiar vocabulary; to read forfeits and carry out a small task in pairs to the class; to take turns; to develop self-confidence.

Language focus familiar language and vocabulary, imperatives

Materials *Essential:* small pieces of paper; 6–10 forfeit cards (see examples below)

Procedure

1 Ask the children to sit in a circle, if possible, and divide them into pairs, with the children in a pair sitting next to each other.

2 Place the forfeit cards you have prepared face down in the centre of the circle.

3 Start the game by naming a lexical set, eg animals. Write one word from the set on a small piece of paper without the children seeing what the word is.

4 Ask the pairs to think with their partner and take turns to say one word from the lexical set you have named clockwise round the circle, eg *tiger, cat, crocodile, snake.* As soon as a pair says the word you have written on the piece of paper, hold this up and say *Forfeit!*

5 Ask the pair to take a forfeit card from the centre of the circle. The pair read the forfeit card out loud and carry out the task.

6 The pair then choose and announce the next lexical set, eg food, write one word from it secretly on a piece of paper and the game starts again and continues in the same way.

7 Forfeits you can use include instructions to revise any language the children know, eg *Say the*

alphabet. / Count from 80–100. / Sing a song. / Name eight colours. / Say the months of the year. / Say three facts about elephants. / Describe the weather today.

Comments and suggestions

- This game provides practice in recalling familiar vocabulary as well as enjoyable revision of other language the children know.
- By organizing the class in pairs, children do not feel threatened either when recalling vocabulary in turn round the circle or carrying out the forfeit tasks.
- If appropriate, you can encourage the rest of the class to clap when pairs do the forfeit tasks successfully or to join in and help if this proves necessary.

5.20 Revision tennis

Level All   **Age** 9–12   **Organization** pairs, teams

Aims To prepare questions related to a recently completed unit of work; to ask and answer questions in order to revise a unit of work; to collaborate in teams; to keep a score of the game as in real tennis.

Language focus present simple, *Wh-* questions, any relevant vocabulary
Alternatives: past simple

Materials *Essential:* course book or other materials the children are using

Procedure

1 Divide the class into two teams. If you like, ask them to choose the names of real tennis players for their team.

2 Within each team divide the children into pairs.

3 Ask the children to look through the unit(s) of work they have just completed in their course book or other materials and to prepare 6–8 revision questions to ask the other team. Elicit or give examples of the kinds of questions they can ask, related to the language, eg *How do you spell …? What's the English for …? What's the opposite of …?,* or related to the course or story characters, eg *What's the name of Spike's pet? Where does Sporty live?* or related to the real world content, eg *How many legs has a spider got? What is a chrysalis?* Explain that the children must know the answers to the questions they prepare.

4 Set a time limit, eg 5–10 minutes, and monitor the children carefully as they prepare and write their questions.

5 Once they are ready, explain that one team must 'serve' a question to the other team, who try and answer it. Allow the questions and answers to go backwards and forwards between the teams and keep a score of the game as in real tennis (eg Love–15, 15 all, 15–30, 30 all, 30–40, Deuce, Advantage …, Game).

6 It is then the turn of the other team to 'serve' the first question. Continue playing in the same way for several 'games'.

7 At the end, the team who has won the most games is the winner.

Comments and suggestions

- This game is a motivating way to get children to review and revise recently completed work. It is best played with children who are already familiar with the scoring system in tennis in their own language, even though the English terminology for this may be new.
- If the children are not familiar with real tennis, it may be best to play 'revision football' instead, with each team scoring a goal whenever the other side can't answer one of their questions. In this version of the game, you can also include 'yellow cards', eg if children call out answers. It is best not to use 'red cards', however, as these will exclude children from the game and may negatively affect the way you manage the class.

5.21 Dice games

Level A1.1, A1.2   **Age** 6–10   **Organization** whole class, pairs

Aims To associate numbers on a dice with vocabulary (or instructions); to practise counting; to cooperate and take turns in a game.

Language focus numbers 1–6, *be*
15.21a clothes, *have got*
15.21b, 15.21c, 15.21d parts of the body (animals/human/monster), *have got*
15.21e imperatives

Materials *Essential:* large-size dice (for you), dice (or spinner) for each pair (see 7.5 or 7.3) / *Optional:* photocopies of a picture for children to complete, eg a human body, an animal torso or a human face

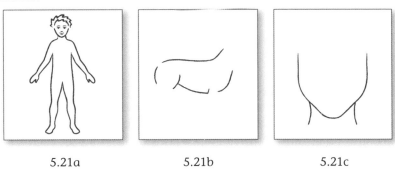

5.21a   5.21b   5.21c

Procedure

Divide the class into pairs. Either get children to make a dice or give one to each pair. Use a large-size dice to play the game you choose with the whole class first:

5.21a Clothes dice

1 Draw an outline of a human body and write the following on the board: 1 = hat, 2 = trousers, 3 = socks, 4 = T-shirt, 5 = trainers, 6 = bag.

2 Ask the children to draw the picture or give them a copy of this.

3 Demonstrate the game by throwing the large-size dice and saying, eg *One … two … three … four. It's four. It's a T-shirt!* and draw a T-shirt on the figure on the board.

4 Children take turns to throw the dice and draw the clothes with their partner. If they throw the same number twice, they say, eg *No. He's already got a T-shirt!*

5 The first child to complete their picture wins.

5.21b Animal dice

1 Draw an outline of an animal torso (see middle picture above) and write the following on the board: 1 = head, 2 = legs,
3 = tail, 4 = ears, 5 = eyes, 6 = teeth.

2 Children play the game as above. They can make their picture into any animal they like, eg cat, dog and then compare these at the end of the game.

5.21c Face dice

1 Draw an outline of a face (see the picture on the right above) and write the following on the board: 1 = eyes, 2 = ears, 3 = nose, 4 = hair, 5 = mouth, 6 = teeth.

2 Children play the game as above.

5.21d Monster dice

1 Explain that the children are going to use dice to draw a monster and write the following on the board: 1 = head, 2 = body, 3 = arm(s), 4 = leg(s), 5 = eye(s) or ear(s), 6 = free choice. Explain the meaning of 'free choice' and elicit or give a few examples, eg tail, whiskers, toes.

2 Children play the game, drawing their monster according to the numbers they throw.

3 After about 10 or 12 throws, children stop and compare their monsters, eg *My monster has got two heads, three eyes, four arms, two legs and a tail.*

15.21e Instructions dice

1 Write suitable instructions for the game on the board, eg 1 = Jump six times! 2 = Hop to the door! 3 = Touch your toes! 4 = Walk round the classroom! 5 = Wave your arms in the air! 6 = Run on the spot! Check children understand the meaning of each instruction.

2 Children take turns to throw the dice and give their partner instructions. Children carry out each instruction once.

3 The child who carries out all the instructions first wins.

Comments and suggestions

- Simple games using dice provide a framework for children to cooperate and take turns with a partner.

- In order to maximize number practice, it is a good idea to get children to count the numbers each time they throw the dice. You can also teach them to use other language as they play, eg *It's my/your turn. / Give me the dice, please. / Here's the dice.*

- If you want the instruction dice game to be less active, you can use different instructions, eg 1 = Spell your name! 2 = Count to 100 in tens! 3 = Name six colours! 4 = Name your clothes! 5 = Say three sentences about you! 6 = Say three sentences about your family!

- For making dice and further suggestions and ideas for using dice see 7.5.

5.22 I don't believe you!

Level A1.2, A2.1, A2.2, B1.1, B1.2   **Age** 9–12   **Organization** whole class, groups

Aims To make statements giving personal information; to ask and answer questions to ascertain whether or not the statements are true; to use any language you know to try and present a convincing case.

Language focus *In the example:* present simple statements, questions and answers; free-time activities, sports, adverbs of frequency, *have got,* pets, *can* (for ability), skills
Alternatives: past simple

Materials *Essential:* none

Procedure

1 Explain that you are going to tell the children three things about yourself. Two of the things are true and one is false, eg *I've got a pet hamster. I can play the organ. I sometimes go mountain biking at the weekend.*

2 Explain that the aim of the game is to ask questions and find out which statement is false, eg T: *I sometimes go mountain biking at the weekend.* P1: *Where do you go?* T: *To the mountains near Segovia.* P2: *What's your bike like?* T: *It's blue. It's an old bike.* P3: *How many kilometres do you ride?* T: *Oh, usually about twenty or thirty.* P4: *I don't believe you!* T: *You're right! I only ride my bike in the park!*

3 Ask the children to write two true sentences and one false sentence about themselves in the same way.

4 Once they are ready, divide the class into groups of 3–4.

5 Children take turns to tell each other their sentences and find out which one is false. At the end, the children in each group who have not been challenged on their false sentences are the winners.

Comments and suggestions

- This game encourages children to use any language they know in order to elaborate on their own statements and ask questions to find out whether other people's statements are true or false.

- The level of challenge in the game can be reduced by getting the children to use one language pattern and topic or lexical area only and to write, for example, sentences about things they do to help at home, eg *I sometimes make my bed* or things they can do, eg *I can swim underwater.* Children can then respond to each others' statements by simply saying *I think it's true!* or *I don't believe you!* rather than asking further questions.

5.23 Treasure

Level A1.1, A1.2, A2.1, A2.2   **Age** 9–12   **Organization** pairs

Aims To ask and answer questions using numbers and letters of the alphabet; to recognize and use coordinates in a grid; to cooperate and take turns with a partner.

Language focus *have got,* numbers, letters of the alphabet

Materials *Essential:* none / *Optional:* photocopies of two identical grids (one for each child)

	10	20	30	40	50	60	70	80	90	100
A										
B			T	T	T					
C									T	
D		T							T	
E				T					T	
F					T					
G										
H							T			
I							T	T		
J										

Procedure

1 Draw the grid for the game on the board. Either ask the children to draw two identical grids like the one on the board or give out the photocopies of these.

2 Divide the class into pairs. Explain that the children have got ten pieces of treasure (each worth three squares) which they must hide in one of the grids. Explain and demonstrate in the grid on the board that children can hide the treasure in any way they like, eg vertically, horizontally, diagonally, in an L-shape, etc, as long as all three squares of each piece of treasure are touching. (See examples in the grid above.)

3 Give the children a few minutes to 'hide' their 'treasure' and insist that they must keep this a secret.

4 Once the children are ready, explain and demonstrate that they should take turns to ask their partner questions to find each other's treasure and record the answers in the second grid, eg P1: *Have you got treasure in 70F?* P2: *No, I haven't. Have you got treasure in 20D?* P1: *Yes, I have.*

5 They should write a cross (X) in the squares which haven't got treasure and a 'T' in the squares which have treasure. Set a time limit for the game, eg 8–10 minutes.

6 At the end, children compare their grids. The child in each pair who has found most treasure is the winner.

Comments and suggestions

- This game is based on the traditional game of Battleships which the children may already know.
- The game encourages active listening and turn-taking. It also familiarizes children with recognizing and reading coordinates in a grid.
- You can vary the numbers and letters you use for the coordinates depending on what you want the children to practise, eg the numbers could be 1–10 and the letters from M–V in the alphabet instead of A–J. Equally, instead of treasure, children can hide anything in the grid from, eg chocolate to UFOs from outer space to 500 euro notes.

5.24 Fruit salad

Level A1.1, A1.2, A2.1, A2.2   **Age** 4–12   **Organization** whole class

Aims To listen and respond as quickly as possible to a specific word; to follow and respect the rules of the game.

Language focus *In the example:* fruit
Alternatives: any lexical set, eg animals, food; present simple questions for personal information

Materials *Essential:* none

Procedure

1 Arrange the chairs in a circle and ask the children to sit down. Make sure that there are no spare chairs.
2 Stand in the middle of the circle and assign a fruit to each child going round the circle, eg *Apple, Banana, Strawberry, Peach / Apple, Banana, Strawberry, Peach.* Get the children to join in repeating the words with you rhythmically as you do this.
3 Check that children know the fruit they have been assigned before playing the game, e.g *Hands up, apples!*
4 Explain and demonstrate that when you say, eg *Strawberries!* all the children assigned that word should immediately change chairs. When you say *Fruit salad!* everyone should change chairs.
5 Play a few rounds of the game until the children are responding confidently. Then say, eg *Peach!* and as the *Peach* children are moving, sit on one of the chairs in the circle.
6 The child who doesn't have a chair then takes over as leader and the game starts again. Repeat several times.

Comments and suggestions

- This well-known game familiarizes children with specific vocabulary and allows for movement and a non-verbal response.
- With very young children, it may not be appropriate for you to take a chair in the circle and for the children to take over as leader.
- When using other lexical sets in the game, you can decide on a suitable equivalent to 'fruit salad'. For example, if the game is based on food vocabulary, children change chairs when you say *Dinner time!* If the game is based on wild animals, children change chairs when you say *Safari!*
- With older, higher level children, an alternative version of the game is for the leader to ask closed questions, eg *Are you 10 years old? / Is your birthday in May? / Have you got long hair? / Are you wearing black shoes?* In this version, any child who answers 'yes' to the question asked has to change chairs. Questions which get everyone changing chairs are those to which everyone answers 'yes', eg *Do you go to … school? Are you learning English now?*

5.25 Enchanted forest

Level A1.1, A1.2   **Age** 8–12   **Organization** whole class, pairs

Aims To listen and follow instructions; to give directions; to build up cooperation and trust between children.

Language focus imperatives, directions, eg *Turn left/right. / Stop. / Go straight on.*

Materials *Essential:* one (or two) blindfold(s), eg sleeping masks from international airlines

Procedure

1 Divide the class into pairs.
2 Ask one pair to come to the front and assign them the roles of traveller and forest guide. Ask the rest of the class to move to a space away from their desks and 'freeze' as if they are trees in the enchanted forest.
3 Blindfold the child who is the traveller.
4 Explain that the object of the game is for the forest guide to direct the traveller through the enchanted forest without touching any of the trees, eg *Go straight on. Stop. Turn right. Stop. Now go straight on. Stop. Turn left.*
5 If the traveller touches a tree, the pair are out. They then become enchanted trees in the forest and another pair has a turn being the traveller and forest guide.
6 Depending on the size of the class, you may be able to have two pairs guiding travellers through the enchanted forest at any one time.
7 The pairs who get the 'travellers' through the forest without touching any of the trees are the winners.

Comments and suggestions

• This game makes giving directions meaningful to children and helps to familiarize them with the concepts of left and right. However, it does need space and may be best done in the playground or gym.
• If you like, you can build in an additional rule to the game whereby when you say *Enchanted forest! One… two… three!* all the trees change their positions, in order to make it harder for the traveller and forest guide, and then freeze again as you finish saying *three*.

5.26 Classroom language sentence race

Level A1.1, A1.2, A2.1, A2.2   **Age** 8–12   **Organization** groups

Aims To establish the use of some basic classroom language; to order and write classroom language sentences and questions; to collaborate in groups.

Language focus *In the example:* classroom language
Alternatives: any relevant language pattern or structure

Materials *Essential:* 10 envelopes (numbered 1–10) with word cards to make classroom language sentences (one set) (see examples below)

Procedure

1 Divide the class into groups.

2 Ask the children to write the numbers 1–10 down the page in their notebooks.

3 Show the children the ten numbered envelopes containing word cards. Explain that they must take turns with the members of their group to come and ask you for an envelope, eg *Can I have number eight, please?*

4 They should then take the envelope back to their group, order the words it contains as fast as they can and write the question or sentence they make against the appropriate number in their notebooks.

5 The next child in the group then returns the envelope to you and asks for another.

6 The first group to have ordered the words in all ten envelopes correctly are the winners.

7 Examples of classroom language you can use for the word cards are: *Can you repeat that, please? / I've finished. What shall I do now? / Can you help me, please? / I don't understand. / I'm sorry I'm late. / Is this right? / How do you spell that? / What does … mean? / Can I go to the toilet, please? / Can I borrow your pencil sharpener, please?*

Comments and suggestions

• This game raises children's awareness about the importance of classroom language. By the end of the game, children have all the sentences and questions correctly written in their notebooks. They can then refer back to these if necessary in subsequent lessons.

• As part of the game, children use classroom language to ask you for the envelopes. This provides an opportunity for a natural communicative exchange with individual children and also allows you to reinforce the value of, eg asking politely, using 'please' and 'thank you'.

• Alternative versions of sentence race games can include, for example, children ordering words to make sentences either based on a newly introduced language pattern or from a story or text they have previously read. In the latter case, it may also be appropriate to ask children to sequence the text once they have ordered the words within each sentence.

5.27 Sketch!

Level All   **Age** 8–12   **Organization** teams

Aims To draw pictures of known vocabulary in order to convey the meaning to others as fast as possible; to guess and identify pictures that other people draw; to collaborate as part of a team.

Language focus any familiar language and vocabulary

Materials *Essential:* a dice, coloured paper squares (one for each team), sticky tac / *Optional:* stop watch or timer, word cards with items for the game in the categories you choose (see step 1)

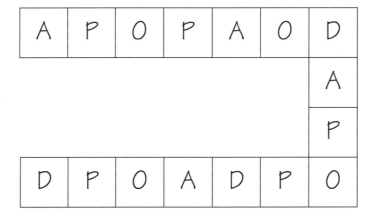

Procedure

1 Decide on your categories for the game, eg A = animals, P = people/places, O = objects/food, D = difficult words, and note these on the board.

2 Divide the class into teams.

3 Draw a simple game board as on the previous page on the board. Draw lines either side of this to assign drawing space for each team.

4 Have ready either a list of suitable words for the age/level of the children or word cards of the selected words with the category letter on one side and the word on the other.

5 Assign a colour to each team. Stick the coloured paper squares to be used as counters for each team at the start of the game on the board.

6 Hold the dice behind your back and ask a child to guess which hand it is in to decide which team starts.

7 Ask a member of the starting team to throw the dice and move their coloured square along the game board.

8 Depending on where it lands, either give the child a word card in that category or whisper them a word from your list. Set your timer or stopwatch for one minute.

9 The child then draws a picture to show the word on the board while the rest of the team guesses what it is. The child drawing is not allowed to talk but can nod or shake their head in response to guesses. They are also not allowed to include numbers or letters as part of their drawing.

10 If the team guess the word within a minute, they have another turn, but with a different child drawing. If they don't guess the word, it is the turn of the other team.

11 The first team to get their coloured square to the end of the game board is the winner.

Comments and suggestions

• This game is a simplified, whole class version of a popular commercial game. The degree of challenge in the game can be increased or decreased depending on the age and level of the children. With younger children, for example, you may decide not to have a D category at all and to simplify the others to, eg A = animals, F = food, C = classroom objects.

• With younger children, vocabulary you include in the game should be mainly concrete objects, eg *ruler, strawberry, penguin, mother*. With older children, D category words can include more abstract concepts that are trickier to draw, eg *love, help, beautiful*.

5.28 Basic board games

Level A1.1, A1.2, A2.1, A2.2   **Age** 6–12   **Organization** pairs

Aims To recall vocabulary within a lexical set; to follow the rules of a game; to cooperate and take turns in pairs.

Language focus *In the example:* clothes, *be*, *Wh*-questions, determiners *this/these*
Alternatives: any relevant lexical set, eg classroom objects, animals, food; any relevant language, eg *have got, want, I'd like*

Materials *Essential:* photocopies of the board game (one for each pair) (pictures from magazines could be cut out or copied to make this), coin and counters, eg rubber, pencil sharpener (for each pair) / *Optional:* a photocopy of an outline of a human body (see 5.21)

Procedure

1 Divide the class into pairs.

2 Give out the *Clothes* board game you have prepared. Make sure the children have a coin and counters to play the game.

3 Check children know all the vocabulary by asking, eg T: *What's number three?* P: *Trainers*.

4 Explain that children will take turns to spin the coin. If it lands on *heads*, they move one square; if it lands on *tails*, they move two squares.

5 Choose one of the options below for playing the game. Explain and demonstrate the game with one child at the front of the class before the children begin.

5.28a Name the clothes

Children have to name the clothes on the square on which they land, eg *Socks!* If they can do this, they spin the coin and have another turn (up to a maximum of two). If they can't do this, they stay where they are. The child who gets to the end of the board first wins.

5.28b What's this? / What are these?

When a child lands on a square, their partner asks: *What's this? / What are these?* and the child must answer, eg *It's a jacket. / They're trainers.*

5.28c My favourite …

When a child lands on a square, they say, eg *My favourite trainers are white. / My favourite T-shirt is red and yellow.*

5.28d Have you got …?

When a child lands on a square, they ask their partner, eg P1: *Have you got a coat?* P2: *Yes, I have.* P1: *What colour is it?* P2: *Blue.*

5.28e Dress the boy/girl

1 Either get children to draw or give them a copy of an outline human body (see 5.21).

2 Children play the game as for *Name the clothes* or *What's this? / What are these?* but additionally they draw the clothes on the boy or girl outline.

3 The child in each pair who has a complete set of clothes (either trousers or jeans, either boots or trainers, etc) on their figure at the end of the game is the winner.

Comments and suggestions

- As well as providing useful language practice and/or revision, basic vocabulary board games are very helpful in training children to work together and take turns in pairs. As the examples above show, they are also flexible in the way they can be set up and the different language demands made.

- Alternative versions of basic board games can be made using any vocabulary which has been introduced. For example, with food vocabulary children can either say their favourites, or what they like or don't like, or offer and accept or decline the food they land on; with animal vocabulary children can collect animals to keep as pets or to have in a zoo.

- It is useful to keep an empty template of a basic board game and then draw pictures of whatever vocabulary you want to practise on the squares before photocopying the game.

- With younger children in particular, you will find that by using basic vocabulary board games regularly, they will become increasingly confident at turn-taking and playing independently in English.

5.29 Question board games

Level All　　　**Age** 8–12　　　**Organization** pairs

Aims To ask and answer questions; to follow the rules of a game; to cooperate and take turns.

Language focus *In the example: can* (for ability), any known language and vocabulary
Alternatives: Wh- questions, comparative and superlative adjectives

Materials *Essential:* a coin, counters and a copy of the board game for each pair

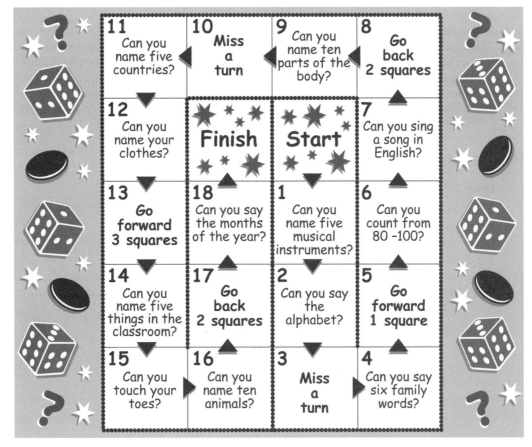

Procedure

1 Divide the class into pairs.

2 Give a copy of the question board game you have prepared to each pair. Make sure the children have a coin and counters to play the game.

3 Check children understand all the questions and instructions in the game.

4 Explain and demonstrate the game as follows. Children take turns to spin the coin. They move one or two squares depending on which side the coin lands: heads – one square, tails – two squares.

5 They either read and show they can answer the question on the square or follow the instruction. If they can answer the question (to their partner's satisfaction) they move forward three squares (but do not answer another question). If they can't answer the question, they stay where they are.

6 The child who gets to the end of the board first wins.

Comments and suggestions

• This version of the game with *Can you …?* questions is a useful revision activity. When playing the game, children are usually very strict with each other about answering the questions correctly!

• As a follow-up, you may like to give children an empty template of the game and ask them to write 6–10 more similar questions, eg *Can you name three American singers?* in order to make a similar board game of their own. Children generally find writing questions in this context very motivating as there is a real purpose and audience. They can also invent a name for their game, eg *The Super Champions Game* and add instructions to some of the squares, eg *Miss a turn.* When they are ready, children can then play each other's games.

• Question board games are easy to make and can be based on a wide range of different language, topics or stories. For example, it might be suitable to make a board game with questions containing comparative and superlative adjectives after children have done a unit of work on this, eg *What's the fastest animal in the world? / Which river is longer – the Mississippi or the Nile?* Children also usually enjoy question board games based on stories, films or books they have read (whether in English or L1), eg *What's the name of Harry Potter's owl? Where does Harry Potter catch the train to school?*

5.30 Design a board game

Level A2.1, A2.2, B1.1   **Age** 10–12   **Organization** groups

Aims To plan and design a board game based on a journey or quest; to write sentences or instructions to include in the game; to develop creative thinking skills; to collaborate in groups.

Language focus any known language and vocabulary, eg present simple, *there is/are, Wh-* questions, imperatives

Materials *Essential:* none / *Optional:* A3 paper or enlarged A3 photocopies of a board game template (one for each pair), blank cards, eg 10 per pair (to write forfeits, questions or chance cards for the game), counters and dice to play the games

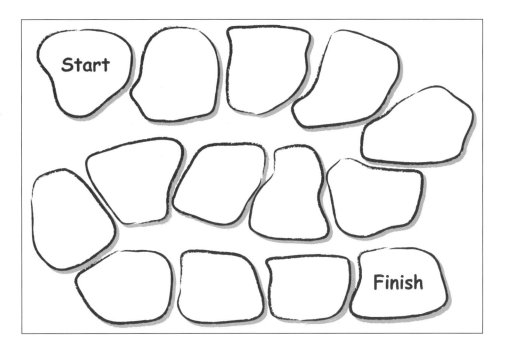

Procedure

1 Divide the class into groups.

2 Either give a photocopy of the board game template to each group or draw this on the board.

3 Explain that you want the children to design a board game based on the idea of a quest or journey. Elicit or give examples to get the children thinking of possible ideas, eg a game where you have to cross the red sea on Mars and meet dangerous aliens and other hazards, or a game where you have to follow a track through a rainforest and avoid dangerous animals, mud swamps, flesh-eating plants and other hazards.

4 Elicit possible things to include in the game, such as squares which say, eg *There is a dangerous snake in a tree. Go back 2 squares.* Or *You meet a rain forest guide. Go to square 6.* Draw the children's attention to the possibility of also including, eg forfeits, questions or chance cards in their games.

5 Ask the children to plan and prepare the game in draft form first. Either set a time limit for this, eg 20–30 minutes, or explain that designing the game will be part of an ongoing mini-project over several lessons.

6 When the children are ready, get them to write and illustrate a final version of their game.

7 In subsequent lessons, children can then take turns to play each others' games.

8 If you like, children can also have a class vote to decide which game they think is best.

Comments and suggestions

• This activity provides purposeful writing practice and also encourages children to think strategically about the way games are designed. Children also generally find playing each others' games very enjoyable.

• When children are planning their games, don't worry too much if they resort to L1 some of the time, as long as this is being used 'on-task' to decide how their games are going to work.

• Depending on the outcome, you may decide to laminate the children's games with a plastic covering. These can then be stored in the classroom and used for independent play whenever there is a suitable moment, eg towards the end of lessons after children have completed more formal work.

Section 6 **Rhymes, chants and songs**

Children love rhythm, music and movement, and it is widely recognized that the use of rhymes, chants and songs contribute to young children's overall social, linguistic, physical, cognitive and emotional development. When starting to learn a foreign language, rhymes, chants and songs play a special role in drawing children into producing language in ways which are natural, spontaneous and enjoyable. As well as enhancing children's learning and acquisition of language, the use of rhymes, chants and songs promotes the development of positive attitudes and motivation towards learning a foreign language in both the immediate and longer term. Given their many potential benefits for learning, there is a strong case for making rhymes, chants and songs a fully integrated component of any programme to learn English at primary school.

Learning through rhymes, chants and songs

Young children are usually already familiar with rhymes, songs and chants in L1. Using them in English lessons provides a link between home and school, and helps to create a secure environment for learning. Rhymes, chants and songs allow for both verbal and non-verbal participation through physical movement, actions, drama and play. By building on children's pleasure in rhythm and sounds, they engage children in responding to and producing language in ways which develop their confidence and self-esteem and lead to a sense of achievement and success.

Rhymes, chants and songs are communal, social events which add variety and a change of pace to classroom activities and build up a sense of group identity and belonging within the class. They can be used as a ritual part of starting and ending lessons, or as an integrated part of language, story or topic-based work (see 6.1, 6.10, 6.13, 6.23). They can also be used to reinforce knowledge and skills in other areas of the curriculum, for example, numeracy (see 6.4, 6.21) or citizenship issues, such as looking after the environment (see 6.18). Rhymes, chants and songs frequently provide an opportunity to introduce children to aspects of traditional children's culture from the English-speaking world. They also develop social

skills, such as turn-taking, eg in interactive chants (see 6.7, 6.15), rhyme or singing games (see 6.5, 6.22), and motor skills, for example, through finger play (see 6.4). With younger children, rhymes, chants and songs can also play a crucial role in managing the class effectively by helping to set up behavioural parameters and establish lesson routines. Rhymes can signal story time, (re)focus attention or allow children to let off physical energy, help them to concentrate or calm them down (see 6.1).

Rhymes, chants and songs can be used to introduce new language or to consolidate, recycle and extend the contexts in which children use structures and vocabulary that are already familiar. They develop listening comprehension and speaking skills, both spoken production and spoken interaction. In some cases, they can also be used to develop reading and writing skills, for example, when children read a short poem or rhyme (see 6.16), or write their own version of a chant (see 6.15).

Above all, rhymes, chants and songs help to improve all aspects of children's pronunciation. With younger children, this is usually an implicit part of the activity itself, whereas with older children it may be appropriate to focus on a particular aspect of pronunciation more explicitly, such as sentence stress or intonation. Through repetition of rhymes, chants and songs, children develop their ability to imitate and produce individual sounds, eg the vowel sound /aʊ/ in a word like *brown*, in a natural way. They also acquire the ability to produce features of connected speech, such as when words are linked together, eg when *put on* becomes /pʊtɒn/ or a question such as *Do you like …?* sounds /dʒʊˈlaɪk/, or the simplification of consonant clusters as when, eg *First touch your toes* becomes /fɜːstʌtʃjəˈtəʊz/.

In addition to individual sounds and sounds in connected speech, rhymes, chants and songs also help to develop children's awareness of stress, rhythm and intonation patterns in English. Children can easily be made aware, for example, by clapping the rhythm of a rhyme, that it is 'content' words such as the nouns that tend to be given the main stress, eg *I like <u>choc</u>olate / I like* _cheese_, and that other words and syllables are unstressed in order to maintain the same rhythm or stress pattern, eg _So not for /fə/me, please_. Older children can also be made explicitly aware of weak forms and the frequent use of schwa /ə/ as in, eg _When I was /wəz/ one_ and how this makes their own speech sound more natural. The use of chants which replicate patterns of everyday communication encourage children to 'lift' their voices and speak with natural pitch and intonation patterns, such as the falling intonation in _Wh-_ questions, eg _Where did he go ↘?_, or rising intonation in a yes/no question, eg _Do you like it↗?_ Such chants also provide an initial controlled framework for children to practise taking turns in interactive speech, a skill which they can increasingly transfer to other activities and everyday communication in class.

The use of rhythm and music in rhymes, chants and songs aids memorization and children are frequently capable of recalling extensive chunks of language in the context of rhymes, songs and chants, which they would not otherwise be able to do. Children also very often naturally transfer language they have met in a rhyme, song or chant to another relevant communicative context in the classroom. When children spontaneously make the connection between language they have learnt in one context and its potential for use in another, this gives them a sense of personal choice and 'ownership' of language and arguably may help them to internalize and commit to long term memory what they are learning.

As in first language learning, it is likely that familiarity with rhymes, chants and songs, and an awareness of sounds, word patterns, rhythm and stress may also contribute to the foundations of early literacy and help children once they start learning how to read in English. Rhymes, chants and songs also frequently provide a vehicle for English going out of the classroom and into the playground and/or home. This also helps to reaffirm in children (and their parents and families) the intrinsic pleasure and value of what they are learning.

Integrating songs, rhymes and chants in sequences of work

In order to maximize the benefits of using songs, rhymes and chants with children, it is usually best to integrate them into sequences of work which develop a range of skills, rather than use them in an isolated way. An example of how a chant (see 6.12b) can be used as the springboard for a whole sequence of work is as follows:

Pizza train chant

Mushrooms, mushrooms
Cheese, tomatoes, cheese, tomatoes
Sausages, bacon, sausages, bacon
Chicken and ham, chicken and ham
Chicken and ham, chicken and ham
Red and green peppers, red and green peppers
Olives, onions, olives, onions
Tu-u-una, tu-u-una
(C. Read and A. Soberón)

1 Draw the shape of a pizza in the air. Ask children to guess the food.

2 Elicit things you can have on a pizza. Use this to revise vocabulary.

3 Ask focus questions: _How many things are on the pizza? What are they?_ Listen to the chant.

4 Check the answers. Stick flashcards on the board in the order of the chant.

5 Children 'read' the flashcards and say the chant with you.

6 Children practise the chant in pairs, saying it rhythmically and doing train movements with their arms.

7 Children stand up and act out the pizza train chant. (Classroom management note: individual carriages are less 'risky' than a whole class train!)

8 (Optional) Children write the chant using the flashcards as a prompt. They then check spelling in pairs and with the whole class.

9 Give out a handout with a picture of an empty pizza frame. Children secretly choose three food items from the flashcards on the board and draw or write the names on the pizza.

10 Pizza partner: Children find their pizza partner, ie someone with the same pizza ingredients as themselves. They can either ask in groups or stand up and mingle to do this, eg P1: _Have you got bacon on your pizza?_ P2: _Yes, I have._

11 Once they've found their partner, children invent a name for their pizza, eg the Super giant pizza and write or complete a simple description, eg *The Super giant pizza has got cheese, bacon and sausages. It's delicious!*

12 Circulate the descriptions and the children make a class menu of all the different pizzas.

13 Children prepare and act out a role play in a pizza restaurant, eg P1: *Can I have a super giant pizza, please?* P2: *Yes, here you are.* P1: *Thank you.*

14 Children observe, investigate and categorize what goes on a pizza in terms of food groups (meat and fish / fruit and vegetable / cereals / dairy products).

When planning sequences of work such as the above, Howard Gardner's *Theory of Multiple Intelligences* (see Further reading) can provide a useful framework for ensuring a balance of activities which will appeal to different children. Examples of the way activities based on the *Pizza train chant* above engage multiple intelligences are as follows:

- **Verbal–linguistic:** repeating the chant, writing the chant, writing a description, doing the role play
- **Musical:** the rhythm of the train and the crescendo on the hoot (tu-u-u-na) in the last line
- **Kinaesthetic:** moving like the train, the mingle activity
- **Visual–spatial:** 'reading' the pizza flashcards, drawing food items on the pizza
- **Logical–mathematical:** deducing the food items to ask about in the mingle
- **Interpersonal:** inventing the name of the pizza; preparing and doing the role play
- **Intrapersonal:** reflecting on what you want on your pizza
- **Naturalist:** observing and categorizing food in different food groups.

Through integrating rhymes, chants and songs into lessons and providing a varied balance of activities which engage children in different ways, we can help to maximize the learning which takes place.

Reflection time

As you use the suggested activities for rhymes, chants and songs in this section with your classes, you may like to think about the following questions and use your responses to evaluate how things went and plan possible improvements for next time:

1 **Rhythm / music:** How did the children respond to the rhythm/music? In what ways did this influence the mood of the class and their willingness to participate?

2 **Pronunciation:** What particular aspects of pronunciation did the activity help to improve? Did you notice these improvements subsequently in other activities or lessons as well?

3 **Memorization:** How easily were children able to remember the rhyme, chant or song? What were the features that made it memorable?

4 **Transfer:** Have there been opportunities for children to transfer language from the rhyme, chant or song to another context? If so, when?

5 **Confidence:** Have you noticed any impact on the children's level of confidence through using the rhyme, chant or songs?

6 **Multiple intelligences:** In what ways did the rhyme, chant or song and related activities appeal to children with different intelligence profiles?

6.1 Routine rhymes

Level A1.1, A1.2   **Age** 4–6   **Organization** whole class

Aims To encourage children to follow classroom routines; to familiarize children with classroom and other language; to create a positive socio-affective atmosphere and secure learning environment.

Language focus see below:
6.1a greetings
6.1b goodbyes
6.1c things in the classroom
6.1d numbers, actions
6.1e, 6.1g parts of the body
6.1f story time

Materials *Essential:* none / *Optional:* a puppet

Procedure

Teach the children one or more of the following rhymes. Say them rhythmically and use them, with or without a class puppet, whenever appropriate as part of your lesson routines.

6.1a Greetings rhyme

You (or a puppet) and children taking turns to say each line.
Good morning.
Good morning.
How are you?
I'm fine, thanks.
And me too!

6.1b Goodbye rhyme

Time to finish now
Stop our work and fun
See you on … (name day of next lesson)
Goodbye, everyone!

6.1c Classroom action rhyme

Use this rhyme to familiarize children with things in the classroom.
Point to the window
Point to the door
Point to the ceiling
Point to the floor!

Point to the clock
Point to the shelves
Point to the board
Point to ourselves! (traditional, adapted)

Substitute words in lines 1 and 3 of each verse for any furniture or other things that are prominent in your classroom, eg *cupboard, plants, carpet.*

6.1d Energetic action rhyme

Use this rhyme to allow the children to let off physical energy.
Ask the children to stand up. Make a beckoning gesture as you say the rhyme and do the actions.
Follow, follow, follow me.
Jump, jump, jump,
One, two, three!

Repeat with other actions, eg *run* (on the spot), *hop, clap, wave.*

6.1e Calming action rhyme

Children do the actions sitting down, to help them calm down.

I can wiggle my fingers
I can wiggle my toes
I can wiggle my elbows
I can wiggle my nose.

No more wiggles
Look at me
I'm as still
As still can be!
(Leonora Davies and Frankie Leibe, adapted)

6.1f Story rhyme

Use this rhyme to focus children's attention before a story.
It's time for a story.
One, two, three.
Are you ready?
Can you see?

Be very quiet.
Let's open the book.
What's going to happen?
Let's have a look.

6.1g Tapping chant

This chant is to aid concentration and practise ear training. Children slap their knees or clap lightly. They follow the rhythm and repeat each line exactly as you do and say it.

Tap. Tap. Touch your nose.
Tap-tap. Tap-tap. Touch your knees.
Tap-tap-tap. Tap-tap-tap. Touch your toes.

Comments and suggestions

- The use of short rhymes such as the above help you to establish learning routines and behavioural expectations with very young children. They also provide opportunities for children to become familiar with the sounds, stress patterns and rhythm of English and acquire language in a natural spontaneous way.

- The ritual use of rhymes to mark stages or moments in lessons appeals to very young children and makes them feel secure. If you forget to say a rhyme, such as the pre-story rhyme, that has become part of your regular lesson routine, they will very probably remind you!

6.2 Introductions chant

Level A1.1, A1.2   **Age** 6–10   **Organization** whole class, pairs

Aims To practise asking and giving personal information in a chant; to acquire features of pronunciation, eg intonation in *Wh-* questions, linking between words, in a natural way; to practise turn-taking; to build confidence and develop fluency in producing chunks of language.

Language focus introductions, personal information, present simple

Materials *Essential:* none / *Optional:* finger or pencil puppets (see 7.12), maracas or a tambourine to keep the rhythm of the chant

Procedure

Use the chant to practise familiar questions and answers related to personal information.

1 Build up the chant with the whole class first. As you do this, either click your fingers and encourage the children to join in, or use maracas or a tambourine to keep the rhythm.

2 Count to three in order to signal to the children when to start the chant.

3 Say the chant at natural speed and in a very rhythmic way. If you like, you can use finger or pencil puppets of story or course book characters or animals from a particular country, eg Australia, to take the parts.

What's your name?	*I'm Kangaroo.*
How old are you?	*I'm eight.*
Where do you live?	*In Australia.*
Do you like it?	*Yes, it's great!*

4 Repeat the chant several times with different characters or different animals from Australia, eg *koala, cockatoo*.

5 Use different interaction patterns, eg you and the whole class, dividing the class in half, inviting 4–6 children to come and take one part at the front. Once the children are saying the chant confidently, they can also do it in pairs.

6 If appropriate, as a follow-up, children can also write the chant as a dialogue.

Comments and suggestions

- The use of simple chants such as the above help to make familiar chunks of language memorable and have a positive impact on all aspects of children's pronunciation.

- Through interacting in the safe, predictable context of a chant, children also develop confidence in transferring this skill to real life.

- You can easily invent other simple interactive chants using any language that you want the children to practise. For example, a chant to practise asking about food and likes could be simply:

Do you like cheese?   *Yes, I do.*
Do you like eggs?   *No, I don't.*
What's your favourite?   *Chocolate cake.*
Yum, yum, yum, chocolate cake.

Children can then substitute the names of food they like and don't like when practising the chant.

6.3 The name rap

Level A1.1, A1.2   **Age** 8–12   **Organization** whole class, pairs

Aims To give personal information keeping the rhythm of a rap; to develop awareness of rhythm and stress; to create a positive socio-affective atmosphere.

Language focus introductions, present simple, any familiar language and vocabulary

Materials *Essential:* none

Procedure

1 Explain to the children that they are going to create a rap in which everyone says their name and one thing about themselves.

2 Demonstrate clapping and saying the chorus of the rap in a very rhythmic way, eg *Everyone clap! Say the name rap!* and give an example of a sentence to introduce yourself which keeps the rhythm of the rap, eg

My name is Jane and I can dance.
I'm Miss Taylor and I like dogs.
My name's Pete and I've got a bike.

3 Ask the children to prepare a sentence to introduce themselves for the rap. Point out that they can say *My name is …* or *My name's …* or *I'm …* depending on what will best fit the rhythm.

4 Monitor to ensure that children have understood the idea of keeping the rhythm of the rap.

5 Once children are ready, get them to practise saying or whispering their sentences rhythmically to each other in pairs.

6 Then do the rap with the whole class. Encourage children to say their sentences clearly and to make them sound as interesting as possible. Ask the children to listen closely to what everyone says and see how many things they can remember.

7 Get everyone to clap and alternate saying the chorus of the rap, with individual children saying their sentences. Point to different children round the class in random order during the chorus in order to prepare them to say their sentence next.

8 At the end, elicit what children can remember about others in the class, eg *Isabel can swim. David likes cats.*

Comments and suggestions

- This rap is useful for learning children's names and something about them.
- As well as developing a sense of rhythm, the rap encourages children to lift their voices in a natural way. Children also enjoy the personalization and instant creativity of the rap.
- If you have a large class, it is probably best to repeat the rap on two or three occasions inviting only half or a third of the children to say their sentences each time. Alternatively children can say their raps in groups.

6.4 Finger rhymes

Level A1.1, A1.2 **Age** 4–8 **Organization** whole class

Aims To follow and show understanding of a rhyme using your fingers; to say a rhyme associating language and finger movements; to develop concentration skills; to develop familiarity with traditional children's culture.

Language focus present simple and
6.4a *caterpillar,* numbers 1– 5
6.4b *spiders,* numbers 1– 5
6.4c determiners *this/these, grandma, grandad*
Alternatives: any, depending on the rhyme

Materials *Essential:* none / *Optional:* a counting cut-out to use instead of fingers (see 7.4)

Procedure

Use finger rhymes as appropriate to fit in with topics, stories or language you are currently working on with the children. Repeat the rhymes in several lessons until children can say the rhyme and do the actions confidently.

6.4a Caterpillar counting rhyme

1 Show the children a picture of a caterpillar and leaf or draw these on the board.

2 Hold out your left hand flat so that it is like a leaf and wiggle the index finger of your right hand so that it is like a caterpillar and get the children to do the same.

3 Say the rhyme, encouraging the children to follow the finger movements and to join in.

One little caterpillar (wiggle your finger)
Hungry for lunch
Finds a tasty leaf (hold your left hand flat, move your finger towards it)
Munch, munch, munch! (move your finger as if eating the 'leaf')

4 Repeat with two, three, four and five little caterpillars raising another finger each time and for five, raising your thumb.

6.4b Spider countdown rhyme

1 Hold up all your fingers on your right hand, pretending that each one is a little spider.

2 Get the children to do the same and to count the 'spiders' with you. Say the rhyme.

3 At the end of each verse, lower one of your fingers on your right hand and use your left hand to run away like a spider behind your back.

Five little spiders
Going out to play,
One says goodbye
And runs away.

Repeat with *four, three* and *two*, then:

One little spider
Playing all alone
Feels very sad
And runs back home!

4 In the last verse, make your left hand run in a circle to your right hand and hold up your fingers to show all five 'spiders' again. Say, eg *And guess what? All the spiders are there!*

6.4c Grandma's glasses

1 Say the rhyme and do actions, getting children to join in.

2 Repeat, if you like, getting girls to be Grandma and boys to be Grandad.

These are Grandma's glasses (make circles round your eyes with your fingers)
And this is Grandma's hat (pretend to pull on a hat)
And this is the way she claps her hands (clap your hands)
And puts them in her lap. (put your hands in your lap)

These are Grandad's glasses (make circles round your eyes with your fingers)
And this is Grandad's hat (pretend to pull on a hat)
And this is the way he folds his arms (fold your arms)
And has a little nap. (put your head on one side and give a gentle snore) (traditional)

Comments and suggestions

• Finger rhymes provide an opportunity for kinaesthetic learning and children find the rhythm, stress and sounds very appealing. They also usually become very absorbed in following the movements of finger rhymes and this helps them to focus and listen to the rhyme with attention.

• Language learnt in rhymes such as the ones above can often be usefully transferred to everyday classroom communication, eg *Fold your arms. / Put your hands in your lap.* when getting children to sit quietly in a circle or, at break time, *We're going out to play.*

• When children learn finger rhymes, they also often spontaneously say them to their families at home. This can help to strengthen connections between parents and the school and increase support for English lessons.

6.5 Rhyme games

Level A1.1, A1.2   **Age** 4–8   **Organization** whole class

Aims To say a rhyme as part of a game; to follow and respect the rules of a game; to become familiar with traditional children's culture.

Language focus 6.5a *have got, ball, big, small*
6.5b *have got, bear, honey*

Materials *Essential:* a soft ball (6.5a); a cut-out of a honey jar (6.5b)

Procedure

Use rhyme games for variety and as appropriate if they relate to the language, topic or story you are doing with the children. Teach the children the rhyme and actions that go with the game first. Then play the game with the whole class.

6.5a Queenie

1 Ask the children to stand up and move away from their desks.

2 Explain and demonstrate the game. Take the role of Queenie yourself at first. Turn away from the children and throw the ball over your shoulder.

3 One child picks up the ball.

4 Children then stand in a line with their hands behind their backs.

5 Turn back to face the children and get them to say to you:
   Queenie, queenie, who's got the ball?
   Is she (or *he*) *big or is she* (or *he*) *small?* (children raise and lower one hand to show big and small) (traditional)
   Encourage the children to say *he* or *she* depending on whether it is a boy or a girl who has got the ball.

6 The children show one hand (keeping the other behind their backs) and say: *I haven't got it!*

7 The children show the other hand (keeping the other behind their backs) and say again:
   I haven't got it! (the child who has the ball simply swops it to the other hand)
   Queenie, queenie, who's got the ball?

8 You then have three turns to ask *Have you got the ball?* to either the boys or the girls who may have the ball. If you guess correctly, that child has the next turn as Queenie.

6.5b Buzz, buzz, buzz

1 Get the children to stand close together in a circle facing towards the centre and with their hands behind their backs.

2 Choose one child to be the 'bear' and to pretend to be asleep in the middle of the circle (they don't need to lie down).

3 Give the cut-out jar of honey to one child in the circle.

4 Get the children to pass the 'honey' clockwise round the circle behind their backs as they say the rhyme:
   Isn't it funny
   A bear likes honey?
   Buzz, buzz, buzz
   I wonder why he does.

5 They then call *Wake up, bear! Someone's got your honey!* and stop passing the cut-out round behind their backs in the circle. The 'bear' pretends to wake up and has three turns to ask *Have you got my honey?* If they guess correctly, that child has the next turn as the bear.

Comments and suggestions

- Rhyme games provide an enjoyable context for repetition of a rhyme for a reason children can relate to. They also engage children in using a repeated language pattern or chunk for a real and immediate communicative purpose.

- As well as developing language, rhyme games develop children's social skills, such as turn-taking, and physical motor skills, eg through passing the honey or changing hands with the ball.

6.6 Learn a chant with rods

Level A1.1, A1.2   **Age** 4–8   **Organization** whole class

Aims To learn a chant using coloured sticks or Cuisenaire rods™; to associate words in the chant with the length and colour of the sticks or rods; to develop recall, memory and concentration skills.

Language focus *In the example:* imperatives, *put on,* clothes
Alternatives: any, depending on the rhyme

Materials *Essential:* coloured sticks or Cuisenaire rods™

Procedure

1 Choose rods or sticks to correspond to the words in the chant. Choose short sticks for words like *on* and longer sticks for words like *everybody*.

2 Get the children to sit in a circle with you.

3 Teach them the chant by laying out the rods or sticks word by word and line by line on the floor facing the children. Use mime to convey the meaning of each word and line.

4 Go back over the lines you have already taught the children frequently, pointing to the rods in turn and getting the children to say the words in chorus with you.

5 As the same words are repeated in new lines, hold up the rods which represent each word and elicit these from the children. As they make the association between the rods and the words, they will almost be able to construct the chant themselves:

Everybody put on your hat,
Put on your hat,
Put on your hat.
Everybody put on your hat,
Just like me!

6 Once you have taught the children the whole chant, ask them to stand up and say it with you and act it out. For 'everybody' point round the group, then mime putting on a hat for each line and point to yourself three times as you say each word in the last line.

7 Repeat several times substituting different clothes words and corresponding actions, eg *boots, coat, gloves* or getting the children to suggest these.

Comments and suggestions

- The use of coloured sticks or rods provides variety in the way you teach rhymes or chants and may be particularly memorable for children with strong visual–spatial intelligence.

- This technique works best for rhymes and chants that include several repetitions of the same word. Children can then predict the words as you show them the rods or sticks in each line.

- If you have a whole box of different coloured sticks or Cuisenaire rods™, instead of choosing the rods for each word, you can invite the children to do this. As they do this, you can encourage them to make the connection between the length of words and the size of rods and also, if appropriate, colour and meaning, eg orange for the sun.

6.7 I don't want to!

Level A1.1, A1.2   **Age** 6–10   **Organization** whole class

Aims To develop familiarity with classroom language instructions; to listen and respond in a chant; to practise saying you don't want to do, or will do, something.

Language focus *In the example:* imperatives, classroom language, *want, will*
Alternatives: food vocabulary

Materials *Essential:* none / *Optional:* a picture or photo of a (very appealing looking) dog, maracas or a tambourine

Procedure

1 Show the children a picture or photo of a dog or draw one on the board.

2 Explain that you are going to say a chant including classroom language instructions. The children can reject all the instructions by saying *No, I don't want to!* but whenever you give an instruction that refers to the dog, eg *Feed / Walk / Stroke / Play with the dog!* they must agree and say *Yes, I will!*

3 Get the children to practise the responses in chorus a few times. Then do the chant with the whole class. Use maracas or a tambourine or click your fingers to keep the rhythm of the chant.

4 Either use the classroom language instructions below or any others that are familiar to the children and fit the rhythm of the chant. Hold up the photo of the dog in the last line of each verse.

Sit on your chairs!	*Stand in a line!*
I don't want to!	*I don't want to!*
Open your books!	*Put away your pens!*
I don't want to!	*I don't want to!*
Tidy the class!	*Put on your coats!*
I don't want to!	*I don't want to!*
Walk the dog!	*Feed the dog!*
Yes, I will!	*Yes, I will!* (adapted from a rhyme by Max de Bóo)

Comments and suggestions

- Children usually enjoy saying *I don't want to!* with gusto in this chant, since this is not how they are usually expected or able to respond in the classroom.

- If appropriate, you may like to talk to the children, either in English or in L1, about how none of us always want to do things that we have to do, and that it's fine to express this, even though we may not always be able to avoid doing them.

- With older children, it may be appropriate to ask them to work in groups and think of three more classroom language instructions to include in the chant. The groups can then take turns to come to the front of the class and do their verse of the chant with the whole class.

- An alternative version of this chant can be done with food vocabulary. For example, children can reject all kinds of fruit and vegetables and only say yes to chips, eg *Eat your peas! I don't want to! Eat your chips! Yes, I will.*

- Children are likely to transfer language from the chant to the classroom. This may give you an opportunity to find out why children do not want to do particular things and you can use their responses to reevaluate, although not necessarily change, what you ask them to do.

6.8 Instructions rhyme

Level A1.1, A1.2   **Age** 4–8   **Organization** whole class

Aims To listen and follow instructions in an action rhyme; to build up confidence in responding to English and participating actively in class.

Language focus *In the example:* imperatives, numbers, colours
Alternatives: parts of the body, actions, shapes, classroom objects, any other familiar vocabulary

Materials *Essential:* none / *Optional:* a poster, or a picture in the course book

Procedure

1 Ask the children to stand up.

2 Demonstrate by saying the rhyme in a rhythmic way and giving an instruction in line 3, eg
Everybody listen
And look at me.
Touch something ... RED
When I count to three.
One... two... three... (traditional)

3 Get the children to wait until you finish counting to three before they do the action and then respond all together as fast as they can.

4 Repeat the rhyme several times giving different instructions in line 3 each time.

Comments and suggestions

- Counting to three at the end of the rhyme gives children thinking time before responding and helps ensure that everyone can participate successfully.

- The instruction in the rhyme can be adapted to many other lexical areas, for example, parts of the body (eg *Touch your nose*), classroom objects (eg *Show me your pen*), actions (eg *Jump three times*), shapes (eg *Touch something round*), pictures on a poster or in the course book (eg *Point to the tree*).

- This rhyme is useful as part of a familiar repertoire of activities that you do regularly with the children using different vocabulary, for example, as a warmer or closer or if you need to refocus attention during the lesson.

6.9 Clapping chants

Level A1.1, A1.2   **Age** 6–10   **Organization** pairs

Aims To say a chant as you play a clapping game; to improve pronunciation and awareness of rhythm and stress; to cooperate with a partner.

Language focus *In the examples:* present simple, days of the week, *like*, food
Alternatives: any language and vocabulary that fits the clapping rhythm of the chant

Materials *Essential:* none

Procedure

Use the following procedure for either of the chants below.

1 Stand facing a partner.
Clap your own hands together.
Clap both hands with your partner.
Clap your own hands together.
Clap right hands with your partner.
Clap your own hands together.
Clap left hands with your partner.
Clap your own hands together.
Repeat over and over.

2 Ask a child to the front to demonstrate this with you, as you say the chant. Get children to repeat the chant with you a few times.

3 Speed up playing the clapping game as the child becomes familiar with this.

4 Divide the class into pairs.

5 Children stand facing their partner and say the chant as they play the clapping game several times.

6 If you like, children can repeat the chant and clapping game with a different partner.

7 Alternatively, children can add their own clapping procedures to the game, eg clapping their thighs, clapping behind their backs, clapping above their heads.

8 At the end, you can ask any pairs who have been particularly creative and worked well together to demonstrate saying the chant and doing the clapping game to the whole class.

Examples of chants which work well using this procedure are:

Days of the week chant
Monday, Tuesday
Wednesday, Thursday
Friday, Saturday, Sunday

I like chocolate chant

I like chocolate	*I don't like cabbage*
I like cheese	*I don't like peas*
I like biscuits	*I don't like carrots*
Lots for me, please!	*So not for me, please!*

You can substitute any suitable food vocabulary in lines 1 and 3 of each verse. Alternatively children can invent their own versions of the chant.

Comments and suggestions

• Children generally focus on perfecting the clapping movements with their partner during this activity. In this way it provides for lots of enjoyable repetition practice almost without the children realizing.

• The activity also encourages the children to work together cooperatively. You may be surprised by the creative clapping routines some children produce!

6.10 Animal noises

Level A1.1, A1.2, A2.1   **Age** 4–8   **Organization** whole class, groups, pairs

Aims To practise asking and answering a question in a rhyme; to practise the names of farm animals and the sounds they make in English; (to learn and associate the names of baby animals with the words for adult animals).

Language focus farm animals, animal noises, (names of baby animals), present simple, *Wh*- question

Materials *Essential:* none / *Optional:* flashcards of farm animals, picture cards of farm animals (one set for each pair)

Procedure

1 Either hold up the flashcards of the farm animals you are going to use in the rhyme or draw pictures on the board.

2 Elicit or teach children the names of the animals and the noises they make in English, eg *duck – quack, cow – moo, dog – woof, cat – miaow, sheep – baa.*

3 Say the first two lines of the rhyme and demonstrate that the children should respond by saying the second two lines. Repeat for all the animals.

The duck has a baby
What does it say?
Quack, quack, quack,
All the day. (traditional)

4 Divide the class into two groups.

5 Repeat the rhyme, this time getting one group to say the first line and ask the question about each animal and the other group to reply.

6 The groups then change roles.

7 Divide the class into pairs. Children say the rhyme with their partner.

8 If you have picture cards available, children can lay these face down on their desks and then take turns to turn over a card and say the rhyme, asking their partner about each animal.

Comments and suggestions

• This rhyme provides a framework for getting children to interact and take turns in pairs.

• The question *What does it say?* is a useful chunk which can easily be transferred to other contexts, eg in a story *What does the wolf say?* or *What does it mean?*

• With higher levels, you can use the rhyme to introduce the names of baby animals by saying these instead of *baby* in the first line, eg *The duck has a duckling (cow – calf, cat – kitten, dog – puppy, sheep – lamb).*

6.11 Who's got the chocolate?

Level A1.1, A1.2 **Age** 6–12 **Organization** whole class

Aims To ask and respond to questions in a chanting game; to follow the rhythm and the rules of the game.

Language focus *Who ...?, have got, chocolate, box*
Alternatives: past simple

Materials *Essential:* none / *Optional:* an empty box of chocolates

Procedure

1 Get the children to stand or sit in a circle. Either number the children round the circle or use their names.

2 Show the children the empty chocolate box if you have one. Ask the first question and get children to repeat this. Then demonstrate how the chanting game works.

Everyone: *Who's got the chocolate from the chocolate box?*
You: *Number three's got the chocolate from the chocolate box.*
Number three: *Who? Me?*
Everyone: *Yes! You!*
Number three: *Not me! Number ten's got the chocolate from the chocolate box.*
Number ten: *Who? Me?*
Everyone: *Yes! You!*
Number ten: *Not me! Number seven's got the chocolate from the chocolate box,* etc.

3   Once the children have got the idea, set up a rhythm for the chanting game either by slapping knees, tapping toes or clicking fingers. Explain that children should try as best they can to keep up the rhythm of the chanting game (take this quite slowly at first). They also should not repeat any numbers or names. The chant ends when everyone has had a turn.

Comments and suggestions

- This chanting game is adapted from a traditional West Indian game: *Who stole the cookie from the cookie jar?* It can be played using either the present or past tense and any suitable vocabulary that fits the rhythm, eg *Who stole the sandwich from the picnic box?*

- In the traditional game, children are out if they miss a beat or make a mistake in the words or say the number of a child who is already out. They then turn to face the outside of the circle but carry on clicking their fingers to keep the rhythm of the chant. The chant starts again every time someone is out and goes faster each time. The winners are the last two children still in the game. With older, more confident children, it may be appropriate to do the chant in the traditional way once they are familiar with the game.

- If you use children's names instead of numbers, this makes the chant easier. It may also be a useful way to familiarize yourself with everyone's names.

6.12 Vocabulary train chants

Level A1.1, A1.2, A2.1, A2.2   **Age** 4–10   **Organization** whole class

Aims To practise saying familiar vocabulary from a lexical set in a rhythmic way; to improve pronunciation of individual words; to develop vocabulary recall, memory and concentration skills; to develop visual literacy (with very young children).

Language focus *In the examples:* colours, food on a pizza
Alternatives: any suitable vocabulary

Materials *Essential:* none / *Optional:* flashcards of vocabulary in the chant, maracas or a tambourine to keep the rhythm

Procedure

1   If you have flashcards of vocabulary in the chant you are going to do, elicit the words and stick these on the board in rows to show the order of the chant.

2   Explain that the children are going to say a 'train chant'. Click your fingers and say <u>Ch</u>-ch-ch-ch placing the stress on the first 'ch' in a repeated way to set up the rhythm of a train.

3   Get the children to join in clicking their fingers and saying the chant with you, quite slowly at first (say *and* in both of the chants below in an unstressed way, ie /ən/). Speed up the rhythm towards the end of the chant and raise your voice and elongate the last words to sound like the whistle of a train.

4   Repeat the chant with the children once or twice. Then ask them to stand up and act out the chant by moving up and down on the spot in a rhythmic way and making circular movements with their arms bent at the elbows, like the wheels of a train.

Two examples of vocabulary train chants are as follows:

Colour train chant (age 4–8)
Red and yellow
Red and yellow
Orange and green
Orange and green
Pink and purple
Pink and purple
Blu-u-u-e! Blu-u-u-e!

(C. Read and A. Soberón)

Pizza train chant (age 6–10)
Mushrooms, mushrooms
Cheese, tomatoes, cheese, tomatoes,
Sausages, bacon, sausages, bacon,
Chicken and ham, chicken and ham
Chicken and ham, chicken and ham
Red and green peppers, red and green peppers
Olives, onions, olives, onions
Tu-u-u-na! Tu-u-u-na!

Comments and suggestions

- Children usually enjoy the rhythm of vocabulary train chants and acting them out. From a classroom management point of view, individual carriages rather than a whole class train are usually advisable!

- If you use flashcards, younger children have an opportunity to develop visual literacy as they 'read' the flashcards from left to right.

- You can easily invent vocabulary train chants to fit in with any topic or unit of work, eg clothes, ending in *sho-o-o-es!*

- See also the introduction to Section 6 for an example of how to use the pizza train chant in the context of a whole sequence of work.

6.13 Echo chant

Level A1.1, A1.2, A2.1, A2.2   **Age** 8–12   **Organization** whole class

Aims To listen and echo the words and actions of a chant; to associate the words and actions of the chant; to develop close observation and imitation skills; to improve pronunciation skills.

Language focus *In the example:* Where's the ...?, be, present continuous, questions, can't, rainforest, animals, prepositions of place
Alternatives: any, depending on the chant

Materials *Essential:* none

Procedure

1 Ask the children to move their chairs so that they aren't sitting behind their desks and have room to move their arms and legs. Sit on a chair yourself facing the class.

2 Set the context for the chant. Explain that you are going to say the chant and that the children should imitate your actions and repeat each line of the chant in exactly the same way.

3 Set up the rhythm for the chant by moving your arms and legs and pretending to walk rhythmically through the rainforest. Say the chant and do actions as below. Pause after each line and children 'echo' each sentence in turn and everything you say and do. Act becoming increasingly scared in each verse.

   Rainforest chant
   We're walking in the rainforest. (do walking movements with your arms and legs)
   We can't see the animals. (put your hand to your forehead and look all around)
   Where's the parrot? Where's the parrot? (open your arms questioningly)
   Oh, look! It's in the tree! (point to an imaginary parrot)

4 Repeat as above for other animals: monkey – behind the tree; snake – on the rock.

5 Then do the last verse:
   We're walking in the rainforest. (do walking movements, sound and look scared)
   We can't see the animals. (put your hand to your forehead and look all around)
   Where's the crocodile? Where's the crocodile? (open your arms questioningly)
   Oh, look! It's under me! (stand up suddenly and look down terrified)
   He-e-e-lp! (put your hands to your mouth as if calling for help)
   (C. Read and A. Soberón)

Comments and suggestions

- The use of the echo technique encourages children to imitate all aspects of your pronunciation closely within an enjoyable, dramatic context.

- It is best not to look at the children directly while you do the chant and ignore any minor disruptions or giggles which may occur at the start while children get used to the activity. If you do the actions as if you really are in the rainforest, the chances are the children will too.

- You can use the echo technique with other chants, particularly chants which contain a narrative or tell a story. The best known traditional example of using the echo technique in a chant is *The bear hunt* or *The lion hunt*. See *We're going on a bear hunt,* by Michael Rosen and Helen Oxenbury (Walker Books), for a story book version of this.

6.14 Spot the rhyming words!

Level A1.2, A2.1   **Age** 8–12   **Organization** whole class, pairs

Aims To identify rhyming words; to say a rhyme with rhythm; to improve pronunciation skills.

Language focus *In the example:* was, past simple, numbers, actions
Alternatives: any, depending on the rhyme

Materials *Essential:* none / *Optional:* photocopies of the rhyme with gaps (one for each child)

Procedure

1   Check children understand the concept of rhyming words by saying a series of words, eg *cat, dog, red, mat / book, luck, cook, kick* and asking them to identify the words which rhyme.

2   Set the context for the rhyme. Write the following words in jumbled order on the board: *dive, fun, late, heaven, mine, door, knee, fun, pen, late.* Explain the meaning of any words the children don't know. Check children know how to pronounce all the words.

3   Say the rhyme. Say *was* in an unstressed way, ie /wəz/. Pause before the last word in the second line of each verse and children supply the missing words.

4   Repeat the procedure, this time seeing if children can remember the whole sentence in the second line of each verse.

5   If you have photocopies of the rhyme with gaps, give these to the children. Ask them to write the missing words.

6   When they are ready, divide the class into pairs and ask them to read the rhyme with their partner, taking turns to say the first or second line of each verse and then reversing roles.

When I was one *I had fun.*	*When I was six* *I built bricks.*
When I was two *I lost my shoe.*	*When I was seven* *Life was heaven.*
When I was three *I hurt my knee.*	*When I was eight* *I arrived late.*
When I was four *I locked the door.*	*When I was nine* *The world was mine.*
When I was five *I learnt to dive.*	*When I was ten* *I had a new pen.*

(adapted from *The End* by A. A. Milne)

Comments and suggestions

- Identifying rhyming words provides ear-training and develops children's awareness of sound–spelling correspondences.
- As a follow-up to this rhyme, you may like to ask the children to write true sentences about when they were younger, eg *When I was six, I visited my grandmother in the USA.*

6.15 Adventure chant

Level A1.2, A2.1, A2.2, B1.1, B1.2   **Age** 9–12   **Organization** pairs, whole class

Aims To ask questions and respond in a chant using the past simple; to improve pronunciation skills; to memorize the past simple form; (to create and write a similar adventure chant)

Language focus *In the example:* past simple, *Wh-* questions, continents/countries, geographical features
Alternatives: any vocabulary depending on the chant

Materials *Essential:* none / *Optional:* a picture or photo of a boy or girl, photocopies of the chant (one for each child), maracas or a tambourine to keep the rhythm of the chant

Procedure

1 Show the children a picture or photo of the character in the chant or draw this on the board. Give the character a name, eg Jack.

2 Explain to the children that they are going to find out about 'Jack's adventure'. Ask the children the four questions in the chant in turn. Write each question on the board in order as you do this and encourage children to predict possible answers. Then say *Let's do the chant and find out!*

3 Explain that the children should ask you the four questions in turn in chorus and you will reply. Click your fingers or use maracas or a tambourine to set up the rhythm of the chant and count the children in to three.

4 At the end, compare the chant with the children's predictions.

5 Divide the class into four groups and assign the answer to one question to each group.

6 Either give out photocopies of the chant if you have these or dictate the answer to their question to each group in turn. Get the children to say the chant again. This time everyone asks all the questions and the four groups take turns to answer.

7 At the end, ask the children if they would feel like Jack and listen to their ideas.

What did Jack do?
> *He said goodbye to his friends one day.*
> *He wanted to travel far away.*

Where did he go?
> *He went to Africa and Asia too.*
> *He went to Mexico and Peru.*

What did he see?
> *He saw volcanoes, deserts and seas.*
> *He saw high mountains and tropical trees.*

Why was he sad?
> *He wanted his friends, he wanted his home.*
> *He didn't like seeing the world alone!*

Comments and suggestions

- The rhythm and rhyme of this chant helps children to memorize the form of *Wh-* questions and past simple statements using regular and irregular verbs. It also helps them to use a falling intonation pattern for *Wh-* questions in a natural way.

- As a follow-up, children can invent and write their own 'adventure chants' in pairs (these do not need to rhyme) and then take turns to say them to the class.

6.16 A rhyme a month

Level A1.2, B1.1, B1.2   **Age** 9–12   **Organization** whole class

Aims To develop enjoyment in saying and memorizing short rhymes, limericks or poems; to develop positive attitudes towards learning English; to become familiar with aspects of English-speaking children's culture.

Language focus any, depending on the rhyme, limerick or poem

Materials *Essential:* one copy for you of the text of the rhyme, limerick or poem you wish to use / *Optional:* a copy of the rhyme, limerick or poem on a large piece of paper or card (for the whole class to see)

Procedure

1   Choose a rhyme, limerick or poem you are going to use. This can either relate to the work children are doing or be completely different.

2   At the beginning of each month or unit of work, either write or stick the copy of the rhyme you have prepared on the board.

3   Either let the children read the rhyme themselves or read it out loud with them. Watch their responses to see if they understand it or, for example, find it funny.

4   Check comprehension and explain the meaning of any words the children don't know.

5   Repeat the procedure of reading the rhyme every now and again during the month with the children. As you do this, either increasingly cover words on the copy you have made or leave gaps on the board. As the month progresses, most children will gradually and naturally learn the rhyme off by heart.

6   At the end of the month, before moving on to a new rhyme, you may like to ask the children to copy the rhyme so that they have a record of it in their notebooks. Some examples of poems and rhymes which children of this age group usually enjoy are as follows:

I eat my peas with honey.	*A thousand hairy savages*
I've done it all my life.	*Sitting down to lunch*
It makes the peas taste funny,	*Gobble, gobble, gulp, gulp*
But it keeps them on the knife. (Anon)	*Munch, munch, munch.* (Spike Milligan)
I'm a grown man now	*A baby sardine saw her first submarine*
Don't easily scare	*She was scared and watched through a peephole.*
(if you don't believe me	*'Oh, come, come, come,' said the sardine's mum,*
ask my teddy bear). (Roger McGough)	*'It's only a tin full of people.'* (Spike Milligan)

Comments and suggestions

• This activity takes very little class time but can be extremely enriching in terms of children's language development and fostering positive attitudes. Children also actively enjoy learning the rhymes, especially when they find them humorous.

• If children have parents or siblings who speak English, they are very likely to share the English rhymes and poems they learn at home. They may also bring in similar rhymes or poems in their first language to share with you. All this helps to strengthen relations between home and school and is likely to impact positively on children's motivation and learning.

• Possible alternatives to 'A rhyme a month' are *either* suitable proverbs *or* jokes.

6.17 Act it out!

Level A1.1, A1.2   **Age** 4–10   **Organization** whole class

Aims To sing (or say) and act out a song (or rhyme); to associate language and actions; to develop concentration and memory skills.

Language focus *In the examples:* elephant, parts of the body, adjectives of size, present simple, *if, crocodile, lunch*
Alternatives: any, depending on the song or rhyme

Materials *Essential:* none / *Optional:* flashcard or picture of elephant or crocodile

Procedure

1 Either show the children a picture of the animal for the rhyme or song you have chosen, or draw this on the board.

2 Say the rhyme or sing the song doing the actions and encourage the children to join in.

3 Repeat once or twice in the same lesson and again in subsequent lessons. Vary the procedure, eg you sing the song and children do the actions; you do the actions only and children sing the song; divide the class into pairs and children take turns to sing the song or say the rhyme and act it out with their partner.

Examples of a rhyme and song to act out are:

The elephant rhyme
An elephant goes like this, like that. (take big strides from side to side)
He's terribly big, he's terribly fat. (make yourself big and fat)
He's got no fingers, he's got no toes. (move your fingers; shake one foot and then the other)
But goodness gracious, what a nose! (make an elephant's trunk with one arm) (traditional)

The crocodile song (sung to the tune of *Little Brown Jug*)
If you see a crocodile today, (put your hands up to your eyes and look around)
Say 'goodbye' and run away. (wave and pretend to run)
If you don't run,
CRUNCH! CRUNCH! CRUNCH! (make three snapping movements with your arms as 'jaws')
He'll eat you for his
LUNCH! LUNCH! LUNCH! (rub your stomach as if eating something delicious)

(C. Read and A. Soberón)

Comments and suggestions

• Acting out songs and rhymes is a standard procedure in primary education which can be applied to many rhymes and songs. Children usually respond enthusiastically and it is often the simplest and most successful way of engaging children's attention and helping them to memorize the words in a natural way.

- With older children, you may like to get them to build up a record of songs and rhymes they learn in a notebook, eg 'My book of songs and rhymes' in which they write the words, or, for example, fill in the gaps, and draw pictures to illustrate the songs and rhymes they know.
- Songs and rhymes which children act out can also be very useful as the basis of a performance for parents or end-of-term show.

6.18 Conduct a song

Level A1.1, A1.2   **Age** 4–10   **Organization** whole class

Aims To sing a familiar song loudly or softly in response to visual signals; to develop concentration and memory skills.

Language focus *In the example:* imperatives *(put, keep), picnic, rubbish, bin*
Alternatives: any, depending on the song

Materials *Essential:* none / *Optional:* a baton to conduct the song

Procedure

1 Ask the children to stand in a semi-circle like a choir.
2 Explain that you are going to 'conduct' them as they sing the song. Demonstrate that they should sing loudly when you raise your hands and quietly when you lower them.
3 Conduct the class as a choir, singing with them at first and raising and lowering your voice as you move your hands.
4 Once children are doing the activity confidently, you can make your hand movements between singing loudly and singing quietly more frequent and sudden. An example of a song you can conduct is as follows (sung to the tune of *Head, shoulders, knees and toes*):

Put your rubbish in the bin, in the bin
Put your rubbish in the bin, in the bin
Picnics in the countryside are fun
Keep it clean for everyone
Everyone!
(adapted from C. Read and A. Soberón)

Comments and suggestions

- This activity is an enjoyable way of varying the way children sing a familiar song.
- With older children, once the class is familiar with the activity, you can ask individual children to conduct the class instead of you. You can also divide the choir into sections and bring different groups in either separately or together.
- When using songs in this way, particularly with younger children, you may want to conduct the last two lines to be sung increasingly quietly in order to settle the class before moving on to the next activity.
- The song in this example can be used with 6–9 year olds to raise children's awareness about the importance of looking after the environment.

6.19 Sing a round

Level All   **Age** 8–10   **Organization** whole class, groups

Aims To sing a familiar song as a round; to develop concentration skills; to promote enjoyment in communal singing.

Language focus *In the example:* weather: *thunder, rain, wet, sunshine, sky, dry*
Alternatives: any, depending on the song

Materials *Essential:* none

Procedure

1 Sing the song you are going to use with the whole class once.

2 Divide the class into two or three groups. Explain that the first group is going to start singing the song; when they get to the end of the first line, the second group should start; when the second group gets to the end of the first line, the third group should start. Explain that the children should sing the song twice (or three times) without stopping.

3 Start the round. Sing with the first group in order to set the pace, rhythm, pitch and tune of the song. Use gesture to bring in the other group or groups when they should start singing.

4 An example of a song to sing as a round (either just one verse or both verses together) is as follows (sung to the tune of *Frère Jacques*):

I hear thunder,	*I see blue sky,*
I hear thunder.	*I see blue sky,*
Oh, don't you?	*Way up high,*
Oh, don't you?	*Way up high.*
Pitter patter raindrops.	*Hurry up the sunshine,*
Pitter patter raindrops.	*Hurry up the sunshine.*
I'm wet through.	*Now I'm dry,*
So are you!	*Now I'm dry.* (traditional)

Comments and suggestions

- Children generally get great satisfaction from successfully singing a song as a round – and the result is often quite impressive!

- Songs that work best as rounds are ones that are short and use traditional tunes that may already be familiar to the children. In addition to *Frère Jacques*, other tunes which work well for rounds are *Row your boat* (see 6.22) and *Kookaburra* (see 6.23).

- You can also invent words to go with traditional tunes based on other language and vocabulary, eg greetings, days of the week or colours.

6.20 Mmm!

Level A1.1, A1.2   **Age** 4–10   **Organization** whole class

Aims To sing a familiar song; to omit and add words to the song; to develop concentration and memory skills.

Language focus *In the example:* snowman, short, fat, hat, nose, play, melt
Alternatives: parts of the body, food, or any familiar vocabulary depending on the song

Materials *Essential:* none / *Optional:* a flashcard or picture of a snowman

Procedure

1 Pre-teach vocabulary as necessary. Sing the song with the whole class doing actions.

2 Once children are familiar with the song, get them to sing it again, replacing key words cumulatively with *Mmm!* but still doing the actions. Once they are just singing *Mmm!* for the

whole song, build it up again until they are singing all the words. An example of a song you can use for this is as follows (sung to the tune of *I'm a little tea pot*):

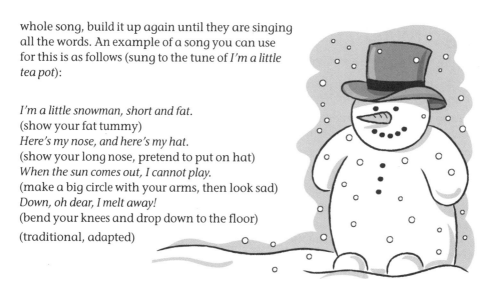

I'm a little snowman, short and fat.
(show your fat tummy)
Here's my nose, and here's my hat.
(show your long nose, pretend to put on hat)
When the sun comes out, I cannot play.
(make a big circle with your arms, then look sad)
Down, oh dear, I melt away!
(bend your knees and drop down to the floor)

(traditional, adapted)

Comments and suggestions

- This word deletion technique works best with short, action songs that contain a lot of vocabulary. It is best known applied to the traditional song *Head, shoulders, knees and toes* which can also be adapted to use with any other vocabulary, eg

  Eggs, bacon, chips and peas, chips and peas
  Eggs, bacon, chips and peas, chips and peas
  Chicken, carrots, salad and cheese
  Eggs, bacon, chips and peas, chips and peas.

  In this case, instead of doing actions, children can point to flashcards of items in the song.

- As well as allowing for variety and enjoyable repetition practice of songs, this technique also provides ear-training as children replace words with *Mmm* while still maintaining the correct rhythm and stress.

6.21 Counting songs

Level A1.1   **Age** 4–8   **Organization** whole class

Aims To practise counting in a song; to build confidence.

Language focus numbers
6.21a *ducks, pond, mother, go swimming*
6.21b *cakes, shop, toys, buy*
6.21c *butterfly*
Alternatives: any, depending on the counting song

Materials *Essential:* none / *Optional:* counting cut-out to go with song chosen (one for each child) (see 7.4)

Procedure

Use any of the following examples to get the children to practise counting in context.

6.21a Five little ducks

1 Introduce the vocabulary of the song by telling the children a little story (see 4.25) either using pictures or a counting cut-out (see 7.4).

2 If the children have made the counting cut-out, they can fold this down as they count the ducks and sing the song. Alternatively, you can assign roles of Mummy duck and the five baby ducks to individual children and they act out the song while everybody sings.

Five little ducks went swimming one day
Over the pond and far away.
Mummy duck said 'Quack, quack, quack, quack'
But only four little ducks came back.

Repeat with four, three, two …

One little duck went swimming one day
Over the pond and far away.
Mummy duck said 'Quack, quack, quack, quack'
And five little ducks came swimming back! (traditional)

6.21b Five chocolate cakes

1 As for *Five little ducks*, you can introduce the vocabulary by inventing a little story based on the song. As you name children in the class in the song, they can come out to your desk and pretend to buy a cake.

2 As a follow-up, children can also act out a role play of buying things in a shop (see 1.9).

The song is sung to the tune of *Five currant buns in a baker's shop*.

Five chocolate cakes in a big cake shop,
Round and brown with a cherry on the top.
Along comes … (child's name) *with money to pay.*
Buys a cake and takes it away (or eats it straight away!) (traditional, adapted)

3 Instead of cakes, you can also sing this song to practise toy vocabulary.

Five new toys in a big toy shop,
Sitting on a shelf right at the top.
Along comes … (child's name) *with money to pay.*
Buys a new … (ball, car, doll, etc) *and takes it away.* (traditional, adapted)

6.21c One little, two little …

1 Children can sing this song with any relevant vocabulary. They can either make a counting cut-out (see 7.4) and fold this up and down as they sing the song and/or act it out themselves. An example is as follows, sung to the tune of *Ten little Indians*:

One little, two little, three little butterflies,
Four little, five little, six little butterflies,
Seven little, eight little, nine little butterflies,
Ten little butterflies!

2 Repeat, counting backwards: *Ten little, nine little …* etc.

Comments and suggestions

• Young children love counting songs. These also provide a link between home and school since children are very likely to already be familiar with counting songs in their own language.

• There are many different traditional counting songs you can use in class in addition to the above, eg *Five little green frogs, There were ten in the bed, Ten fat sausages*. When selecting counting songs, however, it is important to bear in mind the level of difficulty of other language and vocabulary, in addition to the numbers in the song, which may or may not make it suitable to use.

6.22 Singing games

Level A1.1   **Age** 4–8   **Organization** whole class

Aims To sing a song as part of a game; to follow and respect the rules of a game; to build confidence in actively participating in classroom activities.

Language focus 6.22a *Where…?, teddy bear, Here it is!* (*be*, prepositions of place)
6.22b present continuous, any familiar vocabulary
Alternatives: any, depending on the song or game

Materials *Essential:* a teddy bear or flashcard of a teddy bear (6.21a); flashcards of the vocabulary in the game (6.21b)

Procedure

Use games which include songs for variety and as appropriate if they relate to the language, topic or story you are doing with the children. Teach the children the song and actions that go with the game first. Then play the game with the whole class.

6.22a Where's my teddy bear? (age 4–6)

1   Ask the children to close their eyes and put their heads on their desks.
2   'Hide' the teddy bear somewhere in the classroom, not too obvious but visible without moving things.
3   Ask the children to open their eyes and sing the song as they look all round the classroom for the teddy bear.
4   At the end of the song, invite a child who has spotted the teddy bear to get it and say *Here it is!* Alternatively, they can say where the teddy bear is, eg *It's under the table!*

The song is sung to the tune of *Row, row, row your boat*.

Where's my teddy bear?
Where's my teddy bear?
Teddy bear! Teddy bear!
Where's my teddy bear?

(C. Read and A. Soberón)

6.22b We're looking for … (age 4–8)

1   Ask the children to stand in a circle.
2   Lay out 6–8 flashcards face down in the centre.
3   Children walk round in the circle clockwise, singing the song.
4   In the last line, name a child. That child turns over one of the flashcards. If the flashcard matches the word, the child picks it up and has the next turn naming a child in the last line.
5   The game finishes when all the flashcards have been picked up.

This song is sung to the tune of *The farmer's in his den*.

We're looking for a(n) … (name an item, eg *apple, car, tiger*)
We're looking for a(n) … (repeat the item)
Ee-i, ee-i, can you find it … ? (child's name)

Comments and suggestions

• Simple ritualistic games involving songs such as the ones above provide variety in the way songs and games can be used. They also build up children's confidence and sense of security since there is no pressure on individuals to perform on their own.

6.23 Story-related songs

Level A1.1, A1.2   **Age** 6–12   **Organization** whole class, groups, pairs

Aims To recycle language from a story in a song; to aid recall and develop memory skills; to promote enjoyment in stories and songs.

Language focus present simple, questions
6.23a *enormous, turnip, pull,* family, animals
6.23b parts of the body, action verbs, *Why …?*
6.23c present continuous (for future), *zoo*
Alternatives: any, depending on the story and song

Materials *Essential:* none / *Optional:* story books or pictures from the story chosen

Procedure

Use a story-related song once children are familiar with a story in order to recycle and/or extend language it contains. Three examples of story-related songs are as follows.

6.23a The enormous turnip

1   Children sing a verse and do actions for each character in this traditional story. Depending on the version of the story you have used, this may include members of the family, eg *mother, grandfather* and/or animals, eg *cat, dog, cow.*

2   If you like, you can divide the class into groups and each group takes turn to sing verses and do actions for one or two characters each.

This song is sung to the traditional Australian tune of *Kookaburra.*

The enormous turnip song
Here's the … (eg mother)
What does she do?
She pulls and pulls the turnip too.
Pull, everybody, pull
Let's pull the turnip now!

6.23b Little Red Riding Hood

Use the song as preparation for children doing a role play and acting out this part of the story (see 4.28, also 7.12 for making puppets to use for this).

1   Divide the class in half.

2   Children sing the song either as Little Red Riding Hood or Granny / the wolf and then change roles.

3   Children then repeat the procedure in pairs.

Granny, why are your eyes so big? (sung to the tune of *London bridge is falling down*)

Granny, why are you eyes so big,
Eyes so big, eyes so big?
Granny, why are your eyes so big?
To see you little one.

5   Repeat with: *ears – to hear you; arms – to hug you; teeth – to eat you* (and children playing the part of Granny / the wolf pretend to pounce).

6.23c Dear Zoo

Use this song as a bridge between the story (see 4.4) and other activities, eg planning a trip to a local zoo or designing a zoo.

1   Sing the song and do actions with the whole class. Substitute 'Daddy' in line 1 for someone relevant to the children, eg the name of their class teacher or you.

Going to the zoo tomorrow

Daddy's taking us to the zoo tomorrow, (mime driving to the zoo)
Zoo tomorrow, zoo tomorrow.
Daddy's taking us to the zoo tomorrow.
We can stay all day. (move from side to side happily)

We're going to the zoo, zoo, zoo. (put out both arms and turn them over)
How about you, you, you? (pretend to point to different people)
You can come too, too, too. (make a beckoning gesture)
We're going to the zoo, zoo, zoo. (mime driving to the zoo)

(T. Paxton)

Comments and suggestions

- Story-related songs provide an opportunity to recycle and extend children's language using a different medium. This helps to make language memorable and appealing.
- Story-related songs also provide a useful springboard into further work on a story. If they are interactive, as in the case of the Little Red Riding Hood song, they can also prepare children for turn-taking and interacting in a role play independently in pairs.

6.24 Song that tells a story

Level A1.1, A1.2, A2.1　　**Age** 4–10　　**Organization** whole class

Aims To sing and act out a song which tells a story; to associate actions and language in the story; to express opinions and talk about the story at an appropriate level (depending on the age of the children).

Language focus *In the example:* There was …, past simple, story vocabulary
Alternatives: any, depending on the song

Materials *Essential:* none / *Optional:* pictures or flashcards of *princess, tower, witch, forest, prince*

Procedure

1 Either use flashcards or draw pictures on the board and tell the children the story as in the song. Embellish or simplify the language you use to do this depending on the age and level of the children.

2 Sing the song with the whole class and do the accompanying actions using one of the versions following:

There was a princess

For children aged 6–10:
There was a princess long ago, (mime being regal)
Long ago, long ago,
There was a princess long ago,
Long, long ago.

And she lived in a tall, tall tower … (join hands high above your head)

A wicked witch cast a spell … (mime casting a spell)

The princess fell asleep … (put your head to one side on your hands)

A great big forest grew around … (wave your arms like branches of trees)

A handsome prince came riding by … (pretend to ride a horse)

He cut the trees with his sword … (mime cutting down trees)

He took the princess by the hand … (mime taking the princess by the hand)

And everybody's happy now … (mime dancing happily)

(traditional)

For children aged 4–7: Repeat verse 1 for five verses, substituting *princess* with *tower, witch, forest, prince* in each verse and doing the actions in the same way.

3 At the end, talk to the children about the story at an appropriate level. With younger children ask, eg *Do you like the story? Do you know other stories with a prince, princess or witch?* With older children, ask eg *Would you like to be a prince/princess? Why? / Why not? Is the story like real life? Is it a modern story? What would a modern version of the story be like?*

Comments and suggestions

- By simplifying and adapting the language, it is possible to use the same story and song with different ages and levels.

- If you have space, children can act out the song. In order to do this, assign roles of the princess, witch, prince (and horse) to individual children. Get the rest of the class to stand in a circle. The children in the circle sing the song and do the actions, while the other characters come into the centre of the circle and act out their part of the story as they are mentioned in each verse.

- If children act out the story in this way, you may like to reverse the roles, eg the princess can rescue the prince, or the witch can be a troll, in order to give a more balanced gender message. If appropriate, you can talk about this with the children, and also whether the prince should cut down the trees or behave in a more ecologically responsible way.

- See also 4.7 for a sequencing activity which can be used as a follow-up to the song.

6.25 Pop songs

Level All   **Age** 10–12   **Organization** individual, pairs, whole class as appropriate

Aims To develop listening comprehension skills through listening to songs; to sing part or all of the songs; to express opinions and talk about music and songs; to develop positive attitudes towards learning English.

Language focus any, depending on the song

Materials *Essential:* song recordings

Procedure

Use one or more of the following procedures with either pseudo-authentic pop songs, eg in the children's course book, or real pop songs that are currently popular.

6.25a Key words

1 Write 6–8 key words from the song on the board, explaining the meaning if necessary.
2 Children listen and respond non-verbally, eg by putting their hands on their heads, every time they hear one of the words in the song.

6.25b True/false statements

1 Prepare 4–6 true/false statements based on the song.
2 Children listen and say whether they are true or false and give reasons for their answers.

6.25c Listen and order

1 Prepare sets of strips of paper with lines from the song.
2 Divide the class into pairs and give one set to each pair.
3 Children listen and order the sentences as they listen to the song.

6.25d Sing what's next

Use this activity once the children are familiar with the song.
1 Play the song and pause every now and again.
2 Children continue singing as much as they can without the CD.
3 They then listen to check if they have done this correctly before continuing.

6.25e Dance routine

Use as 6.25d above.
1 Divide the class into pairs or groups.
2 Ask them to invent a dance routine to go with the song. Set a time limit for this, eg five minutes.
3 Play the CD and children practise singing the song and doing their dance routines.
4 If you like, ask a few pairs or groups to perform their dance routines to the class.

6.25f Karaoke

If you have a karaoke version of the song available, use as 6.25d above and children sing the song from memory. If appropriate, children can use a karaoke version of the song to do their dance routines in 6.25e.

6.25g Missing words

Use as 6.25d above.
1 Prepare photocopies of the song with missing words. These can focus on either vocabulary or rhyming words or language patterns, eg prepositions or verb forms.
2 Divide the class into pairs. Ask children to write as many of the missing words as they can.
3 They then listen to the song to check their answers and complete any gaps.

Comments and suggestions

- Children at the top end of primary school are interested in real pop music and pop culture and are likely to feel demotivated if you use songs with them that they consider 'babyish'.
- Many children's course books bridge the gap between primary songs and authentic pop culture by including recordings of songs which, although specially written for the classroom, have a convincing contemporary feel. In addition to using these with older children, you can also ask them to bring in recordings of songs that they would like to do in class. Although it is often not possible to agree to their choices if the lyrics are too difficult or unsuitable, it may be appropriate to do this from time to time. If a copy of the lyrics of the song are included in the CD or you can download them from internet, this makes it feasible for you to prepare one or more activities for the children to do such as those suggested above. Although this may prove time-consuming for you, the benefits in terms of the children's motivation, enthusiasm and learning (they often learn the whole song off by heart!) usually make it enormously worthwhile.

Section 7 **Art and craft**

Art and craft activities can be a wonderfully motivating and effective way to develop language skills with children, making English come alive and providing reasons for using language that are immediate, relevant and enjoyable. However, at the same time, art and craft activities may have questionable value if they take up too much precious lesson time, for things such as cutting, sticking and colouring, that could be more efficiently used in other ways. When integrating art and craft activities into English lessons, you need to ensure that they are a valid and effective vehicle for developing language rather than simply keeping children happy and occupied without taking learning further. The focus in this section is on art and craft activities that are feasible in most contexts and which actively enrich and benefit children's language learning.

Art and craft: the pros and cons

Many teachers are understandably wary of doing art and craft activities in English lessons, especially when they may only have two or three lessons with the children a week and the pressure of a syllabus to get through. Art and craft activities can be very time-consuming and, given differing stages of motor skill development, particularly among younger children, some children inevitably take much longer than others to finish their work. Art and craft activities frequently involve materials that may not be readily available or easy to organize in an ordinary classroom. They may also produce a mess and need extra time to get everyone to clear up at the end of lessons. This is especially so if the classroom is not yours and you need to leave it in pristine condition for when the class teacher returns, or for whoever will be working there next.

Some craft activities can also be difficult or fiddly and this can lead either to children feeling a sense of frustration or, in order to avoid this, your becoming directly involved in helping individuals to finish their work. Some craft activities may also have lots of little pieces that are easy to lose, or tabs that children inadvertently cut off. There is also a danger that, unless children are clear about the reasons for doing an art and craft activity, they may perceive it as an opportunity to mess around, with the consequent increases in levels of both noise and L1. Finally, there is no automatic guarantee that art and craft activities will generate very much worthwhile language relative to the time they take to do.

In contrast, on the positive side, art and craft activities are highly appealing to most children. As well as developing visual observation and motor skills, they create immediate reasons for using language in ways which are both purposeful and fun. While following instructions to do a craft activity, there are natural opportunities for children to develop listening skills and use English for real purposes leading to a tangible outcome. Art and craft activities also provide a focus and support for children's initial efforts at using the language and develop social skills by encouraging them to take turns and adhere to the conventions or rules of the activity or game. Art and craft activities allow for personalization and the development of creative thinking skills. They also promote children's feeling of 'ownership' and involvement in their own learning, and this also very often leads to feelings of increased confidence and self-esteem.

Children are usually delighted with the outcome of even a very simple craft activity such as, for example, making a Snap dragon (see 7.8) and this generates interaction in a natural, spontaneous way. As well as helping to make learning memorable, art and craft activities take the focus off language practice for its own sake. Through manipulating, for example, a craft model (see 7.7) or puppet (see 7.12) that they have made themselves, children tend to feel more secure speaking English and this leads them to using language in an increasingly independent way. When children take art and craft home, they are also very likely to do the same language activity that they have done in class with their parents and families. This helps to strengthen connections between home and school as well as making children (and their parents) feel positive about their progress and learning.

The Mad Fox

In order to counter the potential drawbacks of doing art and craft activities and maximize the benefits, it is worth being a little 'crafty' in the choice and use of art and craft activities in English lessons, keeping in mind all the elements of the MAD FOX. These are:

Management: This is vital at all stages: before children start the art or craft activity, while they do the art or craft activity, while they use the art or craft in a language activity, and after this. (See *How to use art and craft activities* below.)

Appropriacy: The art and craft activity needs to be appropriate to children's age, interest, abilities and level of English, and to appeal to both boys and girls. It also needs to fit in appropriately with the story, topic or unit of work you are doing and be a fully integrated part of the lesson.

Design: This needs to be simple, easy, clear, workable and primarily a tool the children will use for interaction and communication. Some questions to ask yourself include: How long is it going to take to make? Can the children do it on their own? Is it fiddly to make? Does it work? Is the language learning benefit relative to the time spent going to be high?

Flexibility: Very often the best art and craft activities lend themselves to a variety of activities. They are multi-level: children can do the activity successfully at different levels (eg when playing with the Snap dragon (see 7.8), children may just say numbers and colours without using the full form to ask questions). They are also multi-purpose: the same art or craft activity may be suitable for practising a range of language (eg the Snap dragon can be used to practise numbers, colours, letters of the alphabet, any other familiar vocabulary or structures such as *can* or *going to*).

Outcomes: When getting children to use an art and craft activity to practise language, it is important to have clear learning aims and outcomes in mind and prepare for the language children will need to use beforehand.

Xcitement: Above all, the art and craft activity needs to spark children's interest, enthusiasm and attention. By engaging children in a visual and kinaesthetic way through art and craft, opportunities to develop their language may be extended and enriched.

How to use art and craft activities

Art and craft activities can be used for a range of purposes, for example, to practise counting (see 7.4) or telling the time (see 7.19), to play language practice games (see 7.3, 7.5, 7.12) to memorize and recall vocabulary (see 7.2, 7.6) as well as to reinforce grammar and encourage children to notice particular language forms (see 7.17, 7.18). They can also be used in role plays (see 7.10, 7.16), to act out stories (see 7.12, 7.13), to personalize learning (see 7.1) and to develop creative thinking skills (see 7.7, 7.14).

Following the four stages mentioned under *Management* opposite, some general tips for using art and craft activities in English lessons are as follows:

Before children start

- Prepare an example of the art or craft activity children are going to do and show it to the class. As well as being motivating for the children, this also ensures you know how it is made.

- Explain the reason and purpose for doing the art and craft activity, eg *We're going to make a … in order to …*

- Make sure children have available any materials they will need, eg scissors, crayons, glue.

While children do the art and craft activity

- Give clearly staged instructions and simultaneously demonstrate how to make the cut-out or model, eg using an enlarged version which you can prepare for this purpose. Include redundancy and use this as an opportunity to develop children's listening comprehension in a natural, purposeful way.

- Monitor the class as they work. Use this time as an opportunity to interact with individual children in a personalized way, giving extra help to those who need it, asking questions, praising children when appropriate, and commenting on their work.

- Get the children to make the cut-out or model before they do any colouring or decorating that is not essential. This can always be done out of class time or at home.

- Ask the children to write their initials in small letters on the reverse side of each part of the cut-out or model they have made so that they do not confuse it with anyone else's later.

- Be ready to give fast finishers additional work to do as soon as they have made their cut-out or model and while waiting for others to finish.

Using art or craft in a language activity

- Explain the game or activity and demonstrate this with the whole class, using the cut-out or model you have made.
- Check the children understand what they have to do.
- Divide the class into pairs or groups depending on the activity.
- Set a time limit if appropriate.
- Monitor the children in order to make sure they are using English and to give help and advice where necessary.
- Observe the children as they work and make any relevant notes.
- Let the children enjoy using their cut-outs to interact in English and remember that a reasonable level of noise is natural for communication to take place.
- Stop the activity before the children's interest peaks.

After the language activity

- Have a place where children can store paper cut-outs and models they make, eg an A5 envelope stuck to the inside back cover of their books. This makes them easily available to be used again, eg in a warm-up activity or for independent play by fast finishers.
- If appropriate, display the art and craft work the children have done and/or get the children to label, write or complete sentences about their work, eg describing the colours.
- Conduct a review of the art and craft activity, eg by asking children whether they have enjoyed it and encouraging them to identify language they have practised and how the activity has helped them to learn (see also Section 10 Learning to learn).

Reflection time

As you use the art and craft activities in this section with your classes, you may like to think about the following questions and use your responses to evaluate how things went and plan possible improvements for next time.

1 **Appropriacy:** Was the art and craft activity appropriate for all the children in terms of its appeal and its creative, cognitive and physical demands?

2 **Manual skills:** Did the use of manual skills affect children's willingness and enthusiasm to participate? If so, in what way(s)?

3 **Language development:** Was the art and craft activity helpful in providing a natural context for developing language? If so, how?

4 **Social skills:** Did the art and craft activity help to develop children's social skills such as, for example, cooperating, showing a willingness to share materials or taking turns in a game?

5 **Self-esteem:** Did you notice any benefits to children's self-esteem as a result of doing the art and craft activity?

6 **Value:** What was the overall value of using the activity, do you think? Will you plan to do more or fewer art and craft activities with the children in future as a result?

7.1 Name cards

Level All   **Age** 4–12   **Organization** individual

Aims To listen and follow instructions; to make and personalize name cards; to create a positive socio-affective atmosphere for learning.

Language focus imperatives, instructions, eg *fold, cut, draw*
7.1b personal information, introductions

Materials *Essential:* A4 paper (one sheet for each child) or a coloured card shape for each child, crayons or coloured pens, scissors / *Optional:* gummed paper shapes, glitter or stars, glue, hole puncher, wool, pegs

Procedure

When you start teaching a new class, ask the children to make name cards. Use these every lesson until you (and the children, if they don't already know each other) are familiar with everyone's names. Two examples of name cards suitable for younger and older children are as follows:

7.1a Shape name cards (age 4–6)

1 Prepare outline shapes of, eg fruit, animals, a star, or a flower on different coloured card.

2 Write the children's first names in large letters on the shapes using a thick felt tip pen.

3 Children cut out and colour or decorate their shape name card with gummed paper shapes, glitter or stars.

4 When they are ready, either punch a hole at the top, thread through and tie the wool in a loose bow, so that the children can attach their name cards to their clothing, or attach them using paper clips or pegs.

5 Give out and collect in the name cards as part of your lesson routine at the beginning and end of every lesson. Use the name cards as an opportunity to provide natural language input and for children to learn the vocabulary for the colours and shapes of their name cards, eg *Here's a green elephant! That's for Marta. Whose is the lovely star with silver glitter? Oh, yes, it's yours, David.*

7.1b Desk name cards (age 6–12)

1 Give a sheet of A4 paper or coloured card to each child.

2 Give instructions and demonstrate that they should fold the card into three equal parts.

3 Children should write their names in large letters in the centre part of the card. In the bottom right they should draw and colour a picture of something they particularly like, eg a football, a cat, a computer, as their personal emblem or symbol.

4 When they are ready, children put their name cards on their desks and either use these to introduce themselves, eg *My name's Natalia and I love football* or you can talk informally about the pictures they have drawn, eg *Is that a picture of your dog, Irene? What's its name?*

5 Children keep their name cards at the back of their books.

Comments and suggestions

- Children enjoy making personalized name cards and the shapes and decorations (7.1a) or pictures they draw (7.1b) lead to natural language use and also help you to remember individual names.

- See also ideas for name games (5.1) and a name rap (6.3) for learning children's names.

7.2 Vocabulary mobiles

Level A1.1, A1.2   **Age** 6–10   **Organization** pairs

Aims To listen and follow instructions; to make a mobile; to make a personalized record of vocabulary; to aid recall and develop memory skills.

Language focus instructions, any vocabulary, eg fruit

Materials *Essential:* plain paper or card, crayons, scissors, wool, plant sticks, an example of a mobile / *Optional:* photocopies of pictures for the mobile (one for each pair), sticky tape, wire coat hangers

Procedure

1 Explain to the children that they are going to make a vocabulary mobile and show them the example you have prepared.

2 Elicit ideas for possible things to go on the mobile, eg for fruit – *apple, banana, strawberry, pear* and specify the number of items, eg 6–8.

3 Divide the class into pairs.

4 Give out the card, crayons and scissors. Explain that the children should agree on the items for their mobile and draw, colour and cut out pictures for half of these each.

5 When they are ready, get them to either make a small hole in each picture and thread through a piece of wool, or attach a piece of wool to the back of each picture with sticky tape. In order to make the mobile, they then use wool to tie two plant sticks together so that they cross at right angles and attach the pictures they have made to the sticks. Alternatively, children can attach their pictures from a wire coat hanger instead.

6 When they are ready, ask the pairs to take turns to show and tell each other about their mobiles, eg *Our mobile has got a peach, a melon ....* The mobiles can then be displayed, eg from a washing line stretching across the classroom.

Comments and suggestions

- With younger children, it is advisable to prepare outline drawings of items for the mobile. Children then colour and cut these out rather than draw the pictures themselves. If you are using plant sticks, it is also best to prepare the crossed sticks tied with wool before the lesson and be ready to help the children attach their pictures to these.

- As well as pictures, children can also write or cut out matching word cards to suspend from the mobile. Alternatively, they can write the words on the reverse side of each picture.
- As well as vocabulary mobiles, children can also make story mobiles, for example for the *Dear Zoo* story (see 4.4) as the illustration on the previous page shows.

7.3 Make a spinner

Level A1.1, A1.2   **Age** 6–12   **Organization** individual, pairs

Aims To listen and follow instructions; to make a spinner; to practise specific vocabulary or language pattern; to interact and take turns in simple games or other activities.

Language focus see below:
7.3a colours
7.3b numbers
7.3c, 7.3d any vocabulary
7.3e *Wh-* questions
Alternatives: any language and vocabulary

Materials *Essential:* stiff card, rulers, scissors, crayons, pencils / *Optional:* photocopies of a spinner shape on stiff card (one for each child), sticky labels

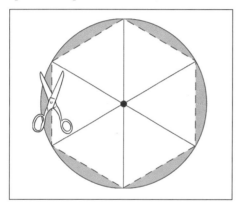 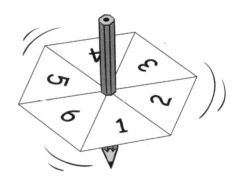

Procedure

1 Explain to the children that they are going to make a spinner, and show them the example you have prepared.

2 Give out the card. With older children, explain and demonstrate on the board that they should draw a circle and divide this into six segments. They should then draw a line across the top of each segment and cut off the curved edge to make the straight sides of the spinner (as in the illustration above). Finally they colour, write or draw on the different segments of the spinner depending on the activity they are going to do (see examples below).

3 When they have done this, they should make a hole in the centre of the spinner and put a pencil through. The spinner is now ready to use.

Some examples of ways in which spinners can be used are as follows:

7.3a Primary colours spinner

Children colour alternate segments of the spinner eg red and yellow / blue and yellow / red and blue. In pairs they then take turns to spin their spinners and identify the colours, eg a red and yellow spinner looks orange when you spin it, a blue and yellow spinner looks green.

7.3b Numbers spinner

Children write numbers 1–6 on their spinner. They can then use the spinner as an alternative to a dice in board games (see 5.28) or dice games (see 5.21).

7.3c Spinner snap

Children draw pictures of six vocabulary items, eg toys, food, clothes, on each segment of their spinner. In pairs, they spin their spinners at the same time and say the word it lands on. When both spinners land on the same item, they score a point. The pair that has the highest score after, say, ten turns wins.

7.3d Spin and guess

Children draw pictures as above. In pairs they take turns to spin the spinner and guess the picture it's going to land on. The child in each pair who gets most guesses correct after, say, six turns each wins.

7.3e Spin a question

Children write question words on their spinners, eg *What? Where? When? Who? How? Why?* In pairs they take turns to spin the spinner and ask each other a question using the word the spinner lands on, eg *What time do you get up? Where do you live?* If possible they must try not to repeat any questions.

Comments and suggestions

- Spinners work best if they are made of stiff card. In order for children to be able to reuse spinners to practise different language, you can get children to draw or write on sticky labels (eg ones used for envelopes) and stick these over previous pictures or words rather than making completely new spinners.

- With younger children, it is advisable to give children photocopies of the spinner shape on card which they cut out rather than asking them to make this themselves.

7.4 Counting cut-out

Level A1.1   **Age** 4–8   **Organization** individual, whole class

Aims To listen and follow instructions; to make a counting cut-out; to provide a visual and kinaesthetic support for counting; to focus attention on numbers while listening to and saying a rhyme or singing a song; to develop motor skills; to develop concentration skills.

Language focus numbers, any vocabulary, depending on the song or rhyme

Materials *Essential:* copies of the counting cut-out (one for each child), scissors / *Optional:* crayons

Procedure

1 Show the children the counting cut-out you have prepared. Give a copy to each child.

2 Explain and demonstrate how to cut along the lines between, eg the ducks or butterflies so that these can be folded up and down when counting. Get the children to practise doing this by saying, eg *Look. Now there's one little duck. And now two little ducks.* as you fold the pictures on the cut-out up to show the ducks.

– – – – cut

· · · · · · · fold

3 Once the children have got the idea, use the counting cut-out to tell a story (see 4.25), to sing a number song (see 6.21) or as an alternative to using fingers for counting in a finger rhyme (see 6.4).

Comments and suggestions

- The counting cut-out is very simple to make and can be adapted to use with any number rhyme or song (see 6.4 and 6.21 for suggestions).

- Folding the pictures up and down gives children a focus and purpose for listening out for numbers and counting. This also makes the cut-out suitable to use even if the rest of the vocabulary of the rhyme or song may be currently beyond the children's productive level.

- As well as to accompany rhymes and songs, you can use the counting cut-out for other activities such as a simple maths activity, eg show ten butterflies on the cut-out, then take away three and ask *How many now?* or for a colour dictation, eg *Colour butterfly 1 purple.*

7.5 Make a dice

Level Al.1, A1.2 **Age** 6–12 **Organization** individual, pairs

Aims To listen and follow instructions; to make a dice; to practise interacting and taking turns in simple games or role plays.

Language focus *In the example: have got*, numbers, toys, shopping
Alternatives: any language and vocabulary

Materials *Essential:* copies of a dice template on paper or card (one for each child), scissors, glue / *Optional:* crayons

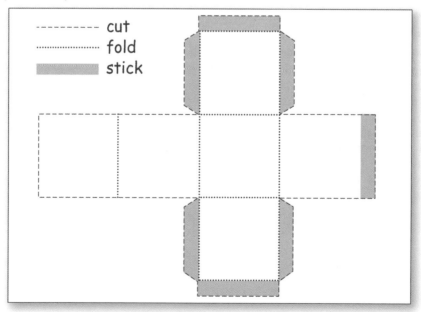

Procedure

1 Show the children the dice you have prepared.

2 Give a copy of the dice template to each child. Explain and demonstrate what you want children to draw or write on each face of the dice, eg numbers, toys (if you have not added this to the template before photocopying).

3 Once the children have done this, ask them to cut out the dice. Explain and demonstrate how to fold and stick the sides in order to make the dice.

Some examples of ways dice can be used are as follows:

7.5a Dice games (see 5.21)

7.5b Board games (see 5.28, 5.29)

7.5c As an alternative to a spinner (see 7.3b–7.3e).

7.5d Simple role plays

For example, dice with pictures of toys can form the basis of a role play in a toy shop.

1 Divide the class into pairs.

2 One child in each pair asks, eg *Have you got a ball, please?* Their partner then throws the dice and responds, eg *Yes, I have* or *No, I'm sorry, but I've got a car.* The role play can either stop there or continue, eg *What colour is it? / How much is it?*

Comments and suggestions

• The use of dice in simple games and role plays helps to provide a framework for children interacting for purposes they can relate to and which they enjoy.

• As with spinners (see 7.3), in order to reuse dice to practise different language, you can get children to draw or write on sticky labels (eg ones used for envelopes) and stick these over previous pictures or words rather than making completely new dice.

7.6 Make a wheel

Level A1.1, A1.2   **Age** 6–12   **Organization** individual, pairs

Aims To listen and follow instructions; to make a wheel; to associate pictures, words and spelling; to recall and memorize vocabulary and/or other language; to interact and take turns in pairs.

Language focus 7.6a determiners, *What's this? It's a ..., Is it a ...?*
7.6b *can* (for ability), superlative adjectives
7.6c weather
Alternatives: any language and vocabulary

Materials *Essential:* copies of a wheel template (one for each child), paper fasteners, scissors

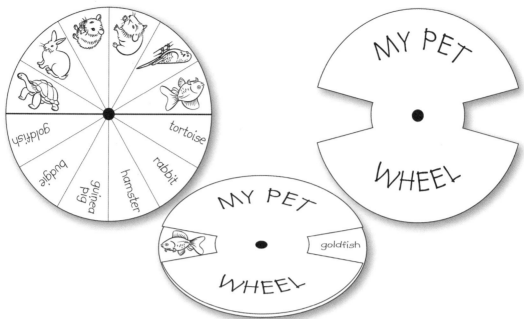

Procedure

1 Show the children the wheel you have prepared.

2 Give a copy of the wheel template, including either pictures or words or both, to each child. If you have left either the pictures or words blank, explain and demonstrate that you want children to add these in the opposite segments of the wheel.

3 Once the children have done this, ask them to cut out both wheels, including the two 'windows' on the second wheel.

4 Once they are ready, give a paper fastener to each child and explain and demonstrate putting the wheel with 'windows' on top of the base and joining the two together with a paper fastener. Children can then turn the top wheel to line up the pictures of vocabulary and the words.

Some examples of ways wheels can be used are as follows:

7.6a Word wheels

Children make the wheels with pictures and words as above. They use the wheels to check they can remember vocabulary and spelling or to 'test' a partner by covering the right side of the wheel and asking, eg P1: *What's this?* P2: *It's a …* or playing a simple guessing game by holding the wheel so their partner can't see, eg P1: *Is it a …?* P2: *No, it isn't.*

7.6b Question wheels

Instead of pictures and words, children write questions and answers, eg *Can a turtle swim? / Yes, it can.* or *What's the biggest desert? / The Sahara.* They then use their wheels to take turns to ask and answer questions in pairs.

7.6c Weather wheels

Children draw pictures and write simple sentences to show different weather on their wheel, eg *It's cloudy. / It's windy.* Children then set their wheels to show the weather at the start of each lesson.

7.6d Story wheels

Children make the second wheel with one larger window rather than two. On the base wheel they draw pictures to show the main sequence of events in a familiar story. They then use the wheel as a prompt to reconstruct the story either with the whole class or in pairs.

Comments and suggestions

- As with spinners and dice, making simple wheels provides a focus and framework for practising language in a purposeful and enjoyable way. Children also often enjoy taking their wheels home and 'testing' their siblings, parents and other friends and family too.

7.7 Junk modelling

Level A1.1   **Age** 4–8   **Organization** individual, whole class, pairs

Aims To listen and follow instructions; to make a junk model; to develop motor skills; to create a character using junk and other modelling material; to talk about the character you create; to act out a dialogue or role play between different characters; to develop creative thinking skills; to develop confidence and self-esteem.

Language focus *have got, be,* present simple, parts of the body, personal information, adjectives to describe people

Materials *Essential:* an example of a junk model head, (eg made out of a milk cartoon, with wool hair, bottle top eyes, plasticine nose etc), junk and other modelling material (eg empty cartons, cardboard tubes, coloured card, wool, bottle tops, plasticine, sticky paper shapes), scissors, glue, crayons

Procedure

1 Show the children the junk model character you have prepared and tell the children a bit about him/her, eg *Look. This is Lenny. He's six years old. He's got big eyes and orange hair. Lenny lives in my house. He loves eggs for breakfast.*

2 Explain to the children that you want them to make their own character like Lenny. Show them the material they can use to make their characters and elicit or suggest ideas for going about it, eg using a cardboard tube for the body, making a plasticine head, making arms out of card.

3 Monitor and talk to the children as they make their characters, eg *I like his hair! What funny eyes! Has he got a name?*

4 When the children are ready, ask them to take turns to show their characters to the rest of the class, eg *This is … He's … He's got ….*

5 If appropriate, children can also act out a simple dialogue or role play between their characters, eg *Hello. / Hello. / What's your name? / I'm Lenny.* etc, either with you or in pairs.

Comments and suggestions

- Children often respond very creatively to inventing and making their own characters – and this also motivates them to talk about them and use language on their behalf!

- If you have space to display the characters in the classroom, you can use or refer to them in subsequent activities, eg to demonstrate an activity, or with younger children to say, eg *I think Lenny and Hilda and everyone liked the song. Shall we sing it again?*

- As a follow-up, older children can complete or write a short description of their character. These can then be written out and displayed with the models.

7.8 Snap dragon

Level A1.1, A1.2   **Age** 8–10   **Organization** individual, pairs

Aims To listen and follow instructions; to make and manipulate a 'snag dragon'; to take turns to ask and answer questions using the 'snap dragon'; to develop confidence and self-esteem.

Language focus *In the example: What's your favourite …?, be,* numbers, colours, letters of the alphabet, adjectives to describe people positively
Alternatives: can, have got, going to

Materials *Essential:* square pieces of paper (one for each child) (Children can make these from a sheet of A4 paper by folding up one corner until both sides are parallel and folding and tearing off the extra piece at the top.)

Procedure

1   Give the children instructions to make a traditional 'snap dragon' and demonstrate each stage as follows:

   – Fold the corners to the centre.
   – Turn the paper over. Fold the corners to the centre.
   – Fold the snap dragon in half. Then fold the snap dragon in half again the other way.
   – Put your index finger and thumb under each flap and push up gently to make the snap dragon.

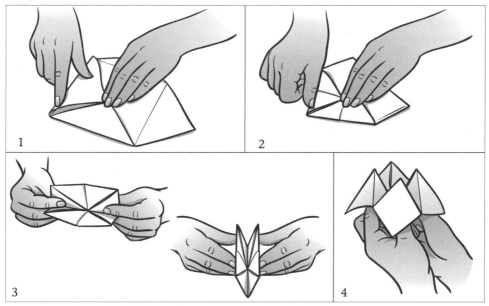

2   Ask the children to colour the four outside squares different colours of their choice, to write numbers 1–8 on the inside and to write positive messages under these, eg *You're great! / You're wonderful!*

3   Once they are ready, children take turns to play with their snap dragons in pairs, eg
   Child A: (holds out the snap dragon) *What's your favourite colour?*
   Child B: (chooses one of the colours) *Red.*
   Child A: *R-E-D* (spells the letters and open and closes the snap dragon three times) *What's your favourite number?*
   Child B: (chooses one of the numbers) *Five!*
   Child A: (opens and closes the snap dragon five times) *One... two... three... four... five* (then reads out the message under the number) *You're great!*

Comments and suggestions

- Following instructions to make the snap dragon provides an opportunity for children to listen with a real purpose and tangible outcome.

- Playing with the snap dragon encourages turn-taking, active listening and a desire to interact with others. Through being positive about others, children tend to see themselves in a positive light too, thus enhancing their self-esteem. Activities like this can also help to make children aware of how they feel when people say nice things to them and to promote care in the way they handle their own relationships.

- Snap dragons can also be used to practise a wide range of other language. For example, instead of the messages under the numbers, you can ask children to write questions using other structures, eg *Can you touch your toes? Have you got a pet?* or sentences making predictions about the future, eg *You're going to be famous!*

7.9 Pop-up cards

Level all **Age** 6–12 **Organization** individual

Aims To listen and follow instructions; to make a card for a special occasion; to write appropriate messages in cards; to develop self-esteem.

Language focus *In the example:* greetings in card, *Christmas*
Alternatives: birthday, Easter, Valentine's day, or any other festival or occasion where it is appropriate to give cards

Materials *Essential:* A4 paper or copies of a pop-up card template (one for each child), scissors, crayons / *Optional:* glitter, glue

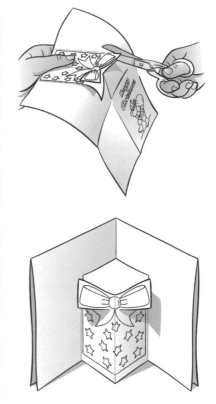

– – – – cut   · · · · · · · · fold

Procedure

1 Show children the card you have prepared. Explain that they are going to make a similar pop-up card to give to their parents or someone else in their family.

2 Give a copy of the pop-up card template to each child. Demonstrate and explain that children should cut out and fold the card. They should then cut around the bow on the present and fold the present down the centre so that it pops out when you open the card.

3 Once they are ready, children can colour and write messages in their cards, eg *To Mummy and Daddy / To Granny and Grandad / Love from ….*

Comments and suggestions

- Children tend to take care in making something to take home to their family. This also creates a sense of pride in their learning.

- Younger children are likely to need a bit of help with the cutting and folding to make the pop-up. If it's too difficult, they can make a simpler card by folding A5 paper in half instead.

- The principle of the pop-up can be adapted to cards for other festivals. The key is to draw a picture which goes across the centre fold of the card and to cut across the top of this, in order to then be able to fold the card the other way and make the pop-up. For birthday cards, you could draw, eg a birthday cake, for Valentine's day a bunch of flowers in a vase and for Easter a rabbit with a basket of eggs.

7.10 Stand-up cut-outs

Level A1.1, A1.2   **Age** 4–10   **Organization** individual, whole class, pairs

Aims To make stand-up cut-outs of animals; to manipulate the cut-outs in simple listening and speaking activities and games.

Language focus *be*, names of animals
7.11a, 7.11b imperatives
7.11b, 7.11d prepositions of place
7.11e greetings, present simple
Alternatives: any language and vocabulary

Materials *Essential:* photocopies of animal cut-outs templates on card, either blank or with animals already drawn (one for each child), example cut-outs, scissors, crayons / *Optional:* one sheet of A3 card for each pair (see 7.10f)

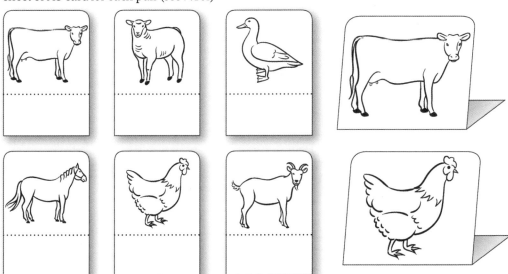

Procedure

1 Show the children an animal cut-out you have prepared.

2 Give a copy of an animal cut-out template to each child. If you have left this blank, elicit suggestions or tell the children the animals they should draw on each cut-out, eg *cow, sheep, duck, horse, hen, goat* for farm animals or *elephant, lion, crocodile, giraffe, parrot, monkey* for wild animals.

3 Set a time limit for children to draw their pictures, eg five minutes.

4 Once children are ready, explain and demonstrate that they should cut round the cut-out and then fold along the folding lines to make it stand up. If there is time, children can also colour their cut-outs as well.

Examples of activities children can do with the cut-outs are as follows:

7.10a Show me!

Say, eg *Show me the …!* and children hold up the correct cut-out.

7.10b Preposition practice

Say, eg *Put the … under your desk! / Put the … on your book!* and children respond.

7.10c Telepathy

In pairs, each child puts their cut-out animals facing them on the table. Together they clap and say *One, two, three …* and immediately pick up one of their animals and say the name.
If they pick up and say the name of the same animal, they put these to one side.
If they pick up and name different animals, they put these down and have another turn.
The game finishes when all the animals have been put to one side.

7.10d Animal line up

In pairs, children put an open book between them as a shield.
One child arranges their paper animals in a line across the table from left to right, starting with the lion.
Then either this child gives instructions to their partner to arrange their cut-out animals in the same way, eg *The elephant is next to the lion.* Or their partner asks questions to find out the order, eg *Is the giraffe next to the lion? Where's the elephant?*

When they have finished, children compare their lines and then change roles.

7.10e Story

Children respond to, and later join in, telling a simple story using two or more of the paper animals, eg

Where's the lion?
Once upon a time, the elephant meets the giraffe. Hello elephant. Hello giraffe. Where's the lion?
I don't know.
Along comes the monkey. Hello, elephant, hello giraffe. Hello monkey. Where's the lion? I don't know.
Along comes the parrot. Hello elephant, hello giraffe, hello monkey. Hello parrot. Where's the lion?
I don't know.
'Here I am,' says the lion. The monkey, the elephant and the giraffe run away. The parrot flies away. And the crocodile smiles. I'm alright, he thinks.

If appropriate, children can use the paper animals to invent their own stories too.

7.10f Stand-up model

In pairs, children make a stand-up model of, for example, a farm by sticking their animals onto a sheet of A3 card. They draw a river or road on the card and colour green for fields. They can also draw and make a farm house, tractor, trees, fence, gate, etc using the same stand-up cut-out technique. If appropriate they can also label the animals and other things on the farm.

Comments and suggestions

- As well as animals, the stand-up cut-out technique can be used to make other things, eg story characters, places or objects.
- Stand-up cut-outs are simple to make and can be used in many ways. The children are also likely to come up with their own creative suggestions which may be suitable to incorporate into lessons.
- With younger children, you need to include pictures on the cut-out templates. It may also be better to use fewer cut-outs, eg 2–4.

7.11 Make a box

Level A1.1, A1.2   **Age** 6 – 12   **Organization** individual, whole class, groups

Aims To listen and follow instructions; to make a box; to ask questions in a game; to guess and deduce the answers.

Language focus imperatives for instructions, *be, can* (for possibility), present simple, yes/no questions, any known vocabulary

Materials *Essential:* photocopies of template to make a box (one for each child); example of box, scissors, glue / *Optional:* crayons, glitter, sticky paper shapes, small picture cards of known vocabulary

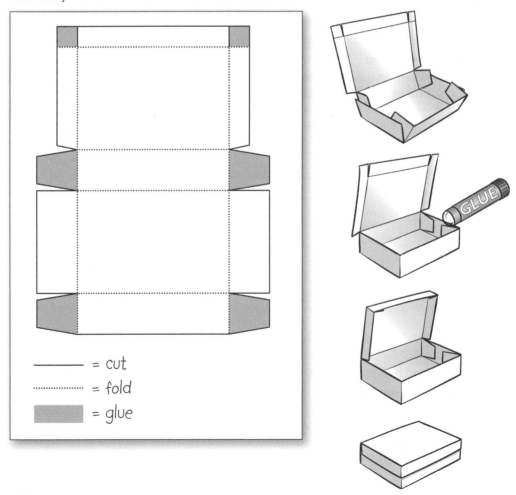

——— = cut

············ = fold

▓▓▓ = glue

Procedure

1 Show the children the box you have prepared. Explain to the children that they are going to make a box and use it to play a game.

2 Give a copy of the box template to each child. Ask them to cut it out.

3 When they are ready, give instructions to make the box. Say, eg *Fold the box like this* and demonstrate folding up the sides of the box. Then say, eg *Now stick the sides of the box like this. And the lid of the box like this.* Children make their boxes.

4 When they are ready, play the game with the whole class first. Either draw a familiar item of vocabulary, eg a banana, on a small piece of paper, or use a picture card, and put it inside your box without the children seeing what it is. Explain that the children can ask you up to ten questions to find out what's in the box and you will answer 'yes' or 'no'.

5 Pretend to wave a magic wand and say, eg T: *Abracadabra! What's in the box?* P1: *Is it an animal?* T: *No, it isn't.* P2: *Is it in the classroom?* T: *No, it isn't.* P3: *Can you eat it?* T: *Yes, you can.* Once children guess correctly, show them the picture in the box.

6 Ask individual children to the front of the class, get them to draw a picture or hide a picture card in their box and play the game several times with the whole class in the same way.

7 Divide the class into groups.

8 Give the children time to secretly draw a picture or choose a picture card and hide it in their box. Make sure they realize that this must be something which they know the word for in English and you may like to restrict it to, eg food, animals or things in the classroom.

9 Children then play the game in their groups.

Comments and suggestions

• This game is similar to the guessing game in 5.17d. However, children find using boxes which they have made themselves additionally motivating and this also ensures that there is something tangible to guess in the game.

• The boxes can also be used in other ways, eg in an activity where children draw presents for each other, either for their birthday or for Christmas, and put them in the box. They then act out a short dialogue as they take turns to give each other and open their 'presents'.

7.12 Puppets

Level A1.1, A1.2   **Age** 4–12   **Organization** individual; any, depending on the activity

Aims To listen and follow instructions; to make a puppet; to develop listening and speaking skills; to develop motor skills; to develop confidence and self-esteem.

Language focus any, depending on how the puppet(s) are used

Materials *Essential:* an example of the puppet; 7.13a, 7.13b cut-out templates, sticky tape, glue; 7.13c (small) paper bags (one for each child) / *Optional:* 7.13a lollipop or plant sticks; 7.13c wool, sticky paper shapes

Procedure

Get the children to make any of the types of puppets below as appropriate and use them to act out dialogues, role plays, stories, songs or rhymes or play games. Show the children an example of the puppet you have prepared and explain what the children are going to use it for before they begin.

7.12a Pencil puppets

Either give children a template for the puppet(s) (essential with younger children) or ask them to draw the character(s) inside a rectangular or oval shape (about 8 x 6cm). Children cut out the puppet(s) and attach them to a pencil using sticky tape. With younger children you will need to help them do this.

7.12b Finger puppets

Give a template of the puppet(s) to each child. Demonstrate and explain that children should cut out the whole rectangle showing both pictures, then fold this in half and use glue to stick down the sides. The finger puppet is then ready to use.

7.12c Paper bag puppet

Give a paper bag to each child and make available wool, sticky paper shapes, etc if you have these. Children draw eyes, ears, nose and a mouth on the paper bag (this can be either of a person or animal, depending on what's relevant) and stick on wool for hair, whiskers or fur. Once they are ready, children put their whole hand inside the bag to use the puppet.

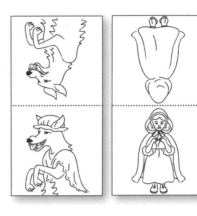

Comments and suggestions

- The use of puppets can have a powerful effect in encouraging shy children to use language, as they feel safe 'hiding' behind the physical presence of the puppet and feeling that it is the puppet speaking rather than themselves.

- If children take puppets home, they will very often also use them spontaneously with their families to show what they have done in class. This helps to reinforce children's sense of achievement and self-esteem.

7.13 Character headbands

Level A1.1, A1.2   **Age** 4–8   **Organization** individual

Aims To listen and follow instructions; to make a character headband; to develop motor skills; to motivate children to listen and speak in character; to develop confidence and self-esteem.

Language focus any, depending on how the headband is used

Materials *Essential:* strips of coloured card (about 8cm wide) to fit round the children's heads (one for each child), photocopies of the character to stick on the card (one for each child), an example of a headband, glue, staples, stapler / *Optional:* crayons, glitter, sticky paper shapes

Procedure

Get the children to make character headbands, as appropriate, and wear them to act out stories, songs or rhymes or in any other activities where they take on the role of the character.

1 Show the children the headband you have prepared and explain what they are going to use it for before they begin.

2 Give a strip of card and a copy of the character to each child. Children stick the picture in the centre of the card. If you like, they can also colour the picture and decorate the headband, eg with glitter or coloured paper shapes.

3 When they are ready, they fold the card so that it fits comfortably on their head and then come to you to have it stapled together. The headband is now ready to wear.

Comments and suggestions

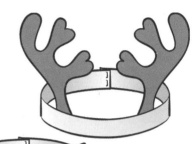

- Depending on the character, it may be appropriate to attach, eg ears to the headbands for three little pigs (see also the class play of this in 4.32) or antlers for Rudolph the reindeer.

- Young children feel special when wearing a headband to act out a story or song and this encourages them to participate actively and take on the character role.

- Headbands play a similar role to masks but they are much more satisfactory as they do not cover children's faces or make it difficult to hear what they say when they speak.

7.14 Make a book

Level All **Age** 6–12 **Organization** individual

Aims To listen and follow instructions; to make a book; to develop motor skills; to practise writing skills; to develop creative thinking skills; to develop confidence and self-esteem.

Language focus any, depending what the book is for

Materials *Essential:* paper and/or card to make the book (enough for each child), an example book ; (7.15a) wool, a hole puncher; (7.15c) scissors, glue; (7.15d) scissors / *Optional:* (7.15b) rulers

7.14a

7.14b

7.14c

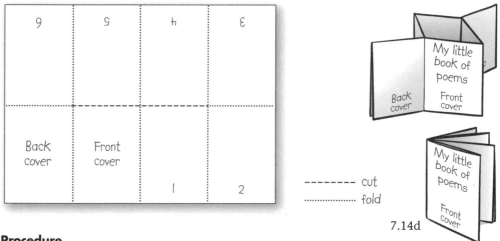

9 | S | h | Ɛ

Back cover | Front cover | |
  | | 1 | 2

My little book of poems
Back cover | Front cover

My little book of poems
Front cover

- - - - - - - cut
· · · · · · · · · · fold

7.14d

Procedure

Get the children to make one of the books below, as appropriate, and use them to, for example, write or reconstruct stories or poems, create parallel versions of stories, write personalized records, eg *I like …, I can …* , keep a diary (see 2.19) or keep a record of favourite songs. Show the children an example of the book you have prepared and explain the purpose of making the book before they begin.

7.14a Basic book

1 Give each child a sheet of coloured A4 card and 2–4 sheets (depending on how long you want the book to be) of A4 paper. Explain and demonstrate that children should cut approximately 2cm off the bottom and one side of the paper (this ensures that the pages of the book stay within the cover).

2 They should then fold the sheets of paper and card in half, punch holes on the side and tie the book together with wool. Alternatively, the book can be stapled.

Basic books are not suitable for younger children to make by themselves and you will need to prepare them yourself in advance.

7.14b Zig-zag book

1 Prepare strips of paper or card (approx 15cms wide) from A2 or A3 size sheets (the larger the sheets, the longer the zig-zag books will be). Either make a pencil mark or rule light lines approximately every 10cm or so on each strip to indicate where the folds should be, before giving the strips to the children (older children can use a ruler and do this themselves).

2 Explain and demonstrate that children should fold the card backwards and forwards, following the marks, to make their zig-zag books. With younger children, you may need to help them to do this.

7.14c Flap books

1 Children make these as for basic books.

2 In addition they cut out flaps using different shapes, eg the shape of a box, if they are creating a parallel version of the *Dear Zoo* story, and stick these over the pictures. The flaps can then be lifted as children read their books.

7.14d Origami book

Given its design, this book always has eight pages (including the covers). It can be made using A4 or A3 paper or card depending on the size you want.

Comments and suggestions

- There are many ways of making books, and the above examples are some of the least time-consuming and most easily manageable.

- Children find it very motivating to make their own books and it helps to develop confidence, creative thinking skills and a sense of achievement. In some cases, such as writing a story, producing a book can be turned into a project which may be done for short periods over several lessons or weeks. When the books are finished, children can take turns to read each others' or, over a period of time, you can read different children's books to the whole class. Younger children in particular tend to feel very proud if you do this.

7.15 Collective mural

Level A1.1, A1.2 **Age** 4–10 **Organization** whole class

Aims To listen and follow instructions; to participate in making a mural; to develop visual observation skills; to develop motor skills; to collaborate with others.

Language focus present simple, questions, *How many…?, Where? What colour …?*, numbers, colours, any relevant vocabulary, eg rainforest or farm animals, things in a city or town

Materials *Essential:* a large, long piece of paper, paints or crayons, cardboard templates (eg for a rainforest mural – tiger, snake, monkey, crocodile, etc, 1 or 2 of each) / *Optional:* photocopies of cut-out pictures for the mural (one for each child or pair)

Procedure

1 Lay the sheet of paper for the mural on the floor or stick it on the board or a wall at the children's height.

2 Draw a basic background for the mural, eg for a rainforest mural draw trees, a river and some rainforest foliage, for a farm draw a farm house, barn, field, fence, gate and pond, for a city street, draw a street with traffic lights, a zebra crossing and park.

3 Get some children drawing more detail and colouring the background. Get other children drawing round the animal templates, colouring and cutting them out to stick on to the mural. If there are not enough templates for everyone, other children can draw and cut out their own pictures to go on the mural, eg birds, butterflies, other insects, flowers.

4 The mural can be built up gradually in short periods of time over several lessons or weeks. When the mural is finished, ask questions, eg *How many monkeys are there? Can you see an orange snake? Where is it?* Children can also prepare questions to ask each other in a group quiz on the mural which they do from memory.

Comments and suggestions

- Making a collective mural provides a wealth of opportunities for natural interaction and acquisition of language as children work on their individual contributions. Some examples of possible teacher language are: *That's a lovely monkey! / Where are you going to put that? / What about a little bit higher so we can see it better?* Some examples of pupil language are: *I want to make a snake. / I'm going to put my tiger here. / Let's colour the flower red. / Give me the green pen, please. / Let's put the snake here.* As far as possible, encourage children to use English as they make the mural and actively look for opportunities to feed in or recast familiar language that is relevant in this context.

- As an alternative to cardboard templates, you can use photocopies of cut-out pictures to go on the mural. Older children can also draw all the pictures themselves.

7.16 Fly away!

Level A1.1, A1.2   **Age** 6–8   **Organization** individual, whole class

Aims To listen and follow instructions; to develop listening and speaking skills; to develop motor skills; to develop confidence and self-esteem.

Language focus 7.16a, 7.16b present continuous, imperatives, prepositions of place, *butterfly*
7.16c greetings, personal information, likes/dislikes
7.16d, 7.16e colours, *butterfly*
7.16f egg, caterpillar, chrysalis
Alternatives: any familiar vocabulary for the cut-out, eg *bird, bee*

Materials *Essential:* Copies of flying butterflies template (one for each child), example of made up pair of flying butterflies, scissors, glue (If possible the template should have the design on both sides, so both surfaces of the wings are patterned.)

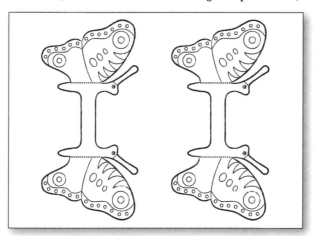 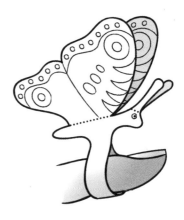

Procedure

1 Show the children the example you have prepared. Put one butterfly on each index finger to demonstrate how they can 'fly'.

2 Give a copy of the butterflies to each child. Explain and demonstrate that they should cut out the butterflies, then fold them in half and stick their bodies, but not the wings, together. They should then fold down the wings, put their fingers through the holes and make the butterflies 'fly'.

Examples of activities children can do using the butterflies are:

7.16a Song: Two little butterflies

This is sung to the traditional tune of *Two little dicky birds*.

Two little butterflies (hold your index fingers with the birds on out in front)
Sitting in a tree,
One named Lucy, (move your right index finger)
One named Lee. (move your left index finger)

Fly away, Lucy. (make your right finger 'fly' behind your back)
Fly away, Lee. (make your left finger 'fly' behind your back)
Come back, Lucy. (make your right finger 'fly' back)
Come back, Lee. (make your left finger 'fly' back)

Repeat the first verse.

(C. Read and A. Soberón)

7.16b Fly under the desk!

Give the children instructions using one of the butterflies, eg *Fly on to your shoulder! Fly into your pencil case!*

7.16c Short dialogue

Children invent a name for one of their butterflies and act out a short dialogue in pairs, using any familiar language, eg for greetings, personal information, likes/dislikes.

7.16d Colour guessing game

Children colour their butterflies any way they like. They then play a guessing game in pairs to find out the colours, eg P1: *Is your butterfly blue?* P2: *No, it isn't.* P2: *Is your butterfly pink?* P1: *Yes, it is.*

7.16e Butterfly display

The butterflies can be stuck on the notice board or, for example, on a collective mural (see 7.15) to make a three-dimensional, pop-up butterfly display. If appropriate, children can also write sentences, eg *My butterfly is pink, purple and blue* and stick these under their butterflies as part of the display.

7.16f Life cycle of the butterfly

Use the cut-outs as part of content-based work on the life cycle of the butterfly (see 8.7).

Comments and suggestions

- This cut-out technique based on symmetry can also be used to make other animals with wings, eg birds, bees.
- Making and using the butterflies as above has similar advantages to using puppets (see 7.12).

7.17 Concertina

Level A1.1, A1.2   **Age** 6–10   **Organization** whole class

Aims To listen and follow instructions; to make a concertina cut-out; to practise making sentences using comparative and superlative adjectives; to reinforce the concept of comparative size; to encourage children to notice the form of comparative and superlative adjectives.

Language focus instructions, comparative and superlative adjectives of size

Materials *Essential:* A4 paper cut in half horizontally (one for each child), an example of a concertina cut-out / *Optional:* photocopies of the caterpillar concertina (one for each child)

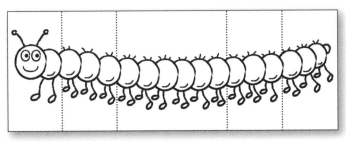 

Procedure

1 Show the children the concertina cut-out you have made. Say, eg *Look. Now the caterpillar is smaller. And now it's bigger.* Explain that you want the children to make their own concertina pictures.

2 Give a strip of paper or a copy of the caterpillar concertina template to each child. Children draw a picture of their choice on the strip of paper either horizontally, eg a snake, a centipede, a fish, or vertically e.g a flower, a tree, a building or a person, or colour the caterpillar (eg as a colour dictation, see 1.5).

3 When they are ready, give the children instructions to fold their strips of paper to make the concertina, eg *First fold the paper here, like this. And now fold the paper the other way, like this. Now fold the paper in the same way on the other side, like this.*

4 When they are ready, ask individual children to show their concertina pictures to the rest of the class and take turns to say, eg *Look. The snake is long* and, as they open the concertina, *The snake is longer.*

5 You can also ask three children who have the same pictures to the front and get them to hold up their concertinas folded in the three possible positions and say with you and the class, eg *This caterpillar is long. / This caterpillar is longer. / This caterpillar is the longest.*

Comments and suggestions

• In this activity, craft is used to reinforce a grammatical concept in a tangible 'hands on' way. By adjusting the size of the concertina, children are also helped to remember the language form.

• The concertina of the caterpillar can also be used as part of content-based work on the life cycle of the butterfly (see 8.7) to show how the caterpillar grows and grows before it becomes a chrysalis and then butterfly.

7.18 Sentence maker

Level A1.1, A1.2, A2.1, A2.2   **Age** 8–12   **Organization** individual, pairs

Aims To listen and follow instructions; to make and use a sentence maker; to make true and false sentences following a language pattern; to notice language patterns and forms.

Language focus *In the example:* present simple, animals, adverbs
Alternatives: questions, any language and vocabulary

Materials *Essential:* a piece of A5 card and three strips of A4 paper about 4cm wide for each child, an example of a sentence maker, scissors

Procedure

1 Show the children the sentence maker you have prepared. Demonstrate how you can move the strips of paper to make different sentences, eg *Lions roar loudly.*

2 Give a piece of card and three strips of A4 paper to each child (or get the children to make these). Write a list of animals, verbs and adverbs on the board, as opposite, and check understanding. Demonstrate and explain that children should write one list on each strip of paper, leaving at least a centimetre between each word. Remind them that the nouns should have a capital letter as they will be at the beginning of the sentence.

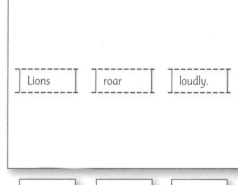

3 When they are ready, they should cut six lines on the sentence maker card and thread the strips through in order: animals, verbs, adverbs.

4 Get children to move the strips to make different sentences and elicit examples, eg *Dogs run fast. Cats purr quietly.*

5 Divide the class into pairs.

6 Explain and demonstrate that they should play a true/false game using the sentence maker, eg P1: *Turtles swim well.* P2: *True!*

7 At the end, you may like to ask the children to use their sentence maker to write one true sentence about each animal in their notebooks.

Lions	swim	slowly.
Dogs	run	quietly.
Mice	move	fast.
Cats	jump	loudly.
Ducks	purr	beautifully.
Turtles	bark	silently.
Birds	roar	easily.
Sharks	sing	well.

Comments and suggestions

- This craft activity provides a framework for practising a particular language pattern and raising awareness of language form. It can be adapted to practise any other structure or pattern, for example, to help children match verb forms with the correct person as in, eg *I was hungry. They were tired.*

- In this example, you may also like to get children to add two additional strips to the sentence maker: one with 'Do' and the other with '?', eg *Do lions roar loudly?* Children can then use the sentence maker to ask and answer questions as well.

7.19 Paper plate clock

Level A1.1, A1.2   **Age** 8–12   **Organization** individual, pairs

Aims To listen and follow instructions; to make and use a clock to tell the time; to reinforce the concept of 'quarter', 'half', 'to' and 'past' using an analogue clock.

Language focus *What's the time? It's …,* numbers, *quarter/half past/to*
7.20c present simple

Materials *Essential:* an example of a paper plate clock, for each child – a paper plate, a paper fastener, two strips of coloured card to make clock hands

Procedure

1 Show the children the paper plate clock you have prepared. Move the hands a few times and ask *What's the time?* Explain that children are going to make their own clocks.

2 Give a paper plate, paper fastener and card to make the hands for the clock to each child.

3 Ask the children to write numbers 1–12 round the plate. In order to space the numbers evenly, get them to write 12, 3, 6 and 9 first and demonstrate this on the board.

4 Draw the shape of the hands for the clock on the board and explain that one should be longer than the other. Tell the children to cut the card to make the hands and then attach these to the centre of the clock using the paper fastener.

Examples of activities children can do with the clocks are as follows.

7.19a Show the time!

You say a time, eg *It's half past eight* and children set the hands on their clocks and hold them up.

7.19b What's the time?

In pairs, children take turns to ask each other the time and set their clocks, eg P1: *What's the time?* P2: *It's ten past seven.* P1 sets their clock and P2 checks that this is correct.

7.19c Daily routines

Children set their clocks and say sentences about their daily routines, eg *I get up at seven o'clock. I go to school at quarter past eight.*

Comments and suggestions

- Manipulating the hands on the clock helps children to associate the concept of telling the time and how to do this in English.

- If you want children to practise the time with a digital rather than analogue clock, you can adapt the sentence maker in 7.18 to become a craft activity to make a digital clock. In this case, children should make two strips of paper. On one they should write numbers 1–24 for the hours, and on the other they should write numbers 00–55 in fives, ie 00, 05, 10, 15 etc. Children can then use their digital clocks to practise the time as in the activities above.

Section 8 **Content-based learning**

The inclusion of content from other areas of the curriculum has long been a feature of some primary foreign language programmes. In recent years, content has been given greater prominence as many countries or regions have lowered the compulsory age of starting to learn a foreign language at school and increased the number of study hours through the introduction of programmes based on *Content and Language Integrated Learning* (CLIL). CLIL is an umbrella term which encompasses many different approaches in which part or all of school subjects are taught through an additional language. As a common feature of CLIL, there are aims, procedures and outcomes which relate both to the subject being taught and to the language. The focus in this section is on including content from other areas of the curriculum in English language learning programmes, rather than on teaching specific subject syllabuses through English. As well as making lessons more intrinsically interesting, the inclusion of content can enhance and extend children's learning and acquisition of language. It can also contribute to their social, cognitive and psychological development.

Throughout their primary education, children are developing their knowledge and understanding of the world. At the same time, they are developing their ability to use language as a tool to investigate, analyse and describe the world. This inter-relationship underpins and links different subject areas across the primary curriculum. On the one hand, language is the medium for learning about all other subjects and, on the other hand, all other subjects are the vehicle for developing language.

When children start learning a foreign language as a school subject, this is often isolated from the mutually reinforcing process of developing knowledge and developing language that enriches all other areas of the curriculum. The reason for this is not surprising perhaps, as, initially at least, it seems difficult to envisage how English may be used as the medium to learn about other subjects when children's language competence is so limited. By adopting an approach which integrates content-based learning from the earliest stages and most elementary levels, learning to use a foreign language becomes part of the holistic developmental and educational process which takes place in all other areas of children's experience and learning at primary school.

How to integrate content into primary language learning

Within English language programmes there are three commonly used approaches to the integration of content. These are:

1 through the organization of the syllabus and learning based on topics from other areas of the curriculum

2 through the organization of the syllabus and learning based on stories

3 through the use of content-based activities from other areas of the curriculum that relate or fit in to an existing language-based syllabus.

Topics chosen from other areas of the curriculum should motivate and interest children and provide a suitably challenging context in which learning can take place. They should relate to and build on children's experience and knowledge of the world and provide opportunities to develop concepts, language and thinking skills in ways that are appropriate to the children's age and level. Topics should also lend themselves to the design of purposeful activities, including opportunities for investigative, factual enquiry and for creative, imaginative work. By organizing learning around topics, children's language development can be integrated with content from other areas of the curriculum in a natural way. Topics provide opportunities for meaningful, experiential learning that appeals to different intelligences and learning styles. Topics also encourage children to be active and constructive in their own learning as they use language as a tool to do things which are relevant, purposeful and enjoyable and which build on their natural curiosity in finding out about the world.

On the next page is an example of a topic web showing how language and content from other areas of the curriculum might be integrated in a topic on bugs.

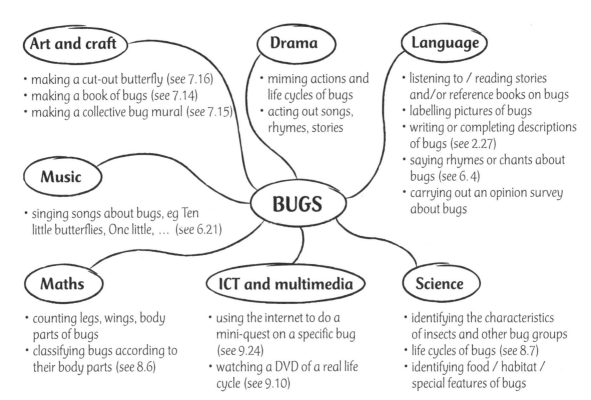

Figure 1 **Topic web on bugs**

A similar kind of web integrating content from other areas of the curriculum may also be used if the children's learning is organized around stories.

When organizing learning which integrates content from other areas of the curriculum based on a topic or story, the use of a web, such as the above, is a flexible initial planning tool. In order to develop a coherent learning sequence, the activities need to be planned in detail and ordered in a logical way. This involves linking them so that each activity consolidates and builds on what has come before and also prepares for what is to follow. Although the activities in the sequence use concepts and skills which draw on different areas of the curriculum, the children experience a seamless series of classroom events. The activities lead children progressively to new learning in a way which is both challenging and achievable. In order to make suitable links between activities you need to analyse and plan each one in terms of:

- **concepts:** what concepts the activity will develop and whether these are already familiar to the children in L1

- **cognitive demands and thinking skills:** whether the cognitive demands are appropriate to the age and level of the children and what these involve, for example, the ability to predict, estimate, classify, describe a process, or interpret and use a graphic organizer

- **language demands and skills:** whether these match the cognitive demands as well as the main sentence patterns, grammar, vocabulary and language functions children will need to use; how much language will be new or recycled, whether it will be receptive or productive, and the language skills, or aspects of these skills, the activity will develop

- **other learning skills and strategies:** apart from language and thinking skills, what other skills, eg social skills, motor skills, learning strategies or metacognitive skills (see Section 10 Learning to learn) does the activity assume or will it help develop?

- **attitudes:** what positive attitudes will the activity help to foster, eg towards the topic itself or in terms of citizenship or individual learning?

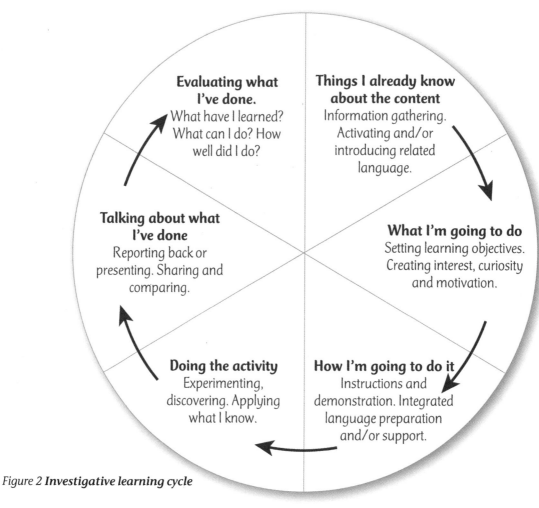

Figure 2 **Investigative learning cycle**

When implementing content-based learning activities as part of topic or story-based work, it is frequently appropriate to follow stages of an investigative learning cycle as outlined above. These broadly reflect the familiar stages of *before*, *during* and *after* activities which have been discussed elsewhere (see Sections 1, 2, 4 and 7) but place an emphasis on ensuring the integration of content and language support needed to carry out the activity.

Many children's course books are based on either topics or stories or a combination of both. In a partial version of the approach suggested in the cycle above, content-based learning sequences can be used to supplement or extend topics and/or stories that already exist within the course book. In a full version of the approach, the detailed planning resulting from initial curriculum-linked webs based on topics or stories can constitute the entire syllabus and learning

programme. While the latter has the advantage of being able to tailor learning very specifically to the children's context, interest and needs, the amount of planning time, effort and additional resources required should not be underestimated.

In situations where children are following a language syllabus which is not based on either topics or stories, content-based activities can also be included to enrich and extend learning, particularly where there is a direct link between the language of the activity and the language in the syllabus. For example, at the moment when the present simple third person 's' appears as part of the syllabus, it may be suitable to do an activity like *Float or sink?* (8.16). Although this represents a much more piecemeal approach to the use of content-based learning, it does nevertheless give children an opportunity to practise language in a meaningful context and may contribute positively to their motivation too.

The content-based activities in this section can either be used as part of a topic- or story-based approach, or provide an alternative means of practising specific language as described above. The activities develop a range of concepts, such as the properties of colour (see 8.1) or materials (see 8.3, 8.16) and the characteristics of animals (see 8.5, 8.7, 8.15) or plants (see 8.8, 8.9). Other concepts explored in the activities relate to, for example, food (see 8.12, 8.13, 8.14), natural phenomena (see 8.2, 8.17) and human biology (see 8.20).

Benefits of content-based learning

In terms of cognitive strategies and skills, the activities develop children's abilities to, for example, estimate, hypothesize, experiment, report, classify, compare, contrast, measure, match, sequence and describe processes, as well as to use different kinds of graphic organizers and charts.

In terms of the CLIL umbrella referred to earlier, integrating content-based learning activities into language lessons where the syllabus, materials and forms of assessment are predominantly language-led, is very much the tip of the 'content' iceberg. There are, however, a number of significant potential benefits which make it extremely worthwhile, even if only on a limited or occasional basis.

- Lessons can be made more interesting, varied and enjoyable.
- Children generally find it extremely motivating to investigate, discover and learn things about the world through English.
- Language is used purposefully and the focus on real meaning is more likely to make it memorable.
- Children use different combinations of intelligences and learning styles which widens the appeal of classroom activities and allows children to build on their strengths.
- It reinforces learning and conceptual development in other areas of the curriculum, thereby bringing English into the mutually reinforcing process of developing knowledge and developing language at primary school described earlier.
- It encourages children to work more

independently and helps them learn how to learn (see also Section 10).
- It provides an approach to learning which takes account of children's whole development in a harmoniously integrated way.
- Additional benefits for individual children also frequently include increased confidence, higher levels of concentration and more positive attitudes towards learning a foreign language at school.

Reflection time

As you use the content-based activities in this section with your classes, you may like to think about the following questions and use your responses to evaluate how things went and plan possible improvements for next time.

1 **Curriculum links:** How did the activity or activities relate to other areas of the curriculum? What was the main value of making such links?

2 **Cognitive / language demands:** Were the cognitive and language demands appropriate to the age/level of the children? Was there a balance or mismatch in the cognitive / language demands? If there was a mismatch, how could you redress this next time?

3 **Interest:** What was the level of interest in the activity or activities? How did the inclusion of content based on another area of the curriculum influence the children's response?

4 **Learning sequence:** What was the rationale for sequencing the activities? Did the sequence allow for a smooth learning progression or would you make any changes next time? If so, what?

5 **Aims and outcomes:** Did the activity or activities fulfill both content learning aims and language learning aims? How were these reflected in the outcomes?

6 **Classroom communication:** How did the use of content-based learning activities influence the way you and the children communicated in class? Did this seem to enhance children's language acquisition and learning? If so, in what way(s)?

8.1 Mixing colours

Level A.1.1, A1.2   **Age** 4–8   **Organization** whole class, pairs

Aims To learn about the effects of mixing colours; to carry out an experiment with mixing colours; to talk about colours and the way they combine.

Language focus colours, present simple

Materials *Essential:* coloured cellophane sheets cut into large circles (red, yellow, blue), paints (red, yellow, blue, eg finger paints, poster paints, water colour), paintbrushes, paper / *Optional:* black and white paints, coloured cellophane sheets (red, yellow, blue) cut into strips, scissors, card

Procedure

1 Stand near a window or against a white or light coloured wall. Hold up the three cellophane circles you have prepared in turn and get children to identify the colours: red, yellow and blue.

2 Then hold up the circles in pairs, with one circle on top of the other, and get children to identify the new colours: red/yellow (orange); blue/yellow (green); red/blue (purple); red/yellow/blue (brown). Encourage the children to say with you, eg *Red and yellow make orange. / Blue and yellow make green. / Red and blue make purple. / Red, yellow and blue make brown.*

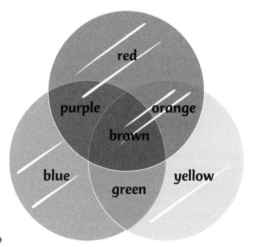

3 Ask the children to predict if they think the same thing will happen when they mix paint. Listen to their response and then say *Let's find out!*

4 Divide the class into pairs.

5 Give paints, paint brushes and paper to each pair. Ask the children to experiment mixing and making new colours.

6 At the end, ask them to report back on what they have found, eg *Red and yellow make orange* but also *Red and a lot of yellow makes lighter orange. / Yellow and a lot of red makes darker orange.* Be ready to feed in vocabulary, eg *lighter, darker* and/or recast and extend what children say as necessary.

7 Younger children can then paint a picture using as many interesting combinations of the three colours as possible. Older children can then draw, colour and label overlapping colour circles (as above) and/or write sentences about the colours they have made.

Comments and suggestions

• In order to keep the activity focused, it is best only to give the children red, yellow and blue paints rather than a paintbox full of colours.

• With younger children, finger paints are easier to use and avoid the need for water on the desks to rinse paint brushes.

• As a separate stage, you may like to give out black and white paints. Children predict what will happen if they add black or white to colours they have mixed, or use these colours together, and then experiment in the same way.

• As an alternative to using paints, older children can cut a frame out of card and use strips of red, yellow and blue cellophane to 'weave' a picture which illustrates the way that the colours combine.

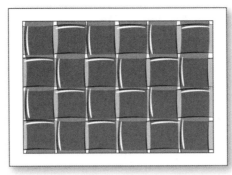

- With older children, it may be appropriate to introduce the terms primary and secondary colours and do further work on colours and the colour spectrum.
- This activity can also be linked to other activities involving colours, eg doing a colour dictation (see 1.5), following colour-related instructions in a rhyme (see 6.8), saying a colour chant (see 6.12), singing a round (see 6.19) or making a colour spinner (see 7.3).

8.2 Rainbows

Level A1.1, A1.2   **Age** 6–10   **Organization** pairs, whole class, individual

Aims To investigate the order of colours in a rainbow; to carry out a simple science experiment by hypothesizing, observing, comparing and reporting; to identify and name the colours in a rainbow.

Language focus numbers 1–7, colours, *What's …?*

Materials *Essential:* a glass of water, a piece of plain white paper, a sunny window

Procedure

1 Ask the children to tell you or guess how many colours there are in a rainbow (7). Write numbers 1–7 in a list on the board. Pre-teach the colour *indigo* (a blend of blue and purple) and write this word next to 6 on the board.

2 Divide the class into pairs.

3 Ask the children to guess the order of the other colours in a rainbow and write a list with their partner. Demonstrate the activity before they begin, eg T: *What's colour number 1?* P1: *(I think) it's orange.* P2: *No, it isn't. It's yellow.*

4 Ask the children to report back and record their guesses on the board. Hold up the glass of water and piece of white paper and say *Now let's find out the order of colours in a rainbow.* Walk over to a sunny window and hold the glass of water over the white paper. Change the angle of the glass until the sun shines through leaving a 'rainbow' on the paper.

5 Invite groups of children to come and have a look at the 'rainbow' and identify the colours in turn. They compare the order of colours with their list and the guesses on the board. (The order is *red, orange, yellow, green, blue, indigo, purple*). Children then draw and colour a rainbow, labelling the colours, based on their observations.

Comments and suggestions

- This activity only works if there is a sunny window in the classroom! The angle that you need to hold the glass and paper for the 'rainbow' to appear varies depending on the time of day and the height of the sun in the sky. Don't give up if you can't make it work at first!
- As a follow-up, you may like to teach children the well-known song *I can sing a rainbow.* As an initial listening task, you can ask children to identify the colours in the song that are wrong.
- With older children, it may be appropriate to do further work investigating the properties of light and colour and the colour spectrum.

8.3 Metal, plastic, glass or wood?

Level A1.2, A2.1, A2.2, B1.1   **Age** 8–12   **Organization** whole class, pairs

Aims To identify different materials; to recognize that everyday objects can be made from the same or different materials; to recognize that materials can be used in different ways; to ask and answer questions about materials and complete a grid.

Language focus questions with *can* (for possibility), *be, made of …*, materials (*metal, plastic,* etc), household or classroom objects and furniture

Materials *Essential:* example objects of different materials / *Optional:* copies of the grid (one for each child)

Procedure

1 Show children examples of objects made of metal, plastic, glass or wood and say, eg *Look at this spoon. It's made of metal. / Look at this pencil case. It's made of plastic.* Check understanding by getting children to identify things in the classroom made of different materials, eg *The door is made of wood. My pencil sharpener is made of plastic.* Ask questions, eg *Can a pencil sharpener be made of metal? Can a door be made of glass?* in order to get the children thinking about the idea that some objects can be made from different materials, and that different materials can be used in different ways.

2 Divide the class into pairs.

3 *Either* draw the grid below on the board (including words or pictures or both for each item) and ask the children to copy this *or* give out copies (one to each child).

4 Explain and demonstrate that children should talk about each item and write ticks (✓) in the grid depending on the materials they can be made of, eg *Can a comb be made of metal? Yes, it can. / Can a comb be made of glass? No, it can't.*

5 At the end, get the children to report back and compare their answers. Use this as an opportunity to discuss the different materials in English or L1 as appropriate, eg *Why isn't a plastic saucepan a good idea (except as a toy)? (It would melt on the stove.) / What's the difference between a metal bucket and a plastic bucket? (The metal one is heavier.)* Listen to the children's responses and be ready to recast or extend their ideas as necessary.

	comb	mug	box	spoon	saucepan	bucket	bowl	pencil case
metal								
plastic								
wood								
glass								

Comments and suggestions

- As a follow-up, in pairs children can think about other objects that may be made of different materials. They prepare their own versions of the grid and then exchange, complete and discuss these, first with the pair who prepared the grid and then with the whole class.

- As an extension, children can do further work on the properties of different materials, eg *Metal is strong / Glass is transparent* and why these properties make them good materials to be used for particular objects. The activity can also be linked to content-based work on recycling.

- In order to reduce the challenge of the activity if necessary, children can complete a grid with fewer items and two materials only, eg metal and plastic. Children can also ask, eg *Can a comb be metal?* rather than *Can a comb be made of metal?* if this is too difficult.

8.4 Hand spans

Level A1.1, A1.2, A2.1, A2.2   **Age** 7–12   **Organization** individual, groups, whole class

Aims To measure your hand span; to record the measurements of other children's hand spans in a chart; to ask and answer questions about the measurements; to compare the measurements; to collaborate with others.

Language focus numbers, *half, quarter, three quarters, be, How long …?*, parts of the body (*hands, feet*), comparative and superlative adjectives of size

Materials *Essential:* rulers (at least two per group) / *Optional:* copies of the hand span chart (each column should be one centimetre) (one for each child), paints and large sheets of paper

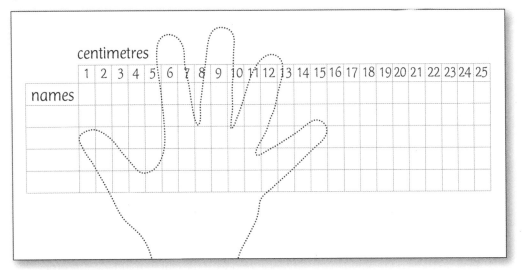

Procedure

1 Hold up your hand, stretching your thumb and your little finger as far apart as possible. Point to the distance between your thumb and little finger and say, eg *Look. This is my hand span.* Explain that the children are going to measure and compare their hand spans.

2 Divide the class into groups of four.

3 Either make sure that each group has rulers or give out copies of the hand span chart (one to each child). Ask the children to write their own name and the names of the members of their group either in their notebooks or in the chart.

4 Explain and demonstrate how children can measure their hand spans either using rulers or the chart.

5 Ask the children to measure their own hand spans and record the result either by writing the number of centimetres in their notebooks or drawing a line at the point their little finger reaches in the chart.

6 When they have done this, explain and demonstrate that they should take turns to find out the measurements of others in their group and record them in the same way, eg P1: *How long is your hand span?* P2: *It's fifteen centimetres.*

7 When they are ready, ask the groups questions, eg *Who's got the longest/shortest handspan?* and ask individual children to report back, eg *My hand span is eighteen centimetres.* / *My hand span is longer/shorter than Jane's.*

8 If appropriate, children can then write a short report about the hand span measurements of their group.

Comments and suggestions

- As a follow-up, children can measure their feet in the same way. They can then compare within their groups whether the children with the longest hand spans also have the longest feet.
- As a further maths activity, children can also measure each others' height and then calculate how many times their hand span or length of their foot fits into their height. If you think some children may feel sensitive about their height, however, it is best not to do this.
- With younger children and lower levels, children can measure to the nearest centimetre. Alternatively, you can introduce fractions, eg *quarter, half, three quarters*.
- If appropriate, as a follow-up to this activity, children can use paints to make a colourful mural display of their handprints.

8.5 Characteristics in common

Level A1.1, A1.2, A2.1, A2.2   **Age** 6–10   **Organization** whole class, pairs

Aims To observe and identify shared characteristics of animals; (to explore and develop the ability to define a term).

Language focus present simple, *can* (for ability), *need*, animals, parts of the body, actions

Materials *Essential:* pictures or flashcards of one human character, eg a child, and a selection of animals, eg dog, rabbit, frog, butterfly, bird, goldfish, snake, spider / *Optional:* copies of true/false sentences about the animals (see step 4, one for each child)

Procedure

1 Stick pictures or flashcards on the board and get the children to identify each one as you do this. Ask the children what all the pictures have in common, using L1 to explain what you mean if necessary (they're all animals; they're all alive).

2 Divide the class into pairs.

3 Explain that you're going to say sentences and see if the children can identify other characteristics the pictures have in common. After you say each sentence the children should confer with their partners and then say *Yes!* or *No!* depending on whether they think it is a shared characteristic or not.

4 Say the following sentences using mime and gesture to convey meaning as necessary: *They're all animals.* (yes) *They're all alive.* (yes) *They all move.* (yes) *They all fly.* (no) *They all need food.* (yes) *They all have legs.* (no) *They all have a heart.* (no) *They all grow.* (yes) *They all produce babies.* (yes) *They all swim.* (no) *They all need water.* (yes) *They all talk.* (no) *They all need air.* (yes)

5 Encourage the children to reconstruct the common characteristics of the animals in the pictures with you, ie *They are alive. They move. They need food, air and water. They grow and they produce babies.*

6 With younger children, you can ask them to draw and colour a picture of another animal which has all these characteristics.

7 Older children can write or complete sentences with the common defining characteristics of the animals in the pictures. You can then ask them if they think all these characteristics apply to all animals. This can lead to a more detailed, discussion of animal characteristics, eg not all animals move – examples are mussels or limpets attached to rocks in the sea; not all animals drink water – examples are frogs, which absorb water through their skin; not all animals see or hear – examples are some fish, worms or bats; not all animals need air – examples are deep sea fish. Be ready to help with vocabulary and recast or extend children's ideas as they contribute to the discussion and explore defining the term 'animal'.

Comments and suggestions

- By saying the true/false sentences one at a time and using mime and gesture to convey meaning, it is possible to do this activity with younger children who are not yet reading in English or familiar with the vocabulary.
- With older, higher level children, you may prefer to give the children true/false sentences on a handout to read and discuss with their partner. Alternatively, instead of using true/false sentences, you can ask the children to work with their partner and write six sentences which they think describe the common characteristics of the animals. The pairs then take turns to say a sentence to the class in order to see whether the others agree, and arrive at a consensus.
- This activity develops children's awareness of common characteristics of animals and can be used as a prelude to doing more detailed work, eg on wild life from a particular habitat such as rainforests.
- A similar activity can also be done with pictures of plants instead of animals, eg tree, flower, plant, grass, vegetable: *They all grow. They all need sunlight. They all need water. They all produce seeds. They all have leaves. They all have flowers.*

8.6 Bug world

Level A1.1, A1.2, A2.1, A2.2   **Age** 6–12   **Organization** pairs, groups

Aims To classify bugs according to observable features; to explore and discuss alternative ways of classifying bugs; to collaborate in groups.

Language focus present simple, *have got,* names of bugs, parts of the body, numbers

Materials *Essential:* pictures of about 12 bugs with their legs (if any) visible, eg butterfly, worm, snail, centipede, spider, millipede, bee, ladybird, grasshopper, fly, ant, cockroach, mosquito, beetle / *Optional:* copies of a 'garden' plan (see below) (one for each child)

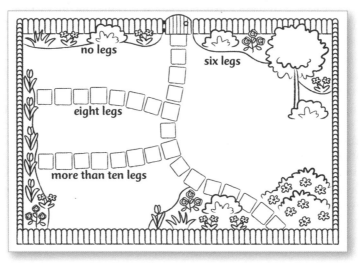

Procedure

1. Show children the pictures of the bugs and elicit or teach the names as you do this. Explain that one of the ways to classify bugs is according to the number of legs they have got. Either draw the 'garden' plan and label the different sections on the board and ask children to copy this or give a copy to each child.
2. Divide the class into pairs.
3. Ask children to either draw pictures or write the names of the bugs in the correct part of the garden depending on the number of legs they have got.

4 When the children are ready, ask them to report back on how they have classified the bugs, eg *Butterflies have six legs.* (no legs: *snail, worm*; six legs: *butterfly, ladybird, beetle, fly, grasshopper, mosquito, bee, ant, cockroach*; eight legs: *spider*; more than ten legs: *centipede, millipede*)

5 Ask which is the biggest group of bugs (the ones with six legs). Elicit or explain that these are insects. If appropriate, point to the pictures and say that all insects have six legs, a head, a thorax, an abdomen, antennae and eyes, and that some insects also have wings.

6 You may also wish to talk about the body parts of the other bugs as well. Snails and slugs have a head with tentacles and eyes. Snails also have a shell. Worms have a head and mouth at one end, a tail at the other, and many body segments which are all the same. Centipedes have many body segments, each with one pair of legs. Millipedes also have many body segments, each with two pairs of legs. Centipedes have about 30 legs; millipedes can have up to 750! Spiders have two body segments (a head and thorax, which are fused together, and an abdomen) and four pairs of legs. Spiders do not have antennae or wings.

7 Explain that counting the legs of bugs is one way of classifying them. Put the pairs together to make groups and ask them how many other possible ways they can think of to classify the bugs. Give them a few minutes to discuss their ideas and then ask them to report back and discuss and compare their suggestions. Examples of possibilities are: bugs which have wings and fly and bugs which don't; bugs which sting or bite and bugs which don't; bugs which help human beings (eg worms aerating earth or bees pollinating flowers) and bugs which don't; bugs which spread disease and bugs which don't; bugs which eat animals and bugs which eat plants; bugs which are colourful and bugs which aren't; bugs which you like and bugs which you don't. Make the point that all these different ways of classifying bugs are valid. If you like, ask the children to draw a second garden plan and classify the bugs in a different way of their choice. If appropriate, they can also use dictionaries and add the names of other bugs which fall into each category.

Comments and suggestions

- This activity develops children's visual observation skills and ability to analyse and classify things in ways which are useful. It also develops their awareness of classification as a helpful tool to aid our understanding, in this case of things in the natural world.

- With younger children, it is unlikely to be appropriate to introduce the names and body parts of all the bug groups. The second part of the activity is also likely to be better done as a whole class activity and eliciting fewer possibilities for classifying the bugs.

- As a follow-up, children can either draw and label a picture and/or write a description of a bug of their choice. This can involve further research either in reference books or on the internet and comprise, eg a description of the bug including any special features, information about its habitat, what it eats and whether or not it is harmful or useful to human beings. The children's work can then either be displayed or made into a class book.

- This activity can also be linked to 2.27, 8.7 or to a websearch activity using one or more pre-selected websites (see 9.24).

8.7 Life cycles

Level A1.1, A1.2, A2.1, A2.2   **Age** 6–12   **Organization** whole class, individual

Aims To identify and sequence stages in the life cycle of an insect or other animal; to label pictures and/or write sentences about each stage.

Language focus present simple, sequencers, name of animal, names of each stage in the cycle

Materials *Essential:* a picture of the animal whose life cycle children are going to study, eg ladybird, butterfly, frog / *Optional:* copies of the life cycle template (one for each child)

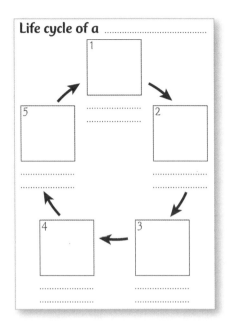

Life cycle of a ....

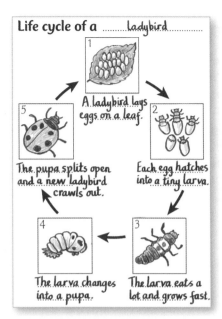

Life cycle of a ....ladybird.........

1

A ladybird lays eggs on a leaf.

2

Each egg hatches into a tiny larva.

3

The larva eats a lot and grows fast.

4

The larva changes into a pupa.

5

The pupa splits open and a new ladybird crawls out.

Procedure

1 Explain that some animals are like their parents as soon as they are born and elicit examples, eg any mammals and some reptiles, eg crocodiles, or bugs, eg snails, which when they hatch out of their eggs both look like tiny adults.

2 Ask the children if they know any animals which go through several changes before they become adults and listen to their response. Hold up the picture of the animal you have chosen to do in the activity, eg ladybird. Elicit and explain the different stages (see above) by drawing the life cycle on the board and labelling the stages with key words (egg, tiny larva, big larva, pupa, ladybird) as you do this.

3 Encourage the children to reconstruct the stages with you using sequencers, eg *First a ladybird lays eggs on a leaf. Next, each egg hatches into a tiny larva. Then the larva eats a lot and grows fast. After that, the larva changes into a pupa. Finally, the pupa splits open and a new ladybird crawls out.*

4 Either get the children to copy the life cycle from the board or give out the life cycle templates. Children draw the different stages in order. They then either label the pictures or write or complete sentences for each one, eg *A ladybird lays ____ on a leaf.*

Comments and suggestions

• If children are doing the life cycle of the butterfly, you can describe the stages as follows:

A butterfly lays eggs on a leaf. / Each egg hatches into a tiny caterpillar. / The caterpillar eats a lot and grows fast. / The caterpillar changes into a chrysalis. / The chrysalis splits open and a new butterfly crawls out.

• If children are doing the life cycle of the frog, you can describe the stages as follows:

A frog lays eggs in a pond. / Each egg hatches into a tiny tadpole. / The tadpole grows big. / The tadpole grows legs and loses its tail. / A new frog crawls out of the pond.

• Learning about the life cycle of animals can be linked to the use of traditional stories, eg *The Princess and the Frog* or story books, eg *The Bad Tempered Ladybird* or *The Hungry Caterpillar* (Eric Carle, Picture Puffin). See also children's reference books or readers, eg *Is it a butterfly?* and *Is it a frog?* (Llewellyn and Parker, Macmillan Children's Readers.) They can also be linked to art and craft (see 7.16, 7.17) as well as counting rhymes and songs (see 6.4 and 6.21) and watching documentary DVDs (see 9.10).

8.8 Growing a plant

Level A1.1, A1.2, A2.1   **Age** 6–10   **Organization** pairs / whole class, individual/ pairs/groups

Aims To recognize the conditions a bean seed needs to grow into a healthy plant; to plant a bean seed and observe and report on its growth; to develop an interest in plants.

Language focus *need*, vocabulary related to plants and growing things (*pot, soil, seed, water, sunlight, warmth, nutrients*)

Materials *Essential:* a plant pot, bean seed, soil (potting compost) / *Optional:* a small green pot plant; pots, bean seeds, potting compost (enough for each child, pair or group), labels to go on the pots

Procedure

1 Either show the children a real pot plant, if you have one, or draw a picture on the board. Say, eg *Plants need four things to grow. What are they?* Either divide the class into pairs, and give them a minute or so to think about the answers before discussing it, or listen to suggestions from the whole class.

2 Draw symbols and/or write the four key words on the board as you explain and establish (in more or less simple terms depending on the age) that plants need:

   a) water: necessary for seeds to germinate and plants to grow
   b) light: plants need sunlight to make food
   c) nutrients: plants need nutrients in the soil to grow
   d) warmth: plants will only grow well in the right temperature; if it's too cold or too hot, they may die.

3 Say, eg *Look. Here's a pot. Here's a bean seed, and here's some soil.* and show these to the children. Say *Let's put the soil in the pot and plant the bean seed like this.* Demonstrate making an indent in the soil with your finger, placing the seed inside and lightly covering it with the compost. Say *Let's give the bean seed water, light, nutrients and warmth. Let's watch it grow and record what happens!*

4 If you have pots, bean seeds and compost for all the children (or for each pair or group), give these out. Get the children to plant their own seeds and label the pots with their names. Monitor carefully as they do this and stress the importance of not planting the bean seed in the earth too deeply or pressing down the compost too hard.

5 Once the children are ready, arrange all the pots on a window sill in the classroom.

6 Draw a picture on the board to show the bean seed in its pot. Ask the children to draw and label a similar picture to show this first stage. If appropriate children can also write a sentence about what they have done.

7 In subsequent lessons, as the bean stem starts to appear, children draw and label further pictures to record the growth of their plant.

pot
bean seed
soil
root
stem
leaf

We planted a bean seed. | The root started to grow. | The stem appeared. | A leaf appeared. | More leaves appeared. The plant grew taller.

Comments and suggestions

- Children find it very motivating if they can plant and watch the progress of their own bean seeds, rather than just one for the whole class. In order to supervise the planting, you can invite individual children, pairs or groups to come and do this in turn at your table, while the rest of the class does other work, rather than getting the whole class to do it simultaneously.

- With younger children in particular, you need to supervise the watering of the plants or, if appropriate, ask the children's class teacher to help with this. It's important not to overwater the plants, which is what children may tend to do.

- This activity can be linked to telling children the traditional story of *Jack and the Beanstalk* and the game *Jumping beans* (see 5.5).

- If you like, children can make a zig-zag or origami book (see 7.14) to record the progress of their bean seed growing into a plant.

8.9 Flower experiment

Level A1.1, A1.2, A2.1   **Age** 6–10   **Organization** whole class, individual

Aims To investigate how quickly a flower drinks water; to predict and observe what happens over several days; to draw a picture and write about the result; to develop an interest in plants; to respect the opinions of others.

Language focus *going to*, past simple, *hour, day*

Materials *Essential:* a white carnation, a plastic cup of water, red food colouring

Procedure

1 Show the children the carnation and the plastic cup of red water. Say, eg *I'm going to put the flower in the cup of red water. What do you think is going to happen?* and listen to the children's ideas. When they say, eg *The flower's going to turn red,* ask *How long is it going to take?* and encourage them to make further predictions, eg *It's going to take six hours / one day.*

2 Ask the children each to write or complete sentences with their predictions, eg *I think the flower is / isn't going to turn red. It's going to take X hours / days.*

3 Children then talk about and compare their predictions. Explain that they must now wait to find out what happens.

4 In the next or a subsequent lesson, once the carnation has turned red, children compare the result with their predictions. (The flower usually takes about two days to go red.) Ask them to draw a picture to show the experiment and write the result, eg *We put a white flower in red water. The flower turned red in … days.*

Comments and suggestions

- Children usually find the process of observing the flower 'drink' water fascinating, and this activity graphically demonstrates the need of a cut flower for water.
- The activity can also be linked to children growing a plant from seed (8.8) and investigating what plants need to live in addition to water.

8.10 Plants we eat

Level A1.1, A1.2, A2.1, A2.2   **Age** 8–12   **Organization** whole class, pairs

Aims To develop awareness of the importance of plants as a source of food; to relate food we eat to different parts of plants; to classify plants according to the part we eat; (to develop reference skills).

Language focus *be*, parts of a plant, fruit and vegetables

Materials *Essential:* none / *Optional:* pictures of fruit and vegetables, copies of the 'Plants we eat' web (one for each child), bilingual dictionaries

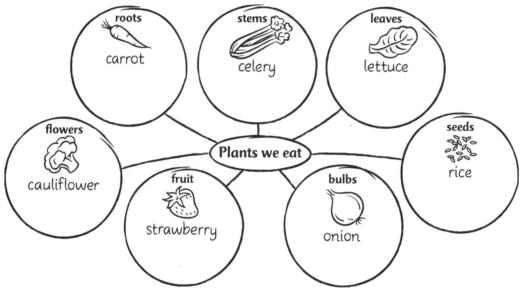

Procedure

1 Ask the children if they think plants are an important source of food and listen to their response.

2 Ask them to give examples of plants we eat, eg *apples, carrots, tomatoes, beans, rice.*

3 Explain or elicit that different food we eat comes from different parts of plants: the seeds, the roots, the bulbs, stems, the leaves, the flowers or the fruit. Draw pictures on the board to explain the meaning of each one.

4 *Either* draw the 'Plants we eat' web on the board and children copy this *or* give a copy to each child.

5 Divide the class into pairs.

6 Ask the children to complete the web by noting as many foods as they can think of which come from different parts of plants. Elicit or give one or two examples before they begin, eg *Carrots are the roots of the plant. / Celery is the stem of the plant.* If you like, you can set a time limit for the activity, eg 10 minutes. If you have bilingual dictionaries available, older children can use these to look up the names of plants they don't know. If you have pictures of fruit and vegetables available, children can also look at these as a prompt for ideas.

7   At the end, ask children to report back on the foods they have identified which go in each category. Some examples are:

roots: carrots, beetroot, sweet potatoes, parsnips, turnips, (not potatoes, which grow off the roots underground and are called tubers)
stems: celery, asparagus
leaves: lettuce, cabbage, spinach, endive
flowers: broccoli, cauliflower
fruit: tomatoes, oranges, strawberries, sweet peppers
bulbs: onions, leeks, spring onions
seeds: rice, beans (eg kidney beans), peas, wheat, maize.

Comments and suggestions

- This activity is particularly motivating for children if it can be accompanied by a visit to a local market where they can observe real fruit and vegetables. If this isn't possible, as an alternative it may be a good idea to give the children the web for homework and ask them to look at fruit, vegetables, pulses, nuts, etc at home and/or in their local market or supermarket and talk about it with their parents and families in preparation for doing the activity in class.

- This activity can be linked with other work on plants (see 8.8) or food and diet (see 8.12, 8.13, 8.14).

8.11 Mystery fruit

Level A1.1   **Age** 4–8   **Organization** whole class, (groups)

Aims To investigate the sense of taste; to make guesses based on sight, smell and texture; to use evidence from experience to draw conclusions; to develop an interest in finding out about the five senses.

Language focus *be,* questions, fruit, *right, wrong*

Materials *Essential:* a blindfold, whole and cut-up fruit (eg banana, apple, pear, peach, melon), containers in which to put the fruit (eg yogurt pots)

Procedure

1 Show the children the whole fruits and pre-teach the names if necessary.

2 Give individual children a piece of cut-up fruit to taste in turn and get them to identify it, eg *(I think) it's a melon.* Ask *Is it easy to identify the fruit?* (Yes.) Then show the children the blindfolds and ask *Is it easy if you can't see?* and listen to their response.

3 Invite a child to the front of the class. Put a blindfold on them and demonstrate the activity. Give the child a piece of fruit to eat (mouthing what it is silently to the rest of the class) and ask the child to try and identify it, eg T: *What's this?* P: *(I think) it's ....* Ask the class *Is he/she right?*

4 Repeat several times with different children, keeping a score of the number of correct guesses on the board.

5 Repeat the experiment, this time asking children to hold their noses as well as wear the blindfold. Keep a score of the number of correct guesses on the board in the same way.

Rosa			
Lena			
Alex			
Dani			

6 At the end, compare the scores for when children were blindfolded and when they held their noses as well (which in theory should be much lower). Ask the children what they can conclude from this. Listen to their ideas, remodelling or expanding them in English where necessary.

7 Use their responses to establish that it's very difficult to identify food if we can't see it or smell it. Our tongue helps us to identify basic taste and texture but we also use our eyes and nose to know what we're eating.

Comments and suggestions

• Check that there are no children with food allergies before doing the activity.

• With older children, you may like to get them to do the activity as an experiment in groups rather than with the whole class. In this case, give a blindfold and cut-up pieces of fruit to each group. Children take turns to blindfold each other and taste three pieces of fruit in turn. They keep a record of their scores in a simple chart (see previous page). Children then repeat the experiment, this time holding their noses as well as wearing the blindfold. At the end, they report back and compare their scores before talking about the conclusions in the same way.

• As a follow-up, younger children can draw or colour pictures of the fruit they found easiest to identify. Older children can do a further activity to identify food which is sweet, sour, salty and bitter and draw a picture to show the taste areas of their tongue.

8.12 Food processes

Level A2.2, B1.1   **Age** 10–12   **Organization** whole class, groups

Aims To develop awareness of processes involved to transform plants into manufactured food products; to sequence stages in the process in a logical order; to design and draw a flow chart to show the process.

Language focus *In the example:* present simple passive, sequencers *(first, then, after that)*, vocabulary to describe making chocolate, eg *cocoa, bean, pod*
Alternatives: present simple active, vocabulary to describe other processes, eg making sugar or cheese

Materials *Essential:* strips of paper describing the process (one for each group) (see below) / *Optional:* a bar of chocolate, sheets of A3 paper (one for each group)

Chocolate comes from cocoa trees which are grown in South America and Africa.

The cocoa pods are picked when they are ripe.

The cocoa beans are taken out of the pods.

The cocoa beans are left under humid banana leaves for 5-6 days.

The cocoa beans are dried in the sun.

The cocoa beans are put into sacks.

The cocoa beans are sent by sea to factories in different countries.

In the factories the cocoa beans are cleaned and roasted.

The inside of the beans is made into a paste.

Sugar and fat are added to the paste to make chocolate.

Procedure

1 If you have a bar of chocolate, show this to the children. Ask where chocolate is from and if they know anything about the process involved in making it. Listen to their ideas and be ready to feed in vocabulary as necessary, eg *cocoa bean, pod.*

2 Divide the class into groups.

3 Give a set of sentence strips in jumbled order to each group. Explain that you want the children to read the sentences and arrange them in the most logical order to describe the process of making chocolate. Tell them the first sentence as an example.

4 When the children are ready, ask them to report back and describe the process.

5 Then explain that you want the groups to design and draw a flow chart to show the stages in the process of making chocolate. Draw one or two examples of how they might go about this on the board. If you have A3 sheets, give one to each group. Children design and draw a flow chart in their groups.

6 When they are ready, they take turns to show their flow charts to the rest of the class. The class then decide which flow chart they think shows the process most clearly.

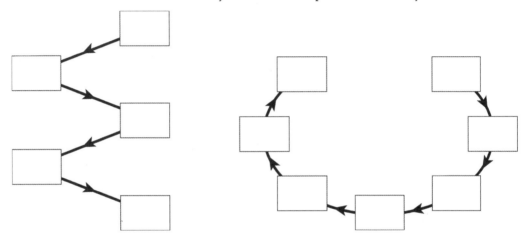

Comments and suggestions

- As a follow-up, children can research another process, eg making sugar or cheese, either using reference books or the internet. They can then write a description of the process and design an accompanying flow chart in the same way.

- If appropriate, you may like to draw the children's attention to the passive forms of the verbs used to describe the process and do further related language practice on this.

- With lower levels, the sentence strips can be written using the present simple active rather than passive voice, eg *People pick the cocoa pods when they are ripe. They put them under banana leaves.*

8.13 Sugar!

Level A1.2, A2.1, A2.2   **Age** 8–12   **Organization** groups, whole class

Aims To guess how much sugar there is in some everyday foods; to listen and compare your guesses with what you find out; to develop awareness of how much sugar is added to foods; to express and exchange opinions with others.

Language focus *be, have (got), there is/are, can* (for possibility), opinions, food

Materials *Essential:* pictures or examples of food items (chocolate biscuit, ketchup, fruit yogurt, cola drink, chocolate bar) / *Optional:* a teaspoon, copies of the grid (one for each child)

	our guess	the answer
chocolate biscuit		
ketchup		
fruit yogurt		
glass of cola		
chocolate bar		

Procedure

1 Tell the children that in a country like Britain, people eat on average approximately 38 kilos of sugar every year. Explain that this works out at approximately 20–22 teaspoons of sugar every day. Show them the size of a teaspoon, if you have one.

2 Divide the class into groups of four.

3 Show the class pictures of the foods in the grid or the real items.

4 Either give out the grid or ask the children to copy this from the board.

5 Explain and demonstrate that you want them to work in their groups and guess how many teaspoons of sugar there are in each food, eg P1: *I think there's one teaspoon of sugar in a chocolate biscuit. P2: I think there are three. P3: Me too!* Clarify that 'ketchup' refers to a helping of ketchup, the chocolate biscuit is, eg a chocolate digestive biscuit (not a sandwich biscuit with cream), the glass of cola is from a small bottle (about 330ml) of normal cola, ie not 'light', and the bar of chocolate is also small (eg 50gm). Explain that the children should come to an agreement about each food in their groups and note their guesses in the grid.

6 When they are ready, ask the groups to report back and compare their guesses for each food.

7 Then say, eg *Now listen and find out!* and read the text below.

> There's a lot of sugar in foods we buy. There are about two teaspoons of sugar in a chocolate biscuit, for example, and next time you have some tomato ketchup on your plate, remember that it's got about four teaspoons of sugar in it! Drinks can have a lot of sugar too. For example, a glass of cola may have seven teaspoons of sugar. That's a lot of sugar in one glass! Of course, sweets also have a lot of sugar but do you know that a chocolate bar can also have about six teaspoons of sugar. Even a snack like a fruit yogurt can also have as many as four teaspoons of sugar in it. So now you can see how easy it is to eat twenty-two teaspoons of sugar in one day!

8 At the end, ask the groups to report back how many guesses they got right. Ask if they are surprised at the amount of added sugar in food and listen to their response.

Comments and suggestions

• Children are usually very interested in finding out if their guesses are correct and this motivates them to listen for the answers. If you like, you can introduce a game element into the activity and the group with most correct guesses at the end is the winner.

• As a follow-up, you can ask children to look on food packets at home and identify other products which also contain sugar. Children may be surprised by how many foods, such as processed ham, peas, cheese biscuits, although they are not intended to be sweet, also contain sugar.

8.14 Food groups

Level A1.1, A1.2, A2.1   **Age** 8–12   **Organization** whole class, individual, pairs

Aims To identify four main food groups; to listen and classify food into the groups; to recognize basic characteristics of each food group; to develop awareness of the importance of a healthy, balanced diet.

Language focus present simple, *be, should,* opinions, food

Materials *Essential:* none / *Optional:* pictures of food (a range from each food group), copies of the plate handout to classify the food (one for each child), copies of the food group descriptions (one for each child)

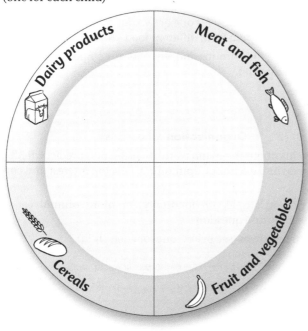

1 The foods in this group are an important source of vitamins, minerals and fibre. They keep you healthy and help you grow. You should eat a lot of food in this group every day.

2 The foods in this group are an important source of carbohydrate. Carbohydrate gives you lots of energy. You should eat a lot of food in this group every day.

3 The foods in this group are an important source of calcium. They keep you healthy and strong. You should eat some food in this group every day.

4 The foods in this group are an important source of protein. You should eat some food in this group every day.

Procedure

1 Elicit or explain that food can be divided into four main food groups. Ask the children if they know what these are. Use their answers to establish that the four main food groups are: Meat and fish, Fruit and vegetables, Cereals, and Dairy products.

2 Either draw and label a large plate on the board (as above) and ask the children to copy this or give a copy to each child. Explain that you're going to say different food words and the children should listen and write them in the correct part of the plate.

3 Dictate 12–16 food words that are familiar to the children in jumbled order and they listen and write them in the correct category. If you have pictures of the food, show these to the children as you do this. Some possible examples are:

Meat and fish: sausages, chicken, tuna
Cereals: spaghetti, rice, bread
Fruit and vegetables: peas, carrots, bananas, oranges, apples
Dairy products: cheese, milk, yogurt

4 Ask children to compare their answers in pairs before checking with the whole class. If you like, you can also ask them to add one or two more foods they know to each group.

5 Ask the children, eg *Is it important to eat foods from all four groups? Which food groups should you eat most food from every day? Why?* Listen to the children's response. Remodel and expand their answers and introduce vocabulary, eg *proteins, vitamins,* etc as necessary. Then either read the descriptions (see previous page) and children identify the food groups, or give children a copy of these and they write the name of the correct food group by each one.
(**Answers:** 1 Fruit and vegetables 2 Cereals 3 Dairy products 4 Meat and fish)

6 Ask the children if they have preferences for food in particular food groups and whether they think they should eat more or less food in any of the food groups and listen to their response.

Comments and suggestions

- As a follow-up, ask children to keep a food diary for one or two days, eg between lessons, in order to work out the balance of food they eat from different food groups every day (see 2.19).

- Children can also find out more about food groups and why they are important for our health using reference books or the internet.

8.15 Living world circuit

Level A1.2, A2.1, A2.2   **Age** 9–12   **Organization** whole class

Aims To take turns to read statements about the living world; to listen and predict whether the statements are true or false; to express and exchange opinions; to develop interest and curiosity in the natural world.

Language focus *In the example:* present simple, *can* (for ability), opinions, animals
Alternatives: any, depending on the topic and questions

Materials *Essential:* living world circuit strips (see below, one for each child)

Fish never sleep.	False. Scorpions have eight legs like a spider.
Tigers can swim.	False. Fish sleep with their eyes open.
Bats lay eggs.	True. Tigers swim to cool down in hot weather.
All plants need sunlight.	False. Bats are mammals and have live babies.
Elephants can jump.	False. About 10% of all plants can grow without sunlight.
Kangaroos can live for weeks without water.	False. Elephants are the only animals in the world that can't jump.
All mosquitoes bite.	True. Kangaroos can survive for months without water if they eat plants.
Frogs never drink water.	False. Only female mosquitoes bite.
All bears hibernate in winter.	True. Frogs absorb water through their skin.
Scorpions have got six legs.	False. Only some bears hibernate in winter.

Procedure

1 Give a strip of paper to each child. Explain that on the left side of the strip, they have a true/false sentence and on the right side they have the correct answer to somebody else's sentence.

2 Explain and demonstrate that one child should read out their sentence to the class. The rest of the class should say whether they think it is true or false and why (the child who has the answer stays quiet), eg P1: *'Fish never sleep.' I think that's true.* P2: *Me too. Fish can't sleep. They can't close their eyes.* P3: *I don't agree. I think it's false. I think fish sleep with their eyes open.*

3 The child who has the answer then reads it to the class and has the next turn at reading a statement. The 'circuit' continues until all the statements have been read and discussed.

Comments and suggestions

- The 'circuit' technique provides a framework for children to listen to each other as well as to predict and provide the answers. It can be used with questions as well as with true/false statements.

- To prepare a 'circuit' you simply need to write the answer to each question or true/false statement on the next strip. In this case, for example, the answer to the statement on the first strip 'Fish never sleep' is on the second strip, the answer to the statement on the second strip 'Tigers can swim' is on the third strip, and so on. The answer to the statement on the last strip is on the first one.

- In order to generate discussion, it is best not to include statements about things that the children won't know at all, as this is likely to close down, rather than open up, discussion.

- As a follow-up to this activity, divide the class into groups and ask them to invent and write three more true/false sentences based on the living world. The only condition is that they must know the answer. The groups then take turns to say their sentences to the rest of the class and predict and discuss whether they are true or false.

8.16 Float or sink?

Level A1.1, A1.2   **Age** 4–10   **Organization** whole class (groups)

Aims To apply understanding of the concept of floating and sinking to classroom objects; to make predictions based on previous knowledge; to carry out an experiment, observe what happens and record the results; to show interest in materials and properties that make things float or sink; to collaborate and take turns in groups.

Language focus *In the example:* present simple, *sink, float,* classroom objects
Alternatives: vocabulary for any other small objects, eg *coin, button*

Materials *Essential:* a large plastic mineral water bottle cut in half and filled with water, small classroom objects (eg rubber, pencil sharpener, paper clip, drawing pin, pencil, elastic band, piece of string) / *Optional:* a sheet of paper to draw and write results

Procedure

1 Pre-teach the verbs *float* and *sink* and the names of any classroom objects you are going to use in the activity that the children don't already know.

2 Put the cut-off plastic bottle filled with water in a central position in the classroom where everyone can see. Hold up each classroom object in turn, ask the children *Does it sink or float?* and elicit their answers, eg P1: *I think it sinks.* P2: *Maybe it floats.* P3: *I don't know.* If appropriate, ask *Why?* and encourage children to justify their views, eg *It's metal.* Be ready to remodel or expand their contributions where necessary.

3 Invite individual children to come and drop each object into the water. The rest of the class watches to see whether or not they predicted correctly, eg *The rubber sinks. / The pencil floats.*

Comments and suggestions

- With older children, you may like to organize the first part of the activity in groups. Children talk about each object in turn with other members of their group and decide whether they sink or float before you carry out the experiment with the whole class.

- As a follow-up, children from 6 years old can draw the objects in the correct place (depending on whether they sink or float) on a picture of the mineral water bottle. Older children can also write sentences about each one, eg *A rubber sinks in water.* They can also experiment with different objects at home and then ask each other or you about them in the next lesson.

8.17 The water cycle

Level A1.2, A2.1, A2.2   **Age** 8–12   **Organization** whole class, groups, pairs

Aims To sequence the stages of the water cycle; to draw and describe the water cycle process; to develop interest and awareness of natural processes; (to investigate and understand the water cycle)

Language focus present simple, weather, temperature, places

Materials *Essential:* water cycle sentence strips (one set per group), A3 sheets of paper (one for each pair) / *Optional:* a large plastic bowl, a small container, plastic film

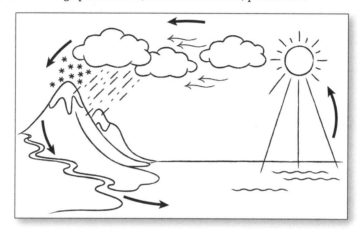

A Large drops of water fall as rain or snow.

B The water vapour cools.

C The sun heats water in rivers, lakes and the sea.

D The wind blows the clouds.

E The water travels back to the sea in rivers.

F The clouds meet cool air above mountains.

G The water vapour forms tiny drops of water in clouds.

H The water evaporates and rises.

Procedure

1 Ask the children if they know about the water cycle and listen to their response.

2 Explain that the water cycle is the continuous recycling of water between the sea, the air and the land. The water cycle is vital in creating the conditions in which life can exist.

3 Draw a simple diagram to show the water cycle on the board (see above) and get the children to identify the key places: *sun, sea, land, cloud, mountain, river.*

4 Elicit the children's suggestions about how the water cycle works and use this as an opportunity to pre-teach vocabulary as necessary, eg *evaporate, heat, cool.*

5 Divide the class into groups.

6 Give a set of the water cycle sentence strips to each group. Explain that the children should look at the diagram on the board, read the descriptions of each stage in the water cycle on the strips of paper and arrange them in order on their desks. Tell children that the first stage in the cycle is sentence C.

7 When the children have ordered the sentences, check the answers. Point to the cycle on the board as children take turns to read the sentences. (**Answers:** C, H, B, G, D, F, A, E)

8 Divide each group into pairs.

9 Give an A3 sheet of paper to each pair. Ask the children to design, draw and colour their own version of the water cycle. Then ask them *either* to label the parts of the water cycle *or* to copy the sentences for each stage into the appropriate place in the cycle.

10 At the end, children can take turns to show their water cycle posters to the rest of the class and these can also be displayed.

Comments and suggestions

- As a follow-up, if feasible in your context, children can make their own mini water cycle to see the principle of how it works. Put a small container of water in a large plastic bowl. Cover the bowl with plastic film and leave this in the sun. After some time (depending on how hot it is), children can then observe how the water in the container evaporates, rises and condenses on the plastic and then falls as 'rain' into the bowl.

- If appropriate, children can use reference books or the internet in order to find out more about the water cycle or, for example, to investigate natural weather phenomena such as storms or hurricanes.

8.18 Save water!

Level A1.1, A1.2, A2.1, A2.2   **Age** 8–12   **Organization** whole class, groups

Aims To identify ways of saving water in our everyday lives; to design a poster to encourage people to save water; to develop awareness of water as a precious resource; to collaborate with others.

Language focus imperatives, *use*, everyday activities and routines

Materials *Essential:* poster-size paper or card (one sheet per group), multi-coloured pens

Procedure

1 Briefly talk about the importance of water in relation to your context, eg if there has been a drought recently.

2 Ask the children to identify all the ways we use water in our daily lives, eg to have a bath or shower, to wash our hands, to flush the toilet, to wash our clothes or use the washing machine, to clean the floors or windows, to make a cup of tea or coffee, to do the washing up or use the dishwasher, to water the plants or garden, to boil potatoes, rice, etc.

3 Ask the children if they think it is important to save water and listen to their ideas.

4 Divide the class into groups.

5 Ask them to think of as many ways as they can to save water and to note their ideas. Set a time limit for this, eg five minutes. Give an example to start them off by saying you use 90 litres of water in a bath, but only 30 litres if you have a five-minute shower.

6 Ask the groups to take turns to report back one idea each. Be ready to help them express and formulate their ideas and note the suggestions on the board. Some possible ways to save water are:
  – have showers and not baths
  – turn the tap off when you clean your teeth
  – use a mug of water to rinse your mouth when you clean your teeth
  – use rain water only for plants
  – use the washing machine or dish washer only when it's full
  – turn the tap off when you do the washing up
  – turn off all taps properly so they don't drip
  – use only the water you need when you cook.

7 Count up and review all the children's ideas.

8 Give out poster-size paper or card and multi-coloured pens to each group. Ask the children to design a poster, including pictures and slogans, to encourage people to save water. Either set a time limit for this, eg 20–30 minutes, or organize the activity so that children make the poster as a mini-project to be done in shorter periods of time, eg after finishing other work, over several lessons.

9 At the end, children can present their posters and water-saving ideas to the rest of the class. You can also encourage children to notice and comment on the features included in each others' posters which give them impact and make them attractive.

10 The posters can then be displayed either in the classroom or elsewhere in the school.

Comments and suggestions

- As the groups make the poster, it is advisable to get them to draft their slogans in their notebooks before writing them on the poster in final form.

- In order to ensure equal participation of everyone, you may find it best to get the children to work on one or two pictures and slogans individually, which they then stick on their group poster.

- Group posters are particularly suitable for topics or issues which send a message, for example, ways to save energy, ways to save the environment or animals in danger or a poster about safety rules in relation to fire. (See also 9.6 for getting children to include digital photos in their posters.)

8.19 The one-minute test!

Level A1.1, A1.2, A2.1, A2.2   **Age** 6–12   **Organization** individual, groups of three

Aims To predict/estimate the number of times you can do an activity in a minute; to count how many times you can actually do it; to record the results in a chart; to collaborate with others.

Language focus *can* (for ability), past simple, numbers, actions

Materials *Essential:* materials to do the activities, eg skipping ropes, bean bags, balls; stopwatches, timers or watches with second hands / *Optional:* copies of the test chart (one for each child)

	my estimate	results
1 throw a tennis ball against a wall and catch it after it bounces once		
2 skip with a skipping rope		
3 bounce the ball on the ground with one hand		
4 throw a ball in the air above your head and catch it		

Procedure

Decide on the activities children are going to do for the one-minute test (see Comments below if the examples above are not feasible).

1 *Either* draw a chart with pictures or a brief description on the board and ask children to copy this *or* give a copy to each child. Explain that the children should estimate how many times they think they can do each activity in the chart in a minute.

2 In order to help them estimate a minute, demonstrate this with a timer or stop watch. Ask the children to count in a whisper until a minute has passed. This also revises numbers and counting in preparation for doing the activities.

3 Ask children to complete the chart with their personal estimates for each activity.

4 Divide the class into groups of three.

5 Children take turns to do each activity, to time the activities and to count the number of repetitions in their groups. After doing each activity, children complete their chart with their personal result.

6 At the end, ask the children to report back on how similar or different their estimates and results were and whether this surprised them.

Comments and suggestions

- If it isn't suitable to include physical exercise in the one-minute test, children can do other activities, eg say the alphabet, count to 100 in tens, write their full name, say a tongue twister (see 1.28).

- As a follow-up, children can practise the activities in order to try and improve their personal results in the next lesson or next week. They can then time the activities and record the results again. This can lead to a brief discussion about the role of practice if you want to improve at something.

- If physical exercise is included in the one-minute test, the activity can be linked to further work on the role and importance of exercise and sport in our lives and its effect, eg through taking and measuring pulse rates before and after physical activity.

8.20 Human body quiz

Level A1.1, A1.2, A2.1, A2.2   **Age** 9–12   **Organization** teams

Aims To predict and guess the answers in a quiz on the human body; to develop interest and curiosity in learning about the human body; to follow and respect the rules; to collaborate with others.

Language focus present simple, parts of the body, numbers

Materials *Essential:* none / *Optional:* copies of the Human body quiz (see next page)

Procedure

1 Explain that the children are going to do a quiz on the human body. Pre-teach vocabulary if necessary, eg *brain, heart, skin, skeleton, bone, nerve, muscle, blood.*

2 Divide the class into two or three teams. Get each team to choose a suitable name for themselves, eg *The Hearts / The Muscles* and write these on the board in preparation for scoring in the quiz.

3 Explain the scoring system for the quiz. Each team scores two points if they get the answer correct first time. If they don't, their turn passes to the other team, who then get one point if they get the answer right. Emphasize that children should put up their hands to answer and must not call out. If necessary, you can introduce a negative scoring system to prevent this, eg anyone who calls out loses a point for their team.

4 Read out a sentence and options to each team in turn. Give the team time to confer before answering, eg 30 seconds.

5 Keep a record of each team's score on the board.

6 At the end, add up the score for each team. The team with the most correct points is the winner.

Human body quiz

1 The human brain weighs less than one kilo / more than one kilo / more than two kilos.

2 Human babies are born with 200 bones / 250 bones / 300 bones.

3 An adult skeleton has 206 bones / 216 bones / 260 bones.

4 A human hand has 17 bones / 27 bones / 37 bones.

5 Young children have 18 / 20 / 22 teeth.

6 Adults have 28 / 30 / 32 teeth.

7 Water makes up 30% of the body / 45% of the body / 60% of the body.

8 The body has more than 500 muscles / more than 600 muscles / more than 700 muscles.

9 Skin has 2 layers / 3 layers / 5 layers.

10 If the skin of a man weighing 75 kilos was laid out flat, it would cover one square metre / two square metres / three square metres.

11 Nerves send messages around the body at speeds up to 90 metres per second / 150 metres per second / 300 metres per second.

12 A child who weighs 40 kilos has a blood supply of about two and half litres / four and a half litres / six and a half litres.

13 The heart pumps the body's supply of blood round the body every minute / every hour / every day.

14 Blood vessels form a branching network in the body of about 55,000 kilometres / 97,000 kilometres / 120,000 kilometres.

(**Answers:** 1 more than one kilo   2 300 bones   3 206 bones   4 27 bones   5 20 teeth
6 32 teeth   7 60%   8 more than 600 muscles   9 three layers   10 two square metres
11 90 metres per second   12 two and a half litres   13 every minute   14 97,000 kilometres)

7 Ask the children if there are any human body facts they found surprising or would be interested in learning more about.

Comments and suggestions

• As a follow-up, children can write or complete some of the sentences with correct information from the quiz, eg *The human brain weighs more than one kilo.*

• This activity can either be used to enrich and extend a unit of work on the parts of the body or as an introduction to doing further work on, for example, the human skeleton, muscles or joints.

Section 9 **ICT and multimedia**

Information and Communications Technology (ICT) and related multimedia applications are a wonder of the age we live in. They are changing the way we think, learn, communicate, access information and use our leisure time in unprecedented ways and at an unparalleled pace. The visually sophisticated world of colourful images, combined with sound and animation, at only one or two clicks away, attracts children like a magnet and can frequently succeed in engaging and motivating them where other more traditional media, such as books, may fail. ICT and multimedia also offer possibilities for instant communication and direct publication in a way that is both personalized and shared. This can help to maximize children's interest and involvement, as well as strengthen their sense of identity and commitment to the class and school community to which they belong.

ICT and related multimedia applications offer a huge and exciting, although at the same time often bewildering, range and variety of tools for learning a foreign language, and learning through a foreign language, at primary level. However, the benefits of using ICT and multimedia are not necessarily automatic and require careful preparation and planning on the part of the teacher. This crucially includes a balanced approach to the integration of ICT and multimedia with face-to-face classroom interaction, which is of prime importance in children's overall development and cannot be replaced.

There are also other attendant risks in the use of ICT and multimedia which necessarily require a cautious approach. These include the whole area of internet security. It is vital to have a robust school policy and strictly enforced computer and internet rules in order to guarantee children's safety. There also needs to be an awareness of the potentially negative effect that stretches of 'screen time' may have on children's mood and behaviour when they experience possibly strident, fast-moving images and sounds. We need to adopt a healthily questioning attitude as to how much actual learning may or may not derive from this.

A further risk, particularly with older children, is the potential that internet access offers to copy chunks of text and present the work of others as their own. Although it is often obvious when this occurs, it is important to set up learning frameworks which actively discourage this. As part of learning to learn (see Section 10) it may also be appropriate to explicitly discuss this with the children.

Ready-made ICT and multimedia material

There is a lot of commercially produced and other ready-made material available for use at primary level. These include interactive whiteboard (IWB) materials, CD-ROMs, DVDs and publishers' or other educational website materials, either specifically produced for children learning English as a second or foreign language or for L1. These provide instant access to interactive games, stories, songs, quizzes, picture dictionaries, graphics, topical information and other activities, such as ready-made webquests or cyber hunts. The main issue very often is finding time to research and track down suitable websites and activities or materials for the age and level of the children you teach and the specific purpose you have in mind. Often the best way to start is to put a suitable search term into an internet search engine such as Google. For example, if you put in a phrase such as 'EFL for children' or 'stories for children', you will immediately have available a range of potentially suitable sites to visit for what you want.

When selecting internet sites for children to visit, it is important to ensure that the presentation of the site is clear, uncluttered and easy to navigate and that the information it contains is correct and comes from a reliable and regularly updated source. It is also important to choose sites where there are plenty of attractive visuals, or film clips, which support children's understanding of the text. There may also be sound effects, music and speech which contribute to their understanding and enjoyment too. It usually helps if the text itself is in a reasonably sized font and chunked into short paragraphs with headings or questions at the start of each one. While the level of the language may be beyond the children's own, the relevant content or information needs to be accessible, or have the potential to be made so, with the support of a suitable task. A further consideration may also be whether the website has diagrams, pictures or other materials which children can download and print out to use as part of a project or display.

In addition to websites for children to visit, there are also a large number of websites with resources for you (see p.320 for examples). As well as articles on all different aspects of teaching and professional development, many websites include, for example, downloadable lesson plans, work sheets, stories, diagrams, graphics or flashcards. Also available for teachers are easy-to-use, online authoring programmes which allow you to create custom-made puzzles or text reconstruction activities at different levels.

Roles of ICT and multimedia

Through the use of specific IWB materials, interactive CD-ROMs and/or ready-to-use website activities and games, children develop language and ICT skills in an integrated and enjoyable way. In this section, there are four main roles of ICT and multimedia in primary English language teaching which are reflected in the activities.

1 Communicating with others

For older children, the use of email, and in particular a class email group, provides a forum for children to communicate with each other, and with you, informally in English on a range of different topics (see 9.16). These topics may or may not be related to what the children are currently doing in class. The immediacy and informality of email increases children's motivation to write, especially if it is made clear that their contributions to the e-group are for their own enjoyment and interest and not part of assessed work.

The advantage of setting up an e-group rather than using individual email accounts is that you moderate and control membership of the group. This makes it easier to communicate with everyone in the class simultaneously and is important from a safety point of view. You can also upload files to the list for everyone to share, for example, if the children produce a class e-zine (see 9.15). Other functions in some e-group set-ups, such as a polling option, may also be useful

to find out collective views on certain issues, and the format of tick-box questions makes it easy for children to participate.

The use of email and/or creation of an e-group can also be used if you set up a partnership exchange with another class or school (see 9.17). There are a number of organizations and websites which facilitate this. Setting up a partnership with another class or school can be a particularly rewarding way of encouraging children to exchange personal information and develop an interest in other countries and cultures. It also brings to life the whole concept of using English as a vehicle to communicate with others in an authentic way.

2 Developing listening skills in context

Through watching DVDs or short extracts of DVDs, for example, films or stories that children have previously read or listened to, children develop confidence and pleasure in listening to English. The visual and situational clues in DVDs help to make language accessible and comprehensible. DVDs also present cultural information in a naturally assimilable way. For example, in the visual context of a DVD, children can see for themselves what English children are like or what an English home, family or town is like, in a way that would be meaningless if it was simply explained. Similarly, the use of short extracts of documentary DVDs (see 9.10) can help to bring topic- or content-based learning alive. The inclusion of subtitle and language options on most DVDs can be used to lead children gradually and naturally into watching a DVD that is beyond their current linguistic level comfortably and with global understanding (see 9.7). Other activities draw children into using some of the language of the DVD (see 9.8), or to focusing on detail (see 9.9) or responding creatively and imaginatively to what it contains (see 9.11, 9.12).

3 Searching, selecting and reporting information

Through searching pre-selected websites in order to find specific information or perform specific tasks, children develop internet and language skills in parallel. In order to maximize the language learning benefits, the search needs to be adequately prepared and the task clearly defined. It also needs to clearly relate to the story, topic or language the children are learning. Similarly, there needs to be a clear outcome and follow-up which integrates the computer-based activity with other class work. For safety reasons, the search needs to be restricted to sites you have previously researched yourself, and it should be clear to children from established computer and internet rules that they are not allowed to access other sites without your permission and approval. The most common websearch activities with children are usually based on educational sites which have information on content related to other areas of the curriculum in an appropriately child-friendly format (see 9.24). Frequently activity types used to develop reading skills may also be suitable to adapt to use with these (see 2.12, 2.13). Other topics with a wide range of websites which can be used to develop websearch skills in conjunction with communicative language skills are shopping (see 9.18) and currency exchange (see 9.20), the weather (see 9.22), local places (see 9.21), bookshops or museums (see 9.19) and holiday courses (see 9.23).

4 Creating and producing materials

The use of ICT and multimedia provides a whole range of exciting opportunities for children to create and produce their own materials. Children generally enjoy experimenting with different software programmes, such as PowerPoint or Creative Writer, to produce work they have previously written or prepared in assorted colours, layouts, fonts and page design. This enhances the quality of presentation of their work (see 9.13, 9.15) and can also be a significant support in developing spoken production skills (see 9.14). The use of a digital camera by the children is inexpensive (once you have a camera) and easy to organize. The inclusion of photos children have taken (see 9.2, 9.3, 9.6) as well as photos of themselves (see 9.1, 9.4, 9.5) personalizes their work and adds to their motivation and enjoyment (as well as incidentally developing visual observation and photography skills). The polished-looking results of electronically produced work can often lead children to make an increased effort and inspire them to produce more ambitious work. This is particularly so if the results can be published, for example, on a class or school website or weblog or, alternatively, sent home to parents as an attachment, or printed out.

Organizing and staging activities

When using DVD or ICT materials, it is frequently appropriate to stage activities into *before*, *while* and *after* in a similar way to procedures described in earlier Sections for developing listening and reading skills (see Sections 1 and 2) and for story telling (see Section 4). Before children watch a DVD or work on computers, it is important to create interest, curiosity and attention, as well as to do any necessary language preparation. While children watch a DVD or extract of a DVD, they may do one or more tasks that engage them in active viewing and lead them from global to detailed understanding and/or interpreting or responding to the content in a creative or personalized way. While children work on computers, they need a clearly defined task that will minimize any possible distraction and keep them focused and engaged in a purposeful way. The period after doing an ICT or DVD activity frequently offers the richest opportunities for the development of language skills, for example, when children report back, share, interpret, compare, exchange opinions and reflect on what they have done.

The activities in this section assume basic ICT knowledge and skills both on your part and on the part of the children. The activities do not relate to specific websites since these may change or move. Detailed technical instructions for carrying out the activities are not included because technology changes so rapidly, systems vary in different contexts and software is constantly being updated.

Apart from 9.1, the activities suggested in this section are not designed to be suitable for 4–6 year old children. Although there are some excellent published IWB materials, CD-ROMS, DVDs and customized sites for this age group with interactive stories, songs and games that are suitable to use in language classes, the activities in this section require greater maturity, basic literacy and ICT skills, as well as an ability to begin to work, at least for short stretches, in an autonomous way.

Reflection time

As you use the ICT and multimedia activities in this section with your classes, you may like to think about the following questions and use your responses to evaluate how things went and plan possible improvements for next time:

1 **Motivation:** Did the use of ICT and multimedia applications affect the children's motivation? In what way(s)? Did this apply to all the children or only some of the children? If so, which children and why, do you think?

2 **ICT skills:** Did the children already have the basic ICT skills needed to do the activity? If not, how did you support them? Was this successful? Can you build on ICT skills the children practised as part of the activity in future? If so, how?

3 **Language skills:** What language skills did the children practise as part of the activity? Did the use of ICT and multimedia applications lead to meaningful and purposeful language use?

4 **'Screen time':** What was the balance of 'screen time' to other class work? Was this balance appropriate to achieve the desired learning aims? Would you make any changes next time?

5 **Personal work:** Has the opportunity to use ICT and multimedia applications improved the quality of children's work and the effort they put into it? Has it had a direct impact on improving their writing skills, do you think?

6 **Your approach:** What impact, if any, has the use of ICT and multimedia applications had on your own approach to teaching and learning? How do you envisage developing this in the future?

NB *For activities 9.1–9.6 you need a digital camera and a computer.*

9.1 Children's portraits

Level All   **Age** 4–12   **Organization** pairs, whole class

Aims To prepare personal portraits and/or profiles using digital photos; to develop self-esteem; to create a positive socio-affective atmosphere; to describe yourself.

Language focus *be,* name, age, personal information, favourites

Materials *Essential:* digital camera, computer / *Optional:* printouts of the photos

Procedure

Do this over the course of the first few lessons of meeting a class.

1 Divide the class into pairs.

2 Children take turns to take a head and shoulders portrait photo of each other. With young children you will need to help and supervise very closely as they do this.

3 Create a slide show of all the photos. Watch the slide show with the whole class. Very young children can simply wave and say, eg *Hello, Maria! / Hello, David!* as they watch the slide show of the photos they have created. Older children can take turns to introduce themselves and say, eg their name, age, where they live and one or two of their favourite things, eg colour, sport, singer, etc.

Comments and suggestions

• Children love taking and seeing photos of themselves. This activity helps to create a sense of class community. It is also very useful for learning the children's names.

• If you have a computer in the classroom, you can make an electronic collage of all the children's photos and use this as wallpaper on the computer. Alternatively you can use a different child's photo or a class photo for this each week.

• If you print out the photos, these can be made into a class display. With very young children you can simply label the photos with their names. Older children can write a paragraph describing themselves to be displayed with the photos.

• Alternatively, older children can create an electronic profile of themselves using the photo and either scanning in or creating text as above.

• This activity can also be linked with other activities for getting to know a new group (see 5.1, 6.2, 6.3, 7.1).

9.2 Alphabet frieze

Level A1.1, A1.2   **Age** 6–12   **Organization** pairs, whole class

Aims To create an alphabet frieze using photos taken by the children; to recall vocabulary; to associate sounds and spelling.

Language focus *be,* the alphabet, classroom objects, any familiar vocabulary

Materials *Essential:* digital camera, computer, printouts of children's photos / *Optional:* a ring binder or plastic envelope file

Procedure

1 Briefly revise the letters of the alphabet. Explain that the children are going to make an English alphabet frieze using photos that they take themselves.

2 Divide the class into pairs.

3 Assign one or two letters to each pair, depending on the size of the class. Ask the children to identify something suitable for their photo(s) that starts with the letter(s) they have been

assigned. These can either be objects in the classroom or pictures in magazines or books. Be ready to help with ideas if necessary.

4 Children then take turns to take a photo of the object or picture they have chosen.

5 Print out the photos and get the children to write a sentence under each one, eg *A is for Art, B is for board, C is for clock, D is for door*, etc. They then arrange their photos and sentences in the order of the alphabet and stick them round the walls of the classroom to make a frieze.

Comments and suggestions

- Children creating their own frieze helps to make the alphabet and related vocabulary more memorable than using a commercially produced one. In subsequent lessons, you can refer to the frieze as a prompt for saying letters and spelling words.

- As an alternative to a frieze, children can make an alphabet album by ordering their photos and sentences in a ring binder or plastic envelope file. If it isn't possible to print out the photos, you can make these into a slide show and the pairs take turns to say, eg *A is for Art* as they watch their photos go by in the alphabet sequence.

- This activity can also be linked with other activities to practise the alphabet (see 2.6, 5.16).

9.3 Seasonal change

Level A1.1, A1.2, A2.1, A2.2   **Age** 6–12   **Organization** pairs, whole class

Aims To identify and describe changes in the environment during different seasons; to develop visual observation skills; to develop interest and curiosity in nature.

Language focus *be*, present simple, *there is/are, have got*, weather, seasons, trees, plants

Materials *Essential:* digital camera, computer / *Optional:* printouts of photos

Procedure

This activity goes over a whole school year.

1 Identify a tree, trees, garden or park near the school to be the subject of the activity. Explain to the children that they are going to take photos of the same spot every two weeks or month over the school year in order to observe and describe the changes that take place during different seasons.

2 Prepare a rota of pairs of children to be in charge of taking the photo each time. As each photo of the same spot is taken, elicit and build up a description with the children, eg *It's early autumn. It's sunny and warm. Some leaves on the trees are green. Some leaves on the trees are brown.* Compare the photo with the one(s) taken previously.

3 Children can also write or complete a description of each photo.

4 Towards the end of the year organize a slide show of all the photos and discuss all the changes which have taken place.

Comments and suggestions

- This activity encourages children to take an interest in their natural surroundings. Through its occasional use it also allows for natural recycling and extension of children's language and vocabulary to describe a scene.

- If you can print out the photos, children can also make a class book of the seasons with written descriptions of the changes in each photo.

- This activity can either be initially introduced as part of a topic on the seasons or linked to a relevant story such as the fable of *The ant and the grasshopper* (see 4.6).

9.4 Photo story

Level All   **Age** 10–12   **Organization** groups

Aims To create and write a photo story using photos of the children taken by each other; to develop creative thinking skills; to collaborate in groups.

Language focus any familiar language and vocabulary

Materials *Essential:* digital camera, computer / *Optional:* examples of photo stories from magazines, printouts of the children's photo stories

Procedure

1 Explain that the children are going to create and write photo stories including speech bubbles and digital photos of themselves. The photo stories can be based *either* on a story the children have listened to or read in class, *or* one that they have previously written themselves, *or* it can be created from scratch.

2 Divide the class into groups.

3 Show the children examples of photo stories from magazines, if you have these available. Set a limit for the number of frames for the photo story, eg 6–8. Explain and demonstrate by drawing on the board that each frame can have two lines of text either above or below the photo and two speech bubbles (or possibly three, if these are very short). Ask the groups to make a rough plan for each frame of their story.

4 When they are ready, get the children to take photos of each other depicting what happens in each frame of the story. When they have done this, children download their photos, add speech bubbles and text and sequence them into a photo story. Children can then read each others' photo stories either on screen or in printed out versions.

Comments and suggestions

- Children tend to take extra care preparing a photo story which they are part of themselves. Their personal involvement also adds to their interest in reading each others' stories.

- If you wish the activity to be more structured, you can build up the story frame by frame with the whole class first. Children then take photos and create the photo story using computers in the same way.

- This activity can be linked to other writing or storytelling activities (see 2.18, 4.15).

9.5 Camera clip

Level All   **Age** 8–12   **Organization** groups, whole class

Aims To write and act out your dialogues; to record the dialogues using the video recording facility of a digital camera; to collaborate with others; to watch and compare your dialogues; to develop self-awareness.

Language focus any familiar language and vocabulary

Materials *Essential:* digital camera, computer

Procedure

1 Choose a relevant context or situation for the dialogue before the activity. For example, the dialogue could be between two characters in a story the children have listened to, or it could relate to particular language functions the children have been practising, eg a dialogue in which children suggest and decide what to do, ask for something in a shop or meet a friend.

2 Divide the class into groups.

3 Explain that the children are going to write, act out and record a dialogue using the video function of a digital camera. Set the context or situation and stipulate the length of the

dialogue, eg 6–8 exchanges. Elicit children's suggestions for possible language to include in the dialogue.

4 Children then either write a dialogue in groups or, with lower levels, you may like to build this up with the whole class.

5 When the children are ready, get them to practise acting out their dialogues and to take turns recording them in their groups. Depending on the size of the class and memory card of the camera, the recordings may need to be done over several lessons.

6 Once the recordings are downloaded, children can watch their own and other dialogues and do a simple listening task. For example, if all the dialogues are based on suggestions, children can watch in order to find out what each pair decides to do.

Comments and suggestions

- Recording a short dialogue using the video facility on a digital camera is easy to organize and increases children's motivation to write accurately and act the dialogue out with conviction.

- When giving feedback, it is important to focus on the positive aspects of children's performance in the recordings.

9.6 Photos for posters and signs

Level A1.1   **Age** 6–10   **Organization** pairs/groups

Aims To take photos and use them to illustrate posters or signs; to collaborate with others.

Language focus imperatives, classroom language
Alternatives: any other relevant language and vocabulary

Materials *Essential:* digital camera, computer, printouts of the photos, paper or card to write signs / *Optional:* poster-size paper

Procedure

1 Elicit or establish typical language for classroom instructions, eg do mimes and children say the words: eg *Listen / Look / Read / Write / Cut / Stick / Draw / Sing / Talk / Colour / Play / Point / Stand up / Sit down / Open/Close your books.*

2 Divide the class into pairs or groups.

3 Assign one or two instruction words to each group. Explain that they should prepare to take a photo which will illustrate the sign(s) as clearly as they can. Give the children a few minutes to plan their photo. Encourage them to think about things like light, colour and background, which will influence how clearly the message of the sign comes across.

4 When they are ready, children take turns to use the camera to take their photos. At the same time, give out paper or card and children write a sign to go with their photo(s).

5 Once the photos are downloaded and printed, children use them and the written signs to make a classroom instruction display. You and the children can then refer to these whenever necessary in subsequent lessons as a reminder or prompt.

Comments and suggestions

- Personalizing signs with the children's own photos contributes to creating a sense of community. It also helps to familiarize children quickly with basic classroom language instructions.

- This activity can be linked to other activities to familiarize children with classroom language (see 5.26).

- Children can also plan and take photos to illustrate signs or posters in other activities, eg making a group poster to encourage people to save water (see 8.18).

NB *For activities 9.7–9.12 you need a DVD player and a computer or DVD player and screen.*

9.7 Subtitle options

Level All   **Age** 8–12   **Organization** whole class

Aims To support children's understanding of DVDs; to develop confidence in watching DVDs in English; to develop awareness of the importance of contextual clues such as gesture and body language as an aid to understanding.

Language focus any, depending on the DVD

Materials *Essential:* a DVD player and screen, a DVD

Procedure

1 Have ready a short DVD extract that the children are going to watch (preferably showing clear action or drama between two or more characters). Explain the general context and ask the children to predict what happens.

2 Play the extract once with the sound down and no subtitles. Ask the children to say what they think happens. Use this as an opportunity to introduce new vocabulary and expand and recast their answers as necessary. Draw children's attention to how much they have understood correctly without listening to any language at all.

3 Play the extract again, this time in English and with sub-titles in the children's L1. Ask more detailed questions and compare children's understanding with the first viewing.

4 Play the extract a third time, possibly in the next lesson, this time with the sound and the subtitles both in English. Pause to give children time to follow the subtitles as they listen and, if appropriate, draw their attention to any key language or vocabulary that they will use as part of any follow-up activity.

Comments and suggestions

• Varying the subtitle options on DVDs provides a natural, enjoyable way of leading children to global and detailed understanding of authentic language spoken at natural speed.

• With very young children who are not yet reading in either L1 or English, you may feel it is appropriate to show them a DVD extract in their own language (also usually an option) before they watch it in English.

9.8 Repeat what they say

Level All   **Age** 4–12   **Organization** whole class

Aims To watch and predict and/or repeat what a character says; to develop pronunciation skills; to develop concentration skills.

Language focus any, depending on the DVD

Materials *Essential:* a DVD player and screen, a DVD, a cut-out card speech bubble

Procedure

1 Play a short extract of a familiar DVD. At key moments when different characters speak, use the pause button. Hold the speech bubble against the screen with the pointer by the character's mouth and children either predict or repeat what the character says.

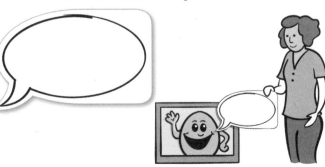

2 If they predict what the character says, continue playing and then pause again after the character speaks so that they can check if they were right.

Comments and suggestions

- If the DVD extract includes two or three characters, you can divide the class into groups and assign a character to each group. Children then predict and/or repeat what their character says when you pause and hold up the speech bubble.

- This activity is a good way of encouraging participation of very young children, eg when they watch a story video with a repeated language pattern. With older children, it can be useful as initial preparation for acting out a dialogue or doing a role play based on the DVD extract.

9.9 DVD Trivia

Level All   **Age** 6–12   **Organization** individual/pairs, teams

Aims To watch a DVD for detail; to develop concentration skills; to ask and answer questions about a DVD extract.

Language focus questions, *be, have got,* present simple

Materials *Essential:* a DVD player and screen, a DVD, question cards based on the DVD or DVD extract (one for each child or pair)

What colour is the piano?

Where's the hippo?

Who's behind the door?

Procedure

Use this activity after the children have watched a DVD or DVD extract once.

1 Give a question card to each child or pair. Check that they understand the question. Explain that they have a special responsibility to find the answer to the question as they watch the DVD and that this will be the basis of a team game afterwards.

2 Play the DVD.

3 At the end, divide the class into two teams.

4 Ask each pair to take turns to ask their question to the other team and then say the answer if the children in the opposing team don't know. The teams score points for correct answers. The team with most correct answers at the end wins.

Comments and suggestions

- This activity provides a specific individualized focus for watching the DVD and helps children to concentrate throughout, especially if they know that the questions will be the basis for a team game afterwards.

- With older children, instead of preparing question cards, you can ask them to prepare one or two questions to ask about the DVD in pairs as they watch. They can then play the trivia team game in the same way.

9.10 Documentary clip

Level All   **Age** 6–10   **Organization** whole class, pairs

Aims To watch a documentary clip closely; to prepare and write a commentary for the documentary clip; to develop curiosity and interest in factual information in a documentary; (to record your commentary).

Language focus any, depending on the DVD extract

Materials *Essential:* a DVD player and screen, a suitable DVD documentary

Procedure

1 Play a very short extract of a documentary DVD which is relevant to the topic the children are doing, with the sound down, eg a documentary on bears or a DVD showing the life cycle of the butterfly.

2 Pause and elicit a description of what's happening at each stage of the DVD extract. Explain that you want the children to write their own commentary to go with this extract of the DVD.

3 *Either* divide the class into pairs and ask them to prepare a commentary with their partner *or*, with younger children, elicit their suggestions and build up the commentary with the whole class writing this on the board.

4 Once the draft commentary is prepared, play the DVD extract with the sound down again. *Either* ask one pair to read their commentary *or* read the class commentary as children watch.

5 At the end, ask the children to make or suggest any further additions or improvements to the commentaries.

6 If the commentary has been prepared by the whole class together, ask the children to write the final version in their notebooks.

7 If you have the facilities, children can record their commentaries as a voice-over to the DVD.

Comments and suggestions

- This activity encourages children to observe a documentary extract closely. It can be a useful activity when you want the children to see real-life documentary footage related to a topic but the original commentary is considerably above their linguistic and conceptual level.

9.11 Music in a DVD

Level A2.1, A2.2, B1.1   **Age** 10–12   **Organization** whole class, pairs

Aims To associate music with actions, moods and types of films; to imagine a scene and characters in response to the music; to develop imagination; to develop creative thinking skills.

Language focus *In the example:* present simple, *there is/are,* types of films, actions, adjectives to describe places and people
Alternatives: any familiar language and vocabulary

Materials *Essential:* a DVD player and screen, a DVD with suitable music

Procedure

Choose a DVD extract with strongly atmospheric or dramatic music.

1 Elicit or pre-teach the names of different types of films, eg *cartoon, thriller, western, comedy, war, science fiction (sci-fi), disaster, adventure, romance, horror, historical drama.* Ask the children to tell you any examples they know of each one.

2 Divide the class into pairs.

3 Explain to the children that they are going to listen to music from an extract of a DVD. Ask them to identify the type of film they think the music is from.

4 Play the extract once (without the image). Ask children for their ideas and encourage them to say why, eg *I think the music is from a thriller. It sounds exciting and scary.* Ask the children to suggest actions that they associate with the music, eg *run, hide, escape, chase.*

5 Explain that the children are going to listen to the music again. This time you want them to imagine the answers to these questions:

   a) Who is in the DVD scene?
   b) What are they like?
   c) Where are they?
   d) What's happening?
   e) Why?

   Write these questions on the board as a prompt and give an example, eg *I think there are two characters in the scene – a man and a woman. The man is tall with blonde hair and dark glasses. He's carrying a red briefcase. The woman is dark and very beautiful. They're on a train. The man has got secret documents in the brief case. The woman is a spy and she wants to get the documents. She follows the man to the restaurant car. He sees her and decides to jump off the train …*

6 Play the music (without the image again). Children work with their partner and prepare their answers to the questions. You may like to set a time limit for this, eg 5–10 minutes.

7 At the end, ask the pairs to take turns to report back to the class. Children listen and decide which they think is the best or most imaginative scenario.

8 Play the DVD extract again, this time with the image and the sound. Children watch and compare the original with their versions.

9 At the end, briefly discuss the role of music in creating an atmosphere and influencing our response to what happens when we watch DVDs.

Comments and suggestions

- In a more extended version of this activity, you can ask children either to create a whole story based on the music or to write and act out a dialogue between the characters based on the scene they have imagined.

9.12 Trailers

Level All   **Age** 10–12   **Organization** pairs, whole class

Aims To watch one or more DVD trailers; to understand what the DVD depicted in the trailer is about; to decide whether or not you would like to watch the DVD and why; to develop critical thinking skills.

Language focus *because, I'd like to,* opinions, any other language and vocabulary depending on the trailer

Materials *Essential:* a DVD player and screen, a DVD with suitable initial trailers

Procedure

1 Explain that a 'trailer' is an advertisement for a film. A trailer includes short extracts of the film to make it look as appealing as possible. Explain that the children are going to watch one or more DVD trailers. Ask them:

   a) What is the title of the film?
   b) What kind of film is it?
   c) What makes the film look appealing?
   d) Would you like to see it? Why? / Why not?

   Write the questions on the board as a prompt.

2 Play the DVD trailer(s).

3 Divide the class into pairs.

4 Give the children time to talk about their answers to the questions with their partner.

5 Ask the pairs to report back to the class. If the children have watched more than one trailer, you may like to organize a class vote to see which film is the most popular.

Comments and suggestions

- Many DVDs include trailers before the actual film. As trailers are short, they can be very convenient to use in class.

- If appropriate, you can use the activity on the trailer as a lead-in to doing more detailed work on the DVD itself. Children can then compare the trailer with the actual film and decide whether or not the claims in the trailer were exaggerated.

NB *For activities 9.13–9.15 you need computers and appropriate software; for 9.14 you need a PowerPoint projector and screen.*

9.13 Creating charts

Level A1.2, A2.1, A2.2, B1.1, B1.2   **Age** 10–12   **Organization** pairs

Aims To record and display information collected, eg in a class survey, in a bar chart or pie chart; to develop awareness of different ways of displaying data; to describe and interpret the data.

Language focus numbers, percentages, any other language and vocabulary relevant to the topic of the survey

Materials *Essential:* computers and software / *Optional:* printed copies of the children's charts

Procedure

Use this activity as a follow-up to a survey the children have done, eg on their favourite things or transport they use to come to school (see 1.8 and 1.20).

1 If the children have carried out the survey in groups, ask each group to report back in turn, and collect and record the results of the survey for the whole class on the board.

2 Ask the children to copy this information into their notebooks. Draw diagrams of the possible charts children can use to display the information (eg bar chart or pie chart) and ask them to suggest which will be best in this case (either may be possible depending on the survey).

3 Divide the class into pairs to work at the computer.

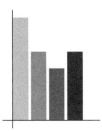

4 Ask the children to open the software programme you want them to use, eg PowerPoint or Excel and create a bar chart or pie chart based on the class survey results. Encourage them to choose colours and font sizes which will have most impact.

5 Either print out the charts or children can compare them on screen. They can also produce a written report of the survey based on their charts.

Comments and suggestions

- This activity integrates a communicative language activity (survey) with the development of basic IT and mathematical skills. Through creating their own colourful charts using computers, children are motivated to both talk and write about the results of class surveys.

- The creation of graphs and charts on computer can also frequently be integrated with topic- and content-based learning. For example, children could produce a chart to show the amount of sugar in food (see 8.13) or a graph to show their improved personal results after doing the one-minute test twice (see 8.19).

9.14 Present your work

Level A1.2, A2.1, A2.2, B1.1, B1.2   **Age** 10–12   **Organization** pairs/individual

Aims To prepare and give a very short presentation on a topic using PowerPoint; to develop awareness of how a computer can help when giving an oral presentation; to develop confidence and self-esteem.

Language focus any, depending on the topic

Materials *Essential:* computers and software, PowerPoint projector and screen / *Optional:* printouts of the PowerPoint presentations (as documents)

Procedure

Use this activity as a follow-up either to investigative work on a topic, eg bugs or food, in which case children work in pairs, or as an opportunity for children to present personalized work, eg on their pets, family or hobbies, in which case they work individually. The activity assumes basic knowledge of working with PowerPoint.

1 Explain that the children are going to take turns to give a short presentation to the rest of the class using PowerPoint.

2 Divide the class into pairs if relevant.

3 Before working on computers, ask them to plan what they are going to say and what is going to go on each slide in their presentation in draft form in their notebooks. Establish that the first slide should contain 3–4 bullet points of the main points of their presentation and the other slides should illustrate these, eg with photos, scanned in pictures, charts, further bullet points or brief text. You may like to specify the number of slides, eg no more than six.

4 Once the children have made their plans, ask them to create their PowerPoint presentations on computer. Encourage them to choose a template and use a combination of colours, eg black text on light background or white text on coloured background, that will make their presentation as clear and attractive as possible.

5 Once they are ready, print out a copy of the presentation for each child or pair in document form (eg with all six slides on one page).

6 Children take turns to give their presentations to the rest of the class. It is best to organize this over several lessons, with one or two pairs giving their presentations in the first or last ten minutes or so of each lesson.

7 Encourage the rest of the class to ask questions and clap at the end of each presentation and say what they particularly like about each one.

Comments and suggestions

• Children can be very creative in the presentations they produce. The use of slides helps them to structure what they are going to say and the visual focus provided by technology makes it non-threatening to speak to the rest of the class.

• This activity helps children to plan and organize a short presentation and can be useful preparation if this is something they have to do for an exam.

• When you give feedback on the presentations, it is important to focus on the positive aspects and use the experience of giving a short presentation to the rest of the class as an opportunity to develop children's confidence and self-esteem.

9.15 Class e-zine

Level All **Age** 9–12 **Organization** pairs/groups, whole class

Aims To prepare, write and/or collate material for an electronic class magazine; to develop creative thinking skills; to collaborate with others.

Language focus any, depending on the topic and/or material

Materials *Essential:* computers and software / *Optional:* printout(s) of the class e-zine

Procedure

1 Explain the idea of producing an electronic class magazine. Ask the children to suggest ideas of things to go in the magazine and write a list on the board, eg class news, articles, letters, poems, recipes, cartoons.

2 Divide the class into pairs or groups.

3 Ask each pair or group to think about what they would specifically like to contribute to the e-zine (this can either be work they have already done and/or new contributions). Give the pairs or groups time to think about this and then ask them to report back.

4 Write a list of everyone's possible contributions on the board. Review this at the end and ask the children if they think this looks a good set of contents for their e-zine. Make any changes or adjustments to the contents and the children's contributions depending on their (and your) response.

5 Children work in their pairs or groups preparing their contributions to the magazine in draft form.

6 When they are ready, and after checking with you, children work on computers formatting the text and scanning in any photos or pictures, using the software or publishing programme you choose.

7 At the end, there will still be work to do collating, ordering and combining everyone's contributions into the final e-zine form. Either you can do this outside class time or you can ask two or three children to help while the rest of the class does other work.

8 When the e-zine is ready, save it in pdf and print out one or more copies for the children to see.

Comments and suggestions

• Creating an e-zine can either be done as a one-off activity or, if the children respond positively, they can produce one more frequently, eg every term.

• If you have set up a class email group (see 9.16) a copy of the e-zine can be sent as an attachment to the group or uploaded to the group file for everyone to share. Alternatively, the e-zine can be linked to the home page of the school or class website.

NB *For activities 9.16 – 9.24 you need computers and internet access.*

9.16 Class email group

Level A1.2, A2.1, A2.2, B1.1, B1.2   **Age** 8–12   **Organization** individual

Aims To provide a forum for informal exchanges of emails between class members; to encourage children to write in English; to develop confidence and self-esteem; to create a sense of class community.

Language focus any familiar language and vocabulary

Materials *Essential:* computers and internet access; children need to have an email account (through the school is best) and you need to set up a group discussion list for the class, eg through Yahoo

Procedure

1 Explain to the children that you have set up a class email group and that the children can use it to exchange informal messages about any topic they like in English.

2 Send an initial welcoming email to the group. Start the discussion off by telling them something about yourself which is appropriate for the age and level of the children and then ask a question inviting them to contribute in a similar way, eg:

3 Encourage the children to respond with descriptions of their pets and to ask you and each other questions about their pets, eg *Does Rasta bite?* You and the children can also attach photos of your pets.

Comments and suggestions

- Use the class email group on a regular basis to encourage children to write informally in English and without fear of being judged or corrected.

- By starting off with a description of your pet (or anything else appropriate, eg what you did in the holidays) you implicitly provide a model which will help children when they write their replies.

- As children start to enjoy and get used to writing messages to the group, you can write fewer messages and they will write more. It is up to you whether to link messages on the class email group to different topics the children are doing in class or whether to keep the two things completely separate.

9.17 Partner exchange

Level A1.2, A2.1, A2.2, B1.1, B1.2   **Age** 8–12   **Organization** whole class, individual

Aims To ask and exchange information with a partner class from another school by email; to motivate children to write in English; to create a sense of class and school community; to develop interest and curiosity in children from a school in another country.

Language focus *In the example:* present simple, *there is/are, have got,* school, places, members of the family
Alternatives: any, depending on the topic of the exchanges

Materials *Essential:* computers and internet access; you also need to have established a partner class in a school in another country for the children to exchange messages with. This does not necessarily need to be an English-speaking country and the exchange may prove richer by exposing the children to greater cultural variety.

Procedure

1 Ask the children what things they think would be interesting to tell their partner class and write a list on the board, eg things about the location of the school; things about the school itself – size, subjects, sports, school day; things about themselves – family, pets, where they live, things they like and don't like.

2 Build up a description of the school and location with the whole class to form part of the general introductory part of the email (see also shared writing 2.8). Then ask the children to complete or write descriptions of themselves individually following a model.

3 When the children have done this, get them to help prepare attachments to go with the email they will send to the partner class, eg either individual photos, class photo, photo of their classroom or school. Alternatively children can draw pictures and scan these as part of the attachments to accompany the message.

Comments and suggestions

- The email and attachments can be kept simple as above or children can make electronic profiles of themselves (see 9.1). The electronic profiles can also include a link to individual children's email addresses with the school account. This will also allow for setting up individual exchanges between pupils in the partner class.

- Depending on your agreement with the partner class or school, the partner exchange can develop in any number of ways. For example, the children can write collaborative stories, research different aspects of the same topic for a project, prepare quizzes for each other, or exchange cultural information such as favourite recipes, famous landmarks or famous historical figures from their country.

- If both schools have or can arrange access to web cams or video conferencing facilities, children can also 'meet' the children from their partner school.

9.18 Best deal

Level A1.2, A2.1, A2.2, B1.1, B1.2   **Age** 8–12   **Organization** pairs, whole class

Aims To scan information on a website; to search and find the best deal for something to buy; to report back and compare prices.

Language focus *How much …?* numbers, prices, shops, shopping, *have got,* comparative adjectives, any vocabulary depending on what the search is for, language for ICT

Materials *Essential:* computers and internet access, pre-selected website addresses in English for the search

Procedure

1 Explain to the children that you want to ask their help in buying something, eg a digital camera to give to your sister for her birthday. Either give some information about the kind of camera you want, eg it doesn't have to be very good quality, but it must be small, it must have a video function and a (limited) zoom lens and/or say the maximum price you want to pay.

2 Divide the class into pairs.

3 Assign one or two websites to each pair for their search. Ask them to look at the digital cameras for sale on the site and find the two or three best deals. Tell them to note a) the make, b) the price, c) what it comes with as part of a pack (if anything).

4 At the end, ask the pairs to report back and recommend the camera they think you should buy your sister as a result of their search. Encourage them to discuss and compare the prices, eg *The X camera is more expensive but it comes with a memory card. / The Y camera is cheaper but it doesn't have a zoom lens.*

Comments and suggestions

• This activity involves a limited websearch which does not take much class time but leads to lots of natural discussion as children recommend and compare different cameras they have found.

• As well as developing computer and language skills, the activity develops children's ability to compare and evaluate consumer offers in a critical way.

• You can vary the context for looking for best deals depending on the age and level of the children, eg younger children can research the price of toys, such as remote control cars, footballs, dolls or computer games.

• If prices on the website are quoted in another currency, eg US dollars, euros or UK pounds, children can use a currency conversion site to find out the prices in their own currency (see 9.20).

9.19 Email a friend about a book

Level A1.2, A2.1, A2.2, B1.1, B1.2   **Age** 8–12   **Organization** whole class, pairs, individual

Aims To send an email to a friend from a website about a book; to say why you think the book is good or looks interesting; to practise writing short messages; to develop interest and curiosity in books.

Language focus present simple, opinions, any other language and vocabulary depending on the book

Materials *Essential:* computers and internet access, pre-selected website addresses in English for the search; children also need individual email accounts / *Optional:* class email discussion group list, examples of reference and story books you have used with the children

Procedure

1 Show children examples of reference or story books if you have these available. Ask children to tell you the books they like and any others they know. This can include stories you have read to them in class, graded readers, picture dictionaries, bilingual dictionaries or reference books they have used for topic- and content-based work.

2 Explain that the children are going to look for a book either that they know or that they think looks interesting on a bookshop website and send an email about it, directly from the website, either to a friend in the class or to the class discussion group.

3 Ask the children for suggestions of what they can say in the email and establish a framework for writing this, eg *Dear …,*
I hope you are well. I'm writing to tell you about a book I like very much / I think looks interesting. It's about … . I think it looks very exciting / good / funny. Please reply and let me know your opinion. Love from …

4 Divide the class into pairs.

5 Ask the children to decide whether they will look for a particular book on the website (in which case they need to note the name of the title and author) or a book on a topic which interests them, eg science or football. When they are ready, ask them to note the address of the website for the activity.

6 Explain that the children in each pair should take turns to find the book they want and send an email. When they first enter the site, they should click on 'children's books' and then type in the title/author or topic that they want to find a book about. When they have found the book they want, or one that they think looks interesting, they should click on 'send an email about this item to a friend' and write their email.

7 Children can then read and reply to each others' emails either individually or via the class group discussion list.

Comments and suggestions

- This activity develops children's awareness and interest in books and they enjoy the feature of being able to send an email to a friend or to the class discussion group directly from the site.

- You may wish to make the point that children can easily get hold of books they are interested in by borrowing them from the class, school or local library. Children can also exchange and borrow books from each other. They do not need to buy every book they want to read.

- The 'tell a friend' via email facility exists on many websites. However, you need to be cautious about using this from commercial websites in order not to encourage consumerism and to avoid children receiving advertising mail. Other websites such as museums which have this facility may be more suitable to use.

- Children can also post book reviews they have written (see 2.20) on some bookshop sites.

9.20 How much is it in …?

Level A1.2, A2.1, A2.2   **Age** 8–12   **Organization** whole class, pairs

Aims To convert money from one currency to another using a website programme; to develop awareness of the relationship between different currencies and countries; to practise asking and saying numbers and prices.

Language focus *How much …?* numbers, currencies

Materials *Essential:* computers and internet access, pre-selected website address in English for the search; prepared currency conversion questions (and answers) to ask the children based on the site / *Optional:* examples of different currencies, copies of the question sheet (one per pair)

How much is 100 US dollars in euros?
How much is 50 GB pounds in yen?
How much is 20 euros in GB pounds?

Procedure

1 Show children examples of different currencies, if you have these available, including their own.

2 Elicit or establish that different currencies have different exchange rates and these vary depending on a range of economic and political factors.

3 Ask children if they know the current rate of exchange between their own currency and, eg the US dollar and UK pound and, if not, tell them what these are.

4 Divide the class into pairs.

5 Give children the website address you have selected and ask them to go into the site.

6 Draw the children's attention to how to do a currency conversion by entering the amount and then scrolling and selecting the currency they wish to convert it from and to. Get the children to practise doing this a few times.

7 Teach the children how to say, eg *one point four six* (1.46) if this is new to them.

8 Then say, eg *OK. Are you ready? I'm going to ask you questions and I want you to tell me the answers as fast as you can! How much is 100 US dollars in euros?* Children perform the conversion with their partner and tell you the answer. Explain they need to say this to the second decimal point only.

9 Continue asking, eg 8–12 questions in the same way. If you like, you can turn the activity into a game. The pair who answer correctly first each time score two points, the pair who answer second score one point. If children finish first but answer incorrectly they lose two points. At the end, the pair with the most points wins.

Comments and suggestions

• This activity develops children's hand–eye coordination in identifying and entering data rapidly and correctly to perform the currency conversion.

• It is best to ask questions about currencies that are most relevant to the children, ie their own and either international currencies or currencies of neighbouring countries.

• Instead of asking the questions orally, you can give children a question sheet to complete as fast as they can instead.

• It may be appropriate to use the same currency conversion site in conjunction with other activities such as Classroom shop (1.9) and Best deal (9.18).

9.21 A visitor in town

Level A1.2, A2.1, A2.2, B1.1, B1.2   **Age** 10–12   **Organization** pairs, whole class

Aims To search websites on local places in English; to complete a grid in order to suggest a two-day itinerary for a visitor; to report back and compare itineraries; (to act out a role play and/or write an email or letter to the visitor suggesting what to see); to develop interest in your own local region and culture.

Language focus *there is/are*, *can* (for possibility), *have got*, addresses, suggestions (*Why don't you …? What about …?*)

Materials *Essential:* computers and internet access, pre-selected website addresses in English for the search / *Optional:* copies of the grid for children to complete (one for each child)

Procedure

1 Ask the children to imagine that a visitor, eg from their partner school, is coming to their city or region for two days. As the visitor is coming for such a short period, they want to make maximum use of their time. You want children to suggest how they should spend their time.

2 Divide the class into pairs.

	Place to go	Address	What to see
DAY 1 Morning			
DAY 1 Afternoon			
DAY 2 Morning			
DAY 2 Afternoon			

3 *Either* draw the grid on the board *or* give the children copies. Elicit and talk about the importance of variety during the visit and explain that children should try and suggest a balance of things to do, eg visits to museums as well as other things, such as a visit to a local market.

4 Ask the children to note the website(s) they should visit in order to plan the itinerary and complete the grid. You may like to set a time limit for this, eg 10–15 minutes.

5 At the end, ask the children to report back and compare their recommended itineraries.

6 If appropriate, these can then form the basis of either a role play in pairs between themselves and a visitor, recommending places to go and/or a letter or email to the visitor outlining their suggestions.

Comments and suggestions

- This activity encourages children to be aware and take a pride in what their local city or region has to offer an outside visitor.

- If you wish to extend the activity, children can be asked to research more detailed information, eg opening times and prices of museums they recommend.

- If you develop the role play, the activity can also be linked with giving directions and following a route (see 1.18).

9.22 Weather check

Level A1.2, A2.1, A2.2   **Age** 8–12   **Organization** whole class, pairs

Aims To search and scan a website in order to find out the weather in a city you want to go to; to ask and answer questions about the weather; to compare the weather in different cities; (to develop awareness of the location of major world cities).

Language focus *In the example:* weather, temperature, cities, countries, *be*, present simple, questions, comparative adjectives
Alternatives: going to, will

Materials *Essential:* computers and internet access, pre-selected website address in English for the search / *Optional:* photocopies of outline world map (one for each child)

Procedure

1 Ask the children to name cities they want to go to e.g. *London, Paris, New York, Tokyo, Mumbai, Istanbul, Beijing* and to say why.

2 Ask them what they think the weather is like in the city they want to visit and encourage them to predict this. Use this as an opportunity to revise weather vocabulary. Elicit and talk briefly about the differences in the weather and climate between the northern and southern hemispheres, if appropriate.

3 Divide the class into pairs.

4 Explain that you want them to use the internet to find out what the weather is like today in both the cities they and their partner want to visit and their own city (or nearest city in their country). Ask them to note the maximum (day) temperature and whether it is sunny, cloudy, raining, etc.

5 Give out the website address that you have pre-selected for the children to use. Children work with their partner and note the information for all three cities. When they have done this, get the children to take turns and ask each other questions, eg *What's the weather like in …? What's the temperature in …? Or How hot/cold is it in …? Is it sunny/cloudy in …?*

6 If appropriate, they can also compare the temperatures, eg *It's colder in Paris than in Madrid. It's hottest in Sydney* and say whether they still want to visit the city they originally chose.

Comments and suggestions

- Most weather websites display information in a very clear visual way which makes it possible for children to do the activity easily.

- This activity can be used to practise *going to* or *will* instead if children find out the weather for tomorrow rather than today.

- As an alternative to finding out the weather for three cities, children can find out the five- (or ten-) day forecast for one city only.

- This activity can be used to follow activities in which children have identified countries they want to go to (see 1.11, 1.19). As a follow-up, children can draw or mark the cities and note the temperatures and draw a weather symbol for each one on an outline world map.

9.23 Holiday course search

Level A1.2, A2.1, A2.2   **Age** 9–12   **Organization** pairs, whole class

Aims To search and scan a website in order to find out details of a holiday course; to say why you would or wouldn't like to do the course.

Language focus present simple, dates, price, opinions, giving reasons, *because*, any other language and vocabulary relevant to the type of course chosen

Materials *Essential:* computers and internet access, pre-selected website address(es) for relevant holiday course(s) in English for the search

Procedure

Before doing the activity, ask the children what kind of holiday course they would most like to do. Choose the suggestion that seems most popular as the basis of research into suitable websites for the activity.

1 Divide the class into pairs.

2 Explain to the children that they are going to look at a website which offers a holiday course they might like to do, eg a horse-riding course in Ireland. Ask children to note the website address. Depending on contents of the website, choose between 4–6 pieces of information that you want the children to find out, eg the length of the course, possible dates, the price, the location, where you stay, how many hours of riding instruction each day.

3 Children work with their partners, visit the site and note the information.

4 At the end, ask the children to report back and check the information they have collected and say why they would or wouldn't like to go on the course, eg *I think it looks great. / I think it's very expensive. / I'd like to ride more than four hours every day. / I wouldn't like to stay with a family.*

Comments and suggestions

- If, in your initial research, you find more than one website suitable for the activity, then half the class can research one course and the other half a different course. Children then compare the information about both courses and decide which one they think sounds best.
- This activity can also be done as a follow-up to 1.19.

9.24 Mini-quest

Level A1.2, A2.1, A2.2, B1.1, B1.2   **Age** 8–12   **Organization** pairs, whole class

Aims To prepare and write questions you would like to know the answers to on a particular topic; to search one or more pre-selected websites to find the answers; to develop curiosity and investigative skills; (to do a quiz and/or write a description or report on the topic based on your findings).

Language focus any, depending on the topic

Materials *Essential:* computers and internet access, pre-selected website address(es) in English for the search

Procedure

1 Divide the class into pairs.
2 Assign, or let children choose, an aspect of the topic they are currently working on in class. For example, if children are working on the topic of bugs, you could ask each pair to identify a bug they are particularly interested in finding out about, eg spiders.
3 Explain to the children that you want them to think about and write 6–8 questions that they are interested in finding out about their bug, eg *Do spiders have blood? Do spiders have hair? What do spiders eat? What is a spider's web made from? What is the most poisonous spider? Can a spider kill you?* Once children have prepared their questions, ask them to note the website address(es) for the activity.
4 Children work with their partner and visit the pre-selected site(s) to find the answers to their questions. If they can't find the answers on the website(s) you have selected, then you may decide to help or let them do a more generalized search.
5 At the end, ask the pairs to take turns to report their findings to the class.
6 If appropriate, they can also write a description or report based on their findings.

Comments and suggestions

- Although there are many web quests or cyber hunts available on the internet, these are often too complex and too long for children learning English as a foreign language.
- This mini-quest activity encourages children to think about a topic in more depth. It also motivates them to search a website for specific information they genuinely want to find out.
- By searching a website to answer questions they have set themselves, children are naturally encouraged to scan the information rather than read in detail and less likely to copy chunks of text directly.
- As an alternative to reporting back to the class at the end of the activity, you can organize a quiz in teams based on the children's original questions and the answers they have found.

Section 10 **Learning to learn**

This section is last, but not least. In fact, learning to learn is arguably the most important aspect of children's overall educational development, of which foreign language learning is just a part. As the proverb goes: *You can lead a horse to water, but you can't make it drink.* In terms of children's learning, we can give children all the opportunities in the world to learn, but ultimately we can't learn for them. To continue the metaphor, learning to learn in a primary context is about guiding children to begin to find the water for themselves, in other words to begin to become autonomous in the way they approach their own learning, and motivating them to be thirsty to learn as much as they can in the most personally effective way possible.

What learning to learn means

An approach which incorporates learning to learn as a specific strand in the syllabus or learning programme focuses on both the *process* and *product* of teaching and learning in an integrated way, by encouraging children to think explicitly about *how* they learn as well as *what* they learn. The value attached to learning to learn is based on the belief and assumption that the more informed and aware children are about their own learning, the more effective and successful they will be as learners. In an age of rapid technological change, shifting knowledge bases and changing employment patterns, there is one thing that we can be sure of for the future. This is that, as a vitally important part of their education, children need to develop awareness, strategies, skills and attitudes that will enable them to constantly adapt to change and meet new learning challenges competently and confidently in a life-long way. The main aim of learning to learn at primary level is to start children off on their own personal journey towards self-knowledge, self-reliance and independence in their learning. Attending to how children learn also helps us to take account of individual differences and needs of children we teach.

Why learning to learn is important

All children have a unique intelligence profile. They also vary in their personality, aptitudes, motivation and emerging learning styles, as well as in their self-concept and in the psychological and emotional support they receive at home. There are no single recipes for being an effective and successful learner. Children who learn effectively and successfully vary hugely in their characteristics, behaviour and preferred emerging learning styles. While some children may be naturally outgoing, sociable and willing to take risks, for example, other children who are equally successful and effective learners may be hard-working, quiet and shy. As children embark on the long haul of education at school, however, we cannot assume that they will automatically grow into effective and successful learners without adequate training and help. As an integral part of lessons, it is therefore important to provide children with opportunities to build on their individual strengths in the service of their own learning, as well as to discover the learning styles and strategies that personally suit them best. It is also important to gradually guide children towards developing self-awareness, positive attitudes and working habits that will enable them to consciously consider, reflect and manage their own learning in an increasingly independent and responsible way.

The teacher's role

In helping children learn how to learn, you, as the teacher, have a central role. This includes a *procedural role* in setting up and following procedures that provide a framework for developing children's learning strategies and metacognitive awareness, in other words children's self-awareness and self-knowledge about the processes involved in their own learning. It also includes a *behavioural role* in explicitly demonstrating and modelling different learning strategies in a way that allows children to experience directly what these involve as a prelude to developing the competence to transfer and apply them to their own learning. These strategies broadly include metacognitive strategies, such as planning or reviewing learning, cognitive strategies required by specific activities, such as predicting or classifying, and socio-affective strategies, such as collaborating and actively listening to what children have to say. In addition to a procedural and behavioural role, you also have an *interactive role* in helping children become thoughtful, responsible and reflective learners by stimulating and responding to their contributions about all aspects of their learning, asking appropriate questions in a way which probes them into further thinking and leads them to greater understanding and self-awareness.

How to incorporate learning to learn in lessons

One way to incorporate a regular focus on learning to learn in your lessons is to establish aims and purposes for doing activities and review what has been done. This can be applied to the whole lesson as well as to activity cycles within the lesson. At the start of lessons, it is important to share with the children what they are going to do in the lesson and the reasons for doing it. It may also be appropriate to write a 'menu' of activities and aims on the board. By explicitly setting learning aims, you show children what to expect and they are encouraged to make the connection between the activity itself and the learning outcome it is intended to achieve. This can be done very simply, for example, by using the phrase *in order to* as in, eg *We're going to do a food quiz in order to remember the food words we learnt last lesson.* Even very young children can understand the aims of doing activities, if these are explained in simple, child-friendly terms.

At the end of activity cycles, lessons or units of work, it is also important to make a link back to the initial setting of aims and conduct a review of what has been done. This calls on your interactive skills to ask children questions, listen to their responses and guide their thinking in order to recall activities and outcomes and explore the ways in which these have helped them to learn. Examples of initial questions you can ask are: *What have we done today / this week? What did we do first/next? Why did we do that? How did it help you? Was it useful? In what way?* as well as further more detailed questions on specific activities, eg *What words did you learn? Why do you think it was easy to remember the story? What helped you?* With younger children and lower levels, it may be appropriate to carry out the review in L1.

Another general way to incorporate a focus on learning to learn in your lessons is to model aloud thinking and verbal reasoning processes that children need to follow in order to carry out an activity or complete a task successfully. By exteriorizing and articulating the cognitive processes and the language involved, you act as a mediator in children's learning and prepare them for performing learning tasks in an independent way. There are many examples of this technique described as part of the procedure for activities in different sections of this book. One example is 3.8, where the children classify clothes in a Venn diagram. An example of modelling the procedure is as follows: *I wear shorts when it's hot. It's hot in summer. So shorts go here. I wear a coat when it's cold. It's cold in winter. So coat goes here. I wear trainers when it's hot and when it's cold. In summer and in winter. So trainers go here.* By talking through the procedure aloud, language and cognitive processes are made explicit and this paves the way for the children to subsequently classify a range of other clothes in an independent way.

Activities for learning to learn

As illustrated above, incorporating a focus on learning to learn is often very much part of the closely woven fabric of your lessons, arising naturally out of general procedures, techniques and interactive discourse that you use as an ongoing, integral part of your teaching. The activities in this section reflect a wide range of other significant aspects of learning to learn which it is also invaluable to incorporate into your lessons on a regular basis. These include activities to develop children's self-esteem and feelings of confidence in their own strengths and abilities, which vitally underpin their receptivity to any kind of learning (see 10.1, 10.2). They also include a relaxation and breathing exercise (see 10.3) which can be used to focus attention and create a state of relaxed alertness and readiness for learning. Other activities focus on introducing children to strategies for recording and memorizing vocabulary (see 10.5, 10.7) and grammar (see 10.10, 10.11) and checking their own learning (see 10.4) as well as exploring specific learning styles and strategies related to different language and skills that may help them learn (see 10.17). Several activities are designed to develop different aspects of metacognitive awareness and positive attitudes towards learning, such as exploring children's reasons for learning English (see 10.16) and their preferred conditions for how they like to work (see 10.18).

Through being offered personal choice, children develop a sense of 'ownership' and responsibility towards their learning and this is explored in two activities related to vocabulary learning and choosing activities to do (see 10.9, 10.12). The setting up of negotiated and agreed parameters for learning in a class contract (see 10.14) as well as the assignment of classroom jobs (see 10.15) are also important for developing a sense of responsibility, establishing good working habits and creating a positive socio-affective atmosphere for learning. Other activities encourage children to set short-term, personal learning goals (see 10.13) and to measure these against what they actually learn as part of topic- or content-based work (see 10.19).

Self-assessment

A further integral aspect of learning to learn is children's ability to assess their own learning. Self-assessment frequently takes the form of 'can do' statements related to a specific unit of work, against which children measure their progress, often using a three-point visual scale of, for example, smiley faces, suns and clouds or a ladder. Two examples of self-assessment formats for younger and older children are included in a self-assessment activity (see 10.20). There are two further activities – getting children to write their own report (see 10.21) and keep a learning diary (see 10.22) – which also encourage children to monitor and measure their progress, as well as reflect on other aspects of their learning.

Self-assessment activities form part of the overall assessment of children's learning. They also give you invaluable information about children's perception of their own progress and activities that they enjoy and that help them learn. This can feed into your own reflective teaching cycle and help you in planning lessons to meet the children's interests and needs in future. If the children are keeping portfolios, then records of their self-assessment can be stored here.

In addition to the activities in this section, there are many other activities throughout the book which also contribute to children's learning to learn, either implicitly or explicitly, in a number of ways. These include a range of activities which build up children's confidence and self esteem as well as activities that are designed to raise children's language awareness, for example, by noticing particular aspects of grammar, develop their understanding of processes involved in reading and writing, or develop concentration and memory skills. They also include many activities which develop socio-affective strategies such as collaborating and turn-taking, and a range of activities which integrate the development of language with cognitive strategies such as predicting, classifying, estimating, hypothesizing, experimenting, sequencing, comparing, investigating and reporting (see Learning skills and attitudes index for detailed references).

Benefits of learning to learn

By adopting an approach which develops language skills and learning to learn in a fully integrated way, there are many potentially significant benefits both for children's overall personal development and education in general, and for their language learning in particular. These potential benefits include:

- increased motivation
- greater self-awareness
- active involvement and commitment to learning
- an open, curious, questioning attitude
- good work habits
- an organized approach to managing their learning
- better concentration
- improved recall and memory
- greater collaboration, sharing and respect between peers
- becoming more responsible, reflective and independent learners.

If we can achieve all this, combined with successful foreign language learning too, then this has to be what makes being a primary teacher such a worthwhile, if challenging, profession to belong to.

Reflection time

As you use the learning to learn procedures and activities in this section with your classes, you may like to think about the following questions and use your responses to evaluate how things went and plan possible improvements for next time:

1 **Self-awareness:** Have you noticed an increase in the children's self-awareness? In what ways? Has this applied to some or all the children? Can you account for the differences between individual children?

2 **Learning strategies:** How helpful has it been to introduce the children to particular learning strategies? Has there been any evidence of children using these independently?

3 **Attitudes / sense of responsibility:** Have you noticed any change in the children's attitudes and/or their sense of responsibility as a result of using learning-to-learn procedures or activities? If so, in what ways?

4 **Learning reviews:** What has the children's response been to learning reviews? If you have conducted these on a regular basis, have you noticed the children becoming more perceptive and insightful about the relationship between classroom activities and their own learning? In what way(s)?

5 **Self-assessment:** What has the children's response been to assessing their own learning? Has this had a positive impact on their subsequent work? In what way(s)?

6 **Independence:** Have you noticed the children are willing and/or able to work more independently as a result of incorporating learning to learn activities and procedures? If so, what impact has this had on the way you teach?

10.1 Rays of sunshine

Level All   **Age** 6–12   **Organization** individual

Aims To recognize your positive characteristics and strengths; to develop confidence in your ability to learn; to develop self-esteem; to create a positive socio-affective atmosphere for learning.

Language focus *be, can* (for ability), *have got,* adjectives to describe people, skills, any other familiar language and vocabulary

Materials *Essential:* none / *Optional:* sun handout (one for each child), children's photos of themselves, glue

Procedure

Do this activity early on when you meet a new class. If you like, ask the children to bring in small photos of themselves before the lesson.

1 Tell the children that you know what a class of great and talented children they are. Ask the children individually to think of their strengths and good points. Give a few examples of what you mean, eg *I am kind. I work hard. I love animals. I try to do my best. I am good at drawing. I can play the piano.*

2 Elicit sentences from individual children round the class.

3 Either draw a sun with six rays on the board or give out the handout. Explain that children should either draw a picture of themselves or stick their photo in the centre of the sun and write different sentences about their good points or strengths on or by the six rays.

4 At the end, children compare their rays of sunshine in pairs. Alternatively these can be circulated round the class so that the children can read what everyone has written. The rays of sunshine can then be displayed.

Comments and suggestions

- This activity encourages children to feel good about themselves (and each other). Positive self-esteem and confidence in their own abilities are a vital foundation for children's learning.

- If appropriate, you can use the activity to talk to the children about how recognizing the things we are good at can help us learn better and achieve what we want.

10.2 Happy tunnel

Level All   **Age** 4–10   **Organization** whole class

Aims To listen and say positive things to others in the class; to develop self-esteem; to create a positive socio-affective atmosphere for learning

Language focus *be, like, good at,* positive adjectives to describe people
Alternatives: proud of, any familiar language and vocabulary

Materials *Essential:* none / *Optional:* CD of instrumental music

Procedure

1 Ask the children to stand facing each other in two lines and raise their arms high with the tips of their fingers touching to make the Happy tunnel. Choose a child to go through the Happy tunnel. Ask the class to think of a positive thing to say to the child who is going to go through the tunnel, eg *I like you! / You're great! / You're nice! / You're good at …*

2 Ask the child to walk slowly through the tunnel. The rest of the class whisper or say their sentences. The child then comes out of the tunnel with a big smile, ie happy!

3 Repeat with one or two other children. In order for everyone to have a turn going through the tunnel, you can repeat the activity once or twice over several lessons.

Comments and suggestions

- This activity makes children feel good about themselves. It also helps them to realize how easy it is to make other people feel good too, thereby creating a positive atmosphere for learning.

- For other activities to develop self-esteem, you can do a sentence round with a starter line such as *I'm good at … / I'm proud of …* (see 1.7) or children can make a 'snap dragon' (see 7.8) in which they write positive comments about each other.

10.3 Ready for learning!

Level All   **Age** 6–12   **Organization** whole class

Aims To listen and follow instructions to do a relaxation and breathing exercise in preparation for learning; to feel focused, alert and energetic.

Language focus *breathe,* present continuous, prepositions, parts of the body

Materials *Essential:* none / *Optional:* a classical music CD, eg Mozart

Procedure

1 Ask the children to move their chairs away from their desks and to sit in a relaxed way with both feet on the floor and their arms by their sides. Sit down yourself as you demonstrate and talk them through the exercise.

2 Ask the children to wiggle their toes and say to them, eg *Imagine you are breathing through your toes. The air is coming through your feet, slowly up your legs, into your back, up your back to your neck, right to the top of your head. And now it's going all the way back, down your neck, down your back, down your legs, into your feet and out through your toes.*

3 Repeat several times, getting the children to breathe deeply from the tips of their toes to the tops of their heads. At the end, the children will be relaxed, energetic and ready for learning.

Comments and suggestions

- It is widely recognized that controlled exercise and relaxed breathing can have huge benefits for children's alertness and readiness for learning. The most well-known and successful techniques are those of Brain Gym ™, a series of movements based on the connections between mind and body which aim to enhance children's experience of learning (see Further reading p.320). In Brain Gym ™, it is also recommended that children should always have water available in order to avoid dehydration, which can impede their learning.

- This activity can be used as a follow-up to a simple gym sequence (see 1.1) in order to focus children's attention and energy in readiness for learning.

10.4 Look, say, cover, write, check

Level All   **Age** 6–12   **Organization** individual

Aims To associate words, pictures, meaning and spelling; to recall vocabulary and memorize how to spell words; to test yourself and check your learning.

Language focus any vocabulary children are learning

Materials *Essential:* pictures of vocabulary with words underneath, eg in course book or picture dictionary / *Optional:* 'Look, say, cover, write, check' handouts (one for each child)

Procedure

1 Ask the children for ideas of what to do if they want to remember how to spell words, and listen to their suggestions (in L1 or English).

2 Introduce, demonstrate and model out loud the technique of 'look, say, cover, write, check' by holding up the course book, picture dictionary page or handout the children are going to use and saying, eg *I want to learn all these words. I'm going to look at the picture and the word. I'm going to say it out loud, or in my head, several times like this: caterpillar, caterpillar, caterpillar. Then I'm going to cover the word. Now I'm going to look up high and try and see the picture and the word in my head and remember how it sounds. Then I'm going to write the word like this (demonstrate this on the board). And now I'm going to uncover the picture and check if I'm right. Yes! Great!*

3 Ask the children if they think that means you'll remember the word forever. Use their response to establish that this technique may help them to remember words and spelling, although they may need to practise it again next week or next month. Tell them that it is very important to try and use the words when they speak English and in their written work if they really want to remember them.

4 Give out the handout pictures and words or ask children to open their course books or picture dictionaries. Give them a set of words which have been recently introduced, but which they don't know very well, and set a time limit, eg five minutes. Ask them to experiment and see if the technique works for them.

5 At the end, ask if the children think this technique might be useful to use if, for example, they need to learn words for a test, and listen to their response.

Comments and suggestions

- This activity appeals to predominantly visual and auditory learners, as children associate the pictures with the shape and spelling of words and repeat them several times either silently or out loud before trying to write them. The activity also encourages children to monitor how they are doing and to check their work.

- Spending short periods of class time modelling a learning strategy such as this one and getting children to practise it lays the foundation for children using it independently later if they find it useful.

- It is helpful to ask children to look up high in order to see the picture and word in their heads as this is what we naturally tend to do when visualizing.

- Children can also do a similar activity to test themselves on vocabulary using word cards. Word cards can have pictures on one side and words on the other. Alternatively, for older children, it may be suitable to have the word in English on one side and L1 on the other.

10.5 Label the picture

Level A1.1, A1.2 **Age** 6–9, (4–6) **Organization** individual, pairs

Aims To draw, colour and label a picture showing vocabulary in visual context; to recall and memorize vocabulary; to record vocabulary learnt.

Language focus any vocabulary learnt recently

Materials *Essential:* none / *Optional:* copies of pictures for the children to label, eg downloaded from the internet (one for each child)

Procedure

1 At the end of a unit of work on a particular story or topic, eg 'On the farm', elicit vocabulary children have learnt and write this on the board.

2 Either give out pictures or ask the children to draw a picture and label it with the words they have learnt. Children can also colour their pictures.

3 Children can then compare their pictures and labels in pairs and test each other on the words.

Comments and suggestions

- By drawing, colouring and labelling pictures at the end of units of work children build up a personalized visual record of their vocabulary learning.

- Over time the pictures can be collated in a file or folder with a title 'My picture dictionary'. Alternatively, if appropriate, the pictures can form part of children's portfolios.

- Very young children (4–6) can simply colour pictures which include vocabulary they have learnt and build up a visual record of their learning in the same way.

10.6 Vocabulary collage

Level All **Age** 4–12 **Organization** groups

Aims To make a vocabulary collage based on a topic or theme; to recall and memorize vocabulary; to show and tell the class about your collage.

Language focus present continuous, any vocabulary, depending on the topic

Materials *Essential:* old magazines, scissors, glue, poster-size card (one sheet for each group)

Procedure

1 Divide the class into groups.

2 Explain that the children are going to make a vocabulary collage based on the topic or theme which they are doing. The groups can either all do the same topic or they can do different aspects of the topic. For example, with very young children working on the theme of colours, each group can make a collage of pictures in a different colour.

3 Give out poster-size card and a selection of old magazines to each group. Make sure the children also have scissors and glue available.

4 As the children make their collage, monitor and use this time as an opportunity to interact with individual children and groups, showing interest, asking questions and (if appropriate) praising their work.

5 At the end, the groups can take turns to show and tell the class about their collage. The collages can also be displayed.

Comments and suggestions

- This activity is a hands-on way for children to identify vocabulary they have learnt based on a topic or theme. It also frequently leads to children extending their vocabulary as they find pictures related to the topic which they do not know the words for in English. With older children, this can also provide a natural opportunity to develop reference skills.

- Once children have made their collages, it may also be possible to use them as the basis of further vocabulary activities or games, eg Kim's game (see 3.3).

10.7 Vocabulary networks

Level All   **Age** 8–12   **Organization** whole class, (pairs)

Aims To create a vocabulary network of related words; to develop awareness of the connections between words; to aid recall and develop memory skills.

Language focus *In the example:* school and classroom objects, furniture, school subjects, actions, jobs
Alternatives: any familiar vocabulary

Materials *Essential:* none / *Optional:* copies of the network diagram for children to complete

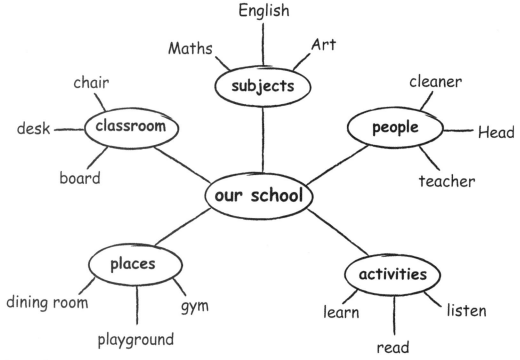

Procedure

1 Prepare a vocabulary network on a familiar theme or topic, eg 'Our school', before the lesson.

2 Write the key word(s) in a circle on the board. Build up the network with the whole class, modelling the process and eliciting the children's suggestions for words to go in each sub-category of the network.

3 Be ready for the children to add other categories that you may not have thought of or intended, eg in this case, clothes we wear at school.

4 At the end, ask the children to copy the network into their notebooks or give them a copy of the network diagram and ask them to complete this. Ask them if they think making a vocabulary network will help them to remember the words, and listen to their response.

5 As a follow-up, if appropriate, divide the class into pairs and ask the children to create a similar vocabulary network on another familiar theme or topic, eg 'My home'.

Comments and suggestions

- This activity encourages children to recognize semantic connections between words rather than perceiving vocabulary to be learnt as isolated items in a list.
- It is important to model the process of creating a vocabulary network with the whole class at least once, and probably several times on different occasions, before asking the children to do this independently. By building up familiarity with the thinking process involved in creating a vocabulary network, children are more likely to adopt it as a personal strategy for learning if they find it helpful.

10.8 Vocabulary cline

Level All   **Age** 4–12   **Organization** whole class, pairs

Aims To develop awareness of the degrees of difference between related items of vocabulary; to order items on a cline; to understand the relationship between the words; to aid recall and develop memory skills.

Language focus any vocabulary or language which can be ordered on a cline, eg adjectives of size, adjectives to describe temperature/weather, adverbs of frequency

Materials *Essential:* none / *Optional:* pictures for children to arrange on a cline (one set for each child)

Procedure

1 Elicit vocabulary that children are going to order on the cline, eg adjectives of size. Use gesture to demonstrate the differences and write the words on the board in jumbled order, eg *enormous, big, medium-sized, small, tiny, minute* (given here in the correct order).

2 Draw a cline on the board, marking six points. Write *enormous* by the first point on the cline as the example.

enormous

3 Divide the class into pairs.
4 Ask the children to copy the cline and work with their partner to arrange the words in order of size on the cline.
5 At the end, ask the children to report back and give you examples of things they know, eg *turnip, elephant, Daddy bear, mouse* to illustrate each size.

Comments and suggestions

- This activity can be used to extend children's vocabulary as part of topic- or story-based work, eg *The Enormous Turnip, The Three Bears.*
- With very young children, the activity can be done with three items and pictures only, as shown below. As a follow-up, children can add pictures of other animals in the appropriate place on the cline.

- With older children, the use of a cline may also help reinforce the relationship between different adverbs of frequency and help the children to use them appropriately, eg when describing their everyday activities and routines.

10.9 Vocabulary choice

Level All   **Age** 6–12   **Organization** individual, whole class / pairs

Aims To identify and choose vocabulary you want to learn; to exercise personal choice in your learning; to develop independence and responsibility for your own learning.

Language focus any vocabulary, depending on the topic

Materials *Essential:* none

Procedure

1 As part of any topic, eg rainforests, pets, seasons, ask the children to choose between 6 and 20 words (whatever is appropriate) related to the topic, which they are particularly interested in learning.

2 Explain that this is their homework and that, as part of the homework, you want them to think about how they will be able to show you and others in the class that they 'know' the words.

3 In the next lesson, ask the children if they have learnt the words and how they can prove it. Listen to their suggestions. These will vary depending on the children's age and level, eg name pictures, translate the word, use the word in a sentence, spell the word, answer questions about the word, describe or define it.

4 Either check individual children have learnt some of their words using the method they suggest with the whole class or, with older children, get them to do this in pairs.

5 At the end, ask the children how well they think they learnt the words and whether choosing the words they wanted to learn themselves and thinking about how they could show or prove that they had learnt them, helped them to learn.

Comments and suggestions

- This activity encourages children to relate what it means to 'learn' vocabulary with how they can actually use it.

- By offering choice in what they learn, children feel a greater sense of 'ownership' and develop an increasingly responsible attitude towards their own learning.

10.10 Grammar mind map

Level All   **Age** 9–12   **Organization** whole class

Aims To create a mind map to remember grammatical forms; to notice the differences between the forms and tenses; to aid recall and develop memory skills.

Language focus any item of grammar

Materials *Essential:* none / *Optional:* skeleton mind map for children to complete (one for each child)

Procedure

Decide on the point of grammar you want the children to create a mind map for, and prepare this before the lesson.

1 If the children are already familiar with mind maps (eg for planning writing, see 2.26), explain that these can also be helpful for learning and remembering grammar.

2 Build up the mind map on the board with the whole class, eliciting the pronouns / verb forms and asking them to suggest example sentences for each tense.

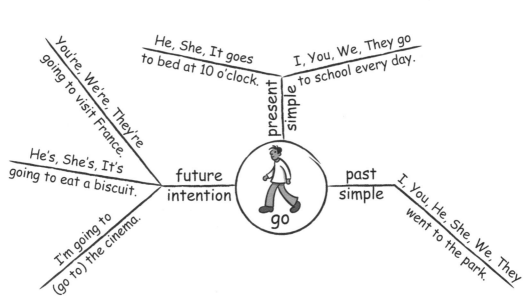

3 Ask the children to copy the mind map into their notebooks or give out photocopies of a skeleton mind map for them to complete.

4 Ask the children if they think noting grammatical information in the form of a mind map will help them to learn and remember it and listen to their response.

Comments and suggestions

- The use of mind maps based on the work of Tony Buzan (see Further reading on p.320) can help some children understand and remember grammatical relationships, eg between pronouns and forms of verbs, more clearly than more usual linear presentations in the form of, for example, a substitution table or box.

- If the children respond positively to grammar mind maps, you may like to use these regularly as a way of helping them to summarize and record different aspects of grammar. However, you will need to build up familiarity with the technique before the children can create their own mind maps independently.

- See also 2.26 and 10.18 for two other activities based on mind maps.

10.11 Magic mind memory stick

Level All   **Age** 9–12   **Organization** individual

Aims To create meaningful, personalized sentences in order to memorize a key grammatical pattern; to refer to the sentences and apply the grammatical pattern as relevant when doing other work.

Language focus any, depending on the grammar to be learnt

Materials *Essential:* none / *Optional:* copies of the 'memory stick' for children to record their key sentences on (one for each child)

Procedure

Use this activity periodically to help the children remember a particular language pattern they have been practising and which they find difficult to use.

1 Elicit or explain that a computer memory stick allows you to store data which you can retrieve anywhere at any time. Explain that the children are going to create their own magic mind memory sticks which will help them to remember sentence patterns in English.

2 Ask them to invent a sentence which means something to them personally and that contains the language pattern they have practised. This can, for example, be humorous, contain alliteration or refer to members of their family.

3 Explain that they are going to 'upload' this sentence onto their magic mind memory stick so that it will be there to help them whenever they need to use the same language pattern in other work. In reality this means that they should learn the sentence off by heart.

4 Elicit or suggest some strategies for doing this, eg using different colours, looking up and visualizing the sentence, repeating it rhythmically or in a silly voice, drawing a picture of the sentence, making a link between the sentence and L1, opening and closing your fist or tapping your foot as you say the sentence.

5 In future lessons refer to the children's magic mind memory stick as a prompt if they need help remembering a particular language pattern. Ask the children if they think their magic memory stick sentences help them to remember language patterns and feel more confident using English, and listen to their response.

Comments and suggestions

- This activity helps children to recognize that the language forms they are learning are generative and can be transferred and adapted to use in other contexts.

- It is important not to overuse the technique, because if there are too many sentences on the memory stick, there will be 'overload' and they will no longer be memorable. Two or three sentences with key language patterns each term is an approximate guide.

10.12 Activity choice

Level All   **Age** 4–12   **Organization** whole class, pairs/groups, individual

Aims To exercise personal choice in deciding what activities to do; to develop a sense of responsibility for your own learning; to develop independence; to respect the decisions of others.

Language focus activity types, *I'd like to, I want to,* any language and vocabulary relevant to the activities

Materials *Essential:* any necessary materials for the activities

Procedure

Use opportunities to offer children a choice of activities to do.

This may be with the whole class together. For example, with very young children, towards the end of lessons, you can ask, eg *Would you like to listen to a story about the elephant or sing a song about the elephant?* Use L1 to explore the reasons for their answers. If there is a lot of disagreement (which may be likely) then you can choose different children to decide what to do on different days.

With older children, it may be appropriate to give options for follow-up activities which children decide in pairs or groups, eg *You can choose whether you want to write the story or prepare a role play.*

Alternatively, it may be possible to write an activity 'menu' on the board at the start of the lesson and, after initial input and plenary work, children individually choose the activities they want to do and the order in which they do them. In this case, you may need to stipulate, for example, that everyone completes at least three activities.

Comments and suggestions

- Offering choice encourages children to think about what they want to do and why they want to do it. If this is accompanied by guided questioning from you, it also encourages children to become aware of the ways in which different activities help them to learn.

- Choice is also empowering: if children at times choose what to do, rather than have it imposed, they feel a greater sense of commitment and investment in their own learning. If you show that you respect children's choices, they also feel valued and this contributes to their confidence and self-esteem.

- By giving children choice regularly, when appropriate and feasible, you can vary activities to appeal to children with different interests, levels, intelligence profiles and learning styles. Through observing the choices children make, this gives you valuable insights into their learning preferences and strengths as well as useful feedback on the activities you use.

10.13 Setting goals

Level All   **Age** 6–12   **Organization** whole class, individual

Aims To identify and set yourself short-term personal learning goals; to review whether or not the goals have been met and the reasons for this; to develop independence, self-motivation and a responsible attitude towards your own learning.

Language focus *In the example: want to, going to*
Alternatives: L1

Materials *Essential:* none / *Optional:* copy of goal setting handout (one for each child)

Procedure

Do this activity at the start of a new topic or unit of work.

1 Ask the children why they think it is important to have learning goals and listen to their response (either in English or L1), eg *It helps us work harder. / We know what we're trying to do. / It makes us feel good if we succeed. / We learn more.*

2 Either draw a goal post and three large footballs (with space to write in) on the board and ask the children to copy this, or give the children a copy of the goal setting handout. Elicit or explain that 'goal' is also the term in football when players score goals for their team.

3 Explain that you want the children to set learning goals for themselves for the next, eg week, two weeks or during the next unit of work.

4 Model the process of setting short term goals yourself, for example, if you are also learning a foreign language, *I want to understand better when people speak, so I'm going to watch two DVDs. I want to increase my vocabulary, so I'm going to learn 20 words related to the topic.* Write your goals in the 'footballs' on the board.

5 Ask the children to think of three learning goals for themselves and to write them in the footballs in the same way (either in English or L1).

6 Invite a few children to share their learning goals if they wish and, if appropriate, collect in the goals to look at and comment on positively yourself.

7 After a week, two weeks or at the end of the next unit of work, ask the children to review their learning goals. If they think they have met their goals, they colour the footballs and draw a matching line into the goal. Monitor and discuss their goals individually with the children as they do this. If you like, invite some children to report back to the class.

Comments and suggestions

- Setting goals develops children's metacognitive strategies through encouraging them to plan and think ahead about their learning. As well as developing self-motivation, goal setting helps children to organize and manage their own learning. Through reviewing whether goals have been met, children also develop self-awareness and a more responsible attitude to their learning.

- With younger children and lower levels, the activity will probably need to be done in L1. Alternatively, you can prepare a selection of options in very simple English, eg *I want to … learn 10 new words / listen to two stories,* which the children then choose from.

10.14 Our class contract

Level All   **Age** 9–12   **Organization** whole class, pairs

Aims To set up parameters for learning and behaviour by negotiating a class contract; to develop awareness of the value of mutually agreed rules; to create a sense of community and positive socio-affective atmosphere.

Language focus *In the example:* opinions, classroom language and activities
Alternatives: must, mustn't

Materials *Essential:* none / *Optional:* a class contract with options, a wax seal or stamp

Our class contract

☺ Children

We agree to

-
-
-
-
-
-

☺ Teacher

I agree to

-
-
-
-
-
-

Procedure

1 Introduce the idea of developing a class contract, with rules that apply to both you as teacher and to the children as learners.

2 Ask the children to identify where you find rules, eg at school, in sports, in games, on roads. Briefly discuss why rules are important, both in general and in English lessons in particular.

3 Draw two columns on the board with the headings *Teacher* and *Children*.

4 Ask for suggestions of rules to include in *Our class contract, eg make the lessons interesting / always do our homework / come to class on time / remember our books / listen when others are speaking / raise our hands if we want to speak / speak quietly in groups / help clear up at the end of lessons / take us to the computer room / show us DVDs / explain if we don't understand.* Children say whether the suggested rules should go in the column under *Children* or *Teacher* or in both columns as you write them on the board.

5 Divide the class into pairs.

6 Ask each pair to choose a maximum of six suggestions they think should be included in the class contract for you and them.

7 Ask the pairs to report back and decide on the rules with the whole class. Veto any rules that you don't think will work or should apply.

8 Write the final version of selected rules on a large poster under the heading *Our class contract* or ask the children to do this. Sign your name under your part of the contract and get the children to sign their names under theirs. If you have a wax seal or stamp, it can be fun to add this to the poster.

9 Keep the class contract on the classroom notice board. Refer to the rules, eg *Hand up, please, Pedro. Remember our rule!* as and when necessary during your teaching.

Comments and suggestions

- Creating a class contract with the children encourages them to 'buy in' to an agreed way of behaving in class and helps to promote a responsible attitude towards learning. For more discussion of rules, see the General introduction, page 12.

- If this is the first time the children have been involved in this kind of class decision making, you are likely to get a range of responses, varying from rules which are too vague and therefore difficult to enforce, eg *We must behave well*, to rules which are draconian, eg *We must never speak Italian,* to rules which are plain jokey, eg *You must let us eat chewing gum.* With your judicious guidance and choice, however, the result is usually a set of sensible rules, which, because the children have (largely) thought them through themselves, they are generally willing to adhere to.

- With younger children, it is more appropriate to elicit and talk about the reasons and importance of key rules (that you have previously prepared) and then ask them to illustrate these for display on the classroom notice board, rather than negotiate them in the way described above.

10.15 Classroom jobs

Level All   **Age** 4–12   **Organization** whole class

Aims To involve children in the organization of learning; to develop a sense of responsibility about carrying out everyday classroom jobs; to create a sense of community and positive socio-affective atmosphere.

Language focus *want to,* classroom jobs

Materials *Essential:* a pre-prepared job rota (one copy) / *Optional:* a poster-size version of the same

Classroom jobs rota	
Job	**Name**
calling the register	
cleaning the board	
giving out books	
writing day and time on the board	

Classroom jobs rota	
Job	**Name**

Procedure

Do this activity when you meet a new class, and thereafter on a regular basis.

1 Identify the classroom jobs which it will be suitable to assign to children on a rota basis and have ready an empty rota that you have prepared.

2 Announce what the jobs are to the children, eg giving out books or work sheets, cleaning the board. Ask *Who wants to …?* Assign individuals or pairs of children to each job and write their names on the rota.

3 Keep the rota on the classroom noticeboard. Refer to the rota as necessary whenever jobs need doing. Praise the children whenever appropriate for carrying out their jobs responsibly and well.

Comments and suggestions

- Children usually enjoy doing classroom jobs and this can help to develop their confidence and self-esteem as well as their sense of responsibility and pride in the way things are organized in their classroom. The assignment of classroom jobs can also encourage children to exert healthy pressure on their peers to do things, eg help clear up in the agreed way.

- It is usually best to assign jobs to children in pairs as they can then support and remind each other and one of them can do the job if the other is away.

- With younger children, jobs need to be assigned and changed frequently, eg every week. The rota should also show pictures or icons for the jobs rather than words. With older children, the time frame can be longer, eg every two months or every term.

- Classroom jobs are likely to vary with older and younger children. With older children jobs which may be suitable include calling the register, collecting in and giving back homework, writing the day and date on the board before the lesson, cleaning the board before and after the lesson, giving out handouts, watering the class plant. With younger children, suitable jobs include table monitors to give out and put back trays of colours, glue sticks and other materials, to give out and collect in the books for their table and put paper in the bin.

10.16 Why I'm learning English

Level All   **Age** 8–12   **Organization** individual, whole class

Aims To reflect on reasons for learning English; to develop self-awareness and self-motivation.

Language focus *In th example: will, want to, because,* giving reasons
Alternatives: L1

Materials *Essential:* none / *Optional:* copies of possible reasons (one for each child)

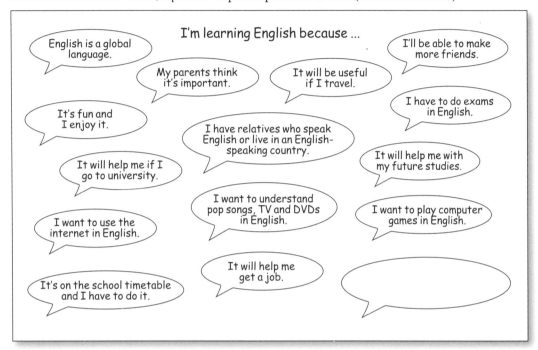

I'm learning English because ...

- English is a global language.
- My parents think it's important.
- It will be useful if I travel.
- I'll be able to make more friends.
- I have to do exams in English.
- It's fun and I enjoy it.
- I have relatives who speak English or live in an English-speaking country.
- It will help me with my future studies.
- It will help me if I go to university.
- I want to understand pop songs, TV and DVDs in English.
- I want to play computer games in English.
- I want to use the internet in English.
- It will help me get a job.
- It's on the school timetable and I have to do it.

Procedure

1 Either ask the children to spend a few minutes individually and note the reasons why they think they are learning English or give them a copy of the handout you have prepared (in English or L1) and ask them to tick the reasons that they think apply to them and/or add any other ideas of their own.

2 When the children are ready, ask them to report back on their views. Use this as the basis of a class discussion on their reasons for learning English. Be ready to ask questions as appropriate, in order to relate their reasons to what you do in lessons and to push the children's thinking further. For example, if they say they want to understand pop songs in English, you may suggest listening to more pop songs in lessons and also ask the children what they can do themselves outside lessons to help with this. Equally, if a child says that they're learning because they have to, agree that this is certainly true and ask how they think they can get more out of it. Use the discussion to establish that we don't often stop and think about our reasons for learning things, especially when we don't have any choice, as is the case at school, but if we know our own personal reasons for learning things, this can often make us feel more motivated and help us learn faster and better.

Comments and suggestions

- This activity encourages children to think about the benefits of learning English and gives you useful insights into their attitudes. Although children's views often directly reflect the attitudes of their parents, you may also be surprised by the maturity of their response.

10.17 Things that help me learn

Level All   **Age** 8–12   **Organization** individual, whole class

Aims To reflect on learning styles and strategies related to specific areas of learning; to develop awareness of your own learning preferences; to begin to develop personalized learning style and strategies.

Language focus *In the example:* present simple, language to talk about vocabulary learning
Alternatives: language to talk about other areas of learning, eg listening, reading, pronunciation; L1

Materials *Essential:* none / *Optional:* copies of yes/no questions (one for each child)

Vocabulary

Which of these help you to learn vocabulary? Circle Yes or No.

• I learn sets of words together.	Yes / No
• I hear the words many times.	Yes / No
• I write the words in my vocabulary book.	Yes / No
• I draw pictures of the words.	Yes / No
• I repeat the words.	Yes / No
• I say the words with rhythm.	Yes / No
• I say the words in my head.	Yes / No
• I walk about as I say the words.	Yes / No
• I tap my fingers or toes as I say the words.	Yes / No
• I translate the words.	Yes / No
• I play with word cards.	Yes / No
• I test myself on the words.	Yes / No
• _____	Yes / No
• _____	Yes / No

Procedure

Use this activity to get the children to explore learning strategies related to specific areas of learning.

1 Elicit possible things that help the children, for example, to learn vocabulary. Either note their ideas on the board or give them a copy of the handout (either in English or L1) and ask them to circle the statements that apply to them and/or add any other ideas of their own.

2 When the children are ready, divide the class into pairs and ask them to compare their views.

3 Discuss their responses with the whole class. Use the discussion to make the point that there are no 'right' answers and that we all have our own preferences for the way we learn. The important thing is to try and identify and use the strategies that work best for us individually.

Comments and suggestions

• This activity helps children become aware of options and choices available to them for learning and to think about and identify their own preferences. It also gives you valuable insights into the children's learning styles.

• With older children, it may be appropriate to introduce them to the idea of the way we use our senses when we learn and that some of us prefer to see (visual learners), some to hear (auditory learners), and others to move about (kinaesthetic learners), and that very often we use a combination of two of our senses to learn, or all three. Children can then reflect on their own learning styles in those terms and discuss their preferences.

10.18 How I like to do homework

Level All   **Age** 10–12   **Organization** individual, whole class

Aims To reflect on the conditions in which you personally work and learn best; to recognize the value of your own personal effort in learning a foreign language.

Language focus *likes/dislikes,* preferences, prepositions of place and time, home, family, activities

Materials *Essential:* none / *Optional:* mind map to complete (one for each child).

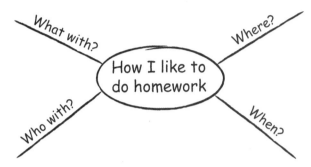

Procedure

This activity is only suitable for older children who are expected to do homework as a regular part of the course.

1 Ask the children why they think doing homework is important and listen to their ideas.

2 Explain that in order for them to do their homework as well as possible and also have time for other things, it is worthwhile organizing and planning when and how they do their homework.

3 Draw the beginning of a mind map on the board (see above). Elicit possible answers to each question, eg Where? *In my bedroom / the kitchen / the dining room / the garden.*
When? *Immediately I get home. / After a snack. / After watching TV. / After my piano lesson. / Before dinner. / Before I go to bed.*
Who with? *On my own. / With my dog/cat/mum/dad/brother/sister/friend.*
What with? *A glass of water / a snack / loud music / soft music / total silence.*

4 Ask the children to complete the mind map with their own personal preferences for how they do their homework. If you like, children can also illustrate their mind maps.

5 When they are ready, ask the children to report back, eg *I like doing my homework in the kitchen. / I prefer doing my homework after a snack. / I don't like listening to music.*

6 At the end, you may like to suggest that the children stick their homework mind maps in their bedrooms at home , for example, and, as far as possible, try and always do their homework in the conditions they prefer.

Comments and suggestions

- The approach towards homework varies in different contexts. Small pieces of homework on a regular basis can reinforce school learning and help children to learn how to concentrate, work independently and manage their time. Homework can also include enjoyable projects and strengthen connections between home and school. However, it should never be onerous for children.

- Being encouraged to think about when and how they do their homework best helps the children to organize their time and take homework in their stride. It also prepares them for moving up to secondary school, where the amount of homework is likely to increase.

10.19 KWL topic grid

Level A2.1, A2.2, B1.1, B2.2   **Age** 10–12   **Organization** individual/pairs

Aims To identify what you already know about a topic; to set goals for what you would like find out about a topic; to reflect and review what you have learnt as a result of doing a topic.

Language focus *In the example:* any language and vocabulary related to rainforests
Alternatives: any language and vocabulary, depending on the topic

Materials *Essential:* none / *Optional:* copies of KWL grids, landscape on A4 sheets (one for each child)

Topic:		
K	W	L
What I already know	What I want to find out	What I've learnt

Procedure

1 *Either* draw a KWL (What I **K**now / What I **W**ant to find out / What I've **L**earnt) grid on the board and ask the children to copy this *or* give out copies at the start of a new topic, eg Rainforests.

2 Ask the children what they already know about rainforests and listen to their ideas, introducing new vocabulary as necessary.

3 Children then either work individually or in pairs and note 3–5 things they already know about rainforests in the first column, eg *Rainforests are near the equator. Rainforests are very hot and it rains a lot. The Amazon rainforest is the largest rainforest in the world.* They then think of 3–5 questions or things they want to find out about the topic and note these in the second column, eg *How high are the tallest trees in a rainforest?*

4 During the topic, ensure that there are opportunities for children to research the answers to their questions, eg using reference books or selected sites on the internet (see 9.24).

5 At the end of the topic, children come back to their grids and note the main or most interesting things they have learnt about the topic in the third column, including answers to their questions, eg *The tallest trees in a rainforest are about 75 metres.*

Comments and suggestions

- The KWL grid provides a useful framework for topic-based learning in which children's previous knowledge is strategically activated (column 1) in order to engage them in setting an agenda for their own learning (column 2) and reflecting on what they have learnt as a result of doing the topic (column 3).

- The use of a KWL grid helps to develop children's metacognitive strategies and awareness through encouraging them to make positive use of prior knowledge during topic work, to identify personal learning goals and work towards these in a responsible way, and to reflect on learning outcomes.

- With younger children, or at a more elementary level, KWL grids can also be completed as part of topic work using L1.

10.20 Self-assessment

Level All   **Age** 6–12   **Organization** individual, whole class

Aims To review, assess and monitor your progress after completing a unit of work; to reflect on your learning; to develop confidence in your own ability to learn; to develop a sense of achievement and self-esteem.

Language focus *can* (for ability), language related to learning and the unit of work

Materials *Essential:* copies of self-assessment sheet (one for each child)

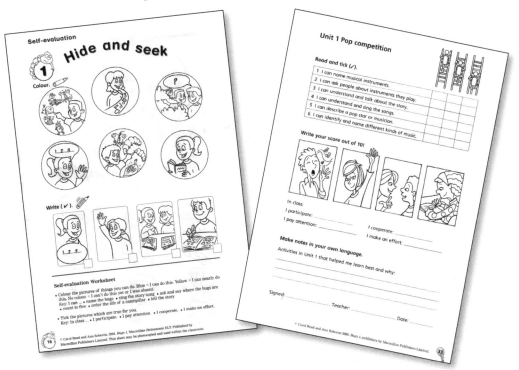

Procedure

Do a self-assessment activity (in English or L1) when children have completed a unit of work. This may either be a unit in the course book or one based on a topic or story.

1 Ask the children what they can do now that they couldn't do at the outset of the unit and listen to their response.

2 Ask them what has helped them to learn and encourage them to identify activities or materials, eg a particular story or song that they found specially helpful.

3 Give out the self-assessment sheets. Make sure the children realize that there aren't 'right answers' and explain, if necessary, that it is the children's personal view and assessment of their own learning that is important. With younger children, if the self-assessment is based on pictures (as in the example above) you will need to say the 'can do' statement that each picture refers to and explain the colouring key, eg blue = *I can do this very well,* yellow = *I can do this,* no colour = *I can't do this yet* or *I was away.* With older children, ask them to read the statements and work individually to complete the self-assessment sheet.

4 At the end, briefly discuss children's responses to the self-assessment sheet on the unit with the whole class and praise the children for their efforts and progress.

5 It is also important to find time to talk to children about their self-assessments and/or take them in and write a positive comment and/or endorse them with your signature and the date.

Comments and suggestions

- Self-assessment develops children's self-awareness and ability to reflect on their own learning. It also encourages children to develop a responsible attitude towards their learning.
- Self-assessment is part of the assessment cycle and affords you valuable insights into children's progress, as well as their own perception of their progress. If children have portfolios, then self-assessment sheets completed on a regular basis can be stored here.
- At times some children can be quite harsh on themselves in their self-assessment, so you need to be ready to counter this with a more positive view.

10.21 Write your own report

Level All   **Age** 10–12   **Organization** individual

Aims To review, assess and monitor your progress after a term/course from your teacher's point of view; to compare your assessment with your teacher's; (to negotiate the final report).

Language focus L1 or present simple, *can* (for ability), language to talk about learning

Materials *Essential:* copies of school report form (one for each child)

Procedure

1 Show the children the school report form. Explain the categories in the report and elicit or remind children of the marking system used at the school.

2 Explain that you want the children to complete a report form for themselves for the term, evaluating their progress as if they were the teacher. In order not to restrict children in their comments, it is likely to be most appropriate to do this activity in L1.

3 When the children have finished, briefly discuss the experience of writing a report about themselves with the whole class.

4 Collect in the reports for comment and, ideally, find time to talk about these with the children individually and either compare them with the report that you have written or use them as the basis for negotiating this.

Name ....

Class ....

	grade	comment
Listening		
Spoken production		
Spoken interaction		
Reading		
Writing		
Effort		
Participation		

General comment: ....
....
....

Signed: .... Date: ....

Comments and suggestions

- This activity can produce some very perceptive, personal insights from the children about their own learning and behaviour which may also be useful and important for you to know.
- As with self-assessment in 10.20, you need to be ready to redress the balance if children have an overly negative view of their progress.
- Children usually enjoy pretending to be the teacher and completing a 'real' report on themselves. It is best to build on this and do the activity in a 'light' way which will allow the humour to naturally come through.
- Instead of doing this activity at the end of a term or course, you might like to do it at the outset. In this case, children complete the form with the kind of report they would like to get. This then gives you an opportunity to discuss with children the criteria they will be assessed on and what they can do to get a good report.

10.22 My learning diary

Level All   **Age** 8–12   **Organization** individual

Aims To monitor your progress by keeping a diary; to review and reflect on your learning; to develop your self-awareness and self-motivation.

Language focus past simple, language to talk about learning
Alternatives: L1

Materials *Essential:* special notebooks or copies of diary sheets stapled into a book (one for each child)

Procedure

1 Introduce the idea of keeping a learning diary. Ask the children if they like the idea and listen to their response.

2 *Either* give out the special notebooks for children to use as their diaries *or* the stapled copies of diary sheets that you have prepared.

3 Explain that the children are going to complete their diaries once a week on …, and name the day, or do this as part of their homework.

4 Children can either write their diaries in English or L1, although in many cases L1 may be preferable so as not to limit the children in what they can write.

5 Explain that the diary is not part of assessed work and the aim is for children to think about and record their learning in English.

6 Model the process involved in completing the diary for yourself for one week before the children write their own entries. Explain that the picture they draw can be anything that will help to make the week's learning memorable, eg a picture of themselves doing an activity they particularly enjoyed or a picture of something they learnt about, eg a butterfly.

This week I learnt ....

My favourite activities were ....

Things that helped me learn were ....

One thing I did very well was ....

One thing I found difficult was ....

Next week I'm going to try to ....

My picture for this week

General comment: ....

Signed: ....

Date: ....

7 Get the children to complete their diaries on a regular basis.

8 Take them in occasionally and respond positively to the entries in writing. Periodically encourage the children to look back over their diaries and see how much progress they have made.

Comments and suggestions

- Keeping a learning diary provides a simple framework for encouraging children to reflect on their learning in a regular and explicit way. Illustrating the diary also helps to make each week's learning memorable.

- You can vary the stem sentences in the diary format depending on the age and level of the children. For example, a simpler diary could be based on the first two sentences in the above example and a picture.

- If children are keeping portfolios, their learning diaries can be part of these. If the portfolios are electronic, an alternative format for the diaries is for children to write them on computer, following a template which you prepare and scanning in their pictures.

Index

Language structures and grammar

Topics and lexical sets

Learning skills and attitudes

Activity titles

Further reading

Aitchison, J. 2003 Words in the mind. (3rd edition) Oxford: Basil Blackwell

Batstone, R. 1994 Grammar. Oxford: Oxford University Press

Bettelheim, B. 1991 The Uses of Enchantment: The meaning and importance of Fairy Tales. Harmondsworth: Penguin

Brewster, J., Ellis, G., Girard, D. 2002 The Primary English Teacher's Guide. (2nd edition) Harlow: Penguin Longman

Buzan, T. 2003 Mind Maps for Kids. London: Harper Collins

Cameron, L. 2001 Teaching Languages to Young Learners. Cambridge: Cambridge University Press

Cook, G. 2000 Language Play, Language Learning. Oxford: Oxford University Press

Dennison, P.E. & Dennison, G.E. 1994 Brain Gym: Teacher's Edition. (Revised) Ventura C.A: Edu-Kinesthetics Inc.

Donaldson, M. 1986 Children's Minds. (2nd edition) London: Harper Collins

Ellis, G., Brewster, J. 2002 Tell it Again! The New Storytelling Handbook for Primary Teachers. Harlow: Penguin Longman

Enever, J. & Schmid-Schönbein, G. (Eds) 2006 Picture Books and Young Learners of English. Munich: Langenscheidt

Faber, A. & Mazlish, E. 2001 How to talk so kids will listen and listen so kids will talk. London: Piccadilly Press

Fisher, R. 2005 Teaching Children to Think. (2nd edition) Cheltenham: Nelson Thornes

Fisher, R. 2005 Teaching Children to Learn. (2nd edition) Cheltenham: Nelson Thornes

Fleetham, M. 2003 How to Create and Develop a Thinking Classroom. Wisbech: LDA

Gardner, H. 1983 Frames of Mind: The Theory of Multiple Intelligences. Fontana

Gardner, H. 1999 Intelligence Reframed: Multiple Intelligences for the 21st Century. New York: Basic Books

Graham, C. 2006 Creating Chants and Songs. Oxford: Oxford University Press

Hannaford, C. 1995 Smart Moves: Why learning is not all in your head. Virginia: Great Ocean Publishers

Lewis, G. 2004 The Internet and Young Learners. Oxford: Oxford University Press

Lightbrown, P., Spada, N. 2006 How Languages are Learned. (3rd edition) Oxford: Oxford University Press

Moon, J. 2005 Children Learning English. (2nd edition) Oxford: Macmillan

Mourão, S. 2003 Using Realbooks in the ELT Classroom. Leamington Spa: Scholastic

O'Grady, W. 2005 How Children Learn Language. Cambridge: Cambridge University Press

Opie, I. & Opie, P. 1967 The Language and Lore of Schoolchildren. Oxford: Oxford University Press

Phillips, S. 1993 Young Learners. Oxford: Oxford University Press

Phillips, S. 1999 Drama with Children. Oxford: Oxford University Press

Pinter, A. 2006 Teaching Young Language Learners. Oxford: Oxford University Press

Read, C. 2001 Instant Lessons: Fairy Tales. Harlow: Penguin Longman

Reilly, J. & Reilly, V. 2005 Writing with Children. Oxford: Oxford University Press

Reilly, V. & Ward, S.M. 1997 Very Young Learners. Oxford: Oxford University Press

Rixon, S. (Ed) 1999 Young Learners of English: Some Research Perspectives. Harlow: Longman

Smith, A., Lovatt, M., Wise, D. 2003 Accelerated Learning: A User's Guide. Stafford: Network Educational press

Vygotsky, L.S., & Vygotsky, L. (1978) Mind in Society. Cambridge Mass: Harvard University Press

Wells, G. 1986 The Meaning Makers. Hodder and Stoughton

Williams, M. & Burden, R.L. 1997 Psychology for Language Teachers. Cambridge: Cambridge University Press

Wood, D. 1997 How Children Think and Learn. (2nd edition) Oxford: Blackwell

Wright, A. 1995 Storytelling with Children. Oxford: Oxford University Press

Wright, A. 1997 Creating Stories with Children. Oxford: Oxford University Press

Useful websites
http://www.bbc.co.uk/children
http://www.bbc.co.uk/cbeebies
http://www.education-world.com
http://www.enchantedlearning.com
http://www.teachingenglish.org.uk
http://www.britishcouncil.org/learnenglish
http://www.iatefl-ylsig.org